HAMAN'S LIES

*Exposing the Ancient Roots of Antisemitism
and Why the Spirit of Esther Must Arise*

JIMMY EVANS &
JOHN ANDERSEN

HAMAN'S LIES

*Exposing the Ancient Roots of Antisemitism
and Why the Spirit of Esther Must Arise*

JIMMY EVANS &
JOHN ANDERSEN

Haman's Lies: Exposing the Ancient Roots of Antisemitism and Why the Spirit of Esther Must Arise

Copyright © 2026 by Jimmy Evans and Dr. John Andersen

Scripture taken from the New King James Version®. Copyright © 1982 by Thomas Nelson. Used by permission. All rights reserved.

All rights reserved. No portion of this publication may be reproduced, stored in a retrieval system, or transmitted in any form by any means—electronic, mechanical, photocopying, recording, or any other—without prior permission from the publisher.

ISBN 978-1-960870-78-0 Paperback
ISBN 978-1-960870-79-7 Hardcover
ISBN 978-1-960870-80-3 eBook
ISBN 978-1-960870-81-0 Audiobook

Tipping Point Press creates resources to help people understand biblical prophecy and the relevance of world events to the End Times. These messages provide hope, peace, and encouragement. For more resources visit EndTimes.com.

Tipping Point Press
1021 Grace Lane
Southlake, TX 76092

While the authors make every effort to provide accurate URLs at the time of printing for external or third-party internet websites, neither they nor the publisher assume any responsibility for changes or errors made after publication.

Printed in the United States of America

26 27 28 29—5 4 3 2 1

Dedication

To Israel, the eternal people of the Covenant, and to the Jewish people everywhere—

You have been scattered, yet never lost. Persecuted, yet never destroyed. Slandered in every generation, yet still you stand.

We dedicate these pages to your resilience, your faithfulness, and your survival against every empire that tried to erase you. We dedicate them to the memory of all who have fallen—from ancient Persia to Bondi Beach—because hatred found them first.

And we dedicate them to the God who made you a promise He has never broken.

> *"Can a woman forget her nursing child,*
> *And not have compassion on the son of her womb?*
> *Surely they may forget,*
> *Yet I will not forget you.*
> *See, I have inscribed you on the palms of My hands;*
> *Your walls are continually before Me."—Isaiah 49:15–16*

Am Yisrael Chai.

Contents

Foreword xi
An Opening Word xv
Introduction — The Spirit of Slander xix
    CHART 1 xxvii
    CHART 2 xxxvi

Part One: The Ancient Pattern

1: The Rising Tide 3
    CHART 3 7
2: Israel—God's Super-Sign 29
3: Haman's Template 37
    CHART 4 49
4: Esther's Template 51
5: The Anatomy of Deception 63

Part Two: Lying Tongues

6: Lie #1 — "The Jews Have No Right to the Land" 77
7: Lie #2 — "Israel Is an Apartheid State" 93
8: Lie #3 — "Israel Was Founded Through the Displacement
    of Palestinians" 105
9: Lie #4 — "Israel Illegally Occupies the West Bank and East
    Jerusalem" 115
10: Lie #5 — "Israel Annexed Territory in Violation
    of International Law" 121

11: Lie #6 — "Israel Is a Settler-Colonial Project" 129
12: Lie #7 — "Israel Is Committing Genocide and Ethnic Cleansing" 139
    CHART 5 143
13: Lie #8 — "Israel Intentionally Targets Civilians" 155
14: Lie #9 — "Israel Uses Disproportionate Force" 167
15: Lie #10 — "Israel Enforces a Punitive Blockade on Gaza" 175
16: Lie #11 — "Israel Systematically Violates Palestinian Human Rights" 183
17: Lie #12 — "Israel Commits War Crimes" 193
18: Lie #13 — "Israel Restricts Access to Muslim and Christian Holy Sites" 203
19: Lie #14 — "Israel Builds Illegal Settlements That Undermine Peace" 211
20: Lie #15 — "Israel Does Not Sincerely Pursue Peace" 223
21: Lie #16 — "Israel Controls American Foreign Policy" 231
22: Lie #17 — "Israel Systematically Discriminates Against Its Arab Citizens" 241
23: Lie #18 — "Israel's Security Measures Are Really Designed to Oppress Palestinians" 249
24: Lie #19 — "Israel Suppresses Journalists and Civil Society" 257
25: Lie #20 — "Israel Fabricates or Exaggerates Security Threats to Justify Its Policies" 265
26: Lie #21 — "Israel Controls Water Resources Unfairly" 273
27: Lie #22 — "Israel Assassinates Political Leaders and Scientists Abroad" 281
28: Lie #23 — "Israel Uses Collective Punishment" 289
29: Lie #24 — "Israel Detains Minors and Uses Harsh Interrogation Methods" 299

30: Lie #25 — "Israel Manipulates Demographics to Maintain Jewish Majority" 309

Part Three: Stepping Into Your Esther Moment
31: America's Best Investment 319
32: A Moment That Demands More Than Understanding 331

Conclusion — The People Who Cannot Be Erased 339
APPENDIX A — The 25 Lies at a Glance 353
APPENDIX B — Key Primary Sources 355
APPENDIX C — Glossary of Key Terms 357
APPENDIX D — Select Bible Passages About Israel 359
APPENDIX E — Answering Haman's Lies 361
References 373

Foreword

There are moments in history when silence becomes complicity. We are living in one of those moments right now.

Since October 7, 2023, we have witnessed something I never thought I would see in my lifetime: the most violent massacre of Jewish people since the Holocaust, followed not by universal condemnation but by a global eruption of hatred against the victims themselves. Synagogues have been defaced. Jewish students have hidden their Stars of David on university campuses. Mobs have chanted for the elimination of the only Jewish state on earth. And in too many pulpits and pews, there has been a deafening silence.

The book you hold in your hands is a shattering of that silence.

I have spent my career studying Bible prophecy, writing about the End Times, and teaching believers how to discern the signs of Christ's return. In all my years of research, I have never seen a topic more urgent, timelier, or more misunderstood than the one Jimmy Evans and Dr. John Andersen tackle in Haman's Lies. The ancient hatred of the Jewish people is not merely a historical curiosity or a political controversy. It is a spiritual battle that runs through the entire biblical narrative—and it is reaching a fever pitch in the days we are living in right now.

HAMAN'S LIES

Understanding antisemitism is not optional. It is essential. Every major prophetic passage about the End Times centers on Israel and the Jewish people. The regathering of the Jews to their ancient homeland, the rising hostility of the nations against them, the covenant with the Antichrist, the Tribulation, and the ultimate return of Christ to rescue His Covenant People—all of these prophetic events revolve around Israel. To ignore antisemitism is to ignore one of the clearest indicators of where we stand on God's prophetic timeline. And to misunderstand it is to risk standing on the wrong side of history—and the wrong side of God.

That is why I am so grateful for this book, and why I am confident that Jimmy Evans and John Andersen are exactly the right people to write it.

Jimmy Evans has been one of the foremost voices in Bible prophecy for decades. His deep study of Scripture, his clarity in communicating complex prophetic truths, and his unwavering commitment to the Word of God have influenced millions of believers around the world. Through his ministry, his books, and endtimes.com, Jimmy has equipped an entire generation to understand the times we are living in. His book *Tipping Point* awakened countless Christians to the convergence of prophetic signs in our day. He brings the same passion, biblical depth, and prophetic insight to this book.

Dr. John Andersen brings a unique and invaluable perspective to this project. With a PhD and years of experience as a pastor and professor of Christian ethics, John combines rigorous academic scholarship with a heart for the church. His research into Israel, antisemitism, biblical studies, and the End Times has given him a depth of knowledge that few possess. He understands not only the biblical foundations of God's Covenant with Israel but also the historical, ethical, and geopolitical dimensions of the hatred that has pursued the Jewish people through the centuries. His expertise allows this book to engage the toughest objections and the most sophisticated propaganda with intellectual honesty

Foreword

and scholarly precision, while never losing sight of its pastoral and prophetic heart.

Together, Jimmy and John have produced a book that is both deeply researched and eminently readable. They expose the ancient template that Haman used to justify genocide—*Different, Disloyal, Dangerous, Disposable*—and trace its echoes through the pogroms, the Holocaust, and into the streets of our own cities today. They answer the lies that are poisoning our culture with the clarity of truth and the authority of Scripture. And they call believers to rise up as Esther did—not to be silent, not to shrink back, but to stand with God's Covenant People in this critical hour.

I must say a personal word about both of these men. I have been part of the endtimes.com family for three years, and in that time I have come to know Jimmy not only as a ministry partner but as a trusted friend. We have researched together, written together, and labored side by side in the work of helping believers understand biblical prophecy. I have seen his integrity up close. I have witnessed his commitment to truth even when truth is costly.

John Andersen has been a tremendous help to me personally on numerous research and writing projects. His scholarship is impeccable, but what sets him apart is the way he combines that scholarship with simplicity, faithfulness, and a genuine love for the church. I trust his integrity completely. I value his friendship deeply. And I am honored to call both of these men my brothers in Christ.

When you read this book, you are not reading the opinions of commentators who have glanced at headlines and formed quick conclusions. You are reading the work of men who have spent decades in the Scriptures, who have studied the history, who understand the stakes, and who love the truth more than they love their own comfort. They have done the hard work so you don't have to. And they have given you a resource that will equip you to stand firm in a world that is increasingly hostile to

Israel and ever more confused about God's purposes for His Covenant People.

I want to tell you plainly: *You need this book.* You need it because the lies are everywhere. You need it because the propaganda is sophisticated. You need it because people of good will and even sincere Christians are being deceived by accusations that sound compassionate but are rooted in an ancient hatred. You need it because we are living in the final days before Christ's return, and what we believe about Israel—and how we respond to the rising tide of antisemitism—matters eternally.

God's promise to Israel has never been revoked. The nations that have persecuted the Jewish people have found themselves on the wrong side of that Covenant, again and again. The believers who have stood with Israel have found themselves aligned with the heart of God.

This is your moment. This is your opportunity to understand the truth, reject the lies, and stand with God's Covenant People. Read this book carefully. Let it inform your thinking, sharpen your discernment, and ignite your courage. And then do what Esther did—rise up, speak out, and trust that God has placed you in this world for such a time as this.

Dr. Mark Hitchcock
Senior Pastor, Faith Bible Church, Edmond, Oklahoma
Research Professor of Bible Exposition,
Dallas Theological Seminary

An Opening Word

We are writing these words with grief in our hearts.

Yesterday evening—while families in Sydney gathered on Bondi Beach to light the first candle of Hanukkah—two gunmen opened fire on a crowd of a thousand people. They killed at least fifteen. They wounded more than forty. They murdered a ten-year-old girl named Matilda, who had come to the beach with her parents and little sister to celebrate the Festival of Lights. They murdered two rabbis. They murdered an eighty-seven-year-old Holocaust survivor named Alex Kleytman, who threw his body over his wife of nearly sixty years to shield her from the bullets.

Read that again. A man who survived the Holocaust—who escaped the Nazi death machine as a child in Siberia, who built a new life on the other side of the world, who raised a family and watched his grandchildren grow—was gunned down eighty years later, at a Hanukkah celebration, in Australia, for the same reason the Nazis wanted him dead so many years before.

Because he was a Jew.

We really don't have words adequate for this moment. We have written this entire book about the lies that fuel hatred against the Jewish people, about the ancient pattern that keeps repeating, about the spiritual warfare that underlies it all. But sitting here on this night, watching the videos of parents running with their children, reading the names of the dead, seeing the images of flowers piling up outside the Bondi Pavilion—theory becomes flesh. Statistics become faces. The chapter you are about to read on the "flood of antisemitism" becomes a beach soaked in blood.

It is almost too much to bear.

Israeli Prime Minister Benjamin Netanyahu responded within hours. He did not mince words. He reminded the world that he had written to Australian Prime Minister Anthony Albanese earlier this year, warning him that Australia's recognition of a Palestinian state was "pouring fuel on the antisemitic fire." He said: "Antisemitism is a cancer. It spreads when leaders stay silent; it retreats when leaders act." And then he added this: "Your government did nothing to stop the spread of antisemitism in Australia. You did nothing to curb the cancer cells that were growing inside your country. You took no action. You let the disease spread and the result is the horrific attacks on Jews we saw today."

Some will call those words too harsh. Some will say this is not the time for blame. But we think Netanyahu understands something that too many Western leaders have refused to see: *Words have consequences. Policies have consequences.* When you reward terrorism with statehood, when you single out the Jewish state for condemnation while ignoring actual atrocities elsewhere, when you allow antisemitic rhetoric to spread unchallenged through your universities and streets and social media platforms—you are not being neutral. You are watering the seeds of violence.

And eventually, inevitably, those seeds bear fruit.

Bondi Beach is what happens when Haman's lies go unanswered.

It is what happens when "from the river to the sea" is treated as free speech instead of a call for genocide. It is what happens when university presidents cannot bring themselves to say that calling for the murder of Jews violates their code of conduct. It is what happens when the international community passes more resolutions condemning Israel than the rest of the world combined. It is what happens when the propaganda we document in this book is allowed to metastasize unchallenged—when Haman's template becomes the accepted narrative about an entire people.

The lies come first. The violence follows. It has always been this way.

We must admit we are devastated tonight. We are angry. We are grieving for people we have never met in a country we have only visited, because their deaths feel like a wound in our own chests. And we know that when the sun rises tomorrow, there will be voices explaining why this attack was "understandable," why the "context" matters, why we shouldn't rush to judgment, why Israel's policies somehow justify the murder of children at a Hanukkah party.

Those voices are the reason this book exists.

We finished the manuscript for this book several days ago. We thought we were done. But as we watched the events of yesterday unfold, we realized we needed to add these words at the beginning—not to update the argument, because nothing that happened yesterday changes the argument. The argument was already proven by October 7, 2023. By the Tree of Life Synagogue. By the Holocaust. By every pogrom and persecution and exile stretching back to Haman himself.

We added these words because we want you to understand, before you read another page, that this book is not an academic exercise. It is not a political argument. It is not an attempt to win a debate.

It is a response to blood crying out from the ground.

Alex Kleytman survived the Holocaust. He lived eighty-seven years. He raised children and grandchildren. And on the first night of Hanukkah 2025, in one of the safest countries on earth, he died the way he would have died in 1943—because the world still has not learned to recognize Haman's lies.

His wife Larisa, who was lying beneath him as he was shot, told reporters: "I think he was shot because he raised himself up to protect me."

HAMAN'S LIES

He raised himself up. Even at eighty-seven. Even as the bullets flew. He raised himself up to protect someone he loved.

That is what this moment requires of all of us. Not to cower. Not to stay silent. Not to hope the hatred passes us by. But to raise ourselves up—to speak, to act, to protect—even when it costs us something.

That is what this book is asking you to do.

May the memory of the Bondi Beach victims be a blessing. And may their blood not have been shed in vain.

Jimmy Evans and John Andersen
December 2025

INTRODUCTION

The Spirit of Slander

Twenty-five centuries ago, a man named Haman stood before the King of Persia and released a lie into the world. It wasn't small. It wasn't careless. It was a crafted accusation designed for one purpose—to justify genocide, to wipe God's Covenant People off the face of the earth.

Listen to what he said:

> Then Haman said to King Ahasuerus, "There is a certain people scattered and dispersed among the people in all the provinces of your kingdom; their laws *are* different from all *other* people's, and they do not keep the king's laws. Therefore it *is* not fitting for the king to let them remain. If it pleases the king, let *a decree* be written that they be destroyed, and I will pay ten thousand talents of silver into the hands of those who do the work, to bring *it* into the king's treasuries" (Esther 3:8–9).

If that sounds familiar, it should. Haman's script has never gone away. The vocabulary has changed, the kingdoms have changed, the geopolitical arguments have changed—but the template has stayed exactly the same. His lie contained a template—a four-part propaganda strategy we will examine in detail in Chapter 3. That template—which we call **Different, Disloyal, Dangerous, Disposable**—has been repeated against the Jewish people in every generation since. Modern activists use updated vocabulary, but the message is identical. The spirit behind it is identical.

It is Haman's voice, echoing through history, calling for **the destruction of God's Covenant People.**

Why This Book?

For over fifty years, I (Jimmy) have studied Bible prophecy. John and I have both written extensively about the signs of the times, the return of Christ, and what Scripture reveals about the last days. My (Jimmy's) book *Tipping Point* examined the prophetic significance of the moment we are living in—how the convergence of signs tells us we are the final generation before the Lord's return.

But we have never seen anything like what is happening right now.

Since October 7, 2023—the deadliest day for Jews since the Holocaust—we have watched in astonishment as the *victims* have been turned into *villains*. We have seen demonstrators in major cities chanting for the elimination of Israel "from the river to the sea." We have watched university professors justify terrorism. We have seen social media flooded with accusations that any previous generation would have instantly recognized as antisemitic propaganda, yet today they are repackaged as "justice," "equity," or "decolonization."

And we've seen many Christians—people who genuinely love Jesus and believe the Bible—struggle to know what to think. They hear these accusations repeated so often, with such confidence and emotion, that they begin to wonder:

Could some of this be true?
Is Israel really an "apartheid state"?

The Spirit of Slander

Are the Palestinians really victims of "genocide"?
If I support Israel, am I supporting oppression?

This book is our answer to those questions. But it is more than that. It is an attempt to show you something almost everyone is missing: **The propaganda assault against Israel is not merely political. It is spiritual.** It is the newest expression of an ancient hatred—a hatred that has pursued the Jewish people through every century, every empire, and every civilization. And it carries profound prophetic significance.

We are not watching random events. **We are watching prophecy unfold in real time.** And the lies being spread about Israel are not peripheral to that story—they are part of it. They reveal exactly where we are on God's prophetic timeline.

A Word to Those Who Wonder Why This Book Is Necessary

Before we go further, we want to address a few objections you may already be forming. We have heard them from friends, from fellow pastors, and even from our own inner critics. They deserve an honest response.

"This book is written for people who already agree with you."

Yes, we are writing primarily for evangelical Christians. We make no apology for that. But here is something that deeply concerns us: Antisemitism is no longer confined to the fringes. It is creeping into conservative churches—churches that should know better, churches that claim to believe the Bible. We are watching pastors stay silent because they don't want to be controversial. We are watching congregations absorb anti-Israel talking points from social media without ever hearing a biblical response from the pulpit. We are watching young believers—raised in the church—adopt positions that previous generations would have instantly recognized as hostile to Scripture and to God's Covenant People.

The infection has reached the household of faith. That is why we are writing to believers first. If the Church does not recover its clarity on this issue, we will have failed at a critical moment in prophetic history. We will have repeated the silence of the German churches in the 1930s. And we refuse to be part of that silence.

"Israeli policy gets criticized everywhere. Why add another voice?"

That objection actually proves our point. Israeli policy is criticized everywhere—on every network, in every newspaper, on every campus, across every social media platform. The criticism is relentless, often one-sided, and frequently indistinguishable from the propaganda we document in this book. But where is the platform for an answer? Where can ordinary Christians hear a thoughtful, biblically grounded response to the accusations they encounter daily?

The mainstream media is not providing that response. The academic community is not providing it. In many cases, even the Church is not providing it. This book exists because someone needs to say clearly what too few are willing to say: These accusations are not merely mistaken—they are part of an ancient spiritual pattern, and they must be answered.

"You don't seem to acknowledge Palestinian suffering."

Let us be clear: The suffering of Palestinian civilians is real, and it is tragic. Every innocent life lost—Jewish or Arab—is an image-bearer of God. Every mother who weeps over a child, every family displaced by war, every person caught in the crossfire of a conflict they did not choose—these realities should grieve anyone with a functioning conscience. They grieve us deeply.

But here is the problem we are trying to address: The narrative of Palestinian suffering has been weaponized. It has been divorced from context, stripped of history, and deployed as a tool to demonize the Jewish state and justify its elimination. Most adults in the Western world have already absorbed this weaponized version. They have heard the accusations of genocide and apartheid repeated so often that they accept them as fact. They have seen the images. They have felt the emotional pull. What they have not heard—what almost no one is telling them—is how those images and emotions are being manipulated to serve an agenda as old as Haman.

This book does not exist to minimize anyone's suffering. It exists to expose the lies that exploit suffering in order to advance destruction. Those are not the same thing.

"Your language is too strong. You seem angry."

We are unapologetic about the strength of what we say in these pages. If some of our words sound forceful, consider what they are responding to. We are responding to calls for genocide chanted openly on American streets. We are responding to the murder of over 1,200 people on a single October morning—and to the global movement that celebrated it. We are responding to Jewish students hiding their identity on campuses their parents are paying tuition for them to attend. We are responding to synagogues firebombed, to mezuzahs torn from doorposts, to the highest levels of antisemitic violence since the Holocaust.

Blood speaks louder than this book ever could. If our words sound strong, it is because we are trying to match the gravity of what is happening—not to exceed it. When people are calling for the elimination of an entire nation, measured tones can become a form of complicity. There is a time for diplomatic language, and there is a time to call a lie exactly what it is. We are living in the second kind of time.

"The book is long. Did you really need to address twenty-five lies?"

Yes, we did.

This subject has been systematically overlooked among American Christians. For decades, support for Israel was assumed in evangelical churches—it was part of the air we breathed. But assumptions are not the same as understanding. When the cultural winds shifted, when the propaganda intensified, when the accusations became sophisticated and emotionally compelling, many believers discovered they had convictions without foundations. They knew they were supposed to support Israel, but they didn't know why. And when the pressure came, their support crumbled.

This book is an attempt to provide the foundations that were never properly laid. It is an attempt to be extensive because the assault is extensive. Every lie we address in these pages is a lie we have heard from real people—including Christians—who have absorbed it without ever encountering a serious response. If we had written a shorter book, we would have left some of those lies unanswered. And unanswered lies do not go away. They metastasize.

So yes, this book is long. It is long because the moment demands it. It is long because too little has been said for too long. And it is long because we would rather give you more than you need than leave you without the answers you are looking for.

Now, with those objections addressed, let us show you the pattern that makes all of this so dangerous—and so predictable.

The Pattern of Propaganda

History teaches us a sobering lesson: **Genocide never begins with gas chambers or machetes. It begins with words.** It begins with a narrative—propaganda that dehumanizes, marginalizes, and demonizes a target group until violence against them feels not only acceptable, but morally justified.

The Spirit of Slander

- Before the Holocaust, there was *Der Stürmer* and *The Eternal Jew*.
- Before the Rwandan genocide, there was Radio Télévision Libre des Mille Collines calling the Tutsis "cockroaches."
- Before the Armenian genocide, the Young Turks spread the lie that Armenians were traitors—an internal enemy that had to be removed.

The pattern never changes. **First come the words. Then comes the violence.**

And that is why the propaganda being unleashed against Israel today is so dangerous. This is not normal political criticism. It is not a neat distinction between "anti-Zionism" and antisemitism. What we are witnessing is the deliberate, coordinated demonization of the Jewish state and, increasingly, of the Jewish people themselves—using the same strategies, the same emotional triggers, and in many cases the same accusations that have preceded every major outbreak of violence against Jews in history.

This isn't just rhetoric. It's the opening stage of a pattern as old as Haman and as deadly as the twentieth century proved it to be.

The Numbers Tell a Story

Consider just one statistic that shows the scope of what we are facing. According to the Anti-Defamation League's Global 100 survey, **approximately 46 percent of adults worldwide—about 2.2 billion people—harbor antisemitic attitudes.**[1]

That number has **more than doubled** since the survey was first conducted in 2014.

Even more alarming is the generational divide. Among adults under 35, antisemitic attitudes reach **50 percent**, compared to **37 percent** among those over 50. The young are more antisemitic than the old. This is not the direction anyone would define as progress.

And consider the institutional bias. According to UN Watch, between 2006 and 2016, the United Nations Human Rights Council (UNHRC) passed **135 resolutions** condemning specific countries. Of those, **68—more than half—were directed at Israel alone.** That is more resolutions against Israel than against Syria, North Korea, Iran, China, Cuba, and Venezuela combined.

The UNHRC even maintains a permanent agenda item—**Agenda Item 7**—dedicated solely to condemning Israel. No other nation on earth is treated this way.

> Not Russia for invading Ukraine.
> Not China for its treatment of the Uyghurs.
> Not Iran for executing political prisoners.
>
> *Only Israel.*[2]

CHART 1

UN Human Rights Council Bias

UNHRC resolutions condemning specific countries (2006–2016): 135 total

COUNTRY	RESOLUTIONS	% OF TOTAL
Israel	68	50%+
Syria, N. Korea, Iran, Myanmar, Belarus combined	~50	~37%
China (for Uyghur genocide)	0	0%
Russia (for Ukraine invasion)	0	0%

These numbers tell a story. And the story is not about proportionate criticism of Israeli policies. The story is about obsession—a double standard so extreme that it points to something far deeper than politics.

The Nazi Roots

To understand where today's anti-Israel propaganda comes from, we have to look at its roots. And those roots lead us to a surprising moment in the middle of Nazi Germany.

On November 28, 1941, Adolf Hitler welcomed a visitor to the Reich Chancellery in Berlin. His guest was Haj Amin al-Husseini, the Grand Mufti of Jerusalem—the highest Islamic authority in Palestine during the

HAMAN'S LIES

British Mandate. The official German record of their meeting still exists today in the *Documents on German Foreign Policy, 1918–1945*.[3]

Al-Husseini had fled British Palestine in 1937 after the British tried to arrest him for stirring up violence. He slipped into Lebanon, then Iraq—where he backed a pro-Nazi coup—and eventually made his way through Italy to Germany. And now he was sitting across from Hitler himself.

According to the German record, the Mufti thanked Hitler for his support and told him that "the Arabs were Germany's natural friends because they had the same enemies ... namely the English, the Jews, and the Communists." Hitler answered by saying that Germany "stood for an uncompromising war against the Jews," including "active opposition to the Jewish national home in Palestine."

Then Hitler made a promise. Germany's goal, he said, was "solely the destruction of the Jewish element residing in the Arab sphere." This wasn't empty talk. The meeting happened just weeks before the Wannsee Conference, where the Nazi leadership would ratify the "Final Solution."

But the Mufti's partnership with the Nazis didn't end with that conversation. All through the war, al-Husseini used radio broadcasts to pump anti-Jewish propaganda into the Arab world.[4] He went even further. He helped recruit Muslims to fight in Nazi military units. And in 1943, the SS brought him in for a recruiting tour through Bosnia.

The result was the 13th Waffen–SS Mountain Division, known as *Handschar*—the Arabic word for a curved scimitar.[5] SS Chief Gottlob Berger reported that the Mufti's visit had "an extraordinarily successful impact." Between twenty-four thousand and twenty-seven thousand recruits signed up. The Mufti spoke to military imams, identifying their "common enemies: World Jewry, England, and Bolshevism."[6]

In total, al-Husseini recruited at least thirty thousand Muslim troops for Hitler across multiple units. Himmler made him an SS officer and gave him an office in the SS Main Office.[7]

After the war, Yugoslavia tried to indict the Mufti for war crimes, but he slipped out of French custody and fled to Cairo. From there, he kept spreading anti-Zionist and anti-Jewish propaganda until he died in 1974.

The point of this history is not to label every critic of Israel as a Nazi. The point is to recognize something important: **The Nazi propaganda playbook didn't disappear with Hitler. It found a new home.**

The Soviet Continuation

After World War II, the baton of anti-Jewish propaganda passed from Nazi Germany to the Soviet Union. The Soviets understood how powerful the Nazi framework had been, and they reshaped it for their own purposes during the Cold War.

In the mid-1960s, the international community was negotiating the International Convention on the Elimination of All Forms of Racial Discrimination. The United States and Brazil pushed to include a clause condemning antisemitism. But the USSR—while actively persecuting Jews and restricting their ability to leave—needed a way to deflect attention.

Their solution was simple, and deeply sinister: *Equate Zionism with racism*.[8] If Zionism could be branded as racism, then opposing Zionism wasn't antisemitism at all—it was "anti-racism." The logic mirrored earlier Nazi propaganda, which claimed that Jewish self-determination was really a conspiracy against the nations.

After the Six-Day War in 1967, the Soviet Union doubled down on this strategy. It built an entire academic field called **"Zionology,"** aimed at "exposing" supposed Israeli racism, imperialism, and—with stunning irony—Nazism. These materials weren't optional. They were assigned reading for Soviet soldiers, students, teachers, and members of the Communist Party.[9]

In 1974, the Soviet Party Central Committee approved a seven-point plan to ramp up anti-Zionist propaganda across the entire society. And in 1975, that effort paid off. The United Nations General Assembly passed Resolution 3379, declaring that "Zionism is a form of racism and racial discrimination."[10]

The resolution passed 72 to 35. Those voting in favor included every nation in the Soviet bloc and most of the Arab states.[11] The US Ambassador to the UN, Daniel Patrick Moynihan, fired back with a blistering response: "The lie is that Zionism is a form of racism. The overwhelmingly clear truth is that it is not."[12]

In 1991, after the Soviet Union collapsed, the resolution was finally revoked. Israel had made its repeal a requirement for taking part in the Madrid Peace Conference. But the damage was already done. The idea that "Zionism equals racism" had been stamped into the world's leading international institution. And from there it spread—into universities, NGOs, and activist networks around the globe.[13]

The vocabulary may have changed. Today we hear terms like "apartheid," "settler-colonialism," and "genocide." But the logic is the same: Delegitimize Jewish self-determination, portray Israel as uniquely evil, and prepare the ground for its removal.

The Spirit Behind the Strategy

Here is something that purely political or historical analysis cannot explain: **Demons do not die.**

When Nazi Germany fell, the demonic spirit that had fueled Hitler's genocidal hatred did not vanish in the bunker with him. It simply looked for another place to operate. And when the Soviet Union collapsed, the spirit behind its anti-Zionist propaganda did not fade away.

The Spirit of Slander

It migrated—into new institutions, new movements, and new voices willing to carry its message.

Jesus taught this principle in Matthew 12:43–45:

> "When an unclean spirit goes out of a man, he goes through dry places, seeking rest, and finds none. Then he says, 'I will return to my house from which I came.' And when he comes, he finds *it* empty, swept, and put in order. Then he goes and takes with him seven other spirits more wicked than himself, and they enter and dwell there; and the last *state* of that man is worse than the first. So shall it also be with this wicked generation."

In the passage, Jesus is speaking about a person, but the principle extends beyond the individual. When a life, a culture, or even a political system is spiritually empty—when it is unguarded and unanchored—the enemy seeks a way back in. And if he cannot return to the same host, he simply looks for another. Demonic influence searches for expression. When one host collapses, it moves to the next available place.

This helps us understand why the same destructive spirit keeps reappearing in history. The spirit of Haman did not die on the gallows. It resurfaced in Antiochus Epiphanes, who desecrated the Temple and attempted to erase Jewish identity. It resurfaced in the Roman emperors who destroyed Jerusalem and scattered the Jewish people. It reemerged in the Crusaders, the Inquisitors, and the architects of the Russian pogroms. It rose again in Hitler. It rose again in Soviet propaganda. And it is active today—in the chants on university campuses, in the resolutions passed at the United Nations, and in the rhetoric spreading across social media. The faces change, the institutions change, the language changes, but the spirit behind them does not.

This is why the lies never fully disappear. This is why each generation finds itself confronting the same accusations wrapped in new vocabulary.

HAMAN'S LIES

The human instruments shift, but the spiritual force driving them remains constant. The ancient serpent—the accuser, the father of lies—has opposed God's Covenant People from the beginning. He understands something many believers overlook: God's promises to Israel form the foundation for all His promises. If the enemy could destroy Israel, he imagines he could discredit God Himself and unravel God's redemptive plan. He cannot. But he never stops trying.

This is why Paul's words in Ephesians 6:12 are so essential:

> For we do not wrestle against flesh and blood, but against principalities, against powers, against the rulers of the darkness of this age, against spiritual *hosts* of wickedness in the heavenly *places.*

The battle we are witnessing—whether in the streets, on our campuses, in political chambers, or online—is not merely political or ideological. **It is spiritual.** And a spiritual battle requires spiritual discernment, spiritual strength, and spiritual weapons.

Haman was not simply a political official. He was animated by a demonic spirit that hated God's Covenant People. That same evil spirit operates today using the same strategy it has always used: Build a narrative, repeat it until it sounds like truth, and then rely on institutions and influencers to give it authority. But just as in the book of Esther, the spirit behind Haman will not prevail. **The God of Israel does not change. His Covenant does not fail. His promises are everlasting.**

What This Book Will Do

In the pages ahead, we want to accomplish seven things.

First, we will show you why Israel matters prophetically. Israel is not just another country. It is what we call God's "super-sign"—the indicator that tells us where we are on the prophetic timeline. What happens to Israel, and how the nations treat Israel, reveal where we are in God's plan.

Second, we will expose Haman's template—the four-part propaganda strategy that has been used against the Jewish people for centuries. Once you see the pattern, you will recognize it everywhere.

Third, we will show you Esther's template—how the spirit of Esther rises in every generation to stand "for such a time as this." Just as Haman's spirit finds new hosts, so does the calling of Esther find new vessels.

Fourth, we will walk you through the anatomy of deception—how good, ordinary, compassionate people can become carriers of destructive ideas without ever intending to. Understanding this pattern will help you recognize how modern anti-Israel narratives take root and gain power.

Fifth, we will take you through twenty-five specific lies that are being told about Israel today. For each one, we will show you the accusation, why it sounds persuasive, and what the historical truth actually is.

Sixth, we will show you why supporting Israel is not a burden on American taxpayers, but one of the best investments America makes anywhere in the world. The returns—in military technology, intelligence, medical innovation, cybersecurity, economic growth, and strategic strength—far exceed the dollars invested. This is not charity. This is partnership that benefits both nations.

Seventh, we will show you why this matters for you as a believer. This is not just about politics or international relations. This is about prophecy, about spiritual warfare, about the blessing and cursing of Genesis 12:3, and about being a faithful witness in the last days.

Most people don't want to become experts in Middle Eastern history or international law. They don't have time to master political science or memorize talking points. They simply want to stop feeling overwhelmed. They want to understand what is true, recognize what is false, and know why Israel matters in God's plan—without needing a degree to do it.

This book is written for them. Our goal is to give you clarity where there has been confusion, confidence where there has been intimidation, and a simple framework you can hold onto when the arguments and accusations feel too complicated. You do not need to be a scholar to stand for truth. You just need the truth made clear. That is what this book will give you.

You'll also notice that this book includes extensive endnotes. That is intentional. Some readers want to dig deeper, verify sources, or explore the history and documentation behind what we have written. Those notes are there for you. But if they distract you from the flow of the book, *feel free to skip them*. Just stay with the main text. The endnotes are simply a resource for those who want more detail, not a burden for those who don't. This book is built so you can read it straight through without getting lost—and return to the notes only when you want to.

By the end of this book, you will be equipped to recognize the lies, answer them with truth, and stand with God's Covenant People in this critical hour. You will understand that you are not a spectator in this drama. You are a participant—positioned by God, for such a time as this.

A Note on the Harder Questions

Throughout this book, you will find sections in some chapters titled "Engaging the Harder Questions." These are not afterthoughts—they are essential to our purpose. We have written this book for believers who want to stand with Israel, but we know that standing requires more than conviction. It requires preparation. Your grandson may come home from college having read serious critics—not social media slogans, but professors who know the history, who acknowledge complexity, and who still reach conclusions hostile to Israel. If we only equip you to answer the slogans, we have failed you. You will win the argument at Thanksgiving and lose it at graduation.

The Spirit of Slander

So we have done something unusual: In the chapters where sophisticated critics would find our basic arguments insufficient, we present their strongest case—not a strawman, but the real argument a serious person would make. Then we give you the honest response, including places where we must acknowledge hard truths and genuine tensions. This is not weakness. This is how you earn the right to be heard. Someone who sees you grapple honestly with difficulty will trust you when you speak with confidence. If they suspect you are hiding something, they will dismiss everything you say. We want you to walk into any conversation—with a skeptic, a critic, or a loved one who has been swept up in the flood—and know that you have heard the hardest version of the case against Israel and found it answerable. Not easy. Not simple. But answerable.

One final note on these harder questions: Any nation under the kind of scrutiny Israel faces daily from the international community would struggle to answer every question. No country's wartime conduct survives examination under a microscope held by hostile observers. The United States, the United Kingdom, and France have all conducted military operations with civilian casualties that would dominate global headlines for months if Israel had done the same. The scrutiny itself is not neutral—it is part of the pressure campaign. That does not mean every question is illegitimate. But it does mean we should notice when Israel is asked to meet standards no other nation is expected to meet, and when the questions themselves are designed not to seek understanding but to delegitimize and ultimately eliminate.

CHART 2

The Recurring Pattern of Antisemitism

This timeline illustrates how Haman's four accusations—Different, Disloyal, Dangerous, Disposable—have recurred throughout history.

ERA	EVENT	HAMAN'S TEMPLATE IN ACTION
~473 BC	Haman's Plot	Original template: Jews accused of being Different, Disloyal, Dangerous, and therefore Disposable.
167 BC	Antiochus Epiphanes	Jews declared too "different"; Temple desecrated; Jewish practice outlawed; mass executions.
70 AD	Roman Destruction	Jews portrayed as disloyal rebels; Temple destroyed; 1,900-year exile begins.
1096–1291	The Crusades	Jews as "Christ-killers" and enemies of Christendom; Rhineland massacres.
1478–1834	Spanish Inquisition	Jews accused of secret disloyalty; 1492 expulsion; torture of "crypto-Jews."
1881–1920	Russian Pogroms	*The Protocols of Zion* fabricated; tens of thousands killed; millions fled.
1933–1945	The Holocaust	Nazi propaganda: Jews racially different, internationally disloyal, existentially dangerous. Six million murdered.
1948–1970s	Arab Expulsions	850,000+ Jews expelled from Arab countries; "fifth column" accusations.
May 28, 1905	UN Resolution 3379	Soviet-backed "Zionism is racism"—Haman's "different" accusation for the modern age.

ERA	EVENT	HAMAN'S TEMPLATE IN ACTION
October 7, 2023	Hamas Massacre	1,200 murdered. Within hours, celebrations in Western cities.
December 2025	Bondi Beach Attack	15+ killed at Hanukkah celebration, including Holocaust survivor. Pattern continues.

Key Pattern: Words come first. Violence follows. Every genocide is preceded by propaganda.

PART ONE

The Ancient Pattern

1

The Rising Tide

We want to tell you about a flood.

You know how it happens. You're standing outside, and you feel a drop. Just one drop. You barely notice it. Then another. And another. Each one so small, so insignificant, that you don't bother to seek shelter. A drop here, a drop there—what's the harm? You go about your business. You check your phone. You have conversations. Life continues.

And then suddenly—*suddenly*—you look up and realize you're standing in water up to your knees. The streets have become rivers. The drops have become a deluge. And you wonder: *How did I not see this coming? When did the rain become a flood?*

That's what happened to the Jewish community in America after October 7, 2023. That's what happened to all of us. Drop by drop, incident by incident—until suddenly we looked up and realized we were standing in a flood of hatred. And the real question every American has to face is this: *How did we not see it coming?*

The late Franklin H. Littell saw it coming. He's often called the "Father of Holocaust Studies," and for good reason. As a twenty-two-year-old in 1939, he stood in Nuremberg and watched a Nazi rally with his own eyes. That moment marked him. He spent the rest of his life trying to understand how a civilized society can sink into hatred. In 1975, he wrote a book called *The Crucifixion of the Jews*, where he warned about the patterns that always show up before a genocide—the layers of antisemitism that build like storm clouds, one on top of another.

After nearly a decade in post-war Germany working to help denazify the country, Littell issued a warning that was decades ahead of its time. He said that many modern universities were turning out people who were highly educated but morally empty—people who knew how to run systems and build technology but had lost their sense of right and wrong. In his later years, he poured himself into developing an early warning system for genocide because he understood something most people ignore: Floods don't arrive without signs. The first drops always fall for those who know how to see them.[1] And take note—Littell developed this early warning system over fifty years ago.

Littell understood that what we're witnessing in America today follows a script as old as civilization itself. Antisemitism is the world's oldest hatred, and when the first drops begin to fall in any society, the wise pay attention. Because those first drops always become a flood.

The Day the Skies Darkened

On October 7, 2023, the world witnessed the deadliest attack on the Jewish people since the Holocaust. In the early morning hours, during the joy of the Simchat Torah holiday, Hamas terrorists poured into Israel through more than a hundred breach points along the Gaza border. They stormed communities, homes, and a music festival—murdering roughly 1,200 innocent men, women, children, and the elderly.[2] At the Nova festival alone, 364 young people were killed while celebrating peace.

The attackers committed atrocities that almost defy description. Entire families were burned alive in their homes. Women were assaulted. Children were tortured. These weren't rumors—independent investigators confirmed what Israel had already shown the world. More than 250 people were dragged into Gaza as hostages, including babies, elderly Holocaust survivors, and citizens from over a dozen nations. The United States later confirmed that forty-four Americans were killed—the largest number of Americans murdered by terrorists since 9/11.[3]

What should have followed was universal outrage. A moment of moral clarity. Instead, something dark awakened. Within hours—not days, but hours—of the massacre, celebrations erupted in American cities. And remember this: At that point, Israel hadn't responded at all. The only thing they had said was that they *would* respond. That's it. Yet pro-Hamas rallies were already filling the streets of New York, Los Angeles, and Chicago. People cheering the slaughter. Holding signs praising the "resistance." Voices shouting in support of the very terrorists who had murdered children only hours before.

Each rally was a drop. Each celebration was a drop. Each voice raised in support of terror was a drop.

Drip ... drip ... drip.

And most Americans didn't even realize the rain had started.

Counting the Drops

Let us give you the numbers because numbers tell a story that emotions cannot dismiss. The Anti-Defamation League (ADL), which has been tracking antisemitic incidents since 1979, began counting the drops. What they found should terrify every American.

In 2024, the ADL recorded 9,354 antisemitic incidents across the United States—the highest number ever recorded in the forty-six years they have been tracking.[4] That's more than twenty-five targeted anti-Jewish incidents every single day. More than one every hour. This represented a 5 percent increase from 2023's already record-shattering 8,873 incidents, a 344 percent increase over the previous five years, and an astonishing 893 percent increase over the past decade.[5]

Think about what that means. In 2014, the ADL recorded roughly 950 antisemitic incidents in America. A decade later, nearly ten times as many. The drops had become a deluge.

But here's what the numbers don't fully capture: *the acceleration.* Before October 7, antisemitism was already rising—drop by drop, year by year. But after October 7, the drops became a downpour. In just the first three months following the Hamas attack, the ADL documented 3,283 incidents—a 360 percent surge from the same period a year earlier.[6] That's more antisemitic acts in three months than they usually record in an entire year.

Assaults rose by 21 percent in 2024, with 196 physical attacks impacting 250 victims. Vandalism rose by 20 percent, with 2,606 incidents of property damage—swastikas spray-painted on synagogues, Jewish cemeteries desecrated, mezuzahs torn from doorways. Harassment remained staggeringly high at 6,552 incidents. Jewish institutions received 627 bomb threats, 89 percent of them targeting synagogues.[7]

For the first time in the history of the ADL's annual audit, a majority of all antisemitic incidents—58 percent—contained elements related to Israel or Zionism.[8] *Anti-Israel hatred had fused with ancient anti-Jewish hatred, creating a toxic new strain of bigotry that spread like wildfire across America.*

According to the FBI's statistics, antisemitic incidents accounted for 68 percent of all religion-based hate crimes in America in 2023—a 63 percent increase from the previous year.[9] Think about that: Jews make up roughly 2 percent of the American population, yet they are the target of more than two-thirds of all religious hate crimes. Each crime was a drop. Each threat was a drop. And the drops kept falling, faster and faster, until the ground could no longer absorb them.

CHART 3

Global Antisemitism by the Numbers

Global Attitudes (ADL Global 100)

METRIC	STATISTIC
Adults worldwide harboring antisemitic attitudes	46% (~2.2 billion)
Antisemitic attitudes among adults under 35	**50%**
Antisemitic attitudes among adults over 50	37%
Americans aged 18-24 siding with Hamas over Israel	**60%**

United States (ADL Audit 2024)

METRIC	STATISTIC
Total antisemitic incidents in 2024	9,354 (highest ever)
Increase over past decade (since 2014)	**893%**
Incidents in 3 months post-October 7	3,283 (360% surge)
Campus incidents (84% increase from 2023)	1,694
Jews: % of population vs. % of religious hate crimes	2% vs. 68%

The Global Flood

But this wasn't just an American phenomenon. The flood was rising across the entire Western world.

According to the World Zionist Organization and the Jewish Agency for Israel, global antisemitic incidents surged 340 percent between 2022 and 2024.[10] The Combat Antisemitism Movement documented

6,326 incidents worldwide in 2024 alone—a 108 percent increase from the previous year.[11] Their report was blunt: "We are now facing the most severe wave of antisemitism since the end of the Second World War."

In the United Kingdom, the Community Security Trust recorded 3,528 antisemitic incidents in 2024—the second-highest ever, following 2023's record of over 4,100 incidents.[12] That represents a 450 percent increase from pre-October 7 levels.[13] There were 201 physical assaults on British Jews, 157 instances of property damage, and 223 incidents specifically targeting synagogues. Jewish Britons reported hiding their mezuzahs, changing their names on ride-sharing apps to sound less Jewish, and avoiding certain neighborhoods of London during the weekly pro-Palestinian marches.

In France, antisemitic acts nearly quadrupled, with 1,570 incidents recorded in 2024—62 percent of all religious hate crimes in the country, despite Jews comprising less than 1 percent of the population.[14] Twenty-eight percent of these incidents involved violence. Physical assaults rose from 85 to 106. A comprehensive survey found that 64 percent of the French population believes Jews have reason to fear for their lives in their own country.[15] France's Ministry of National Education reported a 420 percent increase in antisemitic acts in schools.[16]

In Germany, where the memory of the Holocaust should serve as a permanent warning, police recorded 3,200 antisemitic crimes between January and October 2024. In the three months immediately following October 7, Germany witnessed nearly three thousand incidents—32 per day.[17] The Research and Information on Antisemitism office recorded 1,383 incidents in Berlin alone during the first half of 2024, the highest number in any previous year. The rise of the Alternative für Deutschland party, classified by some German states as right-wing extremist, poses what Jewish organizations call "a major challenge" to Jewish religious life.[18]

The Rising Tide

In Canada, the situation was even more dire. B'nai Brith documented 6,219 antisemitic incidents in 2024—a 562 percent increase from 2022. A quarter of these incidents were violent.[19] Jewish schools were targeted by gunfire. Synagogues received threats. The Jewish community, which represents less than 1 percent of Canada's population, was the target of 19 percent of all reported hate crimes.

In Australia, the Executive Council of Australian Jewry recorded 2,062 antisemitic incidents between October 2023 and September 2024—a 387 percent increase from the previous year.[20] And then came December 6, 2024, when masked arsonists attacked the Adass Israel Synagogue in Melbourne in the early morning hours, destroying much of the building while worshippers were arriving for morning prayers. Two people were injured. The attack was classified as terrorism—the only antisemitic incident in Australia to receive that designation.[21]

The Simon Wiesenthal Center responded by issuing a travel warning advising Jews to exercise "extreme caution" when visiting Australia, stating they were "not convinced that Jews are safe" in the country. A travel warning. For Australia. In 2024.

The European Union Agency for Fundamental Rights surveyed Jews across thirteen European countries and found that 80 percent felt antisemitism had grown in their country over the previous five years. Ninety percent had encountered antisemitism online. Fifty-three percent worried about their own safety, and 60 percent worried about their family's safety.[22] More than three-quarters reported hiding their Jewish identity at least occasionally—not wearing a Star of David, not speaking Hebrew in public, not affixing a mezuzah to their door.[23]

This is what the flood looks like from above: Millions of Jews across the Western world calculating, every day, how much of their identity to reveal and how much to hide.

The Ideological Shift

Perhaps the most alarming aspect of this flood is where the water is coming from.

For decades, antisemitism in America was primarily associated with the far right—neo-Nazis, white supremacists, the kinds of extremists who marched in Charlottesville chanting "Jews will not replace us." That threat hasn't disappeared. The 2018 Tree of Life Synagogue massacre in Pittsburgh, where a white supremacist murdered eleven Jews during Shabbat services, remains the deadliest attack on Jews in American history.

But something fundamental has shifted.

According to the Combat Antisemitism Movement's 2024 report, far-left antisemitism surged by 324.8 percent compared to 2023. Meanwhile, far-right incidents dropped by 54.8 percent. For the first time, the far left became the dominant source of antisemitic incidents globally, with 68.4 percent of all documented cases linked to far-left ideology—compared to just 7.3 percent from the far right.[24]

"Radicalized social movements, media disinformation campaigns, and efforts to target Jewish communities under the guise of anti-Israel activism have primarily fueled this increase," the report stated.[25] Islamist-motivated incidents also rose 44.3 percent.[26]

This is a tectonic shift. For the first time in modern history, the primary threat to Jewish safety in the West is coming not from the political fringe most associated with historical antisemitism, but from movements that *claim* to champion justice, equality, and human rights. The hatred has put on a new mask—but it's the same ancient hatred underneath.

When the Drops Drew Blood

On November 5, 2023, less than a month after the October 7 attack, the drops became something more. Blood mixed with the rising waters.

In Thousand Oaks, California—a quiet suburb of Los Angeles—sixty-nine-year-old Paul Kessler went to a street corner where pro-Israel and pro-Palestinian rallies were occurring simultaneously. Paul was a passionate man, an ardent Democrat who cared deeply about progressive causes. He was also a Jew who loved Israel. That Sunday afternoon, he stood at that intersection holding an Israeli flag, peacefully exercising his First Amendment rights.

Paul Kessler was just one man. One drop in the crowd. But what happened to him showed how dangerous the rising waters had become.

During an altercation with a pro-Palestinian counter-protester, Paul fell (or was pushed, according to some accounts) backward and struck his head on the pavement. He was conscious when paramedics arrived. He spoke with officers at the hospital. But his condition deteriorated through the night, and just after 1 a.m. the next morning, Paul Kessler was pronounced dead. The Ventura County Medical Examiner ruled his death a homicide caused by blunt force head injury.

A professor was charged with involuntary manslaughter and battery. Investigators noted that antisemitic hate speech had been heard at the rally that day—more drops falling on the crowd. Paul Kessler may have been the first American to die in the post-October 7 flood. He was a Jewish man, standing on an American street, holding the flag of Israel—and he paid for it with his life.

The Jewish Federation of Greater Los Angeles called it "an antisemitic crime" and declared, "Violence against our people has no place in civilized society." A memorial was erected at the street corner where he fell.

Flowers were laid. Candles were lit. But by then, the waters were rising everywhere—and Paul Kessler was still dead.

The Flood Reaches the Ivory Towers

If you want to see where the flood waters rose highest, look at our universities. These are supposed to be the sanctuaries of learning, the citadels of enlightenment, the places where young minds are shaped for leadership. Instead, they became some of the most dangerous places in America to be visibly Jewish.

In 2024, the ADL recorded 1,694 antisemitic incidents on college campuses—84 percent higher than in 2023. Campus incidents comprised 18 percent of all incidents nationally, a larger proportion than in any previous audit.[27] But the numbers don't capture the atmosphere of fear that descended on Jewish students across the country.

A Hillel International survey found that 61 percent of Jewish college students had witnessed antisemitic, threatening, or derogatory language during campus protests. A majority said encampments had made them feel less safe. More than half had their classes canceled, interrupted, moved online, or been blocked from attending due to protests.[28] A Tufts University study found that more than a quarter of Jewish students felt they needed to hide their Jewish identity to fit in—nearly double the rate from spring 2022.[29]

At Cornell University, the drops became a torrent of terror. In late October 2023, a twenty-one-year-old junior allegedly posted a series of threats on an online forum. He threatened to "shoot up" the Center for Jewish Living on campus. He threatened to "bring an assault rifle to campus and shoot" Jews. He made explicit threats to stab, behead, and rape Jewish students. Some of his posts were made under usernames that included the word "Hamas."[30]

The Rising Tide

The threats were so severe that Cornell's Hillel organization warned Jewish students and staff to avoid the kosher dining hall "out of an abundance of caution." Think about that: Jewish students at an Ivy League university, in the year 2023, were being told not to eat in their own dining hall because someone had threatened to murder them there.

Governor Kathy Hochul traveled to campus. "If you're going to engage in these harmful actions, hate crimes, breaking our laws, you will be caught and you will be prosecuted to the fullest extent of the law," she declared. The FBI launched a hate crime investigation. The student was arrested and federally charged. Cornell canceled classes for a day. But the message had been delivered: The flood had reached Cornell, and no one was safe.

At Harvard, the waters rose differently but just as dangerously. On October 18, 2023—just eleven days after the massacre—pro-Palestinian protesters staged a "die-in" at Harvard Business School. An Israeli first-year student named Yoav Segev walked past the demonstration. What followed was captured on video that went viral: Protesters surrounded him, shoved keffiyehs in his face, physically blocked his path, and shouted "Shame! Shame! Shame!" as he struggled to escape.

Two graduate students were eventually charged with assault and battery. But Harvard was accused of obstructing the criminal investigation. The victim later filed a lawsuit alleging a cover-up and "systemic antisemitism." And then, in a development that defied belief, Harvard quietly rewarded the very students who had been charged with assaulting their Jewish classmate. In August 2025, one of the attackers—a Harvard Divinity School graduate named Elom Tettey-Tamaklo—was hired as a graduate teaching fellow at Harvard, responsible for advising faculty on curriculum design. The other, law student Ibrahim Bharmal, received a $65,000 fellowship from the *Harvard Law Review* to work with the Council on American-Islamic Relations.

At Harvard, it seemed, the flood was not just tolerated—it was welcomed. It was rewarded.[31]

The Day America Saw the Flood

For weeks, the drops had been falling. For weeks, the waters had been rising. But still most Americans hadn't noticed. They were busy with their lives, checking their phones, having conversations, going about their business. The flood was happening to other people—to Jews, to Israelis, to students at elite universities far away. It wasn't their problem. It wasn't their flood.

Then came December 5, 2023. That was the day America finally looked up and saw the swirl of water rushing toward them.

The House Committee on Education and the Workforce called three university presidents to testify about antisemitism on their campuses: Claudine Gay of Harvard, Liz Magill of the University of Pennsylvania, and Sally Kornbluth of MIT. These were the leaders of three of the most prestigious institutions in the world—schools that had educated presidents, Supreme Court justices, Nobel laureates.

Representative Elise Stefanik of New York, herself a Harvard alumna, asked what seemed like a simple question: Does calling for the genocide of Jews violate your university's code of conduct?

Think about that question. Does calling for the systematic murder of every Jewish man, woman, and child violate the rules of your school? Any decent human being would answer immediately: Yes. Of course. Absolutely. Without hesitation. Without qualification.

"It is a context-dependent decision," replied Penn's Liz Magill.

Context-dependent. In that moment, millions of Americans lifted their heads and suddenly realized they were standing in a flood. The waters hadn't just reached the universities—they had saturated them completely. The leaders of our most prestigious institutions couldn't bring themselves to say that calling for genocide was wrong. The drops had become a deluge so deep that it had drowned their moral compass.

This is exactly what Hannah Arendt meant by "the banality of evil." Watching Adolf Eichmann stand trial in Jerusalem, she saw not a frothing monster but a small, efficient bureaucrat who spoke in clichés and hid behind procedures. She did not mean evil is dull or boring; she meant it becomes ordinary for the people who carry it out. Men who kissed their children goodbye in the morning spent their workday signing deportation orders and scheduling trains to the death camps—and slept soundly because, in their minds, they were only following policy.[32] That is the chilling echo in our own moment: University presidents and cultural elites treating open calls for Jewish genocide as a "context-dependent" question of speech codes, as if the problem were merely administrative and not moral to the core.

The outrage was immediate and bipartisan. Donors withdrew tens of millions of dollars. Alumni demanded accountability. Saturday Night Live parodied the testimony. Within days, Liz Magill resigned. On January 2, 2024, Claudine Gay resigned from Harvard—the shortest tenure in nearly four hundred years. But the flood didn't recede with their departures. If anything, it grew stronger.

The Flood Crests

By spring 2024, what had started as scattered drops had become a raging flood surge that swept across more than 100 American universities. On April 17, students at Columbia University established what they called a "Gaza Solidarity Encampment" in the center of campus.[33] The timing was deliberate: It was the same day Columbia's president, Minouche Shafik, was testifying before Congress about antisemitism. Within days, the waters spread: Harvard, Yale, Princeton, MIT, Northwestern, UCLA, and dozens more.

At Columbia, the flood revealed its true nature. Protesters chanted "Al-Qassam, you make us proud! Take another soldier out!"—praising Hamas's military wing, the same organization that had committed the October 7 massacre. They chanted, "Hamas, we love you. We support your rockets too!"[34] Signs declared "Zionists not allowed here." Students shouted, "Go back to Poland!" at their Jewish classmates—echoing the deportations of the Holocaust. Some called for "10,000 October 7ths."

At one protest, someone held a sign in front of Jewish students that read "Al-Qassam's next targets." A student screamed at Jewish counter-protesters: "Remember the 7th of October? That will happen not one more time, not five more times... but 10,000 more times." Another added: "The 7th of October is about to be every [expletive] day for you."[35]

Rabbi Elie Buechler, who works with Columbia's Jewish students, took the extraordinary step of telling them to go home for their own safety. A rabbi, at an *American* university, telling Jewish students to flee! The flood had made Columbia uninhabitable for Jews.

On April 30, protesters escalated by breaking into Hamilton Hall, smashing windows, and barricading themselves inside with furniture and zip-ties. They locked a facilities worker inside during the takeover.[36] Police were called in twice. Over 100 protesters were arrested. An August 2024 task force report painted a devastating picture: Antisemitism was "common in students' clubs, classrooms and dorms." A Jewish student who placed a mezuzah on her doorway—a simple expression of faith—was harassed until she left her dorm. Professors were reported to have told students that "Jews control the media." The flood had saturated everything.

The Symbol of Death

By now, a particular symbol kept appearing at encampments and protests across the country: the inverted red triangle. This symbol comes directly from Hamas propaganda videos, where it marks Israeli targets moments before they are attacked.[37] It is a death marker. And it was showing up at American universities, on flyers, on banners, spray-painted on buildings—and on Jewish homes.

In June 2024, vandals painted the red triangle on the home of the Jewish director of the Brooklyn Museum. In Pittsburgh—near the Tree of Life Synagogue where eleven Jews were murdered in 2018—vandals painted the red triangle on Chabad of Squirrel Hill, across the street from a Jewish day school.[38] Pennsylvania Governor Josh Shapiro responded: "The Squirrel Hill community witnessed the deadliest act of antisemitism in our nation's history at Tree of Life Synagogue. They should not need to wake up to antisemitic graffiti in their neighborhood."[39]

But they did. And they continued to.

In Philadelphia, Congregation Mikveh Israel—the oldest continuously operating synagogue in America, founded in 1740—older than the Republic itself—was targeted three times in a single day in October 2024. First, arson: a dumpster was set ablaze against the building, damaging a window. Then, attempted burglary: Two men tried to break in through a fence. Then, vandalism: A religious sculpture was defaced with profanity.[40] The Jewish Federation of Greater Philadelphia reported over 130 antisemitic incidents in the city in 2024 alone.

In Melbourne, Australia, masked arsonists attacked the Adass Israel Synagogue at 4:10 in the morning on December 6, 2024, using accelerants to destroy much of the building.[41] The attack was classified as terrorism. Australian Prime Minister Anthony Albanese condemned it as antisemitic, but many in the Jewish community felt his government's response had been "slow and timid." The Australian government allocated 30 million Australian dollars to rebuild the synagogue.

In August 2024, the residential building of a Columbia University administrator was vandalized with red paint that included inverted red triangles.[42] The symbol had moved from Hamas propaganda videos to American streets, from political protests to private homes. What starts with symbols doesn't end with symbols.

The Hidden Jews

One of the most heartbreaking consequences of the flood is what it has done to Jewish identity in America and around the world.

According to the American Jewish Committee's "State of Antisemitism in America 2024" report, 56 percent of American Jews said they had altered their behavior over the past year out of fear of antisemitism.[43] They hid their Star of David necklaces. They covered their kippot with baseball caps. They removed mezuzahs from their doorposts. They changed their names on ride-sharing and food delivery apps to sound less Jewish.

A rabbi in Houston wrote in *Time* magazine that for the first time in his twenty-four years of ministry, he had found himself removing his yarmulke in certain public settings—not because he felt an immediate threat, but because he felt "enough wariness about how it would be received."[44] For the first time in his life, he felt the need for a security escort walking home from Yom Kippur services.

Families in his community elected to tone down their Hanukkah decorations. Several members told him they were considering removing their mezuzahs.[45]

The ADL's senior vice president wrote that she had recently found herself "tucking my Star of David necklace inside my shirt while getting into a taxi."[46] If someone who works professionally in Jewish advocacy feels the need to hide, what does that tell us about what ordinary Jewish students and families are experiencing?

In New York City, a young woman had her Star of David necklace ripped off while riding the subway.[47] On campuses, Jewish students formed "protection squads" to accompany each other. In 2024 America, Jewish students needed escorts.

The European Union's Fundamental Rights Agency found that 76 percent of European Jews hide their identity at least occasionally.[48] Thirty-four percent avoid Jewish events or sites because they don't feel safe. In response to online antisemitism, 24 percent avoid posting content that would identify them as Jewish, and 16 percent reduced their use of certain platforms entirely.[49]

This is what the flood has done: It has made millions of Jews around the world ask themselves, every day, whether it's safe to be who they are.

The Cost of Safety

Jewish schools and institutions across the country have dramatically increased their security spending—up 47 percent since October 7. The average Jewish school now spends over $315,000 annually just to keep children safe. Parents drop their kids off past armed guards and metal detectors. Synagogues install bulletproof glass. Security cameras monitor every entrance. Panic buttons are within reach of every rabbi.

Each expense is an acknowledgment: The flood is here, and no one knows when it will recede.

In the United Kingdom, the government extended the Jewish Community Protective Security Grant, which pays for commercial security guards at synagogues and Jewish schools across the country. In Australia, state and federal police increased patrols around synagogues and Jewish institutions. In France, soldiers patrol Jewish neighborhoods.

This is what Jewish life in the West has become: a constant calculation of risk, a daily assessment of threat, a perpetual state of vigilance that previous generations thought they had left behind in the old country, in the old century, in the old world.

Building the Levees

In March 2025, the federal government finally acted to hold back the waters. Four federal agencies jointly announced the cancellation of $400 million in grants and contracts to Columbia University for its "continued inaction in the face of persistent harassment of Jewish students." Education Secretary Linda McMahon declared it a warning: "Since October 7, Jewish students have faced relentless violence, intimidation, and antisemitic harassment on their campuses—only to be ignored by those who are supposed to protect them. We will not tolerate their appalling inaction any longer."

Columbia paid a $220 million settlement. They disciplined seventy students. They adopted new definitions of antisemitism. The Trump administration revoked student visas and cut federal funding to other colleges and universities accused of tolerating antisemitism.

But we have to ask: *Why did it take hundreds of millions of dollars to build levees that basic human decency should have provided? Why did our universities wait until the flood was catastrophic before acknowledging the rain?*

What the Flood Reveals

The ADL's Jonathan Greenblatt put it starkly: "The American Jewish community is facing a threat level that's now unprecedented in modern history. It's shocking that we've recorded more antisemitic acts in three months than we usually would in an entire year."

Tel Aviv University's authoritative Antisemitism Worldwide Report, which has been published for a quarter century, concluded that while there was a slight decrease in some countries compared to the immediate aftermath of October 7, "around the world, levels of antisemitism remain significantly higher compared to the period before October 7."[50] The report found that in cities like New York, Chicago, Toronto, and London, fewer than 10 percent of antisemitic attacks led to arrests between 2021 and 2023.[51]

"The sad truth," the report stated, "is that antisemitism surged just as the Jewish state appeared most vulnerable and under existential threat."

The flood is still rising. And the question that confronts every American, every person of conscience, and every Christian in the Western world, is simple: *What will we do about it?*

History has shown us what happens when societies allow hatred of Jews to fester unchecked. Every empire that has turned against the Jewish people has eventually been swept away by its own flood. Egypt. Babylon. Rome. Spain. Nazi Germany. The Soviet Union. The hatred that rises against the Jews always eventually consumes the nations that embrace it.

The question is whether America will learn from history or repeat it. Will Christians in America stand up and be counted as defenders of God's Chosen People. The drops are still falling. The waters are still rising. And every day we fail to act, the flood grows stronger.

The hour is late. But it is not too late.

But to understand what we are fighting, we must first understand why it matters. The flood of antisemitism is not random hatred—it is targeted at God's prophetic purposes. In the next chapter, we will see why Israel is not just another nation, but the "super-sign" of Bible prophecy—the indicator that tells us where we are on God's timeline.

A Generational Chasm

Before we leave this chapter, we need to discuss what is perhaps the most disorienting aspect of this flood; what it has revealed within families themselves. Across America, parents and grandparents sit at dinner tables in stunned silence as their children and grandchildren repeat Hamas propaganda as if it were established fact. They hear their own flesh and blood dismiss the murder of 1,200 Israelis as "resistance." They watch teenagers who have never willingly opened a history book lecture them about "colonialism" and "apartheid." They see young people who cannot find Israel on a map demand its elimination "from the river to the sea."

Pastors watch young adults they baptized and nurtured in the faith embrace ideologies that would have been unthinkable a generation ago. Grandparents who remember when "Never Again" meant something—who grew up in the shadow of the Holocaust, who were raised by the Greatest Generation that liberated the camps—cannot comprehend how their grandchildren have come to parrot the very antisemitic tropes their ancestors fought and died to defeat. A 2024 Harvard-Harris poll found that 60 percent of Americans aged 18 to 24 now side with Hamas over Israel—a terrorist organization over a democracy.[52] Among Americans 65 and older, 89 percent support Israel. This is not merely a generational divide. *These are different moral universes.*

The culprit is not hard to identify. TikTok—the Chinese-owned social media platform where a generation now gets its "news"—has become what one researcher called "the biggest antisemitic movement since the Nazis."[53] The hashtag #Palestine has received over 40 billion views; pro-Hamas content floods young people's feeds while algorithms suppress pro-Israel voices. Studies have documented bot networks amplifying antisemitic content and targeting young influencers for radicalization. A generation that cannot name the capitals of neighboring states has been taught to chant slogans about a conflict they do not understand, in a region they have never visited, about a history they have never studied.

For parents and grandparents, for pastors and teachers, the experience is surreal—like watching their children drown in a flood they cannot see. They feel helpless. They feel as if they are living through a nightmare that the Greatest Generation assured them could never happen again in the West. And yet here it is, not imported from some foreign land, but growing in their own living rooms, spreading through the phones in their children's hands, poisoning minds they thought they knew.

Why Your Children and Grandchildren Believe What They Believe

We need to pause right here to say something directly to those of you who are heartbroken about what has happened in your own families.

You raised your children in the faith. You took them to church. You taught them right from wrong. You told them about the Holocaust. You explained why Israel matters. And now you sit across from a grandson who tells you that Israel is committing genocide—and he says it with the same moral certainty you once used to teach him the Ten Commandments.

You feel like you're watching someone you love drown in lies. And the hardest part is that they think *you're* the one who's deceived.

We've heard from hundreds of you. The letters break our hearts. "My granddaughter won't speak to me anymore because I support Israel." "My son says I've been brainwashed by Fox News." "My niece posted something so hateful about Jews that I couldn't believe it came from her." You're not alone. This is happening in families all across America.

We want to help you understand what happened—not to excuse the lies your loved ones have absorbed, but to help you respond with wisdom instead of just grief.

They Were Discipled by a Different Teacher

Here's the painful truth: While we were raising our children and grandchildren in church, someone else was discipling them Monday through Saturday.

The average young person spends seven to nine hours a day consuming digital media. Their phones are the first thing they see in the morning and the last thing they see at night. They scroll through hundreds of images and videos every day, each one carrying an implicit message about what's true, what's good, and what kind of person they should be.

TikTok alone has over a billion users, and its algorithm is designed to keep them watching. It learns what triggers their emotions and feeds them more of it. A teenager who watches one video critical of Israel will be served dozens more within hours. The algorithm doesn't care about truth—it cares about engagement. And outrage engages.

Meanwhile, how many hours did that same young person spend in church last year? How many hours in Scripture? How many hours in conversation with older believers who could have given them context and wisdom?

The math isn't close. We gave them an hour or maybe two on Sunday. The world gave them fifty hours a week.

They Were Never Taught to Think—Only to Feel

When we were young, we were taught to evaluate arguments. We learned to ask: Is this true? What's the evidence? Who's saying this and why? We didn't always do it well, but at least we knew we were supposed to try.

Today's young people have been trained differently. They've been taught that feelings are the measure of truth. If something feels unjust, it *is* unjust. If someone claims to be a victim, they *are* a victim. If an image makes you sad, the cause behind that image must be righteous.

This is why the propaganda works so effectively on them. They see a picture of a wounded Palestinian child, and their hearts break—as they should. But they've never been taught to ask the next questions: Who took this picture, and why? What happened before this moment? Who put this child in danger? Is there context I'm not seeing? Or as we have recently learned—Is this child even in Palestine?

Instead, they've been taught that asking those questions is itself a moral failure. "Why are you defending oppression?" "Why don't you care about children?" The emotional response *becomes* the argument. And anyone who wants to think more carefully is accused of being heartless.

Your children and grandchildren aren't stupid. Many of them are quite bright. But they've been trained to feel before they think—and to treat thinking as a betrayal of feeling. That's not an accident. That's the fruit of an education system and a media environment that has been shaping them for at least twenty years.

They Want to Be Good

Here's something important to understand: Most young people who have absorbed anti-Israel lies are not motivated by hatred. They're motivated by a desire to be good.

They genuinely believe they're standing up for the oppressed. They genuinely believe they're on the right side of history. They look at older generations and see people who were wrong about civil rights, wrong about the environment, wrong about so many things—and they're determined not to repeat those mistakes. They want to be the heroes of their own story.

The propaganda exploits this. It presents the conflict as a simple morality tale: powerful oppressor versus helpless victim. It strips away all context, all history, all complexity. It offers young people a way to feel righteous without doing any hard work. Just post the meme. Just share the video. Just repeat the slogan. Now you're one of the good people.

This is what makes it so hard to reach them. When you challenge the narrative, you're not just challenging their politics—you're challenging their identity as moral people. They experience your disagreement as an accusation that they don't care about suffering. And because they *do* care—because their compassion is real, even if it's been manipulated—they dig in deeper.

They've Been Isolated from Wisdom

There's something else happening that we don't talk about enough: Young people today have been systematically cut off from the wisdom of older generations.

When we were young, we respected our elders. We didn't always agree with them, but we understood that they had lived through things we hadn't. They had perspective we lacked. Their experience meant something.

Today's culture teaches the opposite. Youth is celebrated; age is dismissed. Your grandchildren have been told, implicitly and explicitly, that older people are out of touch, that tradition is oppression, that the past has nothing to teach them. They've been encouraged to trust their peers and their screens more than their parents and grandparents.

This is spiritually devastating. Proverbs is full of warnings about young people who reject the counsel of their elders.

> The way of a fool *is* right in his own eyes,
> But he who heeds counsel *is* wise. (Proverbs 12:15).

When an entire generation is trained to dismiss the wisdom of those who came before, that generation becomes dangerously vulnerable to deception.

Your children and grandchildren aren't rejecting *you* personally—though it feels that way. They're rejecting the entire concept that your experience and wisdom have value. And that rejection was taught to them by people who wanted to separate them from the very sources of truth that could protect them.

What This Means for You

So what do you do with this understanding?

First, *don't give up on them.* The deception is strong, but it's not permanent. Many young people eventually wake up—sometimes through life experience, sometimes through crisis, sometimes through the patient love of family members who never stopped praying for them. The prodigal son came home. Keep the light on.

Second, *don't win the argument at the cost of the relationship.* We know how frustrating it is when someone you love repeats obvious lies. We know the temptation to fire back with facts and watch them squirm. But if you destroy the relationship, you lose your chance to influence them over the long term. Stay in their lives. Let them know you love them even when you disagree. Be the steady presence that contradicts what they've been told about people like you.

Third, *pray for their eyes to be opened.* This is a spiritual battle, and it requires spiritual weapons. The same God who opened Lydia's heart can open your grandson's heart. The same Spirit who convicted Paul on the Damascus road can convict your niece scrolling through TikTok. Don't underestimate what God can do.

Fourth, *be ready with an answer.* When the moment comes—and it often comes unexpectedly—be prepared to share truth with gentleness and respect. That's part of why this book exists. Not so you can win debates, but so you can be ready when someone you love is finally willing to listen.

HAMAN'S LIES

Finally, *don't carry the guilt.* Some of you are blaming yourselves. *"If only I had taught them better. If only I had been more involved. If only I had seen this coming."* Stop. You did the best you could with what you knew. The forces arrayed against your family are immense—spiritual, cultural, technological, institutional. You were outgunned. That's not your fault. And beating yourself up doesn't help anyone.

The battle for the minds of the young people in your family isn't over. As long as they're breathing, there's hope. And the God who preserved His people through Pharaoh, through Haman, through Hitler, is more than able to preserve them through TikTok.

2

Israel—
God's Super-Sign

> "I will bring back the captives of My people Israel;
> They shall build the waste cities and inhabit *them*;
> They shall plant vineyards and drink wine from them;
> They shall also make gardens and eat fruit from them.
> I will plant them in their land,
> And no longer shall they be pulled up
> From the land I have given them,"
> Says the LORD your God.
>
> —Amos 9:14–15

Before we can understand the lies being told about Israel, we must understand why Israel matters. And Israel matters because God said it matters.

In Joel 3:1–2, the Lord declares:

> "For behold, in those days and at that time,
> When I bring back the captives of Judah and Jerusalem,
> I will also gather all nations,
> And bring them down to the Valley of Jehoshaphat;
> And I will enter into judgment with them there

On account of My people, My heritage Israel,
Whom they have scattered among the nations;
They have also divided up My land."

Notice what this prophecy connects: the regathering of the Jewish people to their land and the judgment of the nations for how they have treated Israel and divided the land. These two things are linked in God's prophetic program. And both are happening in our lifetime.

A Nation Born in a Day

On May 14, 1948, something happened that had never happened before in human history. A nation that had been scattered among the peoples of the earth for nearly two thousand years was reborn in a single day.

Through the word of the Lord, the prophet Isaiah had asked:

"Who has heard such a thing?
Who has seen such things?
Shall the earth be made to give birth in one day?
Or shall a nation be born at once?
For as soon as Zion was in labor,
She gave birth to her children" (Isaiah 66:8).

For millennia, the answer seemed to be no. Nations rise and fall gradually. They do not spring into existence overnight.

But on that May afternoon, David Ben-Gurion stood in the Tel Aviv Museum and declared the establishment of the State of Israel.[1] The British Mandate expired at midnight. And by the next morning, President Harry Truman had recognized the new nation—eleven minutes after its declaration.[2]

A nation was born in a day. Isaiah's prophecy was fulfilled.

This was unprecedented. No other people in history had been scattered across the globe for two millennia, maintained their distinct identity, and then returned to reconstitute their ancient nation in their ancestral homeland. It simply does not happen. Except that it did happen—exactly as the prophets foretold.

From the North and from All Lands

The prophet Jeremiah gave another specific prophecy about the regathering:

> "Therefore behold, the days are coming," says the LORD, "that it shall no more be said, 'The LORD lives who brought up the children of Israel from the land of Egypt,' but, 'The LORD lives who brought up the children of Israel **from the land of the north** and from all the lands where He had driven them.' For I will bring them back into their land which I gave to their fathers." (Jeremiah 16:14–15, emphasis added).

"From the land of the north." For centuries, this was a puzzle. What great Jewish population existed in "the land of the north"?

Then came the collapse of the Soviet Union. Between 1989 and 2002, approximately 1.1 million Jews emigrated from the former Soviet states to Israel.[3] They came from Russia, Ukraine, Belarus—"from the land of the north." Jeremiah's prophecy, written over 2,600 years ago, was fulfilled in our generation.

Jerusalem: The Prophetic Timepiece

Jesus himself gave us a prophetic indicator involving Jerusalem. In Luke 21:24, He said: "And they will fall by the edge of the sword, and be led away captive into all nations. And Jerusalem will be trampled by Gentiles until the times of the Gentiles are fulfilled."

"Until." That word tells us that the trampling would end. And on June 7, 1967, it did. During the Six-Day War, Israeli paratroopers captured the Old City of Jerusalem for the first time since AD 70. The iconic radio transmission echoed around the world: "The Temple Mount is in our hands."[4]

For nineteen centuries, Jerusalem had been "trampled by Gentiles"—ruled by Romans, Byzantines, Arabs, Crusaders, Mamluks, Ottomans, British, and Jordanians. But in 1967, Jewish sovereignty was restored to the Holy City.[5]

Jesus also said, in Matthew 24:32–35:

"Now learn this parable from the fig tree: When its branch has already become tender and puts forth leaves, you know that summer *is* near. So you also, when you see all these things, know that it is near—at the doors! Assuredly, I say to you, this generation will by no means pass away till all these things take place. Heaven and earth will pass away, but My words will by no means pass away."

The generation that sees these prophetic signs—including the restoration of Jerusalem—will see all things fulfilled. And Psalm 90:10 tells us a generation is seventy to eighty years.

Do the math. 1948 plus seventy to eighty years. *We are the final generation.*

Some Christians object that modern Israel has nothing to do with biblical Israel—a theological position called supersessionism or replacement theology. We address that objection fully in Chapter 6, where we examine the biblical evidence and the continuity between ancient and modern Israel. For now, we proceed with the prophetic evidence that Israel's restoration is God's work.

God's Land, God's People

Why does God care so much about this particular piece of real estate? Because He calls it His own.

In Leviticus 25:23, God declares: "The land shall not be sold permanently, for the land *is* Mine; for you *are* strangers and sojourners with Me." *The land of Israel belongs to God.* He has the right to give it to whomever He chooses. And He chose to give it to Abraham and his descendants through Isaac and Jacob.

In Genesis 15:18, God made a Covenant with Abraham: "To your descendants I have given this land, from the river of Egypt to the great river, the River Euphrates." This Covenant was confirmed to Isaac, to Jacob, and throughout the Bible.

The Covenant is described as "everlasting" (Genesis 17:7). The land is called an "everlasting possession" (Genesis 17:8). These are not temporary arrangements. They are permanent features of God's redemptive plan.

This is why Joel 3:2 says that God will judge the nations for "dividing up My land." Every peace plan that proposes to carve up the land of Israel, every resolution that denies Jewish sovereignty over Jerusalem, every campaign that seeks to delegitimize Israel's existence—all of these set themselves against God's Covenant. And God takes His Covenant personally and seriously.

The Blessing and the Curse

In Genesis 12:3, God made a promise to Abraham that extends to all who interact with his descendants:

> "I will bless those who bless you,
> And I will curse him who curses you;
> And in you all the families of the earth shall be blessed."

This is not ancient history. This promise is still in effect.

Consider the historical record. Spain expelled its Jews in 1492 and began a long decline from global superpower to secondary nation. The United Kingdom reneged on the Balfour Declaration and restricted Jewish immigration to Palestine even as Jews fled the Holocaust; the British Empire collapsed within a generation. The Soviet Union persecuted its Jews and led the campaign to delegitimize Israel; it no longer exists. Nazi Germany attempted to annihilate the Jewish people; it was destroyed so thoroughly that its crimes became the defining evil of the modern age.

On the other hand, the United States has been Israel's closest ally since 1948. Whatever challenges America faces, it remains the world's preeminent power. Coincidence? The Bible suggests otherwise.

Why the Lies Matter

This is why the propaganda campaign against Israel is so significant. It is not merely unfair. It is not merely biased. It is preparing the world to turn against God's Covenant People in the hour of their greatest need.

The prophet Zechariah tells us what is coming:

> "Behold, I will make Jerusalem a cup of drunkenness to all the surrounding peoples, when they lay siege against Judah and Jerusalem. And it shall happen in that day that I will make Jerusalem a very heavy stone for all peoples; all who would heave it away will surely be cut in pieces, though all nations of the earth are gathered against it" (Zechariah 12:2–3).

"All nations." Not some nations. All nations will ultimately turn against Jerusalem. And Zechariah 14:2 says: "For I will gather all the nations to battle against Jerusalem."[6]

Every lie that is accepted about Israel moves the world one step closer to that prophesied confrontation. Every accusation that delegitimizes

Israel makes it easier for nations to join the final assault. Every repetition of "apartheid," "genocide," and "settler-colonialism" hardens hearts against God's Covenant People.

This is not a political game. This is the setup for the final battle of this age.

And that is why every truth told about Israel matters. That is why every lie exposed pushes back against the darkness. That is why you need to know the truth—not just for Israel's sake, but for your own.

Because the God who blesses those who bless Israel and curses those who curse Israel is still watching. And He still keeps His word.

Now that we understand why Israel matters prophetically, we can examine the propaganda strategy being used against her. The lies we hear today are not new. They follow an ancient template—one that was first articulated twenty-five centuries ago by a man named Haman.

3

Haman's Template
How Lies Become Genocide

"No weapon formed against you shall prosper,
And every tongue *which* rises against you in judgment
You shall condemn.
This *is* the heritage of the servants of the Lord,
and their righteousness *is* from Me,"
Says the Lord.

—Isaiah 54:17

The Ancient Enemy: Haman's Amalekite Heritage

Before we examine Haman's propaganda techniques, we need to understand who he was. His identity is not incidental to the story—it is essential to it. The book of Esther repeatedly identifies him as "Haman the Agagite" (Esther 3:1, 10; 8:3, 5; 9:24). To modern readers, that title might seem like a minor historical footnote. To the original Jewish audience, it was a flashing warning sign. That single word—*Agagite*—connected Haman to the most ancient and relentless enemy Israel had ever faced: **Amalek.**[1]

To understand why this matters, we need to go back to the beginning.

The Origin of Amalek

The story starts with twin brothers: Jacob and Esau, the sons of Isaac and grandsons of Abraham. Before they were even born, they battled in their mother's womb. God told their mother Rebekah:

> "Two nations *are* in your womb,
> Two peoples shall be separated from your body;
> *One* people shall be stronger than the other,
> And the older shall serve the younger" (Genesis 25:23).

Jacob, the younger twin, would become the father of the twelve tribes of Israel. His name was later changed to *Israel,* meaning 'he who strives with God.' Esau, the older twin, became the father of the Edomites, and through one particular grandson, the father of the Amalekites.

Here is the genealogy: Esau had a son named Eliphaz. Eliphaz had a concubine named Timna, and together they had a son named Amalek (Genesis 36:12). This Amalek became the patriarch of a tribe that would set itself against Israel for centuries.

From the very beginning, there was something different about Amalek and his descendants. They were not merely political rivals or territorial competitors. They became the embodiment of irrational, implacable hatred toward the people of Israel.

The First Attack

Shortly after the Israelites escaped from slavery in Egypt, which is one of the greatest miracles in human history, something shocking happened. The Egyptian army had just been destroyed in the Red Sea. The nations around them had heard what God had done and were terrified. No one dared attack this people whose God could split huge bodies of water and drown armies.

No one, that is, except the Amalekites.

At a place called Rephidim, the Amalekites launched an unprovoked assault against the Israelites. But what made their attack uniquely evil was *how* they fought. The Bible records:

> "Remember what Amalek did to you on the way as you were coming out of Egypt, how he met you on the way and attacked your rear ranks, all the stragglers at your rear, when you *were* tired and weary; and he did not fear God" (Deuteronomy 25:17–18).

This is the scene: The Israelites were a nation of former slaves trudging through the desert. Included among them were men, women, children, and elderly. At the back of this vast caravan were the weakest: the sick, the elderly, the exhausted mothers with small children, those too frail to keep up with the main group. And *these* were the people the Amalekites targeted.

They did not challenge Israel's warriors in open combat. They ambushed the defenseless. They slaughtered the weak. They preyed upon those who could not fight back.

This was not warfare. This was terrorism. This was cruelty for cruelty's sake.

And notice the phrase at the end of that verse: "He did not fear God." Every other nation in the region had heard what God had done to Egypt. And those people were afraid. But the Amalekites had heard the same reports, and they attacked anyway. Their assault was not merely against Israel; it was a direct challenge to the God of Israel.

God's Response

God's response to this atrocity was unlike His response to *any* other nation. He declared perpetual war:

Then the LORD said to Moses, "Write this *for* a memorial in the book and recount *it* in the hearing of Joshua, that I will utterly blot out the remembrance of Amalek from under heaven." And Moses built an altar and called its name, The-LORD-Is-My-Banner; for he said, "Because the LORD has sworn: the LORD *will have* war with Amalek from generation to generation." (Exodus 17:14–16).

No other nation received such a sentence. God commanded Israel to destroy other enemies, but only Amalek was marked for total obliteration across all generations. Only Amalek warranted a divine vow of unending warfare.

The Spiritual Dimension

Why such an extreme response to one tribe's attack? Why perpetual war against Amalek when God showed mercy to other enemies?

The answer lies in the spiritual realm.

Ancient Jewish teaching recognized something profound about the conflict with Amalek. According to the Midrash (rabbinic commentary), every nation on earth has a guardian angel overseeing its destiny—*except for two.* Israel rejected the archangel Michael as their guardian, choosing instead to be guarded by God Himself. And Amalek? According to this teaching, **Amalek's guardian angel is Samael—the foremost angel of evil, meaning Satan himself.**[2]

This is why the battle against Amalek is described as continuing "from generation to generation." It is not merely a political or ethnic conflict. It is a spiritual war—the earthly manifestation of a cosmic battle between the forces of God and the forces of darkness.

The *Zohar*, the foundational text of Jewish mysticism, states it directly: "Amalek is Samael." In other words, behind the human enemies who attacked Israel's weakest members stood the accuser—the one the Bible calls "the father of lies" (John 8:44) and "the accuser of our brethren" (Revelation 12:10).

This explains something that has puzzled observers for millennia: *Why does hatred of the Jewish people persist across cultures, centuries, and ideologies?* Empires rise and fall, philosophies come and go, political systems transform—yet antisemitism endures. The names change: Pharaoh, Haman, Antiochus, the Inquisitors, the Cossacks, Hitler, Hamas. The vocabulary changes: religious persecution, racial theory, anti-Zionism. **But the target never changes.**

It is always Israel. It is always the Jewish people. It is always the Covenant Community.

The pattern is too consistent to be coincidental. There is a spirit behind it—an ancient malevolence that predates any modern political conflict.

King Saul's Fatal Failure

Centuries after the first Amalekite attack, God gave Israel an opportunity to fulfill His command. He sent the prophet Samuel to King Saul with specific instructions:

> Thus says the LORD of hosts: "I will punish Amalek *for* what he did to Israel, how he ambushed him on the way when he came up from Egypt. Now go and attack Amalek, and utterly destroy all that they have" (1 Samuel 15:2–3).[3]

Saul went to war and won a decisive victory. But then he made a fateful choice: He disobeyed God's command. Instead of destroying everything,

> But Saul and the people spared Agag and the best of the sheep, the oxen, the fatlings, the lambs, and all *that was* good, and were unwilling

to utterly destroy them. But everything despised and worthless, that they utterly destroyed (1 Samuel 15:9).

Agag was the King of the Amalekites.

When Samuel confronted Saul, the king made excuses. The prophet's response was devastating:

> For rebellion *is as* the sin of witchcraft,
> And stubbornness *is as* iniquity and idolatry.
> Because you have rejected the word of the Lord,
> He also has rejected you from *being* king" (1 Samuel 15:23).

Samuel then executed Agag himself, but the damage was done. Some Amalekites had escaped. The bloodline continued. The spirit of Amalek lived on.

From Agag to Haman

Now we can understand the significance of Haman's title.

Five hundred years after Saul's failure, in the Persian Empire, a man rose to become prime minister to King Ahasuerus. The book of Esther introduces him this way:

> "After these things King Ahasuerus promoted Haman, the son of Hammedatha **the Agagite**, and advanced him and set his seat above all the princes who *were* with him." (Esther 3:1, emphasis added).

The Agagite. A descendant of Agag. An Amalekite.

And notice who opposes Haman in the story. Mordecai is introduced as "the son of Jair, the son of Shimei, the son of Kish, a Benjamite" (Esther 2:5). "The son of Kish, a Benjamite"—the exact same description given to King Saul (1 Samuel 9:1–2). *Mordecai came from Saul's family line!*

The story of Esther is, in one sense, a rematch. The descendant of Saul versus the descendant of Agag. Benjamin versus Amalek once again. What Saul had failed to finish, Mordecai and Esther would complete.

Haman's genocidal rage against all Jews was not merely personal offense at Mordecai's refusal to bow. It was the ancient hatred of Amalek manifesting once again. It was the spirit behind his ancestor Agag, behind his ancestor Amalek, behind his ancestor Esau—the spirit of the one who has set himself against God's Covenant People since the beginning of time. Mordecai stood against Satan himself.

The Geography of Amalek

Where did the Amalekites live? The Bible places them in "the land of the South" (Numbers 13:29)—the Negev desert region. The Amalekites were nomads who roamed the wilderness between southern Canaan, the Sinai Peninsula, and the border of Egypt. Their territory overlapped with and bordered the land of the Philistines.[4]

One passage is particularly striking. During the time of the Judges, when Israel was weak and fragmented, the Amalekites joined forces with the Midianites to raid Israel. Scripture records that they "destroyed the produce of the land *as far as Gaza*" (Judges 6:4, emphasis added).

As far as Gaza.

Does this mean modern Gazans are Amalekites? No. The ancient Amalekites as an ethnic group disappeared from history after the tenth century BC. In rabbinic literature, Amalek comes to represent not a continuing bloodline but a symbolic embodiment of unprovoked hatred, moral inversion, and persistent opposition to the purposes of God.

Over time, Jewish interpretation understood Amalek less as a genealogical identity and more as a spiritual and ethical archetype. Maimonides (Rabbi Moses ben Maimon) taught that the distinct identity of Amalek was lost through historical population mixing, rendering the command concerning Amalek no longer applicable to any identifiable people group. As a result, the concept of Amalek functions within Jewish thought as a moral warning rather than an ethnic designation, emphasizing the eradication of evil dispositions rather than the targeting of human descendants.[5]

Thus the *spirit* of Amalek—attacking the weak, targeting civilians, refusing all peace, seeking the complete destruction of Israel—that spirit has found new hosts in every generation. And it is no coincidence that it manifests today in the same geographic region where Amalek once roamed.

The Spirit That Never Dies

Let us be absolutely clear again: We are not saying that any modern ethnic group *is* Amalek. The physical descendants of Amalek vanished long ago.

But the *spirit* of Amalek—that is a different matter.[6]

Remember what Scripture says about our enemy:

> For we do not wrestle against flesh and blood, but against principalities, against powers, against the rulers of the darkness of this age, against spiritual *hosts* of wickedness in the heavenly *places* (Ephesians 6:12).

The hatred that Amalek embodied did not die when the last Amalekite perished. It found new vessels. It infected new movements. It whispered recycled lies in new languages to new generations.

Different nations. Different centuries. Different ideologies. The same target. The same goal. The same spirit.

This is not coincidence. This is the war that has continued "from generation to generation" since Exodus 17.

Why This Matters for Understanding Haman

Now we can read the book of Esther with new eyes.

When Haman stood before King Ahasuerus and spoke his carefully crafted lies about the Jewish people, he was not merely a political operator pursuing a personal vendetta. He was the latest vessel for an ancient spiritual force. His words were the words of Amalek. His hatred was the hatred that had burned since Rephidim. His goal was the same goal that has driven every enemy of Israel: complete destruction.

And the tactics he used? They were not new. They were the same tactics refined over centuries—the spirit and the same lies Amalek had always employed:

Different. Cast God's people as fundamentally other.

Disloyal. Accuse them of undermining legitimate authority.

Dangerous. Frame their very existence as a threat.

Disposable. Conclude that elimination is the only solution.

This is Haman's template. But it is older than Haman. It is Amalek's template. It is Satan's template.

And it is being used against Israel right now.

Now that we understand why Israel matters prophetically—and now that we understand who Haman was and the ancient spiritual war he represented—we can examine the propaganda techniques he used. His template has been repeated for twenty-five centuries.

Haman's brief speech to King Ahasuerus in Esther 3:8–9 is one of the clearest examples of political propaganda in all of Scripture. In just a few phrases, he builds a case for genocide. What is striking is not only what he said, but how he said it. His strategy has been repeated for twenty-five centuries. It is simple, predictable, and devastating.

In the Introduction, we summarized and have later repeated Haman's template in four words that all begin with D. Here, we will walk through it more slowly, because once you see the pattern, you will recognize every modern lie about Israel for what it is.

Different—"Their laws are different."

Haman begins by marking the Jews as fundamentally "other":

> "There is a certain people scattered and dispersed among the people in all the provinces of your kingdom; their laws *are* different from all *other* people's."

He never names them directly. He speaks instead of "a certain people"—vague, scattered, unfamiliar. This creates suspicion before a single accusation is made. The implication is clear: *They don't fit. They don't belong. They are not like us.*

This is always the first step. Propaganda begins with separating a group from the rest of society.

You see this exact move in modern anti-Israel rhetoric:

- "Israel is not a normal country."
- "Zionism is unlike any other national movement."
- "Israel must be judged by different standards."

The UNHRC has even codified this distinction through Agenda Item 7, which singles out Israel alone for permanent scrutiny. No other nation receives such treatment.[7]

The vocabulary changes. The stage changes. But the goal remains the same: *Isolate Israel by casting it as fundamentally different.*

Disloyal—"They do not keep the king's laws."

Once a group is portrayed as different, the next step is to cast them as disloyal.

Haman moves from identity to accusation:

> "... and they do not keep the king's laws."

This was false. The Jews of Persia had lived peacefully under Persian rule for generations. But propaganda does not require truth. It requires suspicion.

Today the same accusations appear in different forms:

- "Israel violates international law."
- "Israel disregards human rights."
- "Israel destabilizes the region."

The accusation is always that Israel cannot be trusted, that it refuses to obey the rules the rest of the world lives by. *Israel becomes, in the modern narrative, a "rogue state."*

Mark the progression:

First, *different*.

Then, *disloyal*.

This prepares the way for the next step.

Dangerous—"It is not fitting for the king to let them remain."

Haman then escalates:

"Therefore it *is* not fitting for the king to let them remain."

Now the Jews are no longer merely different or uncooperative—they are dangerous. Their very presence is a threat. Their existence creates instability.

This is always how propaganda grows: Difference becomes distrust; distrust becomes fear.

The modern forms are familiar:

- "Israel is the cause of Middle East conflict."
- "Israel provokes violence."
- "Israel is the real obstacle to peace."

HAMAN'S LIES

Once Israel is painted as *the primary source of danger*, calls for pressure, isolation, and punitive measures begin to sound "responsible."

This is the same pattern Haman used.

Disposable—"Let a decree be written that they be destroyed."

The final step is the most chilling:

"If it pleases the king, let *a decree* be written that they be destroyed."

Once a group is portrayed as different, disloyal, and dangerous, the conclusion becomes disturbingly "logical": *Since they cause so many problems, the world would be better off without them.*

Haman doesn't shout for violence. He uses administrative vocabulary: *Let a decree be written.* Genocide becomes a policy suggestion.

Today the equivalents are easy to identify:

- "From the river to the sea …"
- "Zionism must be dismantled."
- "Israel has no right to exist."

The Hamas charter makes an explicit call for Israel's destruction.[8] Iran pledges to eliminate the "Zionist entity" Some statements are shouted; others are hidden behind jargon like "decolonization" or "liberation." But they all point to the same goal: *a world with no Jewish state.*

Twenty-five centuries apart. The same template.

Different. Disloyal. Dangerous. Disposable.

The vocabulary changes, but the structure never does.

CHART 4

Haman's Four Accusations—Then and Now

Haman's speech (Esther 3:8-9) contained four accusations. The same template is used today.

ACCUSATION	HAMAN'S WORDS	MODERN EQUIVALENTS
DIFFERENT	"Their laws are different from all other people's."	• "Zionism is racism" • "Israel is apartheid" • "Settler-colonial project"
DISLOYAL	"They do not keep the king's laws."	• "Israel controls US policy" • "The Israel Lobby" • "Dual loyalty" accusations
DANGEROUS	"It is not fitting for the king to let them remain."	• "Israel commits genocide" • "Greatest threat to peace" • "Zionists are Nazis"
DISPOSABLE	"Let a decree be written that they be destroyed."	• "From the river to the sea" • "Globalize the Intifada" • "10,000 October 7ths"

Why This Matters

Once you see the pattern, you cannot unsee it. Every modern accusation against Israel fits into one of these four categories. And once all four take hold, the final step—removal, elimination, destruction—begins to feel like a reasonable option to the deceived.

This is how lies become violence.

This is how propaganda becomes persecution.
This is how anti-Israel rhetoric becomes antisemitic action.

Our Response

The verse at the beginning of this chapter offers both a promise and a mandate:

> "No weapon formed against you shall prosper,
> and every tongue *which* rises against you in judgment
> You shall condemn.
> This *is* the heritage of the servants of the LORD,
> And their righteousness *is* from Me,"
> Says the LORD. (Isaiah 54:17).

God promises to deal with the weapons. He commands *us* to deal with the lies.

We cannot be passive observers while a new generation repeats the mistakes of the past. We are called to expose falsehood, to confront deception, and to defend truth—just as Esther did "for such a time as this."

The enemy's strategy has not changed. And neither has God's call for His people to stand.

4

Esther's Template
For Such a Time as This

> "For if you remain completely silent at this time, relief and deliverance will arise for the Jews from another place, but you and your father's house will perish. Yet who knows whether you have come to the kingdom for *such* a time as this?"
>
> —Esther 4:14

We have examined Haman's template—the propaganda playbook used against the Jewish people for twenty-five centuries. But there is another template in the book of Esther, one that offers hope and a model for response.

Esther is not merely ancient history. **She is a prophetic template for the last days.** She is what theologians call a "type"—a figure whose story foreshadows greater realities to come.[1] Just as Haman is a type of every enemy who rises against God's Covenant People, Esther is a type of every righteous remnant that stands when Israel faces annihilation.[2]

The story of Esther didn't end in ancient Persia. Its pattern is still unfolding. Every time that ancient hatred rises against the Jewish people, God raises up an Esther to meet it.[3]

The Spirit of Esther

Mordecai's words to Esther—"Who knows whether you have come to the kingdom for such a time as this?"—are among the most quoted in Scripture. But we often miss their full significance.

Mordecai was not speaking only to a young Jewish queen in ancient Persia. He wasn't giving general spiritual advice. Mordecai was speaking to every generation that would face the same specific crisis. That moment of decision is always *now*.

During the Holocaust, there were Esthers who risked everything to hide Jews from the Nazis. Corrie ten Boom[4] and her family in Holland. Raoul Wallenberg[5] in Hungary. Thousands of others whose names are known only to God.

During the Soviet persecution, there were Esthers who smuggled Bibles, who advocated for refuseniks, who refused to be silent when the world wanted to ignore the plight of Soviet Jews.

In October 1943, when word leaked that the Nazis were planning to round up Denmark's eight thousand Jews, an entire nation rose up as Esther. Fishermen, doctors, teachers, police officers, priests, shopkeepers—ordinary Danes who had never considered themselves heroes—suddenly discovered they had "come to the kingdom for such a time as this."[6]

What followed was one of the most remarkable acts of collective resistance in the Second World War and perhaps in all of history. Within three weeks, the Danish underground organized a flotilla of fishing boats, cargo vessels, rowboats, and kayaks to smuggle nearly every Jew in the country across the narrow strait to neutral Sweden.

Jewish families huddled in the holds of fishing boats, hidden beneath nets and tarpaulins. Children were sometimes sedated to keep them quiet during the dangerous crossing through German-patrolled waters. One survivor, who was nine years old at the time, later recalled the terrifying instruction: "When you hear boots on the deck, you have to be absolutely silent." The boots would recede, the boat would continue, and lives would be saved. Years later, that same survivor reflected on the journey and said, "I thought it would smell like fish. But it didn't. *It smelled like freedom.*"[7]

The cargo boat *Gerda III* alone carried some 300 Jews to safety over multiple crossings. The Danish resistance operated under code names—one group called themselves the "Elsinore Sewing Club" to disguise their life-saving purpose. Historians estimate that for every Jew rescued, around fifty Danes played a part—hiding, transporting, funding, standing guard, or simply keeping silent.[8]

In the end, 7,200 Jews and 700 of their non-Jewish relatives were smuggled to Sweden. The success rate was extraordinary: 99 percent of Denmark's Jewish population survived the Holocaust—the highest survival rate of any Nazi-occupied country in Europe. Yad Vashem records that only 102 Danish Jews died in the Holocaust and most of those were too elderly or too infirm to move.[9]

When Israel later sought to honor the rescuers as "Righteous Among the Nations," the Danes declined individual recognition. They insisted on being honored collectively—the entire nation as one. A nation of Esthers. At Yad Vashem today, a single tree stands in honor of the Danish people, alongside an authentic fishing boat from the village of Gilleleje that carried refugees to freedom.

That is what the spirit of Esther looks like when it comes upon a nation. Our sincere prayer is that America too becomes a nation of Esthers.

Modern Esthers

The spirit of Esther is not confined to history books. It is rising today. Consider Pastor John Hagee, who founded Christians United for Israel in 2006 and has mobilized millions of Christians to stand with Israel at a time when such support has become increasingly costly. Consider Shabbos Kestenbaum, a young Harvard student who filed a federal lawsuit against his own university for failing to protect Jewish students—risking his academic career to demand accountability. Consider the anonymous donors who fund security for synagogues, the pastors who preach unpopular truths from their pulpits, the students who wear their Stars of David openly on hostile campuses. These are today's Esthers—ordinary people who have decided that silence is not an option.

Today, as lies about Israel flood university campuses, social media platforms, and even some churches, God is raising up Esthers again. The question is whether you will be one of them. **"Have you come to the kingdom for such a time as this?"**

The Purim Pattern

Every year, Jewish communities around the world celebrate Purim—the holiday commemorating the events of Esther's story. But Purim is more than a memorial. It is a prophetic declaration: *What God did then, He will do again.*

The name "Purim" comes from the word *pur*, meaning 'lot.' Haman cast lots to determine the date for the annihilation of the Jews. But what was this *pur* exactly?

The word is not Hebrew. It is Akkadian, borrowed from the ancient Babylonian world where Persia's religious practices had their roots. Archaeological evidence helps us understand what Haman was doing. The Yale Babylonian Collection preserves a clay cube dating to the ninth century BC, belonging to a minister of the Assyrian king Shalmaneser III. A cuneiform inscription invokes the gods to make the 'lot'—the *pur*—fall favorably.[10]

These clay cubes or small stones were cast toward statues of pagan gods as a form of divination. The way they fell was believed to reveal the favor or disfavor of fate itself.

Picture the scene. Haman, consumed with murderous hatred, stands before the divination instruments of the Persian court. He is not merely picking a convenient date on a calendar. He is appealing to the gods of Persia, to fate, to the forces he believes govern the universe. He is asking them to reveal the most auspicious day to annihilate the Jewish people.

The book of Esther records:

> In the first month, which is the month of Nisan, in the twelfth year of King Ahasuerus, they cast Pur (that *is*, the lot), before Haman to determine the day and the month, until *it fell on the* twelfth *month*, which *is* the month of Adar (Esther 3:7).

The text tells us that Haman cast Pur—the lot—"to determine the day and the month," until it fell on the twelfth month, Adar. The New King James Version does not spell out the process, but the Hebrew phrasing implies repetition over time, moving from day to day and from month to month until a final date was fixed. This was not a single throw of the dice but a prolonged search for the "right" moment, shaped by pagan divination and the belief that fate could be manipulated. What Haman believed he was controlling through chance was, in reality, being governed by a sovereignty he neither acknowledged nor understood. The delay itself became the instrument of deliverance, allowing God's purposes to unfold quietly, without spectacle, and entirely beyond the awareness of those who thought they were in control.

The lot finally fell on the thirteenth day of the twelfth month—Adar. Haman had his date, but God also has His.

That is what Haman did not understand: *The God of Israel is not subject to dice.*

HAMAN'S LIES

The forces of fate and fortune that Haman worshipped do not govern the universe. The Lord God does. And the Lord was about to take those very dice and use them against the man who cast them.

The long delay, nearly eleven months, gave Esther time to act, Mordecai time to rally the Jewish people, and God time to orchestrate a thousand "coincidences" that would lead to a complete reversal.

The *pur* that Haman cast to destroy the Jews became the instrument of their deliverance. The day that was meant for destruction became a day of victory.

This is the Purim pattern: What the enemy plans for evil, God reverses for good. Haman's dice became Haman's doom.

The Jewish people named the holiday after the very weapon that was turned against their enemy! Every year at Purim, when the *Megillah* is read and Haman's name is mentioned, the congregation erupts in noise—stomping feet, shaking the rattles called "graggers"—to drown out the name of the man who tried to drown them in death. It is a celebration of reversal, of tables turned, of God's sovereign power over all the dice that evil men cast.

Another well-attested Purim custom involves the **symbolic blotting out of Haman's name**. Because Haman is understood in rabbinic tradition to be a descendant of Amalek, the Torah's command to "blot out the memory of Amalek from under heaven" (Deuteronomy 25:19) became associated with ritualized acts of erasure during the public reading of *Megillat Esther*.[11]

Beyond the familiar use of graggers and congregational noise to drown out Haman's name, earlier European Jewish communities practiced additional physical forms of symbolic obliteration. Medieval sources describe the custom of writing Haman's name on stones or pieces of wood and striking them together until the name was worn away.[12] Closely related to this was a practice in which Haman's name was written in chalk on the soles of shoes, and worshippers would stamp their feet when his name was read, so that the letters were literally ground into dust.[13]

These practices were never understood as acts of personal vengeance, but as **ritual dramatizations of the biblical mandate to erase the memory of evil.** Over time, many of these physical customs were replaced or simplified into the widespread noise-making traditions used today, yet the theological message remains the same: Haman's plot is overturned, his name is brought low, and the God of Israel is shown to be the ultimate deliverer of His people.[14]

"On the very day when the enemies of the Jews hoped to overpower them," Esther 9:1 declares, **"the opposite occurred."** Those three words tell us almost everything we need to know about this story.

Every time the spirit of Haman rises, God turns the story around. The tables always turn in His timing.

But the story doesn't stop in ancient Persia. Esther's reversal becomes a pattern God will repeat in Israel's final hour—the final days of the Tribulation.

Esther as a Type of the Tribulation Remnant

If Esther is a prophetic type, then what does she foreshadow? We believe she represents the righteous Jewish remnant that will stand during the Tribulation—the period of unprecedented crisis before the return of Christ.[15]

Consider the parallels:

First, a decree of total annihilation. Haman's decree called for the complete destruction of all Jews—"young and old, little children and women"—in a single day (Esther 3:13). During the Tribulation, the Antichrist will launch the most intense campaign against the Jewish people in history. Revelation 12 describes the dragon pursuing the woman

(Israel) with murderous intent. Zechariah 13:8 indicates that two-thirds of the people in the land will perish. It will be the greatest crisis Israel has ever faced.

Second, hidden identity revealed. Esther concealed her Jewish identity until the moment of crisis, when she revealed herself to save her people (Esther 7:4). During the Tribulation, the Jewish people will come to recognize their true Messiah—the One they have not acknowledged for two millennia. "They will look on Me whom they pierced" (Zechariah 12:10). The hidden will be revealed.

Third, "If I perish, I perish." Esther's declaration of total commitment (Esther 4:16) mirrors the 144,000 sealed servants of Revelation 7 and 14. These Jewish believers during the Tribulation are described as those who "follow the Lamb wherever He goes" and are "without fault" (Revelation 14:4–5). They are willing to lay down their lives.[16]

Fourth, intercession for the nation. Esther called for a three-day fast before approaching the king (Esther 4:16). During the Tribulation, Joel 2:17 describes priests "weep[ing] between the porch and the altar," crying out, "Spare Your people, O Lord." There will be a remnant that intercedes for Israel in its darkest hour.

Fifth, divine reversal and destruction of the enemy. Haman died on the very gallows he built for Mordecai.[17] At the end of the Tribulation, Zechariah 12:9 promises: "I will seek to destroy all the nations that come against Jerusalem." The enemies of God's people will fall into the pit they have dug.

Do you see it? Esther is not just ancient history. She is a prophetic picture of what is coming—and what is already beginning to unfold.

The Esther Assignment

Just as demons do not die, the spirit of Esther also rises in every generation. This is not a demonic spirit but a spiritual pattern—a calling that God places on certain people at certain times.

We see this principle in Scripture. The "spirit of Elijah" came upon John the Baptist (Luke 1:17). John was not Elijah reincarnated, but he carried the same prophetic mantle. In the same way, the calling of Esther—to stand in the gap for God's Covenant People at a critical hour—can come upon those in subsequent generations.[18]

What does the spirit of Esther look like?

- It is courage in the face of danger.
- It is speaking truth when lies are everywhere.
- It is risking reputation, comfort, and even life to stand with the Jewish people and the nation of Israel.
- It is saying, "If I perish, I perish—but I will not be silent."

The book of Esther is remarkable for what it does not contain. The name of God is never mentioned directly. Yet His fingerprints are everywhere—in the "coincidences," the timing, the sleepless night that changed history, the reversal that came at the last possible moment.[19]

This "hiddenness" of God in the book of Esther is itself significant. It shows us how God works behind the scenes, orchestrating events even when He seems absent.

In 1845, James Russell Lowell captured this truth in the poem that later became a famous hymn: "Once to Every Man and Nation":

Though the cause of evil prosper,
yet the truth alone is strong;
though her portion be the scaffold,

and upon the throne be wrong;
yet that scaffold sways the future,
and, behind the dim unknown,
standeth God within the shadow
keeping watch above His own.[20]

The same is true today. God may seem hidden. The lies may seem overwhelming. The truth may seem silenced. But God is watching. And He is at work—raising up Esthers, positioning people "for such a time as this," preparing the great reversal.

We return to another verse of Lowell's poem:

Once to every man and nation
comes the moment to decide,
in the strife of truth with falsehood,
for the good or evil side;
Some great cause, some great decision,
off'ring each the bloom or blight,
and the choice goes by forever
'twixt that darkness and that light.[21]

The question is the same one Mordecai asked: *Will you stand?*

The Esther Thread in This Book

As we move through the specific lies about Israel in the chapters ahead, we want you to keep Esther in mind. We will see both templates at work—Haman's and Esther's.

Every lie we examine will bear the marks of Haman's playbook. But for each lie, there is also an Esther response—a truth that can be spoken, a stand that can be taken, a refusal to be silent.

For each of Haman's lies, there is an Esther answer—this time with the letter I:

- Israel is not **different**—Israel is **indigenous.** They are not foreign. They belong to the land God gave them.
- Israel is not **disloyal**—Israel is **innocent.** They are not plotting; they are defending themselves.
- Israel is not **dangerous**—Israel is **indispensable.** Israel is a blessing to the world, not a threat.
- Israel is not **disposable**—Israel is **indestructible.** They cannot be erased because God Himself has made an everlasting Covenant with them.

Indigenous. Innocent. Indispensable. Indestructible.

This is not just academic information. This is equipping for your Esther moment. Because if you are reading this book, it is not by accident. God has positioned you "for such a time as this."

The question is not whether God will raise up an Esther generation. He already has. The question is whether you will be part of it.

Haman Lost. Esther Won.

In the book of Esther, the outcome was never really in doubt.

Yes, there was genuine danger. Yes, the crisis was real. The Jewish people faced annihilation. But Mordecai knew something that gave him unshakable confidence. "If you remain completely silent at this time," he told Esther, "relief and deliverance will arise for the Jews from another place" (Esther 4:14).

Deliverance *will* come. **The only question is whether you will be part of it.**

HAMAN'S LIES

Mordecai understood what Haman did not: God has made a Covenant with Israel that He will never break. "I will bless those who bless you, and I will curse him who curses you" (Genesis 12:3). God would never allow His people to be completely destroyed, because His own faithfulness was at stake.

That is still true today. The lies will fail. The propaganda will be exposed. The spirit of Haman will fall on its own gallows. Israel will survive and thrive because God has promised it.

Haman lost. He died on the very gallows he built for Mordecai. His sons were destroyed. His plot was exposed. His offspring were erased from the earth. His legacy is eternal shame.

Esther won. The young woman who was willing to perish became the instrument of her people's salvation. Her legacy is celebrated every year at Purim. Her courage echoes through the generations.

The same will be true for all who follow in her footsteps. Those who stand with Israel, who speak truth against lies, who refuse to be silent—they are on the winning side. Not just the winning side of history, but the winning side of Bible prophecy. The winning side of God Himself.

For such a time as this, you were born.

5

The Anatomy of Deception

How do good people become the carriers of bad ideas?

In the last chapter, we looked at Esther's template—how God raises up courageous men and women to stand against the spirit of Haman in every generation. Esther shows us what righteous courage looks like when lies are marching toward their deadly conclusion.

But before we examine the specific lies about Israel in the chapters ahead, we need to slow down and ask a deeper question:

How Do Lies Get That Far in the First Place?

How does this ancient pattern gain so much cooperation from people who would never dream of calling themselves antisemites or enemies of God's Covenant People? How do ordinary, decent, even compassionate people become carriers of ideas that endanger the very things they say they care about?

The Bible has a word for this pattern: *deception*.

Deception is not just people believing something that isn't true. Deception is a system. It is a way of thinking, a way of feeling, and a way of belonging that recruits otherwise good people into serving destructive purposes—often while they feel morally superior for doing it.

In this chapter, we want to walk you through some of the recurring patterns that we see—patterns in Scripture, in history, and in our current culture—that explain how good people become the most effective messengers of bad ideas.

Our goal is not to condemn anyone. Our aim is to help us recognize the anatomy of deception so we can resist it when it comes dressed as compassion, justice, or moral courage.

Borrowed Convictions

One of the earliest warning signs that deception is at work is this: **People are absolutely certain about things they have never seriously studied.**

We have met people who can deliver entire speeches in slogan form—and yet, when you ask the simplest follow-up question ("What do you mean by that?" "How did you reach that conclusion?"), the conversation quickly falls apart. The conviction is strong; the foundation is weak.

This is not new.

Religious leaders in Jesus' day could quote traditions, but their understanding of God's heart was shallow. They had memorized conclusions instead of wrestling with truth. They had secondhand certainty instead of firsthand conviction.

We are watching the same pattern unfold today. Entire worldviews are adopted from a viral video or a thread on social media. A phrase that sounds righteous becomes a substitute for wisdom. It *feels* deep, but it has never been tested.

A borrowed conviction cannot survive honest questions. It was never built to.

Symbols Without Substance

There is a difference between **believing something** and **signaling that you believe something**. On the surface, they look similar. On the inside, they could not be more different.

Jesus confronted people who loved the appearance of righteousness but not the reality of it—performing spirituality like a stage play. The problem wasn't that they prayed or gave or fasted. The problem was they turned those things into public performance.

We're surrounded by a modern version of that same performance culture.

People announce their values in their bios, wear cause-themed merch, repeat all the right phrases, and join all the right campaigns. They build an identity out of symbols. But none of those things necessarily produce fruit, sacrifice, or obedience.

Real conviction always costs something.

The people who actually changed history for the Jewish people—men and women like Dietrich Bonhoeffer, Corrie ten Boom, Raoul Wallenberg, and the Danish rescuers you just read about—did not merely *signal* the right virtues. They took risks. They paid a price. Their convictions pushed them out of comfort and into costly obedience.[1]

So when someone's entire moral profile is perfectly in step with whatever is fashionable in their peer group, I don't just ask, *What do they say?* I ask, *What have they risked? What have they sacrificed?*

If the answer is "nothing," what you're seeing is probably performance, not principle.

Allies Who Would Become Enemies

Another sign that deception is at work is when people throw their support behind movements that would crush them if those movements ever gained power.

We see it when Western feminists defend ideologies that strip women of basic rights in other parts of the world. We see it when progressive activists champion regimes that imprison or execute people for living out the very values those activists claim to cherish. We see it when students march side by side with groups whose leaders are on record calling for the destruction of people just like those students.

And again—we've seen this before.

During the twentieth century, Western intellectuals defended Soviet communism while the Soviet system was starving, imprisoning, and killing millions.[2] From their safe distance in London, Paris, and New York, they romanticized the revolution precisely because they never had to stand in a bread line or survive a gulag.

Why does this happen?

Because when people adopt a cause primarily to *feel* righteous, they stop asking the most basic question of all: **If this movement achieved everything it wants, what would happen to people like me?**

- Would I still be free to believe what I believe?
- Would my daughters still have rights?
- Would my faith still be tolerated?
- Would my conscience still be protected?

Wisdom insists that we ask those questions. Deception trains us not to.

The Silencing of Inconvenient Witnesses

Deception cannot endure open testimony. False narratives collapse when people who *actually know* what they're talking about are allowed to speak freely.

So one of the clearest indicators that a movement is built on deception is what happens to dissidents.

They aren't answered—*they're erased.*

Instead of saying, "Let's listen to this person and weigh what they're saying," the crowd says, "We must discredit and destroy this person so no one hears them again." Careers are ruined, reputations shredded, social circles turned against them.[3]

It's even worse when the dissenter comes from inside the group the movement claims to represent: a former insider, a survivor, a defector, a member of the community who refuses to repeat the script. These people are extremely dangerous to deceptive systems because they cannot be dismissed as ignorant or prejudiced. They *were* on the inside. They know the details.

When truth-tellers from within are treated as traitors rather than as witnesses, you are not dealing with a search for truth. You are dealing with a system of control.

- Movements built on truth can afford to let their critics speak.
- Movements built on deception must silence them.

The Rejection of Every Imperfect Solution

Another repeated pattern: **Nothing is ever good enough.**

There is a form of activism that guarantees failure while loudly claiming the moral high ground. It demands perfect outcomes and rejects every realistic path toward improvement.

- Incremental progress? *Not enough.*
- Practical compromise? *Betrayal.*
- Partial solutions? *"Band-aids on a bullet wound."*

The result is paralysis dressed up as purity.

But beneath that stance, something often hides: **Some people are more committed to *having* problems than to *solving* them.** For some people, the grievance itself becomes who they are. If the problem were resolved, they wouldn't know who they are anymore.

Meanwhile, the Bible (and history) are relentlessly practical. God works through partial victories, incremental change, and imperfect people. He doesn't wait for utopia to bring relief. Jesus didn't refuse to feed the five thousand because they'd be hungry again tomorrow. He didn't refuse to heal individuals because sickness still existed in the world.

When someone will only accept a solution that is perfect, total, and immediate, you can be sure of this: They are choosing purity of posture over real help for real people.

Real compassion does what it can today—and it never despises small beginnings.

Compassion as a Weapon

One of Satan's favorite tricks is to weaponize good things. He rarely starts with something obviously evil. He starts with something beautiful and then twists it.

Compassion is one of his favorite tools.

We have watched well-meaning Christians shut off their discernment the moment someone accuses them of not being "loving" or "kind" or "on the right side of history." The accusation works like emotional blackmail:

- If you disagree with my solution, you don't care.
- If you ask questions, you're heartless.
- If you want clarity, you're part of the problem.

But real compassion is not reckless. Real love is not mindless. As Jacques Ellul observed in his classic work on propaganda, emotional appeals—especially appeals to pity—are one of the most powerful tools for manipulating democratic societies.[4]

When compassion is used to shut down thinking instead of guiding it, deception is at work.

The right response isn't to become less compassionate. It's to become more discerning. To care deeply *and* think clearly. To be willing to say, "I care too much to support something that doesn't actually help."

Sometimes the most loving thing you can do is refuse to be emotionally blackmailed into a destructive decision.

The Inversion of Moral Categories

Isaiah described a time when people would call evil good and good evil, when darkness would be renamed light and light would be renamed darkness (Isaiah 5:20). We are watching that inversion in real time.

- People who initiate violence are called "resistance fighters."
- People who defend their families are called "oppressors."
- Terrorists are described as "militants," while their victims are described as "settlers" who had it coming.
- Simple moral distinctions that any child could grasp are buried under academic jargon and political spin.

This doesn't happen by accident.

It requires sustained propaganda, constant repetition of false stories, intimidation of anyone who points out the obvious, and a class of influencers who act as moral referees—blowing the whistle on the wrong team every time.[5]

George Orwell warned that when language is corrupted, thought is soon corrupted as well. Once you no longer have words that clearly name reality, you begin losing the ability to *see* reality.[6]

One test of discernment in days like these is simple: **Can you still recognize who is attacking and who is defending, even when the headlines try to tell you the opposite?**

If you can, hold onto that clarity. It is more precious than you realize.

Trust in Captured Institutions

There was a time when people could reasonably trust certain institutions to pursue truth, even if they sometimes failed. Universities existed to seek wisdom. News organizations existed to report facts. Professional guilds existed to uphold standards.

That time is largely gone.

Many of the institutions that once served truth have been "captured" by ideological agendas. They no longer ask, *Is this accurate?* They ask, *Is this acceptable?* More and more institutions now put narrative ahead of facts—especially on controversial issues.[7]

This does **not** mean every journalist, professor, or leader is corrupt. It means the *system* itself exerts enormous pressure on individuals to conform or be pushed out.

People caught in deception often cling to institutional approval as proof that they're right:

- "All the experts agree."
- "All the major organizations say so."
- "All the right publications support this."

But if those experts, organizations, and publications are all swimming in the same ideological water, their agreement does not prove truth. It proves peer pressure.

The Berean instinct—"I hear what you're saying, but I want to check it"—has to return to the Church. We cannot outsource discernment to captured institutions.

Immunity from Consequences

Another feature of deception is this: **The people pushing the ideas almost never pay the price for them.**

The celebrity who promotes destructive ideologies keeps their mansion, their security team, and their brand deals. The academic who advocates harmful policies keeps their tenure. The influencer who tells entire communities to embrace chaos often lives far from the neighborhoods where that chaos plays out.

Meanwhile, ordinary people carry the cost. Children. Families. Vulnerable communities.

Thomas Sowell has pointed out that many modern "intellectuals" deal only in ideas, never in implementation.[8] Because they never have to live with the consequences, they are free to advocate whatever sounds morally impressive.

So when we evaluate someone's message, we don't just ask, *What are they saying?* We ask, *What do they risk? What skin do they have in the game?*

If the answer is "none," we hold their moral posturing *very* loosely.

Serving the Enemy's Purposes

All of this brings us back to Esther and Haman.

Haman knew exactly what he was doing. His hatred was intentional. His plans were deliberate.

But the Persian court—the scribes who wrote the decree, the messengers who carried it, the officials who prepared to enforce it—were not all animated by genocidal hatred. Many of them were just doing their jobs. They were following procedures. They were trusting a high official who sounded reasonable.

They became participants in an attempted genocide not because they set out to destroy the Jews, but because they cooperated with a man who did.

That is the anatomy of deception:

- borrowed convictions
- performance without substance
- alliances with movements that would harm you
- silencing inconvenient witnesses
- rejecting imperfect solutions
- weaponized compassion
- inverted moral categories
- trust in captured institutions
- leaders immune from consequences

Put all of this together, and you don't just get confused people. You get an entire culture that thinks it is doing good while it is, in fact, doing evil by serving the purposes of the enemy.

Good people become carriers of bad ideas.

That is what happened in Esther's day. It has happened repeatedly throughout history.[9] And it is happening again around Israel and the Jewish people right now.

From Patterns to Lies

So where do we go from here?

In the chapters ahead, we are going to look at specific lies—twenty-five of them—shaped by Haman's template and aimed at Israel today. These are not just abstract ideas. They are narratives that are already shaping policies, protests, sermons, social media posts, and even the way young Christians talk about Israel and the Jewish people.

The chapter you've just read is the "x-ray." It shows the internal structure of deception—how it spreads and why it feels so persuasive.

Now we're going to look at the lies themselves.

And we will begin with the **shield lie**—the one that protects all the others from scrutiny. It is the claim that allows people to say the most vicious things about the Jewish state while insisting they have no prejudice against Jews at all.

You know the line: *"I don't hate Jews. I'm just against Zionism. Anti-Zionism is not antisemitism. Besides, the Israel of today isn't even the same Israel in the Bible."*

In the next chapter, we will put that claim under the microscope and see it for what it is: not a careful distinction, but *the foundational lie* that gives modern antisemitism moral cover.

PART TWO

Lying Tongues

6

Lie #1

"The Jews Have No Right to the Land"

This is the foundational lie that supports all the others. It comes in two forms—one secular, one theological—but both reach the same conclusion: *The Jewish people do not belong in the land of Israel.* The Jewish state is illegitimate. Its existence is a crime that must be corrected.

The secular version is called anti-Zionism. "I don't hate Jews," the formula goes, "I just oppose Zionism. I just criticize Israel. Anti-Zionism is a political position, not bigotry." The theological version says: "Whatever promises God made to ancient Israel have no connection to the modern state. Biblical Israel and modern Israel are completely different things. The prophecies were spiritual, not political."

Both versions sound reasonable on the surface. Both allow people to delegitimize Israel while claiming the moral high ground—one in the name of human rights, the other in the name of proper biblical interpretation. But both collapse under examination. And both serve the same ancient purpose: to deny the Jewish people their place in the land God promised them.

This is Haman's lie in modern dress.

What Zionism Actually Is

Before examining whether anti-Zionism is antisemitism, we must understand what Zionism actually is—not the caricature presented by its opponents, but the actual idea.

Zionism is the belief that the Jewish people have the right to self-determination in their ancestral homeland. That's it. It is the conviction that Jews, like other peoples, are entitled to a nation of their own, and that this nation should be in the land where Jewish civilization emerged and where Jews have maintained a continuous presence for over three thousand years.

Zionism arose in the late nineteenth century as a response to persistent antisemitism in Europe. Despite emancipation, despite assimilation, despite contributions to every field of human endeavor, Jews remained targets of discrimination, persecution, and violence. The Dreyfus affair in France—where a Jewish army captain was falsely convicted of treason amid a wave of antisemitic hysteria—demonstrated that even in the most enlightened European societies, Jews would never be fully accepted.[1] Theodor Herzl, witnessing crowds in Paris chanting "Death to the Jews," concluded that the only solution was a Jewish state.[2]

The Holocaust vindicated this conclusion in the most horrific way imaginable. Six million Jews were murdered while the world largely stood by. Ships full of Jewish refugees were turned away from port after port.[3] Jews who had lived in Europe for a thousand years discovered that when it mattered most, they belonged nowhere. Israel's establishment in 1948 was the Jewish people's answer to this catastrophe—a homeland where Jews could defend themselves, where they would never again depend on others for protection.

Zionism, then, is not colonialism or racism or any of the other labels attached to it. It is a national liberation movement—the national liberation movement of the Jewish people. It asserts for Jews the same right to self-determination that the international community recognizes for every other people on earth.

What Anti-Zionism Actually Means

If Zionism is the belief that Jews have the right to self-determination in their homeland, anti-Zionism is the belief that Jews do not have that right. It is not merely criticism of particular Israeli policies—settlements, military operations, treatment of minorities. It is opposition to Israel's existence as a Jewish state. It is the conviction that of all the peoples on earth, Jews alone should be denied a nation of their own.

Consider what anti-Zionism requires. It requires believing that the French deserve France, the Japanese deserve Japan, the Egyptians deserve Egypt, the Palestinians deserve Palestine—but Jews do not deserve Israel. It requires singling out one people, and one people only, as unworthy of the self-determination granted to all others. It requires insisting that the Jewish state alone is illegitimate, that its existence is a crime that must be rectified through its elimination.

This is not a neutral political position. When you believe that one people—and only one people—should be denied the rights accorded to all other peoples, that is prejudice by definition. When that one people is the Jews, that prejudice has a name: *antisemitism*.

The Double Standard Test

One clear test for antisemitism disguised as anti-Zionism is whether the same standards are applied to others. If criticism of Israel is applied even-handedly—if the critic applies the same expectations to all countries—that criticism may be legitimate. But if standards are applied to Israel that are applied to no other nation, something other than principled criticism is at work.

The critics who call Israel an illegitimate settler-colonial state do not apply that label to the United States, Canada, Australia, or any Latin American country—all of which were established by settlers who displaced indigenous populations far more thoroughly than Israel displaced anyone. Americans calling Israel illegitimate are standing on land taken from others while condemning Jews for living in their ancestral homeland.

The critics who demand that Palestinian refugees and all their descendants have a "right of return" to Israel do not demand the same for any other refugee population. Germans expelled from Eastern Europe after World War 2—roughly twelve million people—have no "right of return" to Poland or Czechoslovakia. The partition of India created millions of refugees who have no "right of return" to the other side. Only Palestinians are granted a perpetual hereditary refugee status designed to demographically eliminate the Jewish state.[4]

The critics who call for boycotts of Israel do not call for boycotts of other nations committing demonstrably heinous acts. Only Israel—the Jewish state—is selected for this treatment. The selectivity reveals that something other than human rights concerns drives the campaign.

The double standard is the tell. When Israel is judged by criteria applied to no other nation, when Israel alone is selected for condemnation that others escape, when the world's only Jewish state receives treatment no other state receives—that is antisemitism, regardless of what the critic claims.

The Effects on Jews

If anti-Zionism were truly distinct from antisemitism, it would target only Israel as a state. In practice, anti-Zionism creates hostile environments for Jews *everywhere*, proving the connection its proponents deny.

When anti-Israel protests occur, synagogues are attacked—not Israeli embassies, but synagogues in countries far outside of Israel. Jewish students on campus are confronted and demanded to denounce Israel as a condition of acceptance—not Israeli students, but Jewish students. Jewish neighborhoods see increased vandalism and harassment during Gaza conflicts. Jewish businesses are targeted for boycotts based on the owners' religion, not their nationality. The overflow from anti-Zionism to antisemitism is not occasional—it is systematic and predictable.

Anti-Zionist activists routinely blur the line they claim to respect. "Zionists" becomes a term applied to any Jew who does not actively denounce Israel, which is the vast majority of Jews worldwide. Polls consistently show that over 80 percent of American Jews consider caring about Israel essential or important to their Jewish identity, even if they criticize particular policies.[5] When "Zionist" becomes an epithet applied to nearly all Jews, the distinction between anti-Zionism and antisemitism collapses. They are one and the same.

Jews are increasingly asked to denounce Israel as a condition of participation in progressive spaces—to pass a political litmus test applied to no other group. No one demands that Chinese Americans denounce China, that Russian Americans denounce Russia, that Iranian Americans denounce Iran. Only Jews are required to condemn the Jewish state to prove they belong. This demand—applied to Jews alone—is antisemitism in action, whatever its proponents call it.

The Language Tells the Truth

Listen to the language of anti-Zionism, and you hear echoes of historical antisemitism. The tropes have been updated, but they remain recognizable.

Jews were accused of killing Christian children for their blood; Israel is accused of deliberately killing Palestinian children.[6] Jews were accused of secretly controlling governments; Israel is accused of controlling American foreign policy through the "Israel Lobby."[7] Jews were accused of dual loyalty; Zionists are accused of caring more about Israel than their home countries. Jews were accused of being rootless cosmopolitans with no legitimate national home; Israel is accused of being an illegitimate settler state with no right to exist.

The blood libel has become the Gaza libel. The conspiracy theory has become the lobby theory. The accusation of disloyalty has become the accusation of Zionism. The denial of Jewish belonging has become the denial of Israeli legitimacy. The pattern is obvious once you know the history—and invisible to those who refuse to see it.

When anti-Zionists chant "From the river to the sea, Palestine will be free," they are calling for the elimination of the Jewish state and, implicitly, the extermination or subjugation of its Jewish population. When they call for "globalizing the intifada," they are calling for deadly violence against Jews worldwide. When they tear down posters of kidnapped Israeli children—Jewish children held hostage by Hamas—they reveal that their concern is not Palestinian welfare but Jewish suffering. The mask slips constantly for those willing to notice.

Legitimate Criticism vs. Antisemitism

None of this means that all criticism of Israel is antisemitic. Israel is a country like any other, and its policies can be criticized like any other country's policies. This isn't complicated.

- Criticizing Israeli settlement policy is legitimate. Calling Israel a settler-colonial state with no right to exist is antisemitic.
- Criticizing a particular Israeli military operation is legitimate. Accusing Israel of genocide while ignoring the terrorism that necessitated the operation is antisemitic.
- Advocating for Palestinian rights alongside Israeli rights is legitimate. Advocating for Palestinian rights instead of Israeli rights—denying Jewish self-determination while affirming Palestinian self-determination—is antisemitic.
- Holding Israel to the same standards as other democracies is legitimate. Holding Israel to standards applied to no other nation—while ignoring far worse abuses by others—is antisemitic.

The line is clear enough: Criticism that treats Israel as a normal country subject to normal criticism is legitimate; criticism that singles out the Jewish state for unique condemnation, denies its right to exist, or applies standards to it that are applied to no other nation crosses into antisemitism. The critics know the difference—they simply refuse to acknowledge it because doing so would expose what they really are.

Anti-Zionism's Theological Cousin

If anti-Zionism is the secular denial of Jewish legitimacy in the land, there is a theological version that reaches the same conclusion through different means. It says: *Whatever promises God made to ancient Israel have no connection to the modern state founded in 1948. Biblical Israel was a spiritual Covenant Community; modern Israel is a geopolitical accident. The two have nothing to do with each other.*

This argument is particularly effective among Christians, even among otherwise conservative believers. It allows someone to affirm the Bible, honor the Old Testament, and still conclude that modern Israel has no special significance. It provides a theological off-ramp for believers who feel pressured to oppose Israel but do not want to reject Scripture. They can say, "I believe the Bible—I just don't believe it applies to *that* Israel."

This theological position has a name: **supersessionism**, also called **replacement theology**.[8] It is the belief that the Church has replaced Israel in God's plan—that the promises made to Abraham, Isaac, and Jacob have been transferred to the Church, and that ethnic Israel no longer has any special role in God's purposes.

Supersessionism has a long and troubling history. As theologians Michael Vlach and Gerald McDermott have documented, it contributed to centuries of Christian anti-Judaism, providing theological justification for persecution.[9] If God has rejected the Jews, why should Christians treat them well? If the Covenant had been transferred, then the Jews were a stubborn relic clinging to an obsolete faith. This theology created fertile ground for the very antisemitism the secular version promotes today.

Supersessionists often cite Galatians 3:28—"There is neither Jew nor Greek... for you are all one in Christ Jesus"—as proof that ethnic distinctions no longer matter in God's plan. But this misreads Paul's point entirely. Paul is speaking about access to salvation, not the nullification of Covenant promises. The same Paul who wrote Galatians 3:28 also wrote Romans 11:29: "The gifts and the calling of God *are* irrevocable." Equality in salvation does not erase God's specific promises to Abraham's descendants regarding the land. A Gentile believer and a Jewish believer are equally saved—but that does not mean God has abandoned the land Covenant He made with Israel.

What the New Testament Actually Says

The New Testament does not teach that God has rejected Israel or transferred His promises to the Church. It teaches the opposite.

In Romans 11, Paul asks the question directly: "Has God cast away His people?" His answer is emphatic: "Certainly not!" (Romans 11:1). This is not ambiguous. Paul anticipates the very argument supersessionists make and rejects it explicitly.

He goes further: "The gifts and the calling of God *are* irrevocable" (Romans 11:29). The Greek word translated "irrevocable"—*ametameleta*—means 'incapable of being changed, not to be taken back'.[10] God does not revoke what He has promised. He does not change His mind about Israel. The gifts He gave and the calling He extended remain in force.

What gifts? Paul lists them in Romans 9:4–5: "the adoption, the glory, the covenants, the giving of the law, the service *of God*, and the promises." Notice the verb tense. Paul does not say these *belonged* to Israel. He says they *belong* to Israel—present tense, decades after Jesus' Resurrection. The gifts and calling had not been transferred. They remained with Israel.

Paul also warns Gentile believers against arrogance toward Israel. Using the image of an olive tree, he reminds them: "You do not support the root, but the root *supports* you" (Romans 11:18). The Church does not replace Israel; it is grafted into Israel's story. Branches can be broken off for unbelief—a warning that should give pause to any theology that dismisses Israel's ongoing significance.

The Prophecies Speak of Physical Return

The prophets did not speak in abstractions when they foretold Israel's restoration. They spoke of physical return to physical land.

Ezekiel reported what God had said: "For I will take you from among the nations, gather you out of all countries, and bring you into your own land." (Ezekiel 36:24). Jeremiah prophesied according to God's Word: "For I will bring them back into their land which I gave to their fathers" (Jeremiah 16:15). Amos wrote that the Lord says:

> "I will bring back the captives of My people Israel;
> They shall build the waste cities and inhabit *them;*
> They shall plant vineyards and drink wine from them;
> They shall also make gardens and eat fruit from them.
> I will plant them in their land,
> And no longer shall they be pulled up
> From the land I have given them" (Amos 9:14–15).

Building cities. Planting vineyards. Making gardens. Being planted in the land and *never again pulled up*. These are not spiritual metaphors. They describe physical realities in a physical place.

Isaiah asked:

> Who has heard such a thing?
> Who has seen such things?
> Shall the earth be made to give birth in one day?
> *Or* shall a nation be born at once?
> For as soon as Zion was in labor,
> She gave birth to her children (Isaiah 66:8).

For millennia, the answer seemed to be no. Nations do not spring into existence overnight. But on May 14, 1948, that is exactly what happened. A nation was born in a day—exactly as the prophet foretold.

The Continuity That Cannot Be Denied

Consider what continuity actually exists between biblical Israel and modern Israel.

The Jewish people today pray in the same language—Hebrew—that Abraham, Moses, and David spoke. They read the same Scriptures, celebrate the same festivals established in the Torah, observe the same Sabbath, and gather in the same land. The very word *Jew* derives from *Judean*—a person from Judea, the biblical heartland.

Former US Ambassador David Friedman observed: "The nation of Israel today comprises a people that pray in the same language, in the same places and with the same liturgy as in ancient times."[11] No other people on earth can make such a claim. The Greeks of today do not worship Zeus. The Egyptians do not build pyramids for their pharaohs. The Romans do not offer sacrifices to Jupiter. But the Jews of today maintain the faith, the language, the calendar, and the identity of their ancestors from three thousand years ago.

Genetic studies confirm what history already demonstrated. A landmark 2010 study published in *Nature* analyzed Jewish populations worldwide and found they share significant genetic ancestry tracing to the ancient Middle East. Ashkenazi, Sephardi, and Mizrahi Jews—scattered across Europe, the Mediterranean, and the Middle East for centuries—are more closely related to each other and to other Levantine populations than to the peoples among whom they lived.[12] The Jews did not become Europeans or Arabs. They remained a distinct people, genetically connected to the ancient inhabitants of the land.

The same double standard we saw with anti-Zionism appears here. No one questions whether modern Greece is connected to ancient Greece, whether modern Egypt is connected to ancient Egypt, or whether modern China is connected to ancient China. National continuity is assumed for every people—except the Jews. When the same denial of legitimacy appears in both secular and theological forms, it reveals that something deeper than principled analysis is at work.

What Continuity Does Not Mean

Affirming continuity between biblical and modern Israel does not mean endorsing every policy of the Israeli government. Israel is a democracy, and Israelis themselves debate their government's decisions constantly. Christians who recognize Israel's prophetic significance are not obligated to approve every military operation, every settlement decision, or every political choice.

Biblical Israel had kings like Ahab, Jezebel, and Manasseh—and God remained faithful to His Covenant despite their wickedness. Faithfulness to the Covenant does not require approval of every leader. Jeremiah 31:35–37 declares that God will never reject Israel as a nation, regardless of the behavior of individual leaders or generations.[13]

Nor does continuity mean that modern Israel has achieved its final, messianic form. The prophets speak of a future restoration that goes beyond what exists today—a time when Israel will recognize its Messiah, when the nations will stream to Jerusalem. Modern Israel is a fulfillment of prophecy, but not the *complete* fulfillment. More is yet to come.

But the fact that more is coming does not negate what has already arrived. The same people to whom God made promises have returned to the same land where those promises were made. They have rebuilt the waste cities and planted the vineyards, exactly as Amos prophesied. The nation that was scattered has been regathered. The valley of dry bones has come back to life.

Why the Lie Persists

The claim that Jews have no right to the land—whether expressed as anti-Zionism or as replacement theology—persists because it is useful. It provides cover for prejudice that would otherwise be unacceptable. It allows people to express hostility toward Jews while maintaining a self-image as progressive or as theologically sophisticated. It permits discrimination against Jews in spaces that would never tolerate discrimination against any other group.

The lie also reflects genuine confusion among some who repeat it. They have been taught that antisemitism looks like Nazi Germany—that it requires jackboots and gas chambers to qualify. They do not recognize antisemitism when it appears in progressive language or theological vocabulary. They are antisemites who do not know they are antisemites, which may be the most dangerous kind.

Antisemitism has always adapted to the moral language of its era. In Christian Europe, it spoke of Jews as Christ-killers. In nationalist Europe, it spoke of Jews as racial contaminants. In progressive circles today, it speaks of Zionists as colonizers. In theological circles, it speaks of Israel as spiritually obsolete. The language changes; the structure remains. The Jew is always the exception—the one group that does not deserve what all others deserve.

The Question of God's Faithfulness

The theological version of this lie ultimately raises a question about God Himself. Did God mean what He said? When He promised Abraham that his descendants would possess the land forever, was that a real promise or a metaphor? When He declared through Amos that Israel would be planted in their land and *never again pulled up*, was that binding or provisional? When He said through Jeremiah that His Covenant with Israel would stand as long as the sun and moon endure, did He mean it?

If God's promises to Israel can be spiritualized away, transferred to another group, or simply allowed to lapse, what confidence can we have in any of His promises? If "everlasting" does not mean everlasting when applied to Israel, why should it mean everlasting when applied to us? The reliability of God's Word is at stake.

Michael Vlach concludes: "There are compelling scriptural reasons in both testaments to believe in a future salvation and restoration of the nation Israel."[14] Gerald McDermott demonstrates that Christian support for Israel's restoration has deep roots predating modern dispensationalism—going back to Puritan theologians who read the same Scriptures and reached the same conclusion: God's promises to Israel remain in force.[15]

The Mask and the Face

Whether expressed as anti-Zionism or replacement theology, the claim that Jews have no right to the land is the foundational lie that makes all the other lies possible. It provides cover for hatred that would otherwise be recognized and rejected.

Zionism is simply the belief that the Jewish people have the right to self-determination in their ancestral homeland. The Bible affirms that God gave this land to Abraham's descendants through an everlasting Covenant. To deny Jewish rights to the land—whether on political or theological grounds—is to single out one people for treatment applied to no other. When that denial leads to chants calling for Israel's elimination, to harassment of Jewish students, to attacks on synagogues, to Jews hiding their identity across the Western world—the true nature of the denial becomes impossible to hide.

"The Jews Have No Right to the Land"

Yes, people can criticize Israeli policies without being antisemitic. Israelis do it constantly. But there is a difference between criticizing what Israel does and denying that Israel should exist. There is a difference between disputing a policy and disputing a people's right to their homeland. When criticism applies standards demanded of no other nation, when it denies Jewish history, when it holds all Jews responsible for Israel's actions, when it spiritualizes away God's explicit promises—it has crossed from criticism into bigotry.

Under all the updated language—secular and theological alike—it still paints Jews as different, illegitimate, and ultimately disposable. The same pattern Haman used, dressed in modern words.

The very existence of modern Israel is a testimony that the God of the Bible keeps His promises. A people scattered among the nations for two thousand years maintained their identity, returned to their homeland, and reconstituted their nation. This has never happened before in human history. Empires that tried to destroy them have fallen into history. Yet Israel remains—still reading the same Scriptures, still praying in the same language, still celebrating the same festivals, still connected to the same Covenant, still in the same land.

The claim that Jews have no right to the land asks us to believe that the world's oldest hatred has simply vanished, that hostility to the Jewish state has nothing to do with hostility to the Jewish people, that God's promises have quietly expired. History teaches otherwise. Scripture teaches otherwise. The evidence before our eyes teaches otherwise.

The mask is new. The face behind it is ancient.

Once the foundational lie is accepted—that Jews have no right to the land—other accusations become easier to believe. The next lie we will examine takes the delegitimization further, branding Israel with one of the most morally toxic labels in modern history.

7

Lie #2

"Israel Is an Apartheid State"

People use the word "apartheid" because it is emotional and powerful. It makes Israel sound like a country built on racism, like South Africa once was. The word carries enormous moral weight. It evokes images of pass laws,[1] separate facilities, systematic dehumanization. By applying this label to Israel, critics tap into a reservoir of moral outrage and place Israel in the same category as one of history's most reviled regimes.

But when you look at what apartheid actually was—and what Israel actually is—the comparison falls apart immediately. The accusation is not a description of reality. It is a propaganda weapon designed to delegitimize Israel—to place it in a category so morally toxic that its destruction becomes not just acceptable but righteous.

What Apartheid Actually Was

In South Africa, apartheid was not simply discrimination. It was a system of codified racial segregation, written into law, designed to enforce white supremacy and exclude non-white populations from political participation, civil rights, public institutions, and geographic freedom.

Black citizens could not vote. They could not serve in government. They could not live in certain areas. They could not marry whom they wanted. They could not use the same hospitals, schools, beaches, buses, or neighborhoods as whites. Their entire lives were controlled by racist laws.[2]

The Population Registration Act of 1950 classified every South African by race. The Group Areas Act designated where each race could live. The Bantu Education Act ensured inferior education for Black children. Pass laws required Black citizens to carry documents at all times and restricted their movement. Separate Amenities Acts created segregated public facilities—separate parks, beaches, restrooms, even benches.

This was apartheid: a comprehensive legal system designed to keep races apart and ensure white dominance in every area of life.

What Israel Actually Is

None of that exists in Israel. Not even close.

The contrast could not be starker:

Under South African Apartheid:

- Black citizens could vote: No
- Black members of parliament: 0
- Black Supreme Court justices: 0
- Integrated public facilities: None
- Interracial marriage: Illegal

In Israel Today:

- Arab citizens can vote: Yes (since 1948)
- Arab members of Knesset: Currently 10+ across multiple parties

- Arab Supreme Court justices: Yes (Salim Joubran served seventeen years)
- Integrated public facilities: All (hospitals, universities, beaches, transportation)
- Interracial marriage: Legal

This is the opposite of apartheid.

Inside Israel, Arab citizens, who make up approximately 21 percent of the population, have full legal equality.[3] They vote in national elections. As of 2024, Arab citizens serve in the Knesset across multiple parties including the Joint List coalition and Ra'am (United Arab List).[4]

Arab justices sit on the Israeli Supreme Court and have authored majority decisions binding on the entire country, including Jewish citizens. Justice Salim Joubran served on Israel's Supreme Court for seventeen years and was part of the panel that convicted a former Israeli president.[5] An Arab judge presiding over the conviction of a Jewish head of state—this is the opposite of apartheid.

Arab doctors comprise a significant percentage of Israel's physicians—in some hospitals, as high as 40 percent.[6] Arab professors teach at Israeli universities. Arab diplomats represent Israel abroad. Arab police officers serve in Israel's security forces. Arab citizens run major businesses and hold positions throughout Israeli society.

Arabs and Jews share the same hospitals, universities, public transportation, beaches, malls, and parks. There are no segregated institutions, no segregated roads, no segregated residential zones, and no laws that allocate different civil rights based on ethnicity.

What About Military Service?

Critics sometimes point to Israel's mandatory military service as evidence of unequal treatment. The reality is the opposite of what they suggest. Jewish citizens are *required* to serve in the Israel Defense Forces—it is a legal obligation, not a privilege. Arab citizens are *exempt* from this requirement. This exemption was established out of sensitivity to the position of Arab citizens, recognizing the difficulty of asking them to potentially fight against neighboring Arab nations or populations.[7]

In other words, Jewish Israelis carry a burden that Arab Israelis do not. If anything, the military service requirement is an *obligation* placed on Jews, not a *right* denied to Arabs. Arab citizens who wish to serve may volunteer, and increasing numbers do—particularly from the Druze and Bedouin communities, who serve with distinction.[8]

Arab citizens have the same civil rights as Jewish citizens—but *fewer mandatory duties*.

The Apartheid Accusation Collapses Under Examination

The apartheid accusation collapses the moment critics are asked to name a single apartheid law Israel has enacted. They cannot because none exist. Israel's Declaration of Independence guarantees "complete equality of social and political rights to all its inhabitants irrespective of religion, race, or sex."[9] This principle is upheld in Israeli Basic Laws.

Israel is the most diverse nation in the region—Jews from over 100 nations, two million Arab citizens, Druze, Bedouin, Christians, Muslims, Circassians, and more. Do inequalities exist? Yes, like in every democracy. But discrimination is not state policy. Social and economic gaps are being addressed through multi-billion shekel government programs to invest in Arab communities.[10]

So Why Do People Still Call It Apartheid?

Because they shift the conversation away from Israeli citizens and talk instead about Palestinians in the West Bank. Palestinians in the West Bank *are not citizens of Israel. They do not want to be citizens of Israel.* They live under the civil authority of the Palestinian Authority, not Israel.

This setup came from the Oslo Accords—an agreement Palestinian leaders themselves signed.[11] It was not Israel imposing racial separation. It was both sides agreeing that Palestinians would govern themselves. Under Oslo, the West Bank was divided into Areas A, B, and C:

- **Area A:** The Palestinian Authority has full civil and security control.
- **Area B:** Palestinian Authority civil control, shared Israeli–Palestinian Authority security.
- **Area C:** Israeli administrative control with responsibilities gradually transferring.

Palestinians are governed by Palestinian Authority courts, not Israeli courts, because Palestinian leadership demanded it. Israel did not create this dual system to enforce ethnic superiority. It was created to give Palestinians self-rule—ironically, the opposite of apartheid. Under full Israeli sovereignty, this dual system would disappear entirely.

But critics of sovereignty oppose that solution while simultaneously complaining about the legal separation they insist on maintaining. It is a circular argument: *They oppose sovereignty, then blame Israel for the legal fragmentation that exists because sovereignty is absent.*

Where Do the Checkpoints and Barriers Come From?

Not from racism. Not from apartheid. They were built after more than a thousand Israelis were killed in suicide bombings during the Second Intifada (see Chapter 17 for the full scope of this terrorism campaign).[12] Before that, movement between Israel and the West Bank was mostly open.

The barrier and checkpoints were built-in responses to terrorism. And the test of this reality is simple: *When violence decreases, Israel reduces restrictions. When violence increases, restrictions increase.* Ethnicity plays no role in the process—security does.

Following construction of the security barrier, terrorist attacks from the West Bank decreased by over 90 percent.[13] It was built because buses, restaurants, and families were being blown up. Any country facing those threats would take similar steps to protect its people. These measures are about security, not racial hierarchy.

What Do South Africans Say?

South Africans who lived under real apartheid—people who know exactly what it looked and felt like—reject the comparison outright. Even they say the accusation is false.

Judge Richard Goldstone, a South African who is openly critical of Israeli policy and who led the controversial UN investigation into the 2008–2009 Gaza conflict, stated explicitly that Israel is not an apartheid state. He wrote in *The New York Times*: "In Israel, there is no apartheid. Nothing there comes close to the definition of apartheid."[14] The legal, social, and political realities are so different that equating them trivializes the suffering of South Africans and distorts the truth.

Where Did the Accusation Come From?

The apartheid charge is a political import, manufactured not by South Africans but by Soviet propaganda campaigns in the 1970s and 1980s.[15] The goal was not to describe Israel but to morally delegitimize it. If Israel can be cast as inherently evil, then its very existence—its sovereignty—becomes negotiable, and resistance to it becomes morally justified.

The Soviet Union's campaign to equate Zionism with racism culminated in a Soviet-backed "Zionism is racism" resolution in 1975 (see Introduction). The resolution was revoked in 1991 after the Soviet Union collapsed—but the propaganda framework it created lives on in the apartheid accusation.

This is why the apartheid accusation always collapses when you return to the fundamental question: What is Israel? A sovereign Jewish state. The real objection is not checkpoints or military administration. Those are symptoms of a larger conflict. The real objection is Jewish self-determination in the Jewish homeland. Everything else is a rhetorical wrapper.

The Real Apartheid in the Region

Israel is the freest, most diverse, most democratic nation in the Middle East—the only place where Arab citizens have full political rights, Christians are protected and growing rather than persecuted, minorities have equal legal status, and women have full equality.[16]

The real apartheid regimes in the region are those where Christians cannot worship freely, women cannot vote or drive, and minorities are not citizens. Saudi Arabia, until recently, did not allow women to drive. Iran executes homosexuals. Gaza under Hamas has no elections and no tolerance for dissent. Syria under Assad massacred hundreds of thousands of its own people.

Israel stands alone as the exception. Calling it an apartheid state is not just wrong—it is a moral inversion that ignores the actual human rights situation across the Middle East.

Engaging the Harder Questions

We have shown that Israel is not apartheid South Africa. Inside Israel proper, the comparison fails completely. But sophisticated critics will shift the argument. They will say: "We're not talking about Arab citizens of Israel. We're talking about Palestinians in the West Bank. They live under Israeli military control but have no vote in the government that controls their lives. That's the apartheid."

This argument deserves a serious response.

"Palestinians in the West Bank Live Under a Two-Tiered System"

The critique:
Palestinians in the West Bank live under Israeli military law while settlers nearby live under Israeli civil law. They drive on different roads, pass through different checkpoints, face different courts. An Israeli settler who commits a crime goes before a civilian court with full due process; a Palestinian goes before a military tribunal. Whatever you call it, this is a system where rights depend on ethnicity.

The honest response:
The legal differentiation exists—but its cause is not racial hierarchy. It exists because the Oslo Accords created a temporary framework pending a final-status agreement, and that agreement never came.

Under Oslo, which Palestinian leadership signed, the West Bank was divided into Areas A, B, and C. Area A is under full Palestinian civil and security control. Area B has Palestinian civil control with shared security. Area C is under Israeli administration. *This was negotiated, not imposed.* Palestinians govern Palestinians in Areas A and B; Israel administers Area C, where most settlers live.

The "different roads" claim is largely outdated. In the early 2000s, during the worst of the suicide bombing campaign, some roads were restricted. Most of those restrictions have been lifted. Today, Palestinians and Israelis generally use the same road network in the West Bank, with some exceptions near settlements and military zones.

The legal differentiation—military courts for Palestinians, civil courts for settlers—exists because extending Israeli civil law to Palestinians would mean annexation, which Palestinians reject. They don't want to be Israeli citizens; they want their own state. The alternative to military administration isn't civil rights under Israeli law—it's either annexation (rejected by Palestinians) or withdrawal (rejected by security realities). The current situation is an interim arrangement that persists because the final status was never agreed.

The honest concession:
The interim has lasted nearly thirty years. What was designed as temporary has become semi-permanent. Whatever the legal justifications, the lived experience of a Palestinian in Hebron is materially different from the experience of a settler in Kiryat Arba nearby. The explanation—that this results from a failed peace process—doesn't change the daily reality.

The honest answer:
This situation exists because peace negotiations failed, not because Israel designed a system of ethnic hierarchy. Every Israeli offer included ending

this dual system through Palestinian statehood. Every offer was rejected. The differentiation is a symptom of unresolved conflict, *not evidence of apartheid ideology*. Apartheid was a permanent system designed to maintain racial supremacy forever. The West Bank situation is an interim arrangement that Israel has repeatedly offered to resolve through Palestinian statehood.

"The Comparison to South Africa Is Valid Because the Effect Is the Same"

The critique:
Intent doesn't matter—effect does. Whether Israel designed the system to be racist or stumbled into it through failed negotiations, the outcome is that one group has rights and another doesn't based on ethnicity. That's apartheid in practice.

The honest response:
The analogy fails because the situations are structurally different in ways that matter morally and legally.

South African apartheid was designed to be permanent. The entire ideology was that racial separation was natural, right, and eternal. There was never an offer to end apartheid—it was the goal, not a problem to be solved.

Israel's situation in the West Bank has produced multiple offers to end it through Palestinian statehood. Camp David (2000), Taba (2001), Olmert (2008)—each proposed ending Israeli military administration through a peace agreement. These offers were rejected.

The effect-versus-intent distinction also matters legally. Apartheid under international law requires discriminatory intent—a system designed for racial domination. A military occupation during unresolved conflict, however prolonged and however imperfect, is not the same legal category.

The honest concession:
The legal distinction may feel irrelevant to a Palestinian waiting at a checkpoint. Academic debates about definitions don't change daily experience. And after thirty years, "temporary" starts to look permanent regardless of stated intentions.

The honest answer:
Call it what you will—the solution is the same. Good faith acceptance of Israel's peace offers would end it. Every Israeli government has offered that path. No Palestinian leadership has ever taken it. The problem isn't that Israel wants apartheid; it's that ending the current situation requires a peace agreement, and no Palestinian leader has been willing to sign one.

8

Lie #3

"Israel Was Founded Through the Displacement of Palestinians"

This is one of the most emotionally powerful claims made against Israel. Many imagine an ancient Arab population living in the land for centuries, suddenly pushed out by foreign Jewish newcomers. The narrative of displacement and dispossession resonates deeply in our cultural moment, fitting neatly into frameworks of colonialism and indigenous rights.

But that picture does not match the historical record, what Arab leaders said at the time, or even the population data from the Ottoman and British periods. Before we can have an honest debate about the future, we must first be clear about the past. If the underlying narrative is wrong, every conclusion built on it collapses.

The Biggest Misunderstanding

People today talk about "the Palestinian people" as if they had a long-established national identity and were fighting for their own independent state in the early 1900s. They were not.

Arab leaders said openly that there was no separate Palestinian nation. In 1937, the Arab Higher Committee declared before the Peel Commission:

> **There is no such country as Palestine. "Palestine" is a term the Zionists invented.**[1]

They identified the land not as a sovereign Palestinian homeland, but as Southern Syria. For decades, the primary political objective of Arab leadership was not to establish an independent Palestinian state, but to prevent Jewish sovereignty in any form. As Professor Kenneth W. Stein explains, surrounding Arab states and Palestinian–Arab leadership were never interested in building a Palestinian–Arab government. Their goal was singular: Prevent the creation of a Jewish state.[2]

Their refusal was not about borders. It was not about settlements. It was not about compromise. It was about Jewish existence.

So when critics today claim that Jewish sovereignty ignores "the national aspirations of people who lived there for generations," they are repeating a narrative invented decades after the fact, not the one expressed by Arab leaders before 1948.

"Israel Was Founded Through the Displacement of Palestinians"

The Arab Higher Committee Rejected All Partition

When the United Nations proposed partition in 1947—one Jewish state, one Arab state—the Jewish leadership accepted it. The Arab Higher Committee rejected it completely and declared before the United Nations:

> The Arabs of Palestine insist upon their right to the whole of Palestine. They do not recognize the legality of the partition or the right of any power to impose it.³

The Arab world rejected any Jewish political presence—no matter how small. Their stated goal, repeatedly, was *to prevent Jewish sovereignty entirely.*

If the Arab world had accepted the UN plan, there would have been a Jewish state, an Arab state, and no refugee crisis—instead of decades of conflict.

What Actually Happened in 1948

After rejecting the UN plan, five Arab armies invaded the new State of Israel on the very next day it declared independence—May 15, 1948.⁴ Egypt, Jordan, Syria, Iraq, and Lebanon attacked with the stated goal of destroying the Jewish state at birth.

A war broke out. In every war, civilians flee battle zones. Some Palestinians fled because Arab leaders told them to leave temporarily so the invading armies could attack more freely. Some fled out of fear, as civilians do in all wars. Some were expelled in local fighting. The causes were mixed, as historians acknowledge.⁵

But here is the part people almost never hear:

At the same time, nearly 850,000 Jews were expelled from Arab countries across the Middle East and North Africa.[6] Their homes, businesses, and property were taken. Jewish communities that had existed for centuries in Iraq, Egypt, Libya, Yemen, Syria, Morocco, and elsewhere were destroyed. Israel absorbed all of these Jewish refugees. The Arab countries refused to absorb the Palestinian refugees.

That political choice—not Jewish aggression—is what created the long-term refugee crisis. The Arab states kept Palestinian refugees in camps for generations as a political weapon, while Israel integrated its refugees.

Arab leaders themselves have acknowledged this reality. Syrian Prime Minister Khaled al-Azm wrote in his 1973 memoirs: "Since 1948, it is we who demanded the return of the refugees... while it is we who made them leave... We brought disaster upon... the refugees, by inviting them and bringing pressure to bear upon them to leave."[7]

Palestinian Authority President Mahmoud Abbas said in a 2008 interview: "The Arab armies entered Palestine to protect the Palestinians from the Zionist tyranny but, instead, they abandoned them, forced them to emigrate and to leave their homeland, and threw them into prisons similar to the ghettos in which the Jews used to live."[8]

These are not Israeli sources. These are Arab leaders acknowledging what actually happened.

Were Palestinians Living There for "Generations Going Back to Ottoman Rule"?

Some were. Many were not.

The population changed dramatically in the late 1800s and early 1900s. British records show that between 1922 and 1931 alone, the Muslim population rose 37 percent—far higher than natural birth rates would explain.⁹ And the biggest growth was in areas where Jews were building new jobs and infrastructure:

- Haifa: +290 percent.
- Jaffa: +158 percent.
- Jerusalem (non-Jewish population): +131 percent.
- Jenin: +78 percent.
- Nablus: +42 percent.
- Bethlehem: +37 percent.¹⁰

Demographic studies show that the late Ottoman period brought waves of migrants from multiple regions:

Bosnian Muslims fled Austrian occupation after 1878, with Ottoman authorities resettling them in Ottoman Palestine. Circassians were expelled from the Caucasus by Russia and resettled across the Ottoman Empire. Algerians came escaping French colonial rule. Armenians fled Turkish massacres after the collapse of the Ottoman Empire.¹¹

Many Christian groups such as Maronites and Syriacs reject the "Arab" label altogether and assert their older ethnoreligious identities.

These groups were later counted as "indigenous Palestinians," even if they arrived only a few years before 1948.

The Broad UN Refugee Definition

To be considered a Palestinian refugee, a person only had to live in the land between June 1946 and May 1948—*just two years!*¹² And that status became hereditary forever. This means that a family who moved to the area in 1946 was suddenly labeled "indigenous," and their descendants are still considered refugees *nearly 80 years later*.

No other refugee population in the world is treated this way. The UNHRC, the UN agency for all other refugees, does not grant hereditary refugee status. Only the United Nations Relief and Works Agency (UNRWA), the agency created specifically for Palestinians, does. This ensures the number of "refugees" grows with each generation rather than diminishing as resettlement occurs.

Where Was the Palestinian State from 1948–1967?

If Palestinian nationalism was ancient and central, then why did no one create a Palestinian state during the nineteen years when Israel did not control the West Bank or Gaza?

From 1948 to 1967, Jordan controlled the West Bank. Egypt controlled Gaza. They ruled those territories for almost a generation. What happened?

Jordan annexed the West Bank and gave its residents Jordanian citizenship. Egypt ran Gaza as an occupied territory without offering citizenship or statehood.[13]

No one talked about a Palestinian state. No Arab leader demanded one. No protests were held to create one. The Palestine Liberation Organization (PLO), founded in 1964, initially called for the "liberation" *of Israel*—not for a state in the West Bank and Gaza, which were already in Arab hands.

The push for Palestinian statehood only became intense when it became politically useful against Israel, not because it had deep historical roots.

Numbers Do Not Determine Sovereignty

Critics often use population figures to argue that Jews were a minority and therefore did not have the right to declare sovereignty. But numbers do not decide who a people are or where they belong.

"Israel Was Founded Through the Displacement of Palestinians"

Jewish legitimacy in Israel is not dependent on census figures. It rests on over three thousand years of historical continuity, documented presence in Judea and Samaria, legal decisions of the post–World War I international system, and cultural, religious, and archaeological inheritance.[14]

Demography is not destiny. Identity is not measured by majority ratios.

Jews Are the Indigenous People of This Land

The idea that Jews are "foreign colonizers" collapses under archaeology and history. You cannot colonize the place you originated from.

Judea and Samaria are not abstract biblical ideas. They are physical, identifiable places with continuous Jewish habitation for millennia. The word "Jew" comes from "Judean"—a person from Judea. Archaeological evidence confirms Jewish presence with extraordinary clarity.

In 2018, at Shiloh, archaeologists uncovered a three-thousand-year-old Hebrew seal impression exactly where the Bible records the *Mishkan* (Tabernacle) stood.[15] Research correlating ancient Hebrew place names with modern geography proves that the biblical landscape and the modern West Bank are the same terrain. The Arabic names that replaced them came after the seventh-century Islamic conquest—*an act of imperial expansion, not indigeneity.*

Jews are not foreigners in Hebron. They are not settlers in Beit El. They are not colonizers in Shiloh. The Jewish people trace their roots in Israel back over three thousand years—long before the Arab conquests of the seventh century AD.[16] They maintained continuous presence in the land throughout the centuries of exile, with significant communities in Jerusalem, Hebron, Safed, and Tiberias.

Jews did not show up in the twentieth century as foreign colonizers. They were returning home.

The Truth About 1948

The real story is this:

The UN voted for two states. Jewish leaders accepted. Arab leaders rejected. Arab armies invaded. Civilians fled as they do in all wars. Arab countries refused to absorb Palestinian refugees. Jewish refugees from Arab lands flooded into Israel. The conflict created two refugee crises—not one.

The narrative of "Jews displaced an ancient people" is not supported by history, demography, leadership statements, or the political actions of the time.

Palestinian nationalism later developed—and people have the right to their identity—but identity formed in the 1950s or 1960s does not rewrite what happened before 1948.

The accusation that Israel's creation was an act of colonial displacement is historically false. Israel was founded through international law—the San Remo Conference, the League of Nations Mandate, the UN partition vote—through millennia of continuous Jewish identity, and through defensive victory against invasion by armies that sought its destruction.[17]

The conflict that followed was the result of Arab rejection of Jewish sovereignty, not a Jewish project of displacement.

What Really Happened

The displacement narrative rewrites history to transform the Indigenous people into colonizers and the victims of aggression into aggressors.

The historical record is clear. The accusation that Israel's founding was an act of displacement ignores all of this. It ignores the Arab rejection of partition. It ignores the invasion by five armies. It ignores the Jewish refugees from Arab lands. It ignores the continuous Jewish presence

"Israel Was Founded Through the Displacement of Palestinians"

in the land for three millennia. It rewrites the return of an indigenous people as a colonial invasion.

But the Jewish people know who they are and where they came from. Israel was not founded through displacement—Israel was restored through return. And no propaganda, however persistent, can change that.

9

Lie #4

"Israel Illegally Occupies the West Bank and East Jerusalem"

This accusation assumes something very simple: that the West Bank and East Jerusalem were once part of a sovereign Palestinian state that Israel invaded and stole. The language of "occupation" suggests a foreign power ruling over another people's land against their will. The phrase "international law" lends an air of legal authority. Together, they paint Israel as a lawless aggressor holding territory that does not belong to it.

But that picture does not match the actual history at all. To understand what is happening today, we need to look at who controlled the land before 1967, how Israel gained it, and what international law actually says.

The Most Important Fact

There has never been a Palestinian state in history. Not in ancient times, not under the Romans, not under the Ottomans, not under the British Mandate, not between 1948 and 1967.[1] No Palestinian government, no

Palestinian borders, no Palestinian currency, no Palestinian king or president. The idea of an independent Palestinian state is modern—it did not exist historically.

This is not a minor detail. It goes to the heart of the "occupation" claim.

Who Controlled These Territories Before Israel?

From 1948 to 1967, Jordan controlled the West Bank and East Jerusalem—not the Palestinians.

Jordan invaded these areas during the 1948 war. Jordan annexed them and declared them part of Jordan in 1950. The international community did not recognize the annexation—not even the Arab League, which explicitly rejected Jordan's claim. Only two countries, the United Kingdom and Pakistan, recognized Jordanian sovereignty over the West Bank.[2]

Jews were expelled from East Jerusalem and barred from the Old City and all Jewish holy sites. The Jewish Quarter was destroyed. Fifty-eight synagogues were demolished or desecrated. Jewish cemeteries on the Mount of Olives were vandalized, with tombstones used as building materials and latrines (see Chapter 18 for comprehensive documentation of religious access under Jordanian versus Israeli control.)[3]

East Jerusalem had a Jewish population for centuries, but under Jordanian rule, Jews were kept out entirely for nineteen years.

So when people say Israel is "occupying Palestinian land," they are ignoring the fact that these areas were controlled by Jordan, not by a Palestinian state.

And what about Gaza? It was controlled by Egypt, not by Palestinians. Egypt never offered to create a Palestinian state there either. No one demanded one.

"Israel Illegally Occupies the West Bank and East Jerusalem"

How Did Israel Gain Control?

In May 1967, Israel was surrounded by hostile armies preparing for war. Egypt amassed troops in the Sinai and expelled UN peacekeepers. Egypt blockaded the Straits of Tiran—Israel's only sea access to Asia—an act of war under international law.[4] Neighboring countries announced their intent to destroy Israel.

President Gamal Abdel Nasser of Egypt declared: "Our basic objective will be the destruction of Israel."[5] Syria shelled northern Israeli communities daily from the Golan Heights. Radio broadcasts across the Arab world called for Israel's annihilation.

Despite Israel begging Jordan to stay out of the conflict, Jordan attacked. On June 5, 1967, Jordan began shelling West Jerusalem and Israeli positions. Israel responded. In the Six-Day War, Israel captured the West Bank and East Jerusalem from Jordan, the Sinai and Gaza from Egypt, and the Golan Heights from Syria.

Israel did not attack Jordan to take land. Jordan attacked Israel, and Israel defended itself. Under international law, *when a country gains territory in a defensive war, that land is considered disputed, not stolen, and its final status must be determined by negotiation.*[6]

That is exactly where things stand today.

What Does International Law Say?

Many activists repeat the phrase "international law says the occupation is illegal," but international law is not as simple as a slogan. It is a complex collection of treaties, customs, precedents, and political interpretations. Several bodies of law matter here:

- The 1920 San Remo Conference and League of Nations Mandate (see Lie #3) gave the Jewish people legal rights to reestablish their national home in what was then known as Mandatory Palestine.[7]
- The League of Nations Mandate of 1922 recognized the Jewish historical connection to the land and encouraged "close settlement on the land" in all areas west of the Jordan River—including what is now called the West Bank.[8]
- UN Charter Article 51 allows nations to defend themselves and take measures necessary for security.
- UN Security Council Resolution 242, passed after the 1967 war, called for Israeli withdrawal from "territories" occupied in the conflict—but notably not "the territories" or "all territories." This wording was deliberate, as confirmed by the resolution's drafters.[9] The resolution envisioned negotiated borders, not a return to the pre-1967 lines.
- Because the West Bank was not Palestinian territory, Israel did not take land from a sovereign Palestinian state. The previous controller—Jordan—was itself not recognized as having sovereignty, and Jordan formally renounced its claim to the West Bank in 1988.[10]

There is no legal foundation for calling Israel's presence "illegal occupation." The land was captured in a *defensive war* from a country whose *control was not internationally recognized.*

The Oslo Accords

Under the Oslo Accords, the parties agreed to divide the West Bank into zones with different control levels.[11] This system—signed by both sides—is the legal framework that governs the area today.

"Israel Illegally Occupies the West Bank and East Jerusalem"

You cannot call something "illegal occupation" when the current arrangement was created by mutual agreement between Israel and the Palestinian Authority. The Oslo framework was negotiated, not imposed. *Palestinians agreed to it.*

Has Israel Tried to End the Dispute?

Yes—multiple times.

Each time, Palestinian leaders rejected offers that would have ended the "occupation" while recognizing Israel's right to exist. The pattern is clear: The "occupation" continues in large part because Palestinian leadership has refused every offer that would end it.

What About Gaza?

Israel completely withdrew from Gaza in 2005. Every soldier was removed. Every civilian was evacuated, some forcibly. Every settlement was dismantled. (For the full history of the Gaza withdrawal and its aftermath, see Chapter 20.)[12]

There is no Israeli occupation of Gaza. It ended in 2005.

What happened next? Hamas seized control in 2007 and began launching rockets at Israeli civilians. Since then, Hamas has fired over twenty thousand rockets at Israeli population centers. The response to Israel's complete withdrawal was not peace but escalating terrorism.

A More Accurate Description

Israel is not occupying "Palestinian land." *Israel is controlling disputed land, gained in a defensive war,* whose final status Palestinians and Israelis agreed would be resolved through negotiation.

That is not illegal. That is the normal outcome of armed conflict in the real world.

The accusation of "illegal occupation" is a political tool—one that ignores history, international law, and the agreements Palestinian leadership itself signed. It is designed to prejudge the outcome of negotiations and frame Israel as criminal regardless of the facts.

The Real Legal Picture

The word "occupation" suggests a foreign power ruling over another people's sovereign territory. But there has never been a sovereign Palestinian state in the West Bank or East Jerusalem. Before 1967, Jordan controlled these areas under an annexation almost no nation recognized. Before 1948, it was the British Mandate. Before that, the Ottoman Empire. At no point was there a Palestinian state from which Israel could have taken land.

Israel gained control of these territories in a defensive war it did not start. Jordan attacked Israel in 1967 despite Israeli pleas to stay out of the conflict. Israel's response was self-defense, not conquest.

The legal status of these territories is genuinely disputed—serious scholars hold different views. But the confident assertion that Israel's presence is "illegal" ignores the complexity of international law, ignores the absence of a prior sovereign, ignores the defensive nature of the war, and ignores the multiple peace offers Israel has made that would have resolved the status of these territories through negotiation.

The final status of these territories should be determined through negotiations—ones that Palestinian leadership has repeatedly abandoned. Until then, Israel administers areas won in a war of self-defense, pending a peace agreement that its enemies refuse to sign. That is not illegal occupation. That is the unsettled outcome of a conflict waiting for resolution.

10

Lie #5

"Israel Annexed Territory in Violation of International Law"

This accusation usually refers to two places: *East Jerusalem and the Golan Heights*. People claim that when Israel applied its law to these areas, it broke international law. The word "annexation" carries heavy implications—it suggests forcible seizure, imperial expansion, the grabbing of land that belongs to someone else.

But the real history is far more complicated—and once you understand it, the accusation stops making sense.

What Does Annexation Mean?

Annexation means a country applies its civilian law to a territory, treating it as part of the state. People hear the word and immediately think: "Israel stole land."

But annexation can be legal or illegal depending on several factors:

Who controlled the land before? Why was the land taken? Was the war offensive or defensive? Was there a recognized sovereign?

Let us look at East Jerusalem and the Golan Heights one at a time.

East Jerusalem: The Historical Context

Was East Jerusalem Palestinian territory? No. From 1948 to 1967, East Jerusalem was controlled by Jordan, not by Palestinians. The international community did not recognize Jordan's control—not even by the Arab League.[1]

Did Jews live there historically? Yes. In fact, *for many decades Jerusalem had a Jewish majority, long before modern Zionism*. Census records from the nineteenth century show Jews as the largest single group in Jerusalem by the 1860s.[2] The Old City's Jewish Quarter had been continuously inhabited for centuries.

But when Jordan took control during the 1948 war, everything changed. Under Jordanian rule, Jews were expelled and their holy sites systematically destroyed (see Lie #4 for full documentation). Jews were blocked from the Western Wall—the holiest site in Judaism where Jews could pray.

For nineteen years, Jews were banned from their holiest places. This was the ethnic cleansing that preceded Israeli control.

How Did Israel Take East Jerusalem?

As we documented in the previous chapter, Jordan attacked Israel in June 1967 despite Israeli pleas to stay out of the conflict. Israel defended itself. Within three days, Israeli forces had liberated the Old City and East Jerusalem from Jordanian control. (For the full context of the 1967 war, see Lie #4.)

"Israel Annexed Territory in Violation of International Law"

Why Did Israel Unify Jerusalem?

Because Jerusalem is the historic and spiritual center of the Jewish people. King David established it as his capital three thousand years ago. Solomon built the Temple there. The prophets walked its streets. For two thousand years of exile, Jews prayed facing Jerusalem and concluded every Passover Seder with the words "Next year in Jerusalem."

Because the city was divided by war, not by consent. The 1949 armistice lines—the "Green Line"—were never intended as permanent borders. They were simply where the fighting stopped.

Because no country divides its capital voluntarily. No one asked Germany to keep Berlin divided after reunification. No one asks any nation to split its capital.

Because the previous controller used the city to exclude Jews from their holiest sites. Under Jordanian rule, Jews could not pray at the Western Wall. Under Israeli rule, all faiths have access to their holy places.

Israel applied its law to the city in 1980 to restore freedom of worship for everyone—Jews, Christians, and Muslims. The Temple Mount remains under administration of the Islamic Waqf. Christians freely access the Church of the Holy Sepulchre. All faiths worship freely.[3]

Is Jerusalem's Unification Illegal?

Not according to serious legal arguments. Israel won the territory in a defensive war, and Jordan had no recognized sovereignty over it. That means Israel did not take land from a recognized owner.

No one demanded a Palestinian state in East Jerusalem before 1967—not once in nineteen years. The claim that East Jerusalem is "Palestinian land" is a post-1967 invention, not a historical reality.

The Golan Heights: The Historical Context

Who controlled the Golan before 1967? Syria.

How did Syria use it? For decades, Syrian forces used the Golan's high ground to terrorize Israeli civilians below. They shelled Israeli farms. They fired on Israeli villages. They sniped at civilians working their fields. They threatened Israel's northern communities with constant attack.

The Golan was a launching pad for aggression, not a peaceful border. Syrian gunners could look down on Israeli towns and farms and fire at will.[4] Life in northern Israel meant living under Syrian guns.

How Did Israel Gain the Golan?

During the 1967 Six-Day War, Syria joined the attack on Israel. Syria shelled Israeli communities from the Golan Heights while Israel was fighting Egypt and Jordan.

Israel defended itself and captured the Golan. The high ground that had been used to terrorize Israeli civilians was now in Israeli hands.

Why Did Israel Apply Its Law to the Golan in 1981?

Because returning the Golan to a hostile regime would threaten Israel's survival. The topography is decisive—whoever holds the Golan dominates northern Israel.

Because Syria continued sponsoring terrorism and calling for Israel's destruction. Syria never recognized Israel's right to exist. It never offered peace. It remained in a formal state of war with Israel.

Because Israel cannot place its northern communities under the gun again. The shelling of the 1950s and 1960s cannot be allowed to resume.

"Israel Annexed Territory in Violation of International Law"

Later events vindicated Israel's decision. When Syria collapsed into civil war under Assad, the regime used chemical weapons against its own people. ISIS and other jihadist groups operated near the Israeli border. Imagine the Golan Heights in the hands of Assad—or worse, the Islamic State of Iraq and the Levant. Even the United States concluded that the Golan must remain under Israeli control for regional stability and security. In 2019, the United States formally recognized Israeli sovereignty over the Golan.[5]

Is the Golan Annexation Illegal?

International law is not as simple as critics suggest. There is no international rule that says a nation must give strategic defensive land back to a hostile regime that has never made peace and continues to threaten its existence.

Syria has never recognized Israel's right to exist—let alone offered peace. Syria remains technically at war with Israel. Returning the Golan to Syria would be strategic suicide.

The Bigger Issue: International Law as a Weapon

Critics treat international law as a weapon, not a standard. Here is why the accusation feels persuasive: People think "international law" is a single book with clear rules. It is not.

International law is a collection of treaties, customs, precedents, and political interpretations. In the Middle East—as with many long-running conflicts—international law is complicated by many factors: defensive versus offensive war, unrecognized annexations like Jordan's, lack of a previous sovereign Palestinian state, ongoing security threats, the failure of peace negotiations, contradictory UN resolutions, and local agreements like the Oslo Accords.

When critics shout, "Israel violated international law," what they are really doing is using a political slogan—not presenting a legally proven fact. They pick the interpretation that condemns Israel and ignore the interpretations that support Israel's position.

The Clear Answer

Israel applied its laws to territories gained in defensive wars, from regimes that either illegally controlled the land or used it to attack Israel. Jordan's control of Jerusalem was not recognized. Syria used the Golan to attack Israeli civilians.

Israel has repeatedly tried to negotiate peace agreements that would have addressed all territorial questions. The Arab side rejected peace at Camp David, at Taba, in Olmert's offer. (These rejected peace offers are documented fully in Chapter 20.) Syria never even came to the table.

These areas remain disputed—not stolen—and their final status can only be resolved through negotiations with partners willing to accept Israel's existence.

The accusation treats "international law" as a simple rulebook with clear answers. It is not. International law regarding territorial acquisition is a complex web of treaties, precedents, and interpretations—and the Middle East's unique circumstances complicate it further.

Jerusalem had a Jewish majority for over a century before modern Zionism. Jordan's ethnic cleansing of Jews from the Old City in 1948—the destruction of fifty-eight synagogues, the desecration of the ancient cemetery on the Mount of Olives—is the crime that preceded Israeli control. Under Israeli administration, all faiths worship freely at their holy sites for the first time in modern history.

"Israel Annexed Territory in Violation of International Law"

The Golan Heights was used by Syria for decades as a platform to shell Israeli farms and villages. Israel captured it in self-defense after Syria attacked. Returning it to Syria—or to whatever now rules the chaos of Syrian territory—would place Israeli communities back under the gun.

When critics invoke international law against Israel, they select the interpretation that condemns while ignoring interpretations that support Israel's position. They apply standards to Israel that are applied to no other nation. The accusation is political—dressed in legal language to give it authority it does not deserve.

11

Lie #6

"Israel Is a Settler-Colonial Project"

This accusation frames Israel as something imposed by European imperialism—a foreign project that displaced an indigenous population, just like European colonization of the Americas, Africa, or Australia. The language is designed to place Israel in the same moral category as history's great colonial criminals.

If this were true, it would make Israel fundamentally illegitimate according to modern progressive sensibilities. Settler-colonial projects are built on theft and displacement. They have no moral right to exist. They must be "decolonized"—which means dismantled.

But the accusation requires ignoring virtually everything about Jewish history, Jewish identity, and the actual circumstances of Israel's founding.

What Is Settler-Colonialism?

Classic settler-colonialism involves a metropolitan power—like the United Kingdom, France, or Spain—sending settlers to exploit a distant territory for the benefit of the mother country. The settlers maintain their primary loyalty and identity with the colonizing power. They extract resources and labor from the indigenous population. They impose foreign culture, language, and religion.

Think of the British in India, the French in Algeria, or the Spanish in Mexico. These were projects of imperial expansion. Settlers came as agents of a distant empire, imposed foreign rule, and exploited local populations for the empire's benefit.

There Was No Mother Country

There was no "mother country" sending Jewish settlers to exploit Palestine. Jews came from over 100 different countries[1]—fleeing persecution in Europe, expulsion from Arab lands, discrimination everywhere. They came not to extract resources for a distant empire but to rebuild their ancient homeland.

Where was the Jewish empire that colonized Palestine? There was none. Jews were the colonized, not the colonizers. For two thousand years, Jews lived as minorities in other people's empires—persecuted, expelled, massacred, and ultimately subjected to industrial genocide in Europe.

The Zionist movement was not an extension of European imperialism. It was a national liberation movement—the same kind of movement that other peoples used to throw off colonial rule. Jews sought self-determination in their ancestral homeland, just as Greeks, Poles, Irish, and dozens of other peoples sought independence.

Jews Are Not Foreign to This Land

This is the central fact the settler-colonial narrative must erase: *Jews are indigenous to the land of Israel.* You cannot colonize the place you come from.

The archaeological, historical, and genetic evidence is overwhelming. Jews originated in the land of Israel. The Hebrew language was born there. Jewish religion took shape there. Jewish holidays commemorate events that happened there—Passover, Sukkot, Shavuot. The Jewish calendar is tied to the agricultural seasons of the land of Israel, not Poland or Morocco.[2]

The word "Jew" comes from "Judean"—a person from Judea. Jewish identity is inseparable from this specific piece of territory. Every synagogue in the world faces Jerusalem. Every Jewish wedding includes the words "If I forget you, O Jerusalem, let my right hand forget its skill." For two thousand years of exile, Jews prayed to return.

Archaeological evidence confirms Jewish presence going back over three thousand years.[3] The Bible is not the only source—inscriptions, coins, buildings, tombs, and artifacts document Jewish civilization in this land centuries before the Arab conquests. The Dead Sea Scrolls, discovered in caves near the Dead Sea, preserve Jewish texts from the Second Temple period. Ancient synagogues have been excavated throughout Israel.

The correspondence between biblical geography and archaeological findings is remarkable.

Jews Maintained Continuous Presence

Even during the long exile, Jews maintained continuous presence in the land. There were always Jews living in Jerusalem, Hebron, Safed, and

Tiberias. The Jewish community in Hebron dated back centuries before it was massacred and expelled in 1929.[4] The "Old Yishuv," the pre-Zionist Jewish community, maintained religious and cultural life under Ottoman rule.

Jews did not arrive in the twentieth century as strangers. They returned to a land where their ancestors had lived for millennia and where their cousins remained.

What About the Mizrahi Jews?

The settler-colonial narrative imagines Israel as a European project. But approximately half of Israeli Jews descend from refugees from Arab and Muslim countries—Mizrahi and Sephardi Jews who were expelled from Iraq, Egypt, Libya, Yemen, Syria, Morocco, Tunisia, and elsewhere.[5]

Between 1948 and the 1970s, approximately 850,000 Jews were expelled from Arab countries. Their property was confiscated. Their communities, some dating back over 2,500 years, were destroyed. They fled to Israel because they had nowhere else to go.

These were not European colonizers. They were Middle Eastern Jews returning to the Middle East. They were refugees from Arab persecution, not agents of Western imperialism. Their presence alone demolishes the settler-colonial framework.

Genetic Evidence

As we saw under Lie #1, genetic studies consistently show that Jewish populations, including Ashkenazi Jews from Europe, share Middle Eastern ancestry with other Levantine populations.[6] Jews are genetically connected to the ancient inhabitants of the land. They did not appear as foreigners from Europe—they are descendants of the people who lived there for millennia.

The genetic evidence confirms what history and archaeology already showed: *Jews are indigenous to the land of Israel.*

What About the Arabs?

Arab presence in the region began with the Islamic conquests of the seventh century—over 1,600 years after Jewish presence was established.[7] The Arab conquest was itself an act of imperial expansion. Arab armies conquered the land from the Byzantine Empire and imposed Arab language, culture, and religion.

This does not mean Palestinians have no rights or legitimate interests. People who have lived somewhere for generations develop connections to the land. But it does mean the "settler-colonial" framework fundamentally mischaracterizes who is indigenous and who is the product of conquest.

If anyone "colonized" the land, it was the Arab conquerors of the seventh century, followed by the Crusaders, the Mamluks, and the Ottomans. The Jews returning in the nineteenth and twentieth centuries were not colonizers—they were the descendants of the original inhabitants, coming home.

What Decolonization Really Means

The "decolonization" that critics advocate is not reform or policy change. It is elimination.

When protesters chant "From the river to the sea, Palestine will be free," they are calling for the removal of Jews from their homeland.[8] The

Jordan River to the Mediterranean Sea encompasses all of Israel. "Free" Palestine in this formulation means no Israel.

When academics call for "decolonizing" Israel, they mean dismantling the Jewish state. The settler-colonial framework provides a theoretical justification for what would otherwise be recognized as ethnic cleansing and genocide.

That is not justice. That is the completion of what ancient empires started—and what the Nazis tried to finish.

The Purpose of the Accusation

The settler-colonial framework provides academic respectability to the delegitimization of Israel. But Israel is not apartheid South Africa. And Jews are not European colonizers. The comparison fails on every factual level. It only works if you erase three thousand years of Jewish history, ignore the circumstances of Israel's founding, pretend Mizrahi Jews do not exist, and define "colonialism" to mean any Jewish presence in the Jewish homeland.

The accusation is not a description of reality. It is a weapon designed to make Israel's existence seem illegitimate, criminal, and reversible.

The Truth

Israel is the national homeland of the Jewish people, restored after two thousand years of exile, persecution, and genocide. It was established through legal processes and defended through wars of survival against enemies who sought its destruction.[9]

Jews are not colonizers in their own homeland. They are the indigenous people who returned after centuries of forced exile. Their language, religion, culture, and identity were born in this land. Their connection to it is not a colonial invention—it is the oldest continuous national claim in human history.

Engaging the Harder Questions

We have documented the Jewish indigenous connection to the land—archaeological evidence, continuous presence, genetic links, historical memory embedded in religion and language. We have explained that there was no "mother country" sending colonizers, that half of Israeli Jews descend from refugees expelled from Arab lands.

But sophisticated critics will complicate this argument. They will acknowledge some Jewish historical connection while arguing that indigeneity claims don't justify dispossession.

"Indigenous Claims Don't Justify Displacement"

The critique:
Even if Jews have ancient roots in the land, so what? Americans have ancestors who lived in Europe or Africa—that doesn't give them the right to reclaim ancestral lands by displacing current inhabitants. The Palestinians living in 1948 weren't responsible for the Roman expulsion two thousand years earlier.

The honest response:
The argument is not that ancient indigeneity alone justifies modern statehood. The argument is that the settler-colonial framework—which portrays Jews as foreign invaders—is factually wrong.

The honest concession:
The Nakba was real, and we should not minimize it.

HAMAN'S LIES

Approximately seven hundred thousand Palestinians left their homes during the 1948 war. The circumstances varied—and this is where honest history requires nuance rather than slogans. Some fled advancing combat, as civilians do in every war. Some left after Arab leaders urged evacuation, expecting to return after the invading armies achieved victory. Some were expelled by Israeli forces in the fog and brutality of war. In some villages, there were atrocities. Deir Yassin, where over 100 villagers were killed by Jewish militias, became a symbol—and Arab leaders broadcast it widely, which increased panic and flight.

The causes were mixed, the experiences were varied, and historians still debate the proportions. But the outcome was displacement, and displacement is traumatic regardless of cause. Families lost homes. Villages emptied. A society was shattered. The keys that Palestinian refugees kept, the deeds they preserved, the memories they passed to children and grandchildren—these are real. The wound is real.

What happened afterward deepened the wound. Israel did not allow return. The reasons were a combination of security (the war was ongoing, and returnees might include combatants), demographics (absorbing seven hundred thousand hostile refugees would have ended the Jewish state before it began), and the reality that their homes and villages were now occupied by Jewish refugees—including 850,000 expelled from Arab countries who had nowhere else to go. Two refugee populations, one land, and a war that never fully ended.

We should also say clearly: The fact that Arab leaders share responsibility for the refugee crisis does not erase Palestinian suffering. The fact that Jewish refugees from Arab lands faced similar dispossession does not make Palestinian dispossession acceptable. Two wrongs do not make a right. The honest accounting includes all of it—the Arab rejection of partition that started the war, the invasion that made it existential, the displacement that followed, the refusal to allow return, and the Arab states' choice to keep refugees in camps as a political weapon rather than integrating them as Israel integrated its refugees.

What we cannot accept is the use of the Nakba to delegitimize Israel's existence entirely. The Nakba occurred in the context of a war launched to prevent Jewish statehood—a war Israel did not start and did not want. Acknowledging the tragedy does not require accepting that Israel should never have existed. It requires accepting that war produces suffering on all sides, and that the path forward is not reversal but reconciliation.

The honest answer:
Jewish indigeneity doesn't erase Palestinian experience. Palestinian experience doesn't erase Jewish indigeneity. Both peoples have claims. The question is how to accommodate both—not how to eliminate one for the other. But the settler-colonial framework rejects any accommodation—it demands the elimination of Jews in the region.

"The Nakba Shows This Was Ethnic Cleansing"

The critique:
Whatever the legal framework, seven hundred thousand people were displaced. Villages were depopulated. Many were never allowed to return.

The honest response:
The 1948 war was a war for survival launched by Arab armies explicitly promising to "drive the Jews into the sea." The displacement of Palestinians must be understood in that context. Some fled warfare. Some were expelled. Some left expecting to return after Arab victory. The historiography is contested.

The honest concession:
The reality on the ground was often brutal. Villages were depopulated. People lost homes. Some were expelled at gunpoint. We should not say "it was war" as though that makes suffering acceptable.

The honest answer:
The 1948 war produced tragedy on all sides. Arab forces also committed wrongs—including the complete ethnic cleansing of Jews from the Old City of Jerusalem and territories Jordan captured. The Nakba is invoked not to contextualize history but to delegitimize Israel's existence entirely. The "return" demanded is not to the West Bank but to Israel proper—a demand designed to eliminate the Jewish state demographically and entirely.

12

Lie #7

"Israel Is Committing Genocide and Ethnic Cleansing"

Two accusations stand at the pinnacle of crimes against humanity: genocide and ethnic cleansing. They are very similar charges, and that's why they are combined in this chapter, but they have important distinctions.

- **Genocide**—the systematic attempt to destroy a people.
- **Ethnic cleansing**—the systematic attempt to remove a people from their land.

These are the gravest charges that can be leveled against any nation. They invoke the Holocaust, the Armenian genocide, Rwanda, Bosnia, Darfur—history's darkest chapters of mass atrocity. To accuse a nation of these crimes is to place it among history's greatest villains.

Both accusations are now routinely leveled against Israel. "Genocide in Gaza" trends on social media. "Ethnic cleansing" appears in academic papers and UN reports. These charges are repeated by politicians, professors, journalists, and protesters until they achieve the status of accepted truth.

Israel, the accusers claim, is systematically destroying the Palestinian people—either by killing them or by driving them from their homeland.

These accusations are not merely false. They are obscene inversions of reality—ancient blood libels recast as human rights claims. They take the crime committed against the Jewish people—genocide—and accuse Jews of committing it. They take the experience of Jewish refugees expelled from Arab lands and erase it while fabricating a narrative of Israeli expulsion. The accusations require ignoring all evidence, inverting cause and effect, and applying definitions so distorted that words lose meaning entirely.

What Genocide Actually Means

The term "genocide" was coined by Raphael Lemkin, a Polish-Jewish lawyer who lost forty-nine family members in the Holocaust.[1] He created the word to describe the Nazi attempt to exterminate the Jewish people—the systematic murder of six million Jews, including 1.5 million children, in gas chambers, mass shootings, and death camps. The word carries the weight of that horror. It should never be used casually or politically.

The UN Genocide Convention defines genocide as acts committed "with intent to destroy, in whole or in part, a national, ethnical, racial or religious group."[2] The key word is intent—genocide requires the deliberate purpose of destroying a people. Killing in war, even large-scale killing, is not genocide unless the intent is destruction of a group as such. A war with civilian casualties, however tragic, is not genocide. A military campaign against a terrorist organization is not genocide. The intent to destroy must be proven, not assumed from casualty figures.

When we speak of actual genocides, we speak of the Holocaust, where Nazi Germany built an industrial infrastructure specifically designed to murder every Jew in Europe. We speak of Rwanda, where Hutu extremists murdered eight hundred thousand Tutsis in 100 days using machetes and clubs, neighbor killing neighbor. We speak of Armenia, where the Ottoman Empire systematically exterminated 1.5 million Armenians through death marches and mass executions. These are genocides—systematic attempts to destroy entire peoples.

What Ethnic Cleansing Actually Means

Ethnic cleansing refers to the forced removal of an ethnic or religious group from a territory[3]—driving people from their homes to change the demographic composition of a region. It differs from genocide in that the goal is removal rather than extermination, though ethnic cleansing often involves mass killing as a means of terrorizing populations into flight.

The term gained prominence during the Yugoslav Wars of the 1990s, when Serbian forces systematically expelled Bosnian Muslims and Croats from territories they sought to control. Villages were surrounded, men were separated and often killed, women were raped, and entire populations were forced to flee. The goal was a Serbia cleansed of non-Serbs—homogeneous territories achieved through terror and expulsion.

Ethnic cleansing has a clear signature: Populations disappear from territories, driven out by systematic violence and intimidation. The demographic transformation is dramatic and intentional. The cleansed population does not return. The territory becomes homogeneous in a way it was not before.

The Palestinian Population: A Decisive Refutation

If Israel is committing genocide and ethnic cleansing against Palestinians, there should be evidence of a population being destroyed or removed. The evidence shows the opposite.

In 1948, approximately 156,000 Arabs remained within Israel's borders after the War of Independence. Today, Israel's Arab population exceeds two million—a more than twelvefold increase.[4] The Arab population of Israel has grown faster than the Jewish population in many periods. Arabs constitute approximately 21 percent of Israel's citizenry. This is not genocide. This is not ethnic cleansing. This is a population thriving within the state accused of destroying it.

The same is true in the West Bank, where the Palestinian population has multiplied several times since 1967 rather than declining.

In Gaza, the population has exploded from approximately 350,000 in 1967 to over two million today—roughly a sixfold increase.[5] Before the October 7, 2023, war, Gaza had one of the highest population growth rates in the world. Life expectancy rose and infant mortality fell. These are the demographics of rapid population growth, not destruction.

The total Palestinian population—in Israel, the West Bank, Gaza, and the diaspora—has grown from approximately 1.4 million in 1948 to over 14 million today. A tenfold increase. In what genocide does the targeted population multiply by ten? In what ethnic cleansing does the population of the cleansed territory grow exponentially? The demographic evidence alone obliterates the accusations.

CHART 5

Population Growth Data

If Israel were committing "genocide," populations would decline. The opposite is true.

POPULATION	1948	2024
Arab citizens of Israel	~160,000	~2,000,000
Palestinians (West Bank/Gaza)	~1,000,000	~5,400,000
Total Palestinian population growth	—	~5x increase

For comparison—actual genocides:

- Holocaust: Six million Jews murdered (population devastated)
- Rwanda: Eight hundred thousand Tutsis killed in 100 days
- Uyghurs: Forced sterilization reducing birth rates 84%

Genocide means population elimination—not fivefold growth.

The Absence of Genocidal Intent

Genocide requires intent to destroy. Where is Israel's intent to destroy the Palestinian people?

Israel provides electricity and water to Gaza—the territory from which Hamas launches rockets at Israeli cities.[6] What genocidal regime provides utilities to the population it is supposedly trying to destroy? Even during military operations, Israel has usually maintained humanitarian corridors, allowed food and medicine to enter, and coordinated with international organizations to provide aid.

Israel has developed the most sophisticated civilian protection measures in military history, detailed fully in Chapter 13.

Israeli hospitals treat Palestinian patients, including from Gaza. Palestinian children receive heart surgeries, cancer treatments, and complex medical care in Israeli facilities. Israeli medical teams—including teams led by Israeli Arabs—perform humanitarian missions providing medical care to Palestinians. This is not the behavior of a state with genocidal intent.

The Post-October 7 Accusation: "Starvation as a Weapon"

Since October 7, 2023, the accusation regarding Israel's genocidal intent has intensified dramatically. Human Rights Watch, Amnesty International, and UN bodies now charge that Israel is deliberately weaponizing starvation—using food and water deprivation as a tool of genocide. They cite statements by Israeli officials and what they characterize as deliberate obstruction of humanitarian aid.

This accusation deserves a direct response.

The Statements in Context

Critics point to statements made by Israeli officials in the immediate aftermath of October 7. Defense Minister Yoav Gallant declared a "complete siege" on Gaza. Energy Minister Israel Katz announced cuts to electricity and water. These statements, made in the raw aftermath of the worst massacre of Jews since the Holocaust, are cited as evidence of "genocidal intent."

But statements made in crisis do not necessarily become sustained policy—and they did not. Within weeks, Israel reopened crossings for humanitarian aid. By late October 2023, aid trucks began entering Gaza. Israel subsequently opened multiple additional crossings and created new routes specifically to increase aid flow.[7]

The Numbers

According to The Coordinator of Government Activities in the Territories (COGAT), by April 2024, Israel had facilitated the entry of nearly twenty thousand trucks of humanitarian aid into Gaza—approximately 370,000 tons of supplies—along with airdrops and the establishment of field hospitals.[8] By August 2025, Israel reported facilitating over ten thousand additional trucks since the resumption of aid in May 2025 alone, with approximately 80 percent carrying food.[9]

These numbers are disputed. The UN reports significantly lower figures. But the discrepancy itself reveals something important: The dispute is over counting methodology, not whether aid is entering at all. Israel counts trucks at crossing inspections; the UN counts trucks collected by UN agencies inside Gaza. The difference—sometimes thousands of trucks—represents aid entering through channels the UN does not track, including private sector deliveries, other international organizations, and airdrops.[10]

A nation intent on starving a population does not open multiple border crossings, coordinate with international organizations, conduct airdrops, pause military operations to allow aid distribution, and publicly document every truck it inspects.

The Real Crisis: Distribution, Not Supply

If massive quantities of aid have entered Gaza, why do hunger conditions persist? The answer lies in what happens after aid crosses the border.

According to UN data from 2025, approximately 88 percent of aid trucks that entered Gaza were intercepted before reaching their intended destinations—either by desperate civilians or by armed groups.[11] The head of COGAT posted video showing 600 trucks worth of aid sitting undistributed on the Gaza side of crossings. In August 2025, Israeli media reported "thousands and thousands of tons of humanitarian aid" sitting at Kerem Shalom, uncollected.[12]

The UN itself has acknowledged the distribution problem. In November 2024, nearly 100 trucks from a single convoy were looted near the Kerem Shalom crossing—described by UNRWA as "one of the worst" such incidents of the war. The UN attributed this to "total breakdown of civil order" within Gaza.[13]

Who bears responsibility for this breakdown? Hamas ruled Gaza for seventeen years. Hamas built hundreds of miles of tunnels while constructing no public bomb shelters. Hamas diverted construction materials to military infrastructure rather than civilian services. And when international organizations try to distribute aid, they face looting, hijacking, and violence—creating conditions that make sustained humanitarian operations nearly impossible.

The Question of Intent

Genocide requires intent to destroy. The accusers claim Israel's intent is proven by its actions. But consider what those actions actually demonstrate:

Israel has facilitated tens of thousands of aid trucks into Gaza during active combat operations. Israel has opened new crossings when existing ones proved insufficient. Israel has coordinated humanitarian pauses in fighting to allow aid distribution. Israel has worked with the United States to establish the Gaza Humanitarian Foundation as an alternative distribution mechanism when UN efforts proved inadequate. Israel has conducted airdrops when ground routes faced obstacles.

These are not the actions of a state seeking to starve a population. These are the actions of a state attempting to balance military necessity against humanitarian obligation—imperfectly, under extraordinary circumstances, while fighting an enemy that deliberately embeds itself among civilians and exploits humanitarian infrastructure. Yet Israel is feeding noncombatant civilians and armed terrorists alike.

Still, the hunger crisis in Gaza is real and tragic. But its cause is not Israeli policy—it is the collapse of civil order in a war zone, the diversion and theft of aid by armed groups, and the deliberate choices of Hamas to prioritize military infrastructure over civilian welfare for nearly two decades.

The Real Ethnic Cleansing: Jews from Arab Lands

While Israel is falsely accused of ethnic cleansing, an actual ethnic cleansing has been erased from historical memory: the expulsion of Jews from Arab countries.

While seven hundred thousand Palestinian refugees are commemorated, the 850,000 Jewish refugees expelled from Arab lands (Lie #3) are forgotten. One displacement generates perpetual outrage; the other has been erased from acceptable discourse.

Who Actually Calls for Genocide?

While Israel is accused of genocidal intent, actual calls for genocide come from its enemies—openly, proudly, and without consequence.

Hamas's founding charter explicitly calls for the destruction of Israel and the killing of Jews—not just Israelis, but Jews worldwide.[14] It cites the antisemitic forgery *The Protocols of the Elders of Zion* and includes religious passages calling for Muslims to kill Jews. The charter does not speak of coexistence or two states—it speaks of elimination.

Iranian leaders have repeatedly called for Israel to be "wiped off the map,"[15] eliminated, destroyed. These are not metaphors—they are expressions of intent, from a regime actively pursuing nuclear weapons. Hezbollah's leader has even expressed regret that Jews gathered in Israel—making it easier to destroy them all at once rather than hunting them down worldwide.[16] These are explicit statements of genocidal intent.

The chant "From the river to the sea" (explained in Chapter 6) calls for Israel's elimination. This is not a call for Palestinian rights alongside Israel; it is a call for Israel's elimination. When protesters chant this at rallies, they are calling for ethnic cleansing at minimum, genocide at worst.

The projection is remarkable: Those who actually call for genocide accuse their intended victims of the crime they themselves proclaim. It is Haman accusing Mordecai of planning what Haman himself intends.

Why the Accusations Persist

If the accusations are so clearly false, why do they persist and spread? Several factors explain their endurance despite their falsehood.

First, the accusations are used strategically. If Israel is committing genocide, then any measure to stop Israel is justified—the Boycott, Divestment, and Sanctions movement (BDS),[17] international isolation, even violence. The accusation is not analysis but a weapon, designed to delegitimize Israel so thoroughly that its destruction becomes morally acceptable. Genocide is the ultimate crime; a state committing genocide has forfeited its right to exist.

Second, the accusations invert Jewish victimhood in a way that serves psychological purposes for some accusers. Jews are no longer victims of genocide but perpetrators of it. The moral weight of the

Holocaust—which constrains criticism of Jews and supports Israel's existence—is neutralized if Jews are now the Nazis. The accusation is a form of Holocaust inversion that relieves pressure on those who might otherwise feel constrained by history.

Third, casualty figures from wars are presented without context in ways that suggest genocide. When Gaza health authorities report deaths, the numbers are repeated without noting that they include combatants, without acknowledging Hamas's practice of using human shields, without comparing the ratios to other urban warfare. Context is the enemy of the accusation, so context is eliminated.

Fourth, the accusations tap into ancient antisemitic tropes about Jews as killers of children, as bloodthirsty murderers, as uniquely evil. These tropes have deep roots in Western and Islamic civilization. The genocide accusation is a *modern blood libel*—it updates medieval accusations for contemporary consumption, using human rights language instead of religious language but serving the same purpose: to mark Jews as uniquely malevolent and deserving of punishment.

The Obscenity of the Accusation

Of all the accusations leveled against Israel, none is more obscene than this one. Genocide—the systematic extermination of a people—was committed against the Jewish people within living memory. To accuse Jews of committing genocide is to weaponize their own trauma against them.

As noted above, this tenfold population increase refutes the genocide accusation. Literacy has risen. Population growth rates exceed regional averages. No genocide in human history has ever produced these outcomes. The accusation does not survive contact with basic demographic data.

Israel's unprecedented civilian protection measures are detailed fully in Chapter 13. When casualties occur, they occur because Hamas builds its military infrastructure in civilian areas—a strategy examined comprehensively in the next chapter.

The genocide accusation is a blood libel—the ancient charge that Jews murder innocents, updated for the modern era. It inverts reality completely: The people who survived the Holocaust are accused of perpetrating one; the military that warns civilians is accused of targeting them; the nation that absorbs terrorist attacks is accused of aggression. The lie is as old as Haman. And like Haman's lies, it will not stand.

Engaging the Harder Questions

We have shown that the Palestinian population has grown tenfold since 1948—the opposite of what genocide produces. We have documented Israel's elaborate civilian protection measures. We have explained the legal definition of genocide and why it requires intent to destroy.

But sophisticated critics will focus on Gaza since October 7, 2023. They will cite the casualty figures, the destruction, the humanitarian crisis. They will argue that regardless of what happened before, what is happening now raises serious questions that deserve answers, not dismissal.

"The Scale of Destruction in Gaza Is Unprecedented"

The critique:

Over forty thousand Palestinians have been killed since October 7. Entire neighborhoods have been leveled. More than half the housing stock has been damaged or destroyed. The scale of devastation is unlike anything in Israel's previous operations. Even if past conduct doesn't meet the definition of genocide, the current campaign might.

"Israel Is Committing Genocide and Ethnic Cleansing"

The honest response:

The numbers are real and the destruction is massive. We do not dispute the scale—we dispute the interpretation.

Urban warfare against an enemy embedded in civilian infrastructure produces devastation. This is true in every conflict of this type—Mosul, Raqqa, Aleppo, Grozny. The destruction of Gaza reflects the nature of the combat environment, not genocidal intent.

Hamas built its entire military infrastructure within Gaza's civilian areas over seventeen years. Tunnels run beneath hospitals, schools, and apartment buildings. Command centers operate in residential basements. Weapons are stored in mosques and UN facilities. When Israel destroys a tunnel network, the surface structures above collapse. When Israel targets a weapons depot, the surrounding buildings sustain damage. The destruction is immense because Hamas made it immense by design.

The casualty figures require context. Hamas-controlled health authorities do not distinguish combatants from civilians. Israel estimates it has killed approximately seventeen thousand Hamas fighters—nearly half the reported total of all fatalities. If accurate, the combatant-to-civilian ratio would be approximately 1:1, which is exceptional for urban warfare. The UN has historically estimated urban warfare ratios at 1:9. If Israel is achieving 1:1, it indicates extraordinary efforts to minimize civilian harm—the opposite of genocide.

The honest concession:

The combatant estimates are disputed. We cannot independently verify Israel's claims about how many fighters it has killed. And even if the ratio is favorable by historical standards, the absolute numbers represent staggering human suffering. Tens of thousands of civilians, including many children, have been killed. Families have been destroyed. A society has been devastated.

We should not become so focused on rebutting accusations that we lose sight of the tragedy. The devastation of Gaza is real, and nothing we say here should minimize the suffering of innocent people caught in a war they did not choose.

"Israeli Officials Have Made Statements Showing Genocidal Intent"

The critique:
Defense Minister Gallant called Palestinians "human animals." Ministers have called for Gaza to be flattened, for Palestinians to be relocated, for collective punishment. These statements, critics argue, reveal the true intent behind Israeli actions—not security, but destruction.

The honest response:
Some Israeli officials made indefensible statements in the immediate aftermath of October 7—the worst massacre of Jews since the Holocaust. Those statements were wrong. They do not represent Israeli policy, and they have been contradicted by Israel's actual conduct.

Defense Minister Gallant clarified that his "human animals" comment referred to Hamas terrorists, not Palestinian civilians. This context matters—though the statement was inflammatory and gave ammunition to critics even with the clarification. Other statements by fringe ministers like Ben-Gvir and Smotrich have been condemned by mainstream Israeli leaders, rejected by the Israel Defense Forces (IDF), and are not reflected in military orders or conduct.

Intent under genocide law is determined by systematic policy and action, not by indiscreet and inflammatory statements from individual politicians. Israel's actual conduct—the warnings, the evacuation corridors, the humanitarian coordination, the pauses for aid delivery—demonstrates the opposite of genocidal intent. You do not warn civilians to flee if your goal is to destroy them.

The honest concession:
The statements were wrong and harmful. They gave credibility to accusations that should have been easily dismissed. Israeli leaders should be held to higher standards, and some have failed to meet them. The fact that politicians all over the world make unwise statements should not normalize making them.

"Starvation Is Being Used as a Weapon"

The critique:
Hunger in Gaza is real. Children are malnourished. The humanitarian situation is catastrophic. Whatever aid enters, it's clearly not enough. If Israel controls the crossings, Israel is responsible for what gets through.

The honest response:
Israel facilitated the entry of tens of thousands of aid trucks into Gaza during active combat—an extraordinary logistical effort during wartime. Multiple crossings were opened. Airdrops were conducted. Humanitarian pauses were implemented. The accusation that Israel was using starvation as a weapon is contradicted by the scale of aid Israel enabled.

The hunger crisis at the height of the conflict was real, but its primary cause was the collapse of distribution systems inside Gaza, not Israeli obstruction at the crossings. The UN itself has reported that aid was looted, diverted, and hijacked after it entered Gaza. Trucks sat uncollected.

Warehouses were raided. Armed groups—including Hamas—intercepted deliveries before they reached civilians.

Hamas ruled Gaza for seventeen years. It built tunnels, not hospitals. It stockpiled rockets, not food reserves. It created no civil emergency infrastructure. When war came, there was no capacity to manage a humanitarian crisis because Hamas had invested everything in war-making and nothing in civilian welfare.

The honest concession:
The explanation doesn't feed hungry children. Whatever the cause—Israeli restrictions, internal looting, Hamas diversion, distribution collapse—people suffered. A child who is malnourished does not care about the legal arguments over who bears responsibility. The moral imperative to prevent starvation exists regardless of who caused the crisis. Explaining why the situation exists is not the same as accepting it.

The honest answer:
Israel did not create this crisis, but Israel has power to affect it. The distribution problem is real, and Israel should reevaluate its capacity to increase aid flow and pressure for better distribution mechanisms. We should not accept accusations of deliberate starvation—they are false—but we should also not be entirely satisfied with explanations when children are hungry.

13

Lie #8

"Israel Intentionally Targets Civilians"

When images of destruction in Gaza appear on television screens and social media feeds, the accusation seems obvious: *Israel must be deliberately killing civilians.* The rubble of apartment buildings, the casualties in hospitals, the grieving families—surely, critics argue, this destruction must be deliberate. No civilized military could produce such devastation by accident.

But this accusation confuses outcomes with intent. Civilian deaths occur in every war; the question—legally, morally, and strategically—is whether those deaths result from deliberate targeting or from the tragic but unavoidable realities of urban combat against an enemy that hides among civilians.

The evidence overwhelmingly shows that Israel does not target civilians. On the contrary, Israel goes to extraordinary lengths to avoid civilian casualties—lengths that no other military in history has matched, and lengths that often cost Israeli soldiers their lives. The real story is not Israeli aggression but Hamas strategy: the systematic, deliberate, openly acknowledged use of Palestinian civilians as human shields.

What Targeting Civilians Would Actually Look Like

If Israel wanted to kill Palestinian civilians, it could do so easily. The Israeli Air Force (IAF) is one of the most capable in the world, equipped with precision-guided munitions, advanced reconnaissance systems, and real-time intelligence capabilities. Israel possesses satellite surveillance, drone technology, and the ability to strike any target in Gaza within minutes of identification.

Gaza is one of the most densely populated areas on earth, with over two million people living in a strip of land approximately twenty-five miles long and six miles wide. If civilian deaths were the goal, the numbers would be staggering. A military with Israel's capabilities, genuinely attempting to maximize civilian casualties, could do so on a catastrophic scale—tens of thousands in a single day. Hundreds of thousands in a week. The technology, access, and capability all exist.

If Israel targeted civilians, no measures to warn civilians would exist. They would be counterproductive—they would reduce civilian casualties rather than increase them. A military that wanted to kill civilians would not call ahead, would not drop warning leaflets, would not provide escape routes, would not pause operations for humanitarian reasons. *Would not even care.*

These are not the actions of a military targeting civilians. These are the actions of a military trying desperately to avoid civilian casualties while fighting an enemy that deliberately, systematically maximizes them.

The Warning Systems

No military in history has developed such elaborate systems for warning enemy civilian populations before strikes. Israel has created an

"Israel Intentionally Targets Civilians"

entire infrastructure of civilian protection that has no parallel in the annals of warfare.[1]

- **Phone calls:** The IDF makes direct phone calls to buildings about to be struck, warning occupants to evacuate. During Operation Protective Edge in 2014, the IDF made over one hundred thousand such calls.[2] Consider the implications: a military telephoning its enemy's population to warn them of impending strikes. No army that wants to kill civilians calls ahead. No army that seeks maximum casualties provides advance notice.
- **Text messages:** The IDF sends mass text messages to cell phones in areas about to experience military operations, warning civilians to leave. These messages often specify safe routes, safe zones, and timeframes for evacuation. Thousands of messages go out before major operations begin.
- **Leaflets:** The IAF drops millions of leaflets warning civilians of operations and advising them where to go for safety. During the 2014 conflict alone, over five million leaflets were dropped over Gaza.[3] These leaflets include maps showing safe areas, instructions for evacuation, and warnings about which neighborhoods will see military activity.
- **Roof knocks:** Before striking a building, the IDF often drops a small, non-explosive or low-explosive munition on the roof—a "knock" that warns occupants the building will be struck in fifteen to twenty minutes. This practice gives civilians time to evacuate while completely sacrificing the element of surprise. Military targets can move. Weapons can be relocated. Fighters can escape. Israel accepts these costs because warning civilians matters more than tactical advantage.
- **Aborted missions:** Israeli pilots and drone operators have standing orders to abort strikes if civilians appear unexpectedly in the

target area. The IDF has documented thousands of aborted missions—strikes that were called off at the last moment because the risk to civilians was deemed too high, even when valid military targets were confirmed and weapons were ready to fire.[4] Terrorists survive. Rocket launchers remain operational. Weapons caches stay intact. Israel accepts these outcomes to protect civilian lives.

Each of these measures imposes real tactical costs. Warning calls give Hamas fighters time to escape. Roof knocks allow weapons to be moved. Leaflets reveal operational plans to the enemy. Aborted missions mean terrorists survive to fight and kill another day. Israeli soldiers face greater risks because the element of surprise is sacrificed.

Israel accepts these costs because protecting civilians—even enemy civilians—is a core value embedded in military doctrine, legal review processes, and the moral framework of the nation. You do not accept tactical disadvantage in pursuit of mass killing.

The Enemy's Strategy

Why, then, do civilian casualties occur? Because Hamas has built its entire military strategy around the production of Palestinian civilian deaths. Hamas maximizes civilian casualties because those deaths serve its strategic interests.

This is documented by the United Nations, international journalists, captured Hamas operatives, recovered documents, and Hamas's own statements.

Rockets are launched from schoolyards. Tunnel entrances are located inside private homes. Command centers operate beneath hospitals. Weapons are stored in mosques and in UN schools and facilities. Fighters wear civilian clothing and operate from residential buildings, from hotels housing foreign journalists, from apartment complexes and shopping areas.[5]

The UNRWA, hardly a pro-Israel organization, confirmed that rockets were found stored in at least three of its schools during the 2014 conflict.[6] International journalists reported seeing rockets launched from civilian neighborhoods. Foreign correspondents described being approached by Hamas fighters operating in plainclothes among civilians.

When Israel strikes a rocket launcher in a school, critics call it targeting civilians. When Israel destroys a tunnel entrance in a home, it becomes an attack on housing. When Israel hits a command center beneath a hospital, headlines scream about hospitals being bombed. The military infrastructure disappears from the narrative; only the civilian setting remains.

Hamas understands that every civilian death—especially deaths they have engineered through their own positioning—becomes a propaganda victory. Dead Palestinian civilians generate international outrage, diplomatic pressure on Israel, calls for ceasefires that allow Hamas to rearm, and sanctions against the Jewish state. Hamas wins when civilians die.

This is why Hamas orders civilians to stay in buildings Israel has warned will be struck—sometimes physically preventing them from leaving. This is why Hamas operates from schools and hospitals. This is why Hamas leaders have openly celebrated the "martyrdom" of Palestinian civilians, calling death "an industry" at which Palestinians "excel."[7]

The accusation that Israel targets civilians inverts reality completely. Israel does everything possible to minimize civilian casualties. Hamas does everything possible to maximize them. The dead are Hamas's strategic asset—and Hamas invests heavily in producing them.

The Legal Standard

International humanitarian law—the laws of armed conflict—does not prohibit all civilian casualties. It prohibits deliberately targeting civilians and requires that military forces distinguish between combatants and civilians to the extent feasible under the circumstances.

The law also recognizes that when combatants operate from civilian areas, some civilian casualties become inevitable. In such cases, the law places responsibility on the party using civilians as shields—not on the party responding to attacks launched from civilian areas.[8]

Multiple military and legal experts have examined Israeli operations and concluded that Israel not only meets but exceeds the requirements of international law.

Colonel Richard Kemp, former commander of British forces in Afghanistan, testified before the United Nations that "no army in the history of warfare has ever taken such extensive measures to protect civilian lives as the IDF."[9] He examined Israeli practices with professional expertise and concluded that Israel sets the standard that other militaries should follow.

General Martin Dempsey, former Chairman of the US Joint Chiefs of Staff, sent a military delegation to study Israeli practices during the 2014 Gaza conflict. He reported that Israel "went to extraordinary lengths" to limit civilian casualties—and that the Pentagon wanted to learn from Israeli methods to apply them in American operations.[10]

These are not Israeli sources. These are Western military commanders with extensive combat experience examining Israeli operations and concluding that Israel's conduct sets the global standard for civilian protection in urban warfare.

The Ratio Question

Critics sometimes point to the ratio of casualties—more Palestinians die than Israelis—as evidence that Israel is doing something wrong. This argument fundamentally misunderstands how military conflicts work and applies a standard that has never been applied to any other conflict in history.

Casualty ratios reflect capability, not morality. Israel has sophisticated air defenses, bomb shelters in every building, early warning sirens throughout the country, and a highly trained military. Gaza has none of these protections—largely because Hamas diverts resources to attack infrastructure rather than civilian protection.[11]

If a homeowner with a security system and a firearm stops a burglar, we do not criticize the homeowner because the burglar was wounded while the homeowner escaped injury. The question is not who suffered more harm—it is who initiated the violence and who acted defensively.

Hamas fires thousands of rockets at Israeli civilians—rockets intended to kill as many people as possible. Israel defends against those rockets. Israel then strikes the launchers, the commanders, the tunnels, the weapons caches. When those strikes cause casualties, they are casualties of Hamas's war—a war started by Hamas, escalated by Hamas, and prolonged by Hamas.

Should Israel be required to lower its defenses to equalize the body count? Should Israel remove its missile defense system so that more Israelis die? Should Israel abandon bomb shelters so that Israeli casualties rise? That is the logical implication of the ratio argument—and it is morally grotesque.

Who Targets Whom

The accusation inverts the moral reality of the conflict completely.

Hamas deliberately targets civilians. Every rocket fired at Israeli cities is aimed at population centers. The October 7 massacre was a systematic campaign of murder, torture, and sexual violence against unarmed men, women, children, and infants. There is no ambiguity about intent. Hamas celebrates civilian deaths—Israeli and Palestinian alike.

Israel does the opposite. Israel targets military infrastructure while taking unprecedented measures to warn civilians away from strike zones. Israeli pilots abort missions when civilians appear unexpectedly. Israeli commanders sacrifice tactical advantage to minimize collateral harm. These are not the actions of a military that targets civilians—they are the actions of a military that values civilian life even at cost to itself.

When critics accuse Israel of targeting civilians, they arm the actual aggressors. They provide moral cover for those who genuinely do target civilians—who name streets after suicide bombers, who pay salaries to terrorists' families, who teach children that martyrdom is the highest calling. The truth cannot be hidden forever. Israel defends. Hamas attacks. The evidence is overwhelming, documented, and undeniable.

When critics invoke international law against Israel, they select the interpretation that condemns while ignoring interpretations that support Israel's position. They apply standards to Israel that have never been applied to any other nation. The accusation is political—dressed in legal language to give it authority it does not deserve.

Engaging the Harder Questions

We have documented Israel's elaborate warning systems—the phone calls, text messages, leaflets, and "roof knocks" that no other military in history has employed. We have explained Hamas's human shield strategy. We have cited Western military experts who praise Israeli practices.

But sophisticated critics will point to specific incidents—strikes on schools, hospitals, refugee camps—and ask: How do you explain those? The general argument about warnings and precautions doesn't answer questions about specific events that produced mass casualties.

"Specific Incidents Suggest Deliberate Targeting or Criminal Negligence"

The critique:

Even if Israel's general policy is to avoid civilians, specific incidents suggest either deliberate targeting or such reckless disregard that the distinction doesn't matter. Strikes on Jabalia refugee camp, on Al-Shifa hospital, on schools sheltering displaced families—these can't all be explained by Hamas presence.

The honest response:

Every significant incident deserves individual examination. The general defense—"Hamas uses human shields"—is true but insufficient when specific strikes produce mass casualties. We should engage the specifics.

Al-Shifa Hospital:

Israel provided extensive evidence—captured documents, tunnel entrances discovered on-site, Hamas fighters found inside, weapons caches recovered—that Hamas operated a major command center beneath Al-Shifa. This was not merely alleged but demonstrated to foreign journalists and verified by multiple independent sources. The hospital was a legitimate military target because Hamas made it one. The tragedy is that patients and medical staff were endangered—but they were endangered by Hamas's decision to operate there, not by Israel's decision to neutralize the military threat.

Jabalia:
The strikes targeted Hamas command infrastructure embedded in the camp. Civilian casualties were high because population density was extreme and because the targets were deliberately placed in civilian areas. Israel argues the military necessity was proportionate—senior Hamas commanders were killed, command and control was disrupted. Critics dispute the proportionality calculation. This is a legitimate debate—but it's a debate about proportionality, not about intent to kill civilians.

Schools sheltering displaced people:
In documented cases, Israel has shown evidence of Hamas military use—weapons storage, tunnel entrances, launch sites. In other cases, intelligence may have been wrong or incomplete. Military operations involve errors. The question is whether errors reflect systematic targeting or the tragic friction of war.

The honest concession:

Military explanations don't bring back the dead. Families who lost children don't care whether the strike was legally proportionate or based on faulty intelligence. Every civilian death is a tragedy, and we should not lose the capacity to grieve with those who suffer.

Some strikes may have been mistakes—intelligence failures, misidentification, disproportionate responses. Israel's system is better than most, but it is not perfect. Errors occur. When they occur, they should be investigated and, where warranted, prosecuted. Israel does investigate and prosecute—imperfectly, but genuinely.

"Israel Intentionally Targets Civilians"

The honest answer:

Specific incidents deserve specific examination, not blanket defenses. The general argument—that Israel takes unprecedented precautions—remains true even when individual operations go wrong. The question is whether civilian deaths result from policy or from the inevitable friction of urban warfare. The evidence shows policy aimed at minimizing harm, not maximizing it.

14

Lie #9

"Israel Uses Disproportionate Force"

The previous chapter addressed a question of intent: Does Israel deliberately target civilians? The evidence showed it does not—Israel's elaborate warning systems, aborted missions, and tactical sacrifices prove that minimizing civilian harm is a genuine priority, not a pretense.

Although we touched on this question briefly in the previous chapter, this one addresses the question more fully: *scale*. Even accepting that Israel does not target civilians, critics argue that its military response is simply too large—that Israel kills too many people, destroys too much, responds with force far beyond what the situation requires. When casualty figures show more Palestinians dead than Israelis, the imbalance is treated as self-evident proof of wrongdoing.

But this understanding of "proportionality" has nothing to do with how the term is actually defined in international law. The accusation relies on a misunderstanding so fundamental that it distorts every conversation about Israeli military operations. Before examining Israel's conduct, we must first understand what proportionality actually means—and what it does not mean.

What Proportionality Does Not Mean

Proportionality in international humanitarian law does not mean what most people assume it means. It specifically does not mean:

- **Equal casualties on both sides.** A military is not required to limit its effectiveness to match the enemy's body count. If an attacker kills ten people and the defender's response kills fifty attackers, that is not inherently disproportionate.
- **Equivalent damage.** A country that can effectively defend itself is not obligated to sustain equal destruction to its attacker. If one side has bomb shelters and air defenses while the other does not, the resulting casualty disparity does not indicate wrongdoing by the defended party.
- **Tit-for-tat responses.** If an enemy fires one rocket, international law does not require you to fire only one rocket back. If an enemy kills one civilian, you are not limited to killing one of theirs. Military operations are not governed by the logic of schoolyard fairness.
- **Matching weapons or capabilities.** A country with precision munitions is not required to use primitive weapons because its enemy lacks advanced technology. A military with superior training is not required to fight poorly to even the odds.

If proportionality meant equal suffering, then every effective military response would be illegal by definition. A well-defended nation could never respond adequately to aggression from a weaker attacker. The doctrine would reward military incompetence and punish effective self-defense. It would incentivize nations to weaken their defenses so they could legally respond to attacks. No nation would agree to that.

What Proportionality Actually Means

Under international humanitarian law, proportionality refers to a specific calculation: whether the expected civilian harm from a particular attack is excessive in relation to the concrete and direct military advantage anticipated from that attack.[1]

In plain terms: Is the collateral damage from this specific strike worth the military objective being pursued? Is the target important enough to justify the risk to nearby civilians?

This calculation happens before every strike—not after, by comparing casualty totals at the end of a conflict. A commander must assess: What is the military value of this target? How many civilians might be affected? What precautions can we take to minimize civilian harm? Is the expected civilian cost excessive relative to what we gain militarily?

If a single low-level terrorist is hiding in a large residential building with hundreds of occupants, destroying the entire building would almost certainly be disproportionate—the military value is low, and the civilian cost would be high. But if that same building houses a major weapons depot supplying rockets that are killing civilians, or a command center directing military operations, or a tunnel junction enabling attacks on Israeli territory, the calculation changes dramatically.

Proportionality is about the relationship between military necessity and civilian harm in each individual operation. The total casualties at the end of a war tell you nothing about whether individual strikes were proportionate.

How Proportionality Is Actually Assessed

As detailed in the previous chapter, Israel's targeting process includes rigorous legal review at multiple command levels, with military lawyers

HAMAN'S LIES

embedded throughout the chain of command. What matters for proportionality is how this process handles the specific calculation the law requires.[2]

Before every significant strike, commanders must weigh the expected military advantage against the expected civilian harm. This is not a post-war calculation comparing total casualties. It happens in real time, for each individual target:

A low-level terrorist in a crowded apartment building? Likely disproportionate—the military value does not justify the civilian risk.

A weapons depot supplying rockets that are killing civilians? The calculation shifts dramatically.

A tunnel network enabling infiltration attacks? The military necessity is high, even if surface structures are affected.

This assessment means many valid military targets go unstruck. Terrorists escape. Weapons caches remain intact. Israel accepts these outcomes because proportionality is treated as a genuine constraint, not a box to check. The previous chapter documented the operational sacrifices Israel makes; this chapter examines whether the strikes Israel does conduct meet the legal standard.

The Tunnel Problem

The previous chapter documented Hamas's deliberate strategy of embedding military infrastructure among civilians—the human shields approach that maximizes Palestinian casualties for propaganda value. This strategy directly affects proportionality calculations, because international law assigns responsibility for civilian harm to the party that deliberately created the dangerous proximity.

Consider the tunnel network. Hamas has built an extensive underground military infrastructure that extends for hundreds of miles. These tunnels are used to store weapons, move fighters undetected, launch surprise attacks, and hold hostages. Some tunnels cross under the border into Israeli territory and have been used to infiltrate Israel for kidnappings and massacres.

The cost of this tunnel network is staggering. Estimates suggest Hamas has spent hundreds of millions of dollars on tunnel construction—money that could have built hospitals, schools, housing, and infrastructure for Gaza's civilian population. Instead, it went underground for military purposes.[3]

These tunnels are deliberately constructed beneath civilian areas—under homes, schools, hospitals, mosques, and UN facilities. Destroying this military infrastructure necessarily affects the surface structures above it. When Israel strikes a tunnel, the buildings above may collapse or sustain damage.

Critics point to the destruction of buildings and call it disproportionate. But what is the alternative? Allow the tunnel network to remain operational and continue enabling attacks? Permit Hamas to use these tunnels to infiltrate Israel and murder civilians? Accept that an entire military infrastructure is immune from attack because it was deliberately built beneath civilian areas?

Under international law, a military facility does not become protected simply because it is placed near civilians or beneath civilian structures. The presence of civilians does not grant immunity to legitimate military targets. The legal and moral responsibility for civilian harm in such cases falls on the party that deliberately placed military assets among civilians—not on the party responding to the threat those assets pose.[4]

The Rocket Equation

The proportionality accusation often rests on a simple comparison: More Palestinians die than Israelis, therefore Israel's response must be excessive. But this comparison ignores a crucial asymmetry—not in military power, but in protection.

Hamas and Islamic Jihad have fired over twenty thousand rockets at Israeli civilian areas since Israel withdrew completely from Gaza in 2005.[5] Each of these rockets was aimed at Israeli cities, towns, villages, and kibbutzim. Each was intended to kill, maim, and terrorize civilians. Each was a war crime.

Most of these rockets do not kill Israelis. Why? Not because Hamas shows restraint or has poor aim—Hamas fires indiscriminately at population centers. Israeli casualties are low because Israel invested billions in the Iron Dome air defense system, in bomb shelters built into every building, in early warning sirens throughout the country, and in reinforced safe rooms.

Should Israel's success at defense be held against it? Should Israel be required to absorb casualties to make the numbers "proportionate"? Should effective protection be treated as evidence of wrongdoing by the protected party?

The logic is perverse. Hamas targets civilians deliberately and indiscriminately—it would kill thousands or tens of thousands if it could. Israel defends its civilians successfully. And somehow Israel is blamed because its defense works while Hamas's attacks fail.

Meanwhile, Hamas invests almost nothing in civilian protection. There are no bomb shelters for Gaza's civilian population. There is no air defense system. There are no warning sirens. The resources that could have provided these things were spent on tunnels and rockets instead. Hamas chose offense over defense—and Palestinian civilians pay the price for that choice.[6]

"Israel Uses Disproportionate Force"

Comparisons to Other Conflicts

When the United States and its allies fought ISIS in Mosul, Iraq, the battle killed an estimated nine thousand to eleven thousand civilians over nine months.[7] Entire neighborhoods were leveled. Ancient heritage sites were destroyed. The coalition used overwhelming force against an enemy embedded in urban areas—precisely the same challenge Israel faces in Gaza.

When Saudi Arabia and its coalition fought in Yemen, tens of thousands of civilians died, and the humanitarian crisis was described as the worst in the world. When Russia attacked Chechnya, entire cities were reduced to rubble, with civilian casualties in the tens of thousands.

None of these conflicts generated the same accusations of "disproportionate force" that every Israeli operation produces. None generated the same protest movements, the same calls for sanctions, the same United Nations resolutions, the same media scrutiny, the same academic condemnation.

Israel, fighting in conditions at least as difficult as any of these conflicts—against an enemy that deliberately maximizes civilian exposure, in one of the most densely populated areas on earth—is subjected to scrutiny that no other military faces. The standard applied to Israel exists for Israel alone. That double standard is itself evidence that something other than genuine concern for proportionality is at work.[8]

What the Experts Say

Military professionals who have studied Israeli operations consistently conclude that Israel meets or exceeds international standards for proportionality and civilian protection.

A detailed study by the High Level Military Group—comprising former military chiefs and senior officers from the United States, Germany, the United Kingdom, France, Spain, Australia, Italy, and Colombia—concluded that "Israel not only met a reasonable international standard of observance of the laws of armed conflict, but in many cases significantly exceeded that standard."[9]

What Proportionality Actually Looks Like

The proportionality accusation misunderstands what proportionality means under international law—and applies a standard that has never been applied to any other nation.

Proportionality does not mean equal casualties. It does not mean matching the enemy's damage tit for tat.

Israel invests billions in protecting its citizens—Iron Dome, David's Sling, bomb shelters, warning sirens, reinforced safe rooms. Hamas invests in attack infrastructure. The resulting casualty disparity reflects those choices, not Israeli wrongdoing. Should Israel remove its defenses to even the body count? Should effective protection be treated as a crime?

The same operations that draw condemnation when Israel performs them pass without comment when conducted by American, British, or French forces. Israel responds to aggression with the force necessary to achieve legitimate military objectives while taking extraordinary precautions to minimize civilian harm. That is not disproportionate. That is what lawful self-defense looks like when facing an enemy that maximizes civilian exposure.

15

Lie #10

"Israel Enforces a Punitive Blockade on Gaza"

Gaza is often described by Israel's detractors as "the world's largest open-air prison." The imagery is powerful and emotionally compelling: millions of Palestinians trapped behind Israeli walls, suffering collective punishment for the sins of Hamas, denied basic necessities by a cruel occupier who delights in their misery.

This narrative omits almost everything relevant to understanding the situation. It ignores why the restrictions exist in the first place. It ignores who else enforces them. It ignores the goods that actually flow into Gaza through Israeli crossings. It ignores what happens when restrictions are loosened. It transforms a complex security situation born from terrorism into a simple morality tale—and gets the morality exactly backward.

HAMAN'S LIES

What Happened Before the Blockade

The history of Gaza since 2005 is essential context that critics consistently omit.

In August 2005, Israel withdrew completely from Gaza. This was not a partial withdrawal or a tactical adjustment—it was total disengagement. Every Israeli soldier left Gaza. Every Israeli civilian left Gaza. Israel dismantled all settlements and evacuated approximately nine thousand Israelis from homes where some families had lived for decades.[1]

The withdrawal was traumatic for many Israelis. Soldiers had to forcibly remove settlers who refused to leave. Synagogues were dismantled. Cemeteries were exhumed and remains relocated. Families lost homes, businesses, and communities they had built over thirty years. Israel did this in the hope that Gaza would develop into a peaceful, prosperous neighbor—a model for future Palestinian statehood that would demonstrate what peace could bring.

Israel even left behind functioning infrastructure. Greenhouses that had produced flowers and vegetables for export—a potential foundation for Gaza's economy—were handed over intact. The hope was that Palestinians would use these assets to build prosperity.

What happened instead?

Within days of Israel's withdrawal, Palestinian mobs looted and destroyed the greenhouses. Equipment was stolen or smashed. Irrigation systems were torn apart. What could have been the foundation of a thriving agricultural export industry was reduced to rubble within hours.[2]

Within months, rocket attacks on Israeli towns increased dramatically. Groups like Hamas and Islamic Jihad used the newly opened territory—no longer constrained by Israeli presence—to expand their arsenals and launch capabilities. In 2006, Hamas won Palestinian legislative elections. In 2007, Hamas seized complete control of Gaza in a

"Israel Enforces a Punitive Blockade on Gaza"

violent coup against the Palestinian Authority, throwing Fatah political opponents off rooftops, executing rivals in the streets, and establishing a terrorist dictatorship.[3]

From 2005 to 2007—before any blockade existed—thousands of rockets were fired at Israeli civilians from Gaza. Hamas and Islamic Jihad used the open borders to import weapons, explosives, and military equipment. Iran began shipping advanced weaponry. Gaza became a launching pad for terrorism.

The blockade was a response to terrorism—not its cause. The sequence matters enormously: Israel withdrew completely, terrorism increased, Hamas seized power, and only then did restrictions begin.

Egypt's Role

The accusation focuses exclusively on Israel, as if Israel alone controls Gaza's borders. This is false. Gaza has two borders—not one. Egypt shares a border with Gaza at Rafah, and Egypt maintains restrictions at least as strict as Israel's—often stricter.[4]

Egypt has kept the Rafah crossing closed for extended periods, sometimes for months at a time. Egypt has flooded smuggling tunnels along its border with Gaza, destroying them and occasionally killing people inside. Egypt has maintained a buffer zone along its border, demolishing Palestinian homes in the process. Egypt has expressed the same concerns Israel has: that Hamas is dangerous, that weapons flow through open borders, that an unrestricted Gaza threatens regional stability.

Egypt—an Arab, Muslim nation—sees Hamas as a threat connected to the Muslim Brotherhood, which Egypt considers a terrorist organization. Egypt does not want Hamas-style Islamism spreading across its border. Egypt does not want Iranian weapons flowing through its territory. Egypt shares Israel's assessment that Hamas poses a genuine danger.

Yet somehow Egypt's restrictions generate almost no international outrage. There are no flotillas challenging Egypt's policies. There are no UN resolutions condemning Egypt's border enforcement. There are no campus protests demanding Egypt open the Rafah crossing. There are no boycott movements targeting Egyptian goods.

The reaction reveals that the accusation is not really about the blockade itself—but about Israel. When Egypt does the same thing, silence. When Israel does it, international condemnation.

What Actually Enters Gaza

Contrary to the "open-air prison" narrative, substantial quantities of goods enter Gaza daily through Israeli crossings. The border is not sealed—it is regulated.

Are there restrictions? Yes. Certain materials are prohibited or limited because they have military applications. This is where the tension between humanitarian needs and security concerns becomes acute.

Cement can build homes and schools—but it can also fortify tunnels and military bunkers. Steel pipes can carry water—but they can also be converted into rocket bodies. Fertilizer can help crops grow—but it can also manufacture explosives. Dual-use materials pose genuine dilemmas, and Israel attempts to balance humanitarian needs against security risks.

When construction materials enter Gaza, some percentage inevitably ends up in Hamas military infrastructure. When fuel enters Gaza, some powers Hamas operations. Every shipment involves risk—because Hamas has proven it will divert civilian goods to military use. Israel tries to maximize humanitarian benefit while minimizing military advantage to terrorist organizations—an imperfect process that critics condemn regardless of outcomes.

"Israel Enforces a Punitive Blockade on Gaza"

The Weapons Problem

Despite the blockade—despite Israel's efforts to prevent weapons from reaching Gaza—Hamas has acquired an enormous arsenal. Where did it come from?

Smuggling tunnels along the Egyptian border brought in rockets, anti-tank missiles, explosives, and small arms for years before Egypt cracked down. Iran has shipped weapons to Gaza through various routes—by sea until Israeli naval interdiction improved, then through Sinai, Sudan, and other channels. Components for rocket construction have been smuggled in disguised as civilian goods. Hamas has manufactured rockets locally using materials diverted from humanitarian shipments—including water pipes repurposed as rocket bodies.[5]

The arsenal speaks for itself. Hamas has fired over twenty thousand rockets at Israel since the 2005 withdrawal. Some of these rockets can reach Tel Aviv and Jerusalem—over fifty miles from Gaza. Hamas has developed sophisticated tunnel networks extending under the border into Israeli territory. Hamas has acquired drone capabilities, naval attack units, and anti-tank missiles that can destroy armored vehicles.[6]

And this occurred even with restrictions in place. The implications of removing restrictions are obvious. An open border would become an expressway for Iranian weapons. Advanced air defense systems could enter, threatening Israeli aviation. Long-range precision missiles could arrive in quantity. Chemical weapons precursors could flow freely. Gaza would transform from a terrorist stronghold into a fully equipped military threat capable of far greater devastation.

The blockade does not eliminate the threat. It limits the threat. Every restriction that critics condemn is a restriction that slows Hamas's military buildup and saves lives—Israeli lives and ultimately

Palestinian lives as well, since every Hamas attack provokes responses that cause casualties.

The "Collective Punishment" Accusation

Critics call the blockade "collective punishment"—penalizing all of Gaza's civilians for Hamas's actions. This accusation misunderstands both the law and the situation.

Under international law, collective punishment refers to penalties imposed on a civilian population for acts they did not personally commit—reprisals against civilians for the actions of combatants. Restricting weapons imports to prevent terrorism is not collective punishment—it is security policy. Every nation on earth restricts dangerous imports. Every nation controls its borders. No country allows unlimited importation of materials that will be used to attack its citizens.[7]

Moreover, the blockade is not a hermetically sealed system. Goods enter daily. Humanitarian programs operate continuously. Medical cases are transferred to Israeli hospitals for treatment unavailable in Gaza. Workers have entered Israel for employment. The border responds to conditions: When violence decreases, restrictions ease; when attacks increase, restrictions tighten. This is security policy calibrated to threat levels—not collective punishment.

The accusation also ignores who is truly responsible for Gazan suffering. Hamas diverts massive resources from civilian needs to military infrastructure. International estimates suggest Hamas spent hundreds of millions of dollars on tunnels alone—resources that could have built hospitals, schools, housing, water treatment facilities, and power infrastructure for Gaza's civilian population.[8] Hamas stores weapons in civilian areas, inviting Israeli strikes. Hamas provokes conflicts that devastate Gaza's infrastructure. Hamas rejects ceasefires that could bring relief.

If Gaza is suffering, the primary responsibility lies with the organization that has ruled it since 2007, that has started multiple wars, that has diverted billions in aid to military purposes, that has rejected every opportunity for peace—not with the country trying to prevent that organization from acquiring more weapons.

The Legal Status

The Palmer Commission, a United Nations panel, examined the legality of Israel's naval blockade and concluded in 2011 that the blockade was legal under international law. The commission found that Israel faced a real security threat from Hamas and had the right to take measures to prevent weapons from reaching Gaza by sea.[9]

This finding came from a UN body, which is hardly a source predisposed to favor Israel given the UN's consistent voting patterns on Israel-related issues. The commission acknowledged that while the humanitarian situation in Gaza was of concern, the blockade itself was a legitimate response to genuine security threats.

The commission did criticize specific Israeli actions, particularly the handling of the 2010 Mavi Marmara incident in which Israeli commandos boarded a ship attempting to break the blockade and nine activists died in the resulting confrontation. But on the fundamental question—does Israel have the right to prevent weapons from reaching Gaza?—the answer was yes.

Security, Not Oppression

The blockade narrative omits the essential context that explains it: Israel withdrew completely from Gaza in 2005. There was no blockade. Borders were open. And within two years, Hamas had seized power, launched thousands of rockets at Israeli civilians, and transformed Gaza into a terrorist base.

The blockade began after the attacks, not before. It was a response to terrorism, not its cause. Egypt maintains similar restrictions on its border with Gaza for similar reasons. Yet somehow only Israel is condemned.

Despite the security measures, hundreds of trucks enter Gaza daily through Israeli crossings. The border is regulated, not sealed. The restrictions target materials with military applications, which include cement that builds tunnels and pipes that become rockets. Meanwhile, Israel allows humanitarian goods to flow.

Even with the blockade, Hamas acquired over twenty thousand rockets, extensive tunnel networks, and sophisticated military capabilities. Imagine what would have happened without restrictions. The blockade does not cause Gazan suffering—Hamas causes it, by choosing war over development, tunnels over hospitals, rockets over schools. The accusation blames Israel for the consequences of Hamas's choices.

16

Lie #11

"Israel Systematically Violates Palestinian Human Rights"

Human rights have become one of the most powerful concepts in modern political discourse. To accuse a nation of systematically violating human rights is to place it in the category of oppressive regimes—dictatorships, authoritarian states, and governments that crush their own people. The accusation carries enormous weight in international forums, in media coverage, and in public opinion. It transforms a political dispute into a moral crusade, making the accused not merely wrong but evil.

Israel faces this accusation constantly. Human rights organizations issue report after report condemning Israeli practices. United Nations bodies pass resolution after resolution. Academic conferences and media outlets repeat the charge until it becomes accepted as obvious truth: "Israel systematically violates Palestinian human rights." The accusation has become so widespread that questioning it seems to mark a person as indifferent to suffering or complicit in oppression. To defend Israel is often treated as defending human rights violations.

But when you examine the accusation carefully—when you compare Israel's actual practices to those of other nations, when you consider the security context Israel faces, when you look at what Palestinian governing authorities actually do to their own people—the accusation collapses. Israel is not a state that systematically violates human rights as a matter of policy. Israel is a democracy operating under the rule of law while facing terrorism that would challenge any nation on earth.

The Institutional Bias

Before weighing the charge, we have to understand the institutional and security context in which it is made. As we noted, the UNHRC has passed more resolutions condemning Israel than all other countries in the world combined. That structural imbalance frames everything that follows. This is not a human rights framework. This is an institutionalized campaign against one nation.

No other country has a permanent agenda item. Not China, which has placed over a million Uyghurs in concentration camps, subjecting them to forced labor, forced sterilization, and cultural eradication. Not North Korea, which operates a system of prison camps where hundreds of thousands suffer in conditions comparable to the Nazi era, where three generations of families are imprisoned for one member's perceived disloyalty. Not Iran, which hangs dissidents from cranes in public squares and shoots protesters in the streets.[1]

This is not a genuine human rights framework. This is an institutionalized campaign against one nation. When the same body that ignores the world's worst atrocities focuses obsessively on Israel, something other than real concern for human rights is at work. The bias is not subtle—it is structural, deliberate, and overwhelming. It is bias built into the very architecture of international human rights institutions.

Many of the countries that vote to condemn Israel are themselves massive human rights violators. Saudi Arabia, which beheads people for sorcery and apostasy, which dismembered a journalist in its own consulate while he was still alive, votes to condemn Israel. Iran, which executes homosexuals by hanging and imprisons women for removing their headscarves, votes to condemn Israel. China, which has eliminated freedom in Hong Kong and operates a surveillance state unprecedented in human history, votes to condemn Israel. Venezuela, whose government has driven millions into exile, pumps tons of drugs into the US, and crushes all opposition with violence, votes to condemn Israel.[2]

Many of the loudest accusers are themselves serial violators, and the institutions are not neutral. The claims must be tested on evidence, not volume. This does not mean Israel is perfect—no nation is. But it means the accusations must be examined on their merits, not accepted because international bodies repeat them. *A lie repeated by the United Nations is still a lie.* An accusation made by dictatorships against a democracy does not become true through repetition.

The Security Context

Every discussion of Israeli security practices must begin with the security context. Israel faces threats that no Western democracy has ever faced on a sustained basis. This is not an excuse—it is an explanation that must be understood before any fair judgment can be made. No country can be fairly judged on its security measures without understanding what those measures are designed to prevent.

During the Second Intifada (2000–2005), Palestinian terrorists carried out over 140 suicide bombings inside Israel. Buses were blown up during morning commutes—mothers taking children to school, workers heading to offices, students going to class, all murdered in an instant. Restaurants were destroyed during Passover seders as families gathered to celebrate their freedom from ancient slavery. Discotheques were bombed during weekend nights as young people socialized after their weeks. Shopping malls, hotels, and public squares became killing grounds. Over a thousand Israelis were killed.[3]

The security measures Israel implemented—checkpoints, barriers, screening procedures—were responses to this campaign of mass murder. They were not created to humiliate Palestinians or violate their rights. They were created to stop the slaughter of Israeli civilians. They were created because the alternative was accepting the continuous murder of innocent people. Any government that failed to implement such measures would be derelict in its most fundamental duty: protecting its citizens.

And they worked. Suicide bombings dropped dramatically after the security barrier was constructed and checkpoint procedures were strengthened. The measures that critics call human rights violations saved hundreds, probably thousands, of lives—Israeli lives and Palestinian lives alike, since Palestinian civilians also died in the violence. The barrier and the checkpoints are not symbols of oppression—they are evidence of what Israel had to do to survive. They are monuments to the terrorism that made them necessary.[4]

When terrorism decreases, restrictions ease. When violence spikes, restrictions tighten. This is not collective punishment—it is security calibration. Every nation on earth adjusts security measures based on threat levels. Airport security tightens after attempted attacks. Police presence increases after terrorist incidents. Only Israel is condemned for doing what every nation does. Only Israel is expected to absorb unlimited attacks without responding, to accept mass murder as preferable to inconveniencing those who might commit it.

What Palestinian Authorities Actually Do

If we are genuinely concerned about Palestinian human rights, we must examine what Palestinian governing authorities do to their own people. The picture is grim—and it receives a fraction of the attention directed at Israel.

In Gaza, Hamas rules as a terrorist dictatorship. There have been no elections since Hamas seized power in 2007. Political opponents are arrested, tortured, and killed. Journalists who criticize Hamas disappear or are shot in the legs as warnings. Gay and lesbian Palestinians face persecution and violence—some have fled to Israel for safety, seeking refuge in the country they are told is their oppressor. Women face severe restrictions on their freedom. Religious minorities have no protection. Civil society does not exist. No independent organizations can operate. No dissent is tolerated.[5]

Hamas has executed Palestinians accused of "collaborating" with Israel, sometimes dragging bodies through the streets as crowds cheer, sometimes throwing accused collaborators from rooftops. These abuses are widely documented—including by major human rights organizations.[6]

In the West Bank, the Palestinian Authority maintains a system of arbitrary detention, torture, and political repression. Palestinians who sell land to Jews can face the death penalty under Palestinian Authority law—think about what that reveals about the nature of the regime, about its values, about what kind of state it would create. The Palestinian Authority pays salaries to terrorists and the families of terrorists—the so-called pay for slay program—incentivizing violence against Israeli civilians. The more Israelis you kill, the more money you receive. The Palestinian Authority arrests journalists and activists who criticize its leadership. There is no independent judiciary, no free press, no political freedom.[7]

Human Rights Watch, Amnesty International, and other organizations that constantly condemn Israel have also documented these abuses by Palestinian authorities. Yet these abuses receive a fraction of the attention directed at Israel. The disparity reveals the true priorities of the accusers. Palestinian suffering at the hands of Palestinian leaders is apparently less important than Palestinian inconvenience at the hands of Israeli security measures. Palestinian torture by Palestinian authorities matters less than Palestinian delays at Israeli checkpoints.

Israel's Legal System

Israel operates under the rule of law. This fundamental fact is consistently ignored in accusations of systematic human rights violations. A state that methodically violates human rights does not create institutions that allow those it is accused of oppressing to challenge the government and win.

Israel has an independent Supreme Court that regularly rules against the government—including on security matters. The Court has ordered the rerouting of the security barrier to reduce impact on Palestinian villages. It has struck down detention practices. It has required changes to military procedures. It has provided remedies to Palestinian petitioners who bring cases before it. No other nation in a comparable security situation grants such access to its highest court. No other country allows those it is accused of oppressing to sue the government and win.[8]

Palestinians can and do petition the Israeli Supreme Court. They have legal representation. They receive hearings. They sometimes win. Lawyers who represent Palestinians are not arrested or disappeared—they practice law freely, often with great success. This is not the behavior of a state that systematically violates human rights—it is the behavior

"Israel Systematically Violates Palestinian Human Rights"

of a state committed to legal process even under conditions of ongoing conflict and constant threat.

Israel has a free press that aggressively investigates and criticizes government and military actions. Israeli journalists have exposed abuses and demanded accountability. Israeli human rights organizations operate freely, often receiving government funding, and publish constant criticism of Israeli policies. Israel's civil society is loud, adversarial, and free—scrutinizing the government in ways that are impossible under Hamas or the Palestinian Authority. This level of internal scrutiny exists in no neighboring country—and in few countries anywhere on earth.[9]

When Israeli soldiers commit abuses, they are investigated and prosecuted. Soldiers have gone to prison for mistreatment of Palestinians. Officers have been disciplined and dismissed. Careers have been ended. The system is imperfect—as all systems are—but it exists and functions. Compare this to Palestinian armed groups, where killing Israeli civilians is celebrated rather than punished, where murderers become heroes rather than criminals, where streets are named after those who blow up buses full of children.

The Checkpoints

As we have discussed, critics point to checkpoints as evidence of human rights violations. Palestinians must wait at checkpoints. They experience delays and inconvenience. This is undeniably difficult and frustrating. No one denies that checkpoints impose burdens on daily life. No one celebrates the necessity of checkpoints.

But why do checkpoints exist? They exist because terrorists used the roads to reach Israeli cities and blow themselves up in crowds of civilians. They exist because weapons were transported in vehicles and hidden in cargo. They exist because ambulances were used to smuggle explosives. They exist because freedom of movement was exploited for mass murder. They exist because without them, Israeli civilians would die in large numbers.

The checkpoints have caught terrorists. They have intercepted explosives. They have prevented attacks. Every inconvenience at a checkpoint represents, in some measure, an attack that did not happen, a bomb that did not explode, lives that were not lost, families that were not destroyed. The checkpoints are not a policy preference—they are a security necessity born of bitter experience, of funerals and hospital wards and broken families.

Israel has worked to reduce checkpoint friction. Humanitarian cases receive expedited passage. Medical emergencies are prioritized. Technology has been deployed to speed processing. When security conditions permit, checkpoints are reduced or removed. The goal is minimum necessary security—not maximum harassment. Israel gains nothing from inconveniencing ordinary Palestinians; it gains everything from stopping terrorists. The incentive is to make checkpoints as efficient as possible while maintaining their security function.[10]

Critics who condemn checkpoints never explain what alternative they would propose. Should Israel simply allow unrestricted movement and accept the resulting attacks? Should Israeli parents send their children to school knowing that the bus could explode because checking vehicles is a human rights violation? The accusation offers no realistic solution—only condemnation of a country trying to protect its people from those who would murder them.

The Regional Comparison

Human rights must be assessed in context. How does Israel compare to other nations in the region? The comparison is illuminating—and devastating to the accusation.

In Syria, the government has killed over five hundred thousand of its own citizens, used chemical weapons on civilian neighborhoods including sleeping children, dropped barrel bombs on markets and hospitals, and created the largest refugee crisis since World War 2. In Iran, the government executes political dissidents by the thousands, crushes protests with lethal force, systematically persecutes religious minorities including Baha'is and Christians, and hangs homosexuals from cranes.[11] In Saudi Arabia, women were only recently allowed to drive, religious freedom does not exist, and criticism of the government can result in imprisonment, torture, or death—sometimes by public beheading.[12]

In Egypt, the government has killed protesters by the hundreds in single incidents, imprisoned journalists and activists by the thousands, and maintains emergency laws that suspend basic rights. In Turkey, the government has imprisoned more journalists than any other country on earth and purged tens of thousands from government positions for suspected disloyalty.[13] In Iraq and Lebanon, militia groups operate outside state control and commit abuses with impunity. Throughout the region, minorities suffer persecution that would be unthinkable in Israel.[14]

Israel, by contrast, has a free press, independent courts, democratic elections, legal protections for minorities, and a civil society that actively monitors and criticizes government actions. Arab citizens of Israel have political rights and legal protections unmatched in most of the region. Israeli Arabs vote, serve in parliament, sit on the Supreme Court, serve as doctors, lawyers, and professors, and hold positions throughout society. And remember, an Arab judge sent a former Jewish president to prison—try to imagine that happening in reverse anywhere else in the Middle East.

The obsessive focus on Israel—while ignoring or minimizing vastly worse abuses throughout the region—reveals that the accusation is not about human rights. It is about delegitimizing the Jewish state. It is about holding Israel to a standard applied to no other nation while giving actual human rights violators a pass. It is about using the language of human rights to pursue ends that have nothing to do with human rights.

17

Lie #12

"Israel Commits War Crimes"

"War crimes" is a term with specific legal criteria. It refers to serious violations of international humanitarian law—the laws of armed conflict—including deliberate attacks on civilians, torture of prisoners, use of prohibited weapons, and other grave breaches of the rules that govern warfare. To accuse a nation of committing war crimes is to accuse it of the most serious violations of international law. It is to place that nation in the company of history's worst offenders.

Israel faces this accusation after every military operation. Gaza conflicts produce immediate accusations of war crimes from UN officials, human rights organizations, media commentators, and political leaders around the world. The accusations are treated as self-evident: If Palestinians died, Israel must have committed war crimes. The assumption is that any Palestinian death is proof of Israeli criminality.

But war crimes are not defined by casualty counts. They are defined by intent, by conduct, by adherence to or violation of specific legal rules. Israel has demonstrated targeting and review procedures designed to meet—and in many cases exceed—the standards required under international law. The real war crimes in these conflicts are committed by Hamas and other terrorist organizations—crimes that are systematically ignored while attention focuses exclusively on Israel. The accusation inverts reality.

What International Law Actually Requires

International humanitarian law, codified primarily in the Geneva Conventions and their Additional Protocols, establishes rules for the conduct of armed conflict. These rules are complex and nuanced, designed for the reality of warfare where civilians are inevitably at risk. The core principles are distinction, proportionality, and precaution.[1]

- **Distinction:** Parties to a conflict must distinguish between combatants and civilians, and between military objectives and civilian objects. Attacks may only be directed at military targets. This does not mean that military targets cease to be military targets because they are located near civilians.
- **Proportionality:** Attacks that may cause incidental civilian harm are not prohibited, but the expected civilian harm must not be excessive in relation to the concrete and direct military advantage anticipated. This requires a judgment about military value versus civilian cost—not a rule that any civilian death is prohibited.
- **Precaution:** Parties must take constant care to spare civilians and civilian objects. Feasible precautions must be taken to minimize civilian harm. This requires reasonable efforts, not impossible guarantees.

Note what these principles do not require.

- They do not require zero civilian casualties.
- They do not require that attacking forces accept unlimited risk to themselves to protect enemy civilians.

- They do not prohibit attacks on military targets located in civilian areas.
- They do not grant immunity to combatants who hide among civilians.
- They do not make every civilian death a war crime.

International law recognizes that war is terrible and that civilians will die even in lawfully conducted operations. The legal question is not whether civilians died, but whether the attacking party made genuine efforts to distinguish between military and civilian targets, assessed proportionality before striking, and took feasible precautions to minimize harm. The question is intent and process, not outcome alone.

How Israel Conducts Operations

Israel's military operates under extensive legal constraints and review processes. Military lawyers are embedded at every level of command.[2] Targeting decisions undergo legal review before strikes are authorized.[3] Rules of engagement are designed to comply with international law and are often more restrictive than the law requires. This legal infrastructure exists because Israel takes the law seriously, not because Israel ignores it.

When incidents occur that may involve wrongdoing, Israel investigates. Military police conduct inquiries. Courts-martial are held. Soldiers have been imprisoned for abuses. Officers have been disciplined and dismissed. The system is not perfect—no system is—but it exists and functions. Accountability is built into the structure.[4]

This is not the conduct of a military committing war crimes. This is the conduct of a military striving to comply with the law while fighting an enemy that deliberately and systematically violates it. This is what distinction, proportionality, and precaution look like in practice.

Hamas's Actual War Crimes

While Israel is accused of war crimes, Hamas commits actual, documented, undeniable war crimes as a matter of deliberate strategy. These crimes are not occasional lapses or unauthorized acts by rogue individuals. They are central to Hamas's method of warfare. They are policy, not aberration.

- **Indiscriminate rocket attacks on civilians:** Hamas and other Gaza-based terror groups have fired rockets deliberately and indiscriminately at Israeli population centers—cities, towns, neighborhoods, schools, and homes. These are not precision strikes on military targets. They are area attacks aimed at civilian life as such.[5] Under international humanitarian law, intentionally directing attacks at civilians—or launching indiscriminate attacks that cannot be directed at a specific military objective—constitutes a war crime. The fact that Israeli defenses often prevent mass casualties does not change the criminal intent or the legal character of the attacks.

- **Massacre of civilians on October 7, 2023:** Hamas carried out a large-scale assault characterized by the deliberate killing of civilians on a massive scale—families in their homes, residents of kibbutzim, and civilians at a music festival.[6] The assault included executions at close range, killings inside homes, and widespread violence against non-combatants who posed no threat. This was not collateral damage from a battle. It was a targeted campaign of murder against civilians, which constitutes a grave breach of the laws of war and fits squarely within the category of war crimes.[7] Victims were burned alive in their homes and tortured before being killed. Others were mutilated after death and subjected to sexual violence of extreme brutality. These were not combatants—they were families in their homes, young people at a music festival, residents of peaceful kibbutzim.[8]

- **Use of human shields:** Hamas deliberately places military infrastructure in civilian areas (see Lie # 8).
- **Taking of hostages:** The seizure of civilians as hostages is a war crime under the Geneva Conventions.[9] Hamas has taken hundreds of hostages over the years, including the mass hostage-taking of October 7, 2023, when over 250 people were dragged into Gaza—babies, elderly, teenagers, families. Hostages were held in inhumane conditions, denied medical care for serious conditions, subjected to psychological torture, and used as bargaining chips. Some were intentionally murdered in captivity.[10]
- **Perfidy:** Hamas fighters operate in civilian clothes, making themselves indistinguishable from non-combatants. They use ambulances to transport weapons and fighters. They exploit protected symbols and locations—the Red Cross, hospitals, schools, mosques. These acts of perfidy—feigning civilian or protected status to gain military advantage—are serious violations of the laws of war. They endanger all civilians by making it impossible to distinguish fighters from non-combatants.
- **Denial of quarter:** On October 7, Hamas fighters executed civilians who attempted to surrender. People who emerged from safe rooms with hands raised were shot.[11] The massacre was not a battle with collateral damage—it was systematic murder of defenseless people who posed no threat and sought no resistance.

These are not accusations or allegations. They are documented facts, recorded on video by Hamas itself, confirmed by forensic investigation, acknowledged by the perpetrators who celebrated rather than denied them. Yet in the international discourse, attention focuses overwhelmingly on Israel while Hamas's crimes are mentioned briefly, if at all, before the conversation returns to condemning Israel.

The Expert Assessments

Military professionals who have examined Israeli operations have consistently concluded that Israel complies with the laws of armed conflict and often exceeds what the law requires. These are people with direct experience in similar operations, people who understand what urban warfare requires and what law permits.[12]

These military experts are not politicians or activists with agendas to promote. They are military professionals with direct experience in similar operations, examining Israeli conduct against professional standards. Their professional assessments consistently conclude that Israel acts lawfully—and that the real violations come from those who accuse Israel while ignoring Hamas.

The Goldstone Retraction

One of the most significant war crimes accusations against Israel came from the Goldstone Report, a 2009 UN investigation of the Gaza conflict that year. The report accused Israel of deliberately targeting civilians and committing war crimes. It was celebrated by Israel's critics as definitive proof of Israeli criminality. It was cited endlessly as authoritative, as the final word, as proof that could not be questioned.

Then something remarkable happened. Richard Goldstone, the South African judge who led the investigation, publicly retracted the report's central conclusions. In a 2011 Washington Post op-ed, Goldstone wrote that subsequent Israeli investigations had shown that civilians were not intentionally targeted as policy. "If I had known then what I know now," he wrote, "the Goldstone Report would have been a different document."

Goldstone acknowledged that Israel investigated alleged abuses and held individuals accountable, while Hamas, which the report also criticized, investigated nothing and continued to celebrate attacks on civilians. The fundamental premise of the report—that Israel deliberately targeted civilians as a matter of policy—was wrong. The accusation was false.[13]

This retraction received far less attention than the original accusations. The damage was done. The report continues to be cited by those who either do not know about or choose to ignore the retraction. But the Goldstone reversal illustrates a crucial point: Accusations are made quickly and loudly; corrections come slowly and quietly; and the accusation continues to be cited long after it has been withdrawn. The lie travels around the world while the truth is still putting on its shoes.

The Purpose of the Accusation

Why is Israel constantly accused of war crimes when the evidence shows it operates lawfully? Because the accusation serves strategic purposes unrelated to truth. Understanding these purposes reveals what the accusation is really about.

First, it delegitimizes Israeli self-defense. If Israel commits war crimes whenever it responds to attacks, then Israel cannot legally defend itself. Every military operation becomes criminal regardless of the provocation or the precautions taken. Israel must simply absorb attacks without response—or face prosecution for responding. The accusation is designed to disarm Israel legally before it is disarmed militarily.

Second, it creates legal exposure for Israeli leaders. War crimes accusations are used to pursue cases in international courts, to issue arrest warrants for Israeli officials, and to create a legal cloud over the

Jewish state. The goal is to criminalize Israel's leadership class, to make Israeli prime ministers and generals afraid to travel abroad, and to turn Israel into a pariah state whose leaders are wanted fugitives.

Third, it provides moral cover for attacks on Israel. If Israel is a war criminal state, then violence against Israel becomes resistance rather than terrorism. The accusation legitimizes the very attacks it purports to condemn. If Israel is committing war crimes, then fighting Israel is not murder but justice.

Fourth, it inverts moral reality. Hamas commits actual, documented war crimes systematically and deliberately. Israel takes unprecedented precautions to avoid civilian harm. By accusing Israel of criminality, the actual criminals escape scrutiny while the law-abiding party stands accused. The guilty go free while the innocent are prosecuted. This inversion is itself a kind of moral crime.

The Law and the Truth

The war crimes accusation functions strategically: to criminalize Israeli self-defense. If every Israeli military response is a war crime, then Israel cannot legally defend itself.

Meanwhile, Hamas commits actual, documented, undeniable war crimes as a matter of deliberate strategy—targeting civilians with rockets, using human shields, taking hostages, executing those who surrender, operating in civilian clothes. These are not allegations; they are recorded facts, often filmed by the perpetrators themselves.

Military professionals who have examined Israeli operations conclude that Israel complies with the laws of armed conflict and often exceeds what the law requires. Richard Goldstone, who led the most famous UN investigation accusing Israel of war crimes, publicly retracted his report's central conclusions after examining the evidence more carefully.

"Israel Commits War Crimes"

The accusation persists not because it is true but because it is useful—useful for delegitimizing Israel, useful for creating legal exposure for Israeli leaders, useful for providing moral cover to those who actually commit war crimes. The law will vindicate those who follow it. The truth will outlast the lie.

18

Lie #13

"Israel Restricts Access to Muslim and Christian Holy Sites"

Jerusalem is sacred to three faiths. For Jews, it is the eternal capital, the site of the Temple, the direction of prayer for three thousand years, the place where Abraham bound Isaac and where Solomon built the house of God. For Christians, it is the place of Christ's crucifixion, burial, and resurrection, the city where salvation history reached its climax, and the place where Jesus will establish His eternal Kingdom. For Muslims, it is the location of Al-Aqsa Mosque, the third holiest site in Islam, the place from which Muhammad is said to have ascended. No city on earth concentrates such religious significance in such a small space.

The accusation that Israel restricts access to holy sites plays on deep religious sensitivities. It suggests that Israel prevents Muslims from praying at Al-Aqsa, prevents Christians from visiting the Church of the Holy Sepulchre, and uses its control of Jerusalem to suppress non-Jewish worship. The accusation portrays Israel as a threat to the religious freedom of billions of people worldwide—a country that would deny sacred access to half the human race.

But this accusation inverts history and ignores present reality. Under Israeli administration and security responsibility, Jerusalem has experienced an unprecedented era of religious freedom and access. All faiths can worship at their holy sites. All religious communities administer their own sacred spaces. The contrast with how these sites were treated when not under Israeli control could not be starker. The accusation is not just false—it is the opposite of the truth.

What Happened Before 1967

To understand religious access in Jerusalem, you must understand what happened when Israel did not control the Old City and its holy sites. The period from 1948 to 1967 provides the comparison that reveals what Israeli control actually means.

From 1948 to 1967, Jordan controlled East Jerusalem, including the Old City, the Western Wall, the Temple Mount, and the major Christian sites. Jordan had signed an armistice agreement with Israel promising to allow Israeli access to Jewish holy sites. That promise was never kept. It was a dead letter from the moment it was signed.[1]

For nineteen years—nearly two decades—not a single Jew was permitted to pray at the Western Wall, the holiest site in Judaism, the last remnant of the Temple compound. Jews were entirely barred from the Old City. They could stand on Mount Zion and look toward the Wall, straining to see the stones their ancestors had touched for millennia, but they could not approach it. The Wall stood empty of Jewish worshippers for the first time in modern memory.[2]

"Israel Restricts Access to Muslim and Christian Holy Sites"

Under Jordanian rule, every synagogue was destroyed and the ancient Mount of Olives cemetery desecrated—a systematic erasure documented in Lie #4. The dead were desecrated to humiliate the living.[3]

This was ethnic and religious cleansing. Every trace of Jewish presence was erased from the parts of Jerusalem that Jordan controlled. Every synagogue, every cemetery, every sign that Jews had lived and prayed there for millennia was systematically destroyed. And the international community said almost nothing. No UN resolutions condemned the destruction. No human rights organizations issued reports. The world watched in silence.

Christian access was also restricted during this period. While Christians could visit holy sites, Jordan imposed significant limitations. Christian institutions faced discrimination. The Christian population of Jerusalem declined under Jordanian rule. Christians were second-class citizens in a Muslim kingdom that had little interest in protecting their rights.[4]

What Israel Did in 1967

In June 1967, during the Six-Day War, Israel captured East Jerusalem from Jordan. Israeli soldiers reached the Western Wall for the first time in nineteen years. The photograph of paratroopers weeping at the Wall became one of the most iconic images in Israeli history—hardened soldiers crying like children at the stones their parents and grandparents had been forbidden to touch.

What Israel did next was remarkable—and historically unprecedented. Rather than treating Muslim holy sites the way Jordan had treated Jewish ones, Israel immediately guaranteed freedom of worship for all faiths. Within days of capturing the Old City, Defense Minister Moshe Dayan announced that all holy sites would be accessible to all worshippers. The army that had just won a stunning military victory chose restraint over revenge.[5]

Even more striking, Israel allowed the Islamic Waqf—the Muslim religious trust—to continue administering the Temple Mount, including Al-Aqsa Mosque and the Dome of the Rock. The holiest site in Judaism, the Temple Mount itself, was left under Muslim religious administration. Jews can visit the Temple Mount during limited hours but cannot pray there under current arrangements—a restriction Israel maintains to preserve religious peace.[6]

Think about what this means. Israel captured the Temple Mount in a defensive war after being denied access to it for nineteen years.

This is where Abraham bound Isaac, where Solomon built the First Temple, where the Second Temple stood until its destruction by Rome, where the divine presence dwelled. And Israel handed day-to-day administration to a Muslim authority.

No conquering power in history has treated the holy sites of other faiths with such deference. Compare this to what happens when ISIS captures ancient sites—they are destroyed, blown up on camera for propaganda. Compare it to what the Taliban did to the Buddhas of Bamiyan—they were demolished with explosives, erased from the earth. Compare it to what Jordan did to the Jewish Quarter—it was systematically erased. Israel's approach has no modern parallel in its generosity and restraint.

Christian Holy Sites Today

Under Israeli control, Christian holy sites are protected and accessible. The Church of the Holy Sepulchre—believed by many Christians to be the site of Jesus's crucifixion, burial, and resurrection—operates freely. The church is administered by six Christian denominations under arrangements that predate Israeli control, and Israel has scrupulously maintained these arrangements. No Israeli government has interfered with Christian administration of what many consider Christianity's holiest site.[7]

Pilgrims walk the Via Dolorosa daily, retracing the steps of Jesus to Calvary. The Garden of Gethsemane is open to visitors who come to pray where Jesus prayed before his arrest. The Mount of Olives churches welcome worshippers from around the world. Bethlehem's Church of the Nativity—while in Palestinian-controlled territory—has been accessible to millions of Christian pilgrims precisely because Israel facilitates their passage. Pilgrims fly into Tel Aviv, travel through Israeli territory, and visit the birthplace of Christ because Israel makes it possible.

The Christian population of Israel has grown, not shrunk. Christians serve in the IDF, in the Knesset, in the judiciary, and throughout society. Christian schools operate freely, educating students of all faiths. Christian holidays are recognized. Christian communities govern their own religious affairs without interference. Churches ring bells, hold processions, and celebrate holy days as they have for centuries. Even more shocking, some churches in Israel have made strongly pro-Palestinian and anti-occupation statements, and yet continue to operate openly.[8]

Contrast this with what has happened to Christian populations elsewhere in the Middle East. The Christian population of Iraq has collapsed from over 1.5 million to under two hundred thousand since 2003—a decline of nearly 90 percent in two decades. The Christian population of Syria has been decimated by civil war, with ancient communities erased overnight. Christians in Egypt face persecution and violence—churches bombed, worshippers killed, communities terrorized. Christians in the Palestinian territories have declined dramatically—Bethlehem, once majority Christian, is now overwhelmingly Muslim.[9]

Israel is the one place in the Middle East where the Christian population is growing. The accusation that Israel restricts Christian access is refuted by the experience of millions of Christian pilgrims who visit every year—and by the thriving Christian community within Israel itself. The evidence is overwhelming and undeniable.

Muslim Access to Al-Aqsa

The accusation focuses most intensely on Muslim access to Al-Aqsa Mosque. Critics claim that Israel prevents Muslims from worshipping there and that Israeli forces invade the mosque. These claims are repeated so often that many assume they must be true.

The reality: Muslims pray at Al-Aqsa every day. Every single day, without exception. On Fridays and during Ramadan, hundreds of thousands of Muslims worship at the mosque. These are among the largest religious gatherings anywhere in the world—and they happen under Israeli sovereignty, with Israeli security facilitating access. The crowds that gather for Ramadan prayers dwarf most religious gatherings on earth.[10]

When do restrictions occur? When violence breaks out. When rioters stockpile rocks and fireworks inside the mosque to attack Jewish worshippers at the Western Wall below. When terrorists use the Temple Mount as a base for attacks. When credible intelligence indicates planned violence. The restrictions are responses to specific threats, not expressions of policy.[11]

These temporary security measures are not restrictions on worship—they are responses to violence. They typically affect young men of military age during periods of heightened tension, and they are lifted as soon as security conditions permit. The routine access of hundreds of thousands of Muslims to Al-Aqsa continues day after day, year after year. The restrictions are the exception, not the rule.

Al-Aqsa stands today as it has stood for over a thousand years—protected, maintained, and open to Muslim worship under Israeli sovereignty.

"Israel Restricts Access to Muslim and Christian Holy Sites"

The Status Quo

Israel maintains the "status quo" on the Temple Mount—an arrangement that restricts Jewish worship while permitting Muslim worship. This arrangement is often criticized by some Israelis who believe Jews should have equal prayer rights at Judaism's holiest site. Why should Jews be forbidden to pray at the place most sacred to Judaism? But Israel maintains the arrangement precisely to ensure religious peace and continued Muslim access.

Under the status quo, the Waqf administers the mosques and the Temple Mount compound. Israeli police provide security but do not enter the mosques except in emergencies. Jews may visit the Temple Mount during limited hours but may not pray visibly—may not move their lips in prayer, may not bring prayer books, may not wear prayer shawls. Muslims have unrestricted access during normal hours.[12]

This arrangement disadvantages Jews more than any other group. Yet Israel maintains it to honor Muslim sensitivities and prevent conflict. The accusation that Israel restricts Muslim access ignores the extraordinary deference Israel shows to Muslim religious concerns—even at the cost of limiting Jewish religious practice at Judaism's holiest site. Israel accepts restrictions on Jewish worship to protect Muslim worship.

The Real Threats to Holy Sites

While Israel is accused of threatening holy sites, the real threats come from those making the accusations. The projection is remarkable and revealing.

Palestinian rioters have repeatedly used Al-Aqsa as a staging ground for violence, stockpiling weapons inside the mosque and using it as a base to attack worshippers at the Western Wall. This is the genuine desecration—using a house of worship as an armory and launching pad for attacks. The mosque is being turned into a fortress, and Israel is blamed for responding.[13]

The Waqf has conducted unauthorized excavations on the Temple Mount, destroying archaeological remains from the First and Second Temple periods. Truckloads of historically significant debris have been dumped as garbage, mixed with modern trash to obscure what was destroyed. This represents the attempt to erase Jewish history at the site most sacred to the Jewish people—a crime against history and against the Jewish connection to the land.[14]

Joseph's Tomb in Nablus—under Palestinian Authority control—has been attacked, burned, and vandalized repeatedly. Mobs have stormed the site, set fires, and destroyed whatever they could reach. The ancient synagogue in Jericho was damaged. Jewish holy sites outside Israeli control are at constant risk. The pattern is consistent: Under Israeli control, sites are protected; outside Israeli control, they are attacked and sometimes destroyed. The accusation against Israel is a projection of what others have done—and continue to do.[15]

19

Lie #14

"Israel Builds Illegal Settlements That Undermine Peace"

No issue in the Israeli–Palestinian conflict generates more consistent international condemnation than Israeli settlements in the West Bank. The word "settlements" has become synonymous with illegality, with colonialism, with the deliberate sabotage of peace. Every construction announcement produces diplomatic protests, UN resolutions, and media denunciations. The condemnation is reflexive, automatic, and overwhelming.

The accusation contains two claims:

- First, settlements are illegal under international law.
- Second, settlements are the obstacle to peace.

Both claims are more complicated than the accusation suggests—and both are used to place all responsibility for the conflict's continuation on Israel while ignoring Palestinian choices that have actually prevented peace. The settlement accusation is *not* analysis—*it is blame assignment*.

The Legal Question

The assertion that settlements are "illegal under international law" is stated as though it were settled fact. It is not. The legal status of settlements is genuinely disputed among legal scholars, and the common assertion of illegality is based on a contestable interpretation of international law. Repeating the assertion does not make it true.

The primary legal argument against settlements is based on Article 49 of the Fourth Geneva Convention, which states that an occupying power "shall not deport or transfer parts of its own civilian population into the territory it occupies."[1] Critics argue that Israeli settlements violate this provision. The argument seems straightforward until you examine it carefully.

However, this argument has significant problems. Article 49 was drafted in response to Nazi Germany's forced transfer of populations during World War II—the deportation of Germans into conquered territories like Poland and the expulsion of local populations to make room for them. Israeli settlers are not deported or transferred by the government; they move voluntarily. No one forces them to live in the West Bank. They choose to live there, just as people choose to live anywhere else. The situations are not analogous.[2]

Moreover, the West Bank's legal status is more complex than the term "occupied territory" suggests. The West Bank was not sovereign territory of any recognized state when Israel captured it in 1967. Jordan had seized it in 1948 in an illegal war of aggression, a war intended to destroy the newly declared State of Israel. Jordan's annexation was recognized only by the United Kingdom and Pakistan—not by the international community, not by the Arab League, not by the United Nations. When Israel captured the territory in a defensive war, there was no legitimate sovereign from whom it was taken.[3]

Some legal scholars argue that under the principle of *uti possidetis juris*, borders of new states are based on prior administrative boundaries. The only prior legal instrument governing these territories is the League of Nations Mandate for Palestine, which specifically encouraged "close settlement by Jews on the land." The Mandate did not distinguish between different parts of Palestine—Jews were to be allowed to settle throughout the entire mandated territory, including what is now the West Bank.[4]

The point is not to argue that settlements are definitively legal. Legitimate legal scholars disagree on these questions, and reasonable people can reach different conclusions. The point is that the assertion of definitive illegality is an advocacy position, not a neutral statement of established law. International law in this area is contested, and the confident declarations of illegality ignore substantial legal arguments to the contrary. The matter is not settled; it is disputed.

The Historical Context

The West Bank—which Israel calls by its biblical names, Judea and Samaria—is the heartland of ancient Jewish civilization. Hebron, Bethlehem, Jericho, Shechem (Nablus)—these are not foreign places to the Jewish people. They are the settings of the biblical narrative, the places where Abraham, Isaac, and Jacob lived, where David was anointed king, where Jewish communities existed for millennia before the word "Palestine" was attached to the land.

Jews lived in these areas continuously until the twentieth century when they were expelled by violence. There was a Jewish presence in the community of Hebron for centuries. Jews lived among their Arab neighbors. But that ended with a massacre and expulsion in 1929 during Arab riots incited by false claims that Jews threatened Al-Aqsa. Sixty-seven Jews were murdered in a single day—men, women, children, elderly—by mobs who had been their neighbors. When Jordan captured the West Bank in 1948, it expelled every remaining Jew. Jewish communities that had existed for generations were erased. Not a single Jew was permitted to remain.

When Israel captured these territories in 1967, it was not entering foreign land for the first time. It was returning to places from which Jews had been ethnically cleansed within living memory. The settlers who returned to Hebron, to Gush Etzion, to other historic sites were in many cases returning to places where their families had lived before being expelled or murdered. They were reclaiming what had been taken from them.[5]

None of this settles the policy question of whether settlements are wise or whether they should be part of a final peace agreement. But it challenges the narrative that settlers are foreign colonizers with no connection to the land. The Jewish connection to the West Bank is older and deeper than almost any other people's connection to almost any other land on earth. Jews are not foreigners in Judea.

What Settlements Actually Are

The word "settlements" conjures images of armed encampments imposed on stolen Palestinian land, of ideological fanatics seizing territory that belongs to others. The reality is more varied and more complex. "Settlements" is a single word used to describe vastly diverse kinds of communities.

Many settlements are suburbs of Jerusalem and Tel Aviv—bedroom communities where Israelis live because housing is more affordable than in major cities. Residents commute to work, send their children to school, and live ordinary suburban lives. They are not ideologues or pioneers; they are families looking for affordable homes near their jobs. Ma'ale

"Israel Builds Illegal Settlements That Undermine Peace"

Adumim, with over forty thousand residents, is essentially a satellite city of Jerusalem, connected to the capital as any suburb to its anchor city.

Some settlements are religious communities established in places of biblical significance—Hebron, where Abraham purchased a burial cave and where the patriarchs and matriarchs are buried; Beit El, where Jacob dreamed of a ladder to Heaven; Shiloh, where the Tabernacle stood for centuries before the Temple was built in Jerusalem. For religious Jews, living in these places is a fulfillment of biblical mandate, a return to the land God promised their ancestors.

Some settlements were established for security reasons—on hilltops and strategic points, providing early warning against attack from the east. Israel's major cities are within a few miles of the West Bank; without strategic depth, Israel would be extremely vulnerable to attack. The Jordan Valley settlements provide a security buffer that Israel has historically considered essential.

The vast majority of settlers—approximately 80 percent—live in settlement blocs close to the pre-1967 lines. Most peace proposals since the 1990s have assumed that these blocs would remain part of Israel in any final agreement, with equivalent land swaps to compensate.[6] The controversial settlements are not the major blocs but small, isolated communities deep in the West Bank, which represent a fraction of the settler population.[7]

Settlements are built primarily on state land or on land purchased legally. When construction does occur on land with disputed ownership, the Israeli legal system provides remedies. The Supreme Court has ordered demolition of structures built on privately owned Palestinian land. Settlers have been evicted; buildings have been torn down. Entire outposts have been removed by force. The system is not lawless, but it has rules and enforces them.[8]

The "Obstacle to Peace" Claim

The second part of the accusation is that settlements are the obstacle to peace—that Israeli construction prevents the two-state solution that would otherwise be achievable. This claim does not survive historical examination. History shows something very different.

In 2000, at Camp David, Prime Minister Ehud Barak offered the Palestinians a state on approximately 94 percent of the West Bank, all of Gaza, a capital in East Jerusalem, and shared sovereignty over the Temple Mount. The Palestinians rejected the offer without making a counter-proposal. There was no issue of settlements preventing this offer—Israel was proposing to dismantle settlements as part of the agreement. The offer was there; it was rejected.[9]

In 2001, at Taba, Israel offered even more—approximately 97 percent of the West Bank with land swaps, a capital in East Jerusalem, and creative arrangements for holy sites and refugees. Again, no agreement was reached. Settlements were not the obstacle; Palestinian leadership's unwillingness to accept any offer that left Israel standing was the obstacle.[10]

In 2005, Israel unilaterally withdrew from Gaza, dismantling every settlement and evacuating every settler—some eight thousand people removed from their homes, synagogues demolished, cemeteries relocated. Rather than responding with peace, Palestinians elected Hamas and used Gaza to launch thousands of rockets at Israeli civilians. The withdrawal demonstrated that removing settlements does not produce peace when the other side is committed to continued conflict.[11]

In 2008, Prime Minister Ehud Olmert offered Palestinian President Mahmoud Abbas approximately 100 percent of the West Bank (with equivalent land swaps), a divided Jerusalem, and a creative solution for refugees. Abbas did not accept. He later admitted he "rejected it out of hand." He did not even take the map home to study. Settlements did not prevent this offer—it was the most generous offer ever made.[12]

The pattern is clear: Israel has repeatedly offered to dismantle settlements as part of peace agreements. The Palestinians have repeatedly rejected those agreements. Settlements are not preventing peace—rejection of Israel's existence and demands that Israel cannot accept are preventing peace.

The Real Obstacles to Peace

If settlements were truly the obstacle to peace, the conflict would have been easily resolved. Israel has shown repeatedly that it will evacuate settlements for peace—it did so in Sinai as part of the peace treaty with Egypt, evacuating every settlement and returning every inch of territory. It did so in Gaza. The pattern is clear: When peace is offered, Israel removes settlements.

The real obstacles to peace are different:

- **Refusal to accept Israel's existence:** Hamas's charter calls for Israel's destruction—not for a Palestinian state alongside Israel, but for Israel's complete elimination. The Palestinian Authority teaches children that all of Israel is "occupied Palestine." Maps in Palestinian schools show no Israel—the entire land, from the river to the sea, is Palestine. The "right of return" demand—that millions of descendants of 1948 refugees be allowed to immigrate to Israel—is designed to demographically eliminate the Jewish state without firing a shot.
- **Incitement and incentivization of violence:** The Palestinian Authority pays salaries to terrorists and their families. Streets and squares are named after suicide bombers. Children's television

glorifies martyrdom. Summer camps teach children to aspire to kill Jews. This culture of violence makes peace nearly impossible.
- **Maximalist demands:** Every Israeli offer has been rejected because it was not enough. Palestinians have demanded not just a state alongside Israel but a "right of return" that would eliminate Israel. They have demanded pre-1967 borders with no modifications, even for major settlement blocs that everyone understands will remain Israeli. They have demanded that Israel accept responsibility for creating the refugee problem, though it was created by Arab armies that started a war to prevent Israel's existence. The demands are designed to be unacceptable.

Blaming settlements for the absence of peace allows these real obstacles to escape scrutiny. It places all responsibility on Israel while ignoring the consistent pattern of Palestinian rejection. It treats the conflict as a real estate dispute when it is actually an existential struggle over whether a Jewish state can exist at all.

A Note on Criticism

None of this means settlements are beyond criticism. Many Israelis oppose settlement expansion for practical, political, or moral reasons. Legitimate debates exist about which settlements serve security needs and which create unnecessary friction. Some settlement activity may be unwise even if it is not illegal. Israelis themselves disagree about settlement policy.

The problem is not criticism of settlements. The problem is the obsessive focus on settlements as the sole obstacle to peace, the confident assertion of illegality that ignores legitimate legal debate, and the use of the settlement issue to delegitimize Israel while giving Palestinian intransigence a free pass. The problem is treating settlements as the cause of the conflict rather than a symptom of unresolved issues that Palestinian leadership has refused to resolve.

If Palestinian leaders accepted Israel's existence, agreed to realistic compromises, and abandoned violence, a peace agreement would be achievable. Settlements would be addressed in negotiations, as they have been in every peace proposal. The obstacle is not settlements—the obstacle is refusal to make peace. The obstacle is the conviction that time is on the Palestinian side, that eventually Israel will be weakened or destroyed, that accepting less than everything is accepting defeat.

Before 1967, when there were no settlements in the West Bank, there was no peace. Before 1948, when there was no State of Israel, there was no peace. The conflict predates settlements by decades. Settlements are a symptom of unresolved issues, not the cause of the conflict.

When Palestinian leaders choose peace—genuine peace that accepts Israel's existence—peace will be achievable. Settlements will be addressed in negotiations as they have been in every peace proposal. Jews living in their ancestral homeland are not the obstacle. The refusal to accept that Jews may live there at all—that is the obstacle.

Engaging the Harder Questions

We have shown that the legal status of settlements is genuinely disputed, that Jews have deep historical connections to the West Bank, and that settlements have not prevented peace—Palestinian rejection has.

But sophisticated critics will press harder. They will argue that settlements are creating facts that foreclose a two-state solution regardless of who is to blame.

"The Geneva Convention Is Clear—Voluntary Transfer Still Violates It"

The critique:
Article 49's prohibition on population transfer doesn't require force. The occupying power need only facilitate transfer—providing housing subsidies, infrastructure, military protection. Israel does all of this.

The honest response:
The Fourth Geneva Convention applies to "occupied territory"—territory belonging to a "High Contracting Party." But Jordan was never the legitimate sovereign of the West Bank. It seized the territory in 1948 through aggressive war, and only the United Kingdom and Pakistan recognized its annexation. If the West Bank was never Jordanian sovereign territory, it is not "occupied" in the technical legal sense but *disputed* territory.

The honest concession:
This is a minority position internationally. The International Court of Justice (ICJ) rejected it in 2004. Most governments accept the "occupation" framework. But advisory opinions are not binding law. When someone declares settlements "clearly illegal," they are taking a side in an unresolved debate—not reporting a verdict.

"Settlements Make a Palestinian State Geographically Impossible"

The critique:
Look at a map. The settlement "fingers," the ring around Jerusalem, the Jordan Valley—these fragment Palestinian territory. A contiguous state is no longer possible.

"Israel Builds Illegal Settlements That Undermine Peace"

The honest response:
Every serious peace proposal since the 1990s included territorial swaps creating a contiguous Palestinian state. Israel offered to evacuate settlements outside the major blocs. Those maps were rejected. The building happened *after* the rejections.

The honest concession:
The distinction between "security-driven" and "ideologically driven" settlement policy is not always clear. Some settlements deep in the West Bank are hard to justify on security grounds. Israeli coalition politics have allowed expansion that may genuinely reduce future options.

The honest answer:
Most settlers—over 80 percent—live in blocs that every peace proposal assumes will remain Israeli with land swaps. If a Palestinian leader had emerged willing to accept a genuine peace agreement, maps could have been redrawn.

"Liberal Zionists Say Settlements Threaten Israel's Future"

The critique:
If Israel absorbs the West Bank population, it faces an impossible choice: grant citizenship and become binational or deny citizenship and become apartheid. Settlements make withdrawal impossible.

The honest response:
The binary—"full annexation or full withdrawal"—assumes these are the only options. Israel has maintained a stable status quo for decades. Withdrawal from Gaza produced rockets. The West Bank overlooks Israel's population centers. A hostile entity there would have capabilities Gaza never had.

The honest concession:
The status quo has costs—moral, diplomatic, strategic. The situation is not sustainable forever.

The honest answer:
Liberal Zionists are often wrong about the solution. "End the occupation" is a slogan, not a policy. Given the history of withdrawal producing attack, the status quo may be the least bad option. That is a tragedy, not a plan. But it is reality.

20

Lie #15

"Israel Does Not Sincerely Pursue Peace"

If Israel wanted peace, critics argue, it could have peace. The conflict continues because Israel prefers expansion over reconciliation, because Israel rejects compromise, because Israel sabotages negotiations whenever agreement seems possible. The accusation portrays Israel as the obstacle—the party that refuses the outstretched hand of peace, choosing conflict when peace is available.

But history tells a different story. Israel has pursued peace consistently, sometimes desperately, often at great risk and cost. Israel has made peace with former enemies who were willing to make peace. Israel has offered far-reaching concessions that would have seemed impossible to earlier generations. Israel has withdrawn from territory, dismantled settlements, and taken extraordinary political risks for the possibility of peace. The obstacle has never been Israeli unwillingness to pursue peace—it has been the inability to find partners willing to accept Israel's existence on any terms.

Peace with Egypt

In 1977, Egyptian President Anwar Sadat made his historic visit to Israel—the first Arab leader to set foot in the Jewish state. He addressed the Knesset, Israel's parliament, and spoke of peace. Two years later, Israel and Egypt signed the Camp David Accords, ending thirty years of war. Four major wars, tens of thousands of casualties, and finally peace. To achieve that peace, Israel made enormous sacrifices.

Israel returned the entire Sinai Peninsula—over twenty-three thousand square miles of territory, more than three times the size of pre-1967 Israel. This was land captured in a defensive war, land containing strategic military assets, land with significant economic value including oil fields that Israel had developed at great expense. The airfields, the strategic depth, the resources—Israel gave up all of it for peace.

Israel evacuated every settlement in Sinai—removing thousands of Israeli civilians from homes they had built, dismantling communities that had been established over more than a decade, relocating families who had built lives in the desert. Some settlers had to be removed by force, dragged from homes they refused to leave. It was traumatic, divisive, and politically costly. Israel did it anyway because peace was worth the price.[1]

The message was unmistakable: When Israel has a genuine partner for peace, Israel will make peace. When an Arab leader is willing to accept Israel's existence and negotiate in good faith, Israel will pay a significant price for peace. The Sinai withdrawal proved that Israel's retention of territory was not ideological—it was conditional on the absence of peace. When peace became possible, territory was returned without hesitation.

Peace with Jordan

In 1994, Israel signed a peace treaty with Jordan, ending decades of formal hostility. The treaty included territorial adjustments, water sharing arrangements, and provisions for economic cooperation. King Hussein of Jordan had been in secret contact with Israeli leaders for years, building trust and exploring possibilities. When the time was right, peace was formalized and made public.

Again, Israel demonstrated its commitment to peace through concrete action. Border disputes were resolved through negotiation rather than war. Resources were shared according to agreed formulas. Diplomatic relations were established. Embassies were opened. The peace has held for three decades—imperfect at times, challenged by events, but enduring. Two nations that had been enemies became, if not allies, at least partners in stability.[2]

Two peace treaties with former enemies. Territory returned. Settlements evacuated. Diplomatic relations established. Economic cooperation developed. Security coordination implemented. This is not the record of a nation that refuses peace. This is the record of a nation that makes peace when peace is offered.

The Oslo Process

In 1993, Israel took perhaps its greatest risk for peace. The Oslo Accords (see Chapter 9 for the legal framework this created) brought the PLO—an organization with a long record of terrorism—into partnership with Israel for a peace process.

Israel agreed to recognize the PLO as the representative of the Palestinian people—an organization that had spent decades trying to destroy Israel. Israel agreed to establish the Palestinian Authority, giving

Palestinians self-governance for the first time in their history. Israel transferred control of cities, towns, and population centers to Palestinian rule. Israel armed Palestinian security forces—literally giving guns to people who had been trying to kill Israelis for a generation.[3]

This was an enormous gamble. Many Israelis, including Prime Minister Yitzhak Rabin himself, had spent careers fighting the PLO. The organization's charter still called for Israel's destruction. The track record of terrorism was long and bloody. Veterans who had lost friends to PLO attacks were asked to shake hands with the people responsible. Yet Israel took the risk, hoping that partnership would transform the relationship, that yesterday's enemies could become tomorrow's neighbors.

Prime Minister Rabin paid with his life—assassinated by an Israeli extremist opposed to the peace process. Rabin became a martyr for peace, killed precisely because he was willing to take risks for reconciliation. His assassination underscored both the political and personal risks Israeli leaders were willing to take for peace, and how far Israel's leadership was willing to go in pursuit of reconciliation.[4]

The Oslo process ultimately failed—but not because of Israeli unwillingness to pursue peace. It failed because Palestinian leadership never fully committed to it, because terrorism continued even during negotiations, because the Palestinian Authority taught hatred and glorified violence even while its leaders negotiated, and because when final-status offers were made, they were rejected without counter-offers.

The Olmert Offer

Mentioned in the previous chapter, it was in 2008 that Prime Minister Ehud Olmert made the most generous offer any Israeli leader had ever presented. Meeting with Palestinian Authority President Mahmoud

"Israel Does Not Sincerely Pursue Peace"

Abbas—a supposed moderate, a man who had criticized violence, a leader the international community had embraced—Olmert proposed:

- Approximately 100 percent of the West Bank territory, with land swaps giving the Palestinians equivalent area for any West Bank land retained by Israel.
- A divided Jerusalem, with Arab neighborhoods becoming the Palestinian capital and Jewish neighborhoods remaining Israeli.
- A creative solution for the Old City involving international oversight rather than either side having complete sovereignty.
- A framework for resolving the refugee issue that would allow some family reunification while preserving Israel's character as a Jewish state.

Olmert showed Abbas a map. He offered to let Abbas photograph it so he could study it with his advisers, take it home, consider it carefully. Abbas declined—he never even took the map home. He did not photograph it. He did not study it. He simply walked away from what would have given the Palestinians virtually everything they claimed to want.

Years later, Abbas admitted in an interview that he "rejected it out of hand." He did not make a counter-proposal. He did not negotiate for modifications. He simply walked away from an offer that would have given the Palestinians approximately 100 percent of the territory, a capital in Jerusalem, and a state of their own.[5] He walked away because accepting would have meant ending the conflict, and ending the conflict would have meant accepting Israel.[6]

Why? The most plausible explanation is that accepting any offer would require accepting Israel's existence—something Palestinian leadership has never been willing to do definitively and finally. An agreement would end the conflict, would require recognizing Israel as legitimate, would mean abandoning the dream of eventual elimination. For Abbas, as for Arafat, that price was too high. The conflict is more valuable than any state.

The Gaza Withdrawal

In 2005, Prime Minister Ariel Sharon—the former general, the builder of settlements, the hardliner who had spent his career fighting Palestinian terrorism—ordered the complete evacuation of Gaza. Every Israeli soldier left. Every Israeli civilian left. Every settlement was dismantled—homes, schools, synagogues, businesses. Israel withdrew unilaterally, without negotiation, without receiving anything in return.

Sharon hoped that the withdrawal would demonstrate Israel's willingness to concede territory, would give Palestinians the opportunity to build a successful society, and would create momentum toward broader peace. If Palestinians could govern Gaza successfully, the argument went, the world would see they deserved a state and pressure would build for further Israeli withdrawals. Critics on the Israeli right warned that withdrawal without agreement would be interpreted as weakness and would lead to more violence, not less.

The critics were right. Within two years, Hamas seized control of Gaza in a violent coup, throwing Fatah rivals off rooftops, dragging bodies through the streets. Gaza became a launching pad for rocket attacks on Israel—thousands of rockets and mortars fired at Israeli cities and towns. Tunnels were dug for terrorist infiltration. The withdrawal—intended as a step toward peace—produced more war, not reconciliation.

The Gaza experience taught Israel a painful lesson: Unilateral concessions do not necessarily produce peace. When territory is vacated without agreement, it can be filled by forces committed to continued conflict. Israel's willingness to take risks for peace was met with violence, not reciprocation. The hand extended in hope was bitten.[7]

The Abraham Accords

In 2020, Israel signed normalization (peace) agreements with the United Arab Emirates, Bahrain, Sudan, and Morocco. These "Abraham Accords" represented a breakthrough—Arab nations making peace with Israel without waiting for resolution of the Palestinian issue, without conditioning relations on Palestinian agreement.

The accords demonstrated that peace with Israel was possible when Arab leaders decided it served their interests. The United Arab Emirates (UAE) and Bahrain saw economic opportunity, security cooperation against Iran, and technological partnership. They chose normalization—and Israel welcomed them enthusiastically. Flights began, embassies opened, business deals were signed, tourists traveled. Peace became real.

The Abraham Accords also revealed the Palestinian leadership's isolation. For decades, Arab states had conditioned relations with Israel on Palestinian agreement—giving Palestinian leaders veto power over regional peace. The accords broke that pattern, showing that the Palestinian leadership's refusal to make peace would not hold the entire region hostage forever. Arab states would pursue their own interests, with or without Palestinian approval.

Israel has made peace with every Arab party willing to make peace. Egypt wanted peace—Israel made peace, returning all of Sinai. Jordan wanted peace—Israel made peace, resolving border disputes and sharing resources. The UAE, Bahrain, Morocco, Sudan wanted normalization—Israel normalized with enthusiasm. The pattern is consistent: When partners emerge, Israel responds. When hands are extended in genuine peace, Israel grasps them.[8]

What Peace Requires

Peace requires two parties willing to accept each other's existence and negotiate in good faith. Israel has repeatedly demonstrated this willingness; Palestinian leadership has not.

Until Palestinian leadership is willing to accept Israel as a permanent reality, to educate for peace rather than hatred, to abandon demands designed to eliminate Israel, and to genuinely commit to ending the conflict rather than just managing it, peace will remain elusive. The obstacle is not Israeli unwillingness to make peace, but Palestinian unwillingness to accept Israel's existence on any terms.

The historical record refutes this accusation completely. The pattern is unmistakable: *Israel takes risks for peace; its enemies exploit those risks for war.*

The accusation that Israel does not want peace projects onto Israel the rejectionism of its enemies. Those who have never accepted Israel's existence, who have never offered recognition, who have walked away from every negotiation, accuse Israel of the failures they themselves produce. When peace becomes possible—when genuine partners emerge—Israel will be ready. It always has been.

21

Lie #16

"Israel Controls American Foreign Policy"

This accusation is whispered in faculty lounges, shouted at protests, and insinuated in think pieces: *Israel controls American foreign policy.* The "Israel Lobby" manipulates Congress through money and pressure. Jewish donors buy politicians and dictate their votes. America fights wars for Israel, sacrificing American blood for Israeli interests. The United States is not a sovereign nation making its own decisions but a puppet dancing on strings pulled from Jerusalem, its Middle East policy dictated by a foreign power and its domestic agents.

This accusation is not new. It is a modern variation of one of the oldest and most dangerous antisemitic tropes in existence—*the belief that Jews secretly control governments, that Jewish power operates behind the scenes manipulating the visible world, which elected leaders are merely fronts for hidden Jewish manipulation. The Protocols of the Elders of Zion,* that infamous forgery fabricated by the Russian secret police and later embraced by the Nazis as justification for genocide, made exactly this claim about Jewish world domination. The accusation about Israel and America is its direct descendant, wearing contemporary clothes but carrying the same poisonous message that has led to mass murder throughout history. Sometimes the accusation names "Jews" directly; sometimes it substitutes "Israel" or "the Israel Lobby," but the structure and implication are identical.

The reality is entirely different. The US–Israel relationship is based on shared values, shared interests, and genuine democratic support among the American people. It is not the product of manipulation but of alignment—two democracies facing common challenges, sharing common principles, and pursuing common goals. Understanding why America supports Israel requires understanding America itself, not imagining Jewish conspiracies pulling strings from the shadows.

The Antisemitic Lineage

The claim that Jews secretly control governments has been used to justify persecution for centuries—it is one of antisemitism's most durable and deadly tropes. In medieval Europe, Jews were accused of manipulating kings through finance, of using hidden influence to advance Jewish interests at Christian expense. In Tsarist Russia, *The Protocols of the Elders of Zion* was used to blame Jews for social unrest and justify violence against them. Pogroms followed—organized massacres that killed thousands across the Russian Empire.[1] In Nazi Germany, the myth of Jewish control was central to the ideology that produced the Holocaust—Jews had to be eliminated because they supposedly controlled banking, media, and governments, using this hidden power to destroy nations from within while enriching themselves.

The modern version simply substitutes "Israel" or "the Israel Lobby" for "the Jews." The structure is identical: A small group with disproportionate power manipulates a great nation against its own interests. The nation's leaders are either complicit in the manipulation—bought off by Jewish money—or too foolish to recognize what is happening. Ordinary citizens are kept ignorant by controlled media, itself supposedly under Jewish influence. Only those brave enough to speak the truth—to name the hidden power that cannot be named—can expose the conspiracy and liberate the nation from its hidden masters.

This framing should immediately raise suspicions among thoughtful people. When an accusation against Jews today mirrors accusations that led to mass murder in the past, careful scrutiny is required. The accusation may be true despite its ugly lineage—historical atrocities do not automatically make their justifications false in all circumstances. But the accusation must meet a high burden of proof precisely because of how such accusations have been used historically. We should be deeply skeptical when we hear echoes of Haman's ancient voice.

The accusation does not meet that burden. It fails on the evidence, fails on logic, and fails to account for the actual reasons American policy takes the shape it does. It is not analysis but prejudice dressed up as political insight, conspiracy theory masquerading as brave truth-telling.

Why Americans Support Israel

American support for Israel is not manufactured by lobbyists—it reflects genuine public opinion held by tens of millions of Americans across the political spectrum, in every region of the country, among people who have never met a lobbyist in their lives. Polls, at least until recently, have consistently shown that Americans sympathize with Israel over the Palestinians by substantial margins, often by ratios of three or four to one. This has been true for decades, across different administrations, through various conflicts, regardless of which party controls Congress or the

White House. The consistency of this support suggests something deeper than lobbying—it suggests values alignment that lobbying alone could never create.[2]

Why do Americans support Israel? Several reasons that have nothing to do with lobbying or manipulation:

- **Shared democratic values:** Israel is a democracy in a region dominated by autocracies, theocracies, and dictatorships. Americans naturally sympathize with a country that holds free elections where outcomes are uncertain, protects civil liberties even under security pressure, maintains an independent judiciary that regularly rules against its own government, allows free press that criticizes leaders in the harshest terms, and provides legal protections for minorities and dissidents. Israel looks like America in ways that its neighbors simply do not. Americans recognize their own values—imperfect, struggling, but fundamentally committed to democratic principles—reflected in Israeli society.
- **Religious connections:** The United States has a large and devout Christian population, many of whom feel deep connection to the Holy Land and to the Jewish people as described in the Bible. Christian Zionism—support for Israel based on biblical beliefs about God's promises to the Jewish people and the role of Israel in salvation history—predates the modern State of Israel by centuries and predates any organized lobbying by decades. Tens of millions of American Christians support Israel for religious reasons entirely independent of any lobby's efforts. They support Israel because they read the Bible, because they believe God's Covenant with Abraham remains in force.
- **Historical memory:** Americans remember the Holocaust—it is taught in schools, memorialized in museums, documented in

countless books and films. They understand that Israel was founded in part as a refuge for a people who had just experienced attempted genocide while the world largely stood by, while ships of refugees were turned away from port after port, while Jews who had lived in Europe for a millennium discovered they belonged nowhere. Support for Israel reflects determination that Jews should have a safe haven where they can defend themselves, that "Never Again" should mean something concrete and tangible. This is moral conviction rooted in historical memory, not manipulation by lobbyists.

- **Counterterrorism solidarity:** After September 11, 2001, Americans understood viscerally what Israelis had long experienced. The threat of terrorism—of enemies who deliberately target civilians, who cannot be deterred or appeased, who celebrate the murder of innocents—became real for Americans in a way it had not been before. Solidarity with Israel against terrorism reflects shared experience and shared values, the bond of nations facing common enemies who wish to destroy their way of life.

These factors explain American support for Israel without recourse to conspiracy theories. When critics claim that support for Israel is manufactured by hidden manipulators, they insult the intelligence and agency of the American people. Americans are not dupes who cannot think for themselves—they support Israel because they genuinely believe it is right to do so, based on values and beliefs they hold independently of any lobby's influence.

How Lobbying Actually Works

Yes, there is an Israel lobby. AIPAC—the American Israel Public Affairs Committee—is a significant organization that advocates for strong

US–Israel relations. Other organizations also work to influence policy in directions favorable to Israel. This is not a secret; it is how American democracy works. Lobbying is legal, constitutionally protected, and practiced by every interest group in the country. There is nothing sinister about it—it is citizens organizing to make their voices heard.

But context matters enormously. Every significant policy area has lobbying organizations, often far larger and better funded than pro-Israel groups. The pharmaceutical industry spends more on lobbying than any foreign policy issue—billions of dollars annually. The oil and gas industry, the technology sector, financial services, labor unions, environmental groups, gun rights advocates, gun control advocates, the healthcare industry—all maintain sophisticated lobbying operations that dwarf pro-Israel spending. Saudi Arabia and other Gulf states spend enormous sums on lobbying and public relations in Washington, hiring former diplomats, funding think tanks, and cultivating media relationships in ways that far exceed what pro-Israel groups do. So do defense contractors, agricultural interests, and countless other groups seeking to influence American policy.

AIPAC is not even close to being the biggest-spending lobby in Washington—it is not in the top twenty, not in the top fifty.[3] It is effective not because of money but because it represents a genuine constituency that politicians want to support anyway. A lobby that aligns with public opinion and shared values is in a fundamentally different position than one trying to manufacture support for unpopular positions. AIPAC succeeds because it amplifies existing sentiment, not because it creates sentiment where none exists. It is pushing on an open door, not forcing one closed.

Moreover, AIPAC and similar organizations are not extensions of the Israeli government—they are American organizations representing American citizens who care about US–Israel relations. Their members vote in American elections, volunteer in American campaigns, donate to

American candidates, and participate in American democracy like any other citizens exercising their constitutional rights. Portraying their political participation as sinister manipulation applies a double standard that is applied to no other group. Irish Americans can lobby for Ireland, Polish Americans for Poland, Armenian Americans for Armenia, Cuban Americans for their preferred Cuba policy—but Jewish Americans lobbying for Israel is somehow uniquely problematic, uniquely suspicious, uniquely dangerous. That double standard has a name: *antisemitism*.

The Strategic Relationship

American support for Israel serves American strategic interests. This is not a favor to Israel extracted through manipulation—it is a calculation of American benefit made by American policymakers pursuing American goals. Understanding these interests explains the relationship without recourse to conspiracy. We will outline these benefits in even more detail in Chapter 31.

- **Intelligence sharing:** Israel provides the United States with intelligence that has saved American lives—intelligence on terrorist networks, on weapons proliferation, on Iranian capabilities, on regional developments that affect American interests. This is a two-way relationship that benefits both countries. Both nations are safer for the partnership.[4]
- **Military technology:** Israel develops military technology that the United States uses and benefits from. The missile defense system, drone technology, cybersecurity tools, armor protection systems, and countless other innovations have emerged from Israeli development. American soldiers are safer because of Israeli innovation. The military relationship flows both ways.

- **Regional stability:** A strong Israel contributes to stability in a volatile region. Israel serves as a counterweight to Iranian expansion. A weakened Israel would invite adventurism from hostile actors in ways that would harm American interests and potentially require American military intervention.
- **Reliable ally:** Israel primarily defends itself with its own soldiers. American support has historically been financial, diplomatic, and in military equipment. However, in recent direct confrontations with Iran (2024–2025), US forces have actively participated in Israel's defense—shooting down Iranian missiles, deploying terminal high altitude area defense (THAAD) batteries with American troops, and in June 2025, directly striking Iranian nuclear sites.

The "Wars for Israel" Myth

The claim that America fights wars for Israel—that the Iraq War was launched at Israel's behest—does not survive scrutiny. The Iraq War was launched by an American administration responding to perceived threats after September 11, debated in Congress, supported by majorities in both houses, and covered exhaustively in American media. Some Americans believe it was a mistake, but if so, it was an *American* mistake. Israeli officials were actually divided on the war—some warned it would strengthen Iran, which is exactly what happened.[5]

The claim requires believing that American presidents, Congress, military leaders, and the public are either dupes manipulated against their interests or corrupt enough to sacrifice American lives for a foreign country. This is conspiracy theory, not analysis.

Disagreements Prove Independence

If Israel controlled American policy, disagreements would not exist. The Obama administration allowed anti-Israel UN resolutions, negotiated the Iran deal over Israeli objections, and maintained tense relations with Netanyahu throughout. These disagreements prove two sovereign nations with overlapping but distinct interests—not control.[6]

An Ancient Trope in Modern Dress

The "Israel Lobby" accusation is one of the oldest antisemitic tropes in modern form—the claim that Jews exercise hidden, disproportionate control over governments and manipulate nations against their own interests.

American support for Israel has genuine roots: shared democratic values, biblical faith among tens of millions of Christians, historical memory of the Holocaust, counterterrorism solidarity after September 11, and strategic interests in a volatile region. These factors explain the relationship without conspiracy theories.

The partnership between America and Israel is built on shared values and mutual benefit, not secret control.

The accusation that Israel controls American foreign policy is not an isolated claim; it is part of a broader pattern that runs through every lie examined in this book. Each accusation removes agency from Israel's enemies, denies moral responsibility to those who reject peace, and replaces complex reality with a simple villain. Whether the charge is war crimes, apartheid, colonialism, or hidden control, the function is the same: to delegitimize the Jewish state by portraying it as uniquely malicious, uniquely dishonest, or uniquely powerful. Together, these lies form a coherent narrative—one that explains away terrorism, excuses rejectionism, and absolves those who refuse peace of accountability. To confront these accusations is not merely to defend Israel; it is to defend truth itself against a worldview that cannot tolerate the existence of a Jewish state under any conditions. What remains is the question each reader must answer: whether these lies will continue unchallenged—or whether truth will be spoken plainly, even when it is costly.

22

Lie #17

"Israel Systematically Discriminates Against Its Arab Citizens"

This accusation portrays Israel as a state that systematically discriminates against its Arab citizens—that Israeli Arabs are second-class citizens denied equal rights, subjected to institutionalized racism comparable to the Jim Crow American South. The accusation feeds into the broader claim that Israel is fundamentally illegitimate, a racist enterprise that cannot be reformed but must be dismantled and replaced with something else entirely. If Israel oppresses even its own Arab citizens—the argument goes—then Israel's very existence is an injustice. As detailed in Chapter 7, Arab citizens vote, serve in parliament and on the Supreme Court, and participate fully in Israeli professional and civic life. The evidence of legal equality is extensive.

The reality is far more complex and far more favorable to Israel than the accusation suggests. Arab citizens of Israel have full citizenship, voting rights, and legal equality—serving in parliament, on the Supreme Court, and throughout Israeli professional life. No Arab citizen of any Arab country enjoys the political rights that Arab citizens of Israel possess.

Like every diverse society, Israel faces challenges of integration, economic disparity, and social tension. But the gap between "Israel has challenges with minority integration" and "Israel systematically discriminates against Arabs" is vast—as vast as the gap between honest analysis and propaganda designed to delegitimize.

The Legal Framework

As established in Chapter 7, Israeli law provides for full equality of all citizens regardless of religion, ethnicity, or national origin—a commitment embedded in Israel's Declaration of Independence and enforced by Israeli courts. Arab judges, including current Justice Khaled Kabub, sit on the Supreme Court bench and rule on cases affecting the entire nation.

Political Participation

Arab political participation in Israel demonstrates the falsity of the discrimination accusation more powerfully than any argument could. Arab citizens vote at high rates—often higher than minority voting rates in other democracies. Arab parties have held significant blocs in the Knesset throughout Israel's history, sometimes holding the balance of power between competing coalitions. In recent years, the Joint List—a coalition of Arab parties—has been one of the largest parties in the parliament, with fifteen seats at its peak.

In 2021, something historic happened that would be impossible in a state practicing systematic discrimination: An Arab party—Ra'am, led by Mansour Abbas—joined an Israeli governing coalition for the first time. An Arab party helped choose Israel's prime minister, participated in

"Israel Systematically Discriminates Against Its Arab Citizens"

cabinet meetings, and helped govern the country. Arab ministers served in the government, making decisions that affected all Israelis. Billions of shekels were allocated specifically to Arab community development as part of the coalition agreement. This is not what systematic discrimination looks like—this is the opposite of discrimination.[1]

Arab members of Knesset engage in the full range of political activity that characterizes healthy democracies. They propose legislation, serve on powerful committees, question ministers during Knesset sessions, and criticize government policy in the harshest possible terms—terms that would result in imprisonment, torture, or death in neighboring Arab countries. Ahmad Tibi, a long-serving Arab member of Knesset, has been one of the most vocal critics of Israeli policy for decades. He exercises his right to free speech from within the Israeli parliament, protected by Israeli law, broadcast on Israeli television, attacking the very state that guarantees his freedom to attack it.

Compare this to political participation for minorities in neighboring countries. How many Jews serve in the parliaments of Arab states? None—because there are virtually no Jews left in Arab states, having been expelled or fled persecution in the years after Israel's founding. How many Christians hold senior positions in Iran's government? None—religious minorities are systematically excluded from power. How many Sunnis held real power in Assad's Syria? How free are Copts in Egypt to criticize the government? The comparison is devastating. Israeli Arabs have political rights that minorities throughout the region can only dream of.

Professional Achievement

Chapter 7 documented Arab achievement throughout Israeli society—in medicine, academia, business, and the professions. These are not tokens but broad patterns of integration. Thousands of Arab doctors, lawyers, professors, and business owners prove through their daily work that systematic discrimination does not exist.

The Military Service Question

Critics point to the fact that most Arab citizens do not serve in the IDF as evidence of discrimination. The reality is more nuanced and actually reflects consideration for Arab citizens, not discrimination against them.

As explained in Chapter 7, Arab citizens are exempt from mandatory military service—an accommodation of their sensitivities, not discrimination against them. What deserves additional attention here is the alternative path of National Service.

Arab citizens who wish to serve in the military may do so voluntarily, and many do. Bedouin Arabs have a long and honored tradition of IDF service, with many serving in elite combat units, in tracking units that use traditional desert skills, and achieving high ranks. Druze citizens are subject to mandatory service like Jewish citizens and serve with distinction throughout the military, including at senior command levels. Christian Arabs increasingly volunteer for military service, seeing it as a path to full integration and to the benefits service provides. The door is open to all who wish to enter.[2]

National Service—civilian service as an alternative to military service—is available to Arab citizens and has become increasingly popular in recent years. Young Arab citizens serve in hospitals, schools, and social services, contributing to their communities and to Israeli society while not bearing arms. This option provides a path to the benefits associated with service without requiring military participation against potential religious or ethnic conflicts of conscience.

Yes, military service in Israel provides certain benefits—preferences for some government jobs, educational scholarships, social connections that help in civilian life. Efforts have been made to decouple these benefits from military service to avoid disadvantaging those who do not serve. The situation is imperfect—genuinely imperfect—but it is not systematic discrimination. It is a complex society working through difficult questions about citizenship, service, belonging, and the obligations that flow from membership in a political community. Where benefits are tied to service, the distinction is civic rather than ethnic—service-based benefits apply equally to all citizens who serve, regardless of background.

Real Challenges

Acknowledging that the discrimination accusation is false does not mean ignoring real challenges. Israeli Arab communities face genuine difficulties that deserve attention, resources, and serious policy effort. Honesty requires acknowledging both what is true and what is false—both the reality of legal equality and the reality of gaps that remain.

Economic gaps exist between Jewish and Arab communities. Average income in Arab towns is lower than in Jewish towns. Unemployment rates are higher in some Arab communities. These gaps reflect historical patterns, educational disparities, economic structures that have developed over decades, geographic factors, and cultural elements that affect labor force participation. They are real and deserve serious attention and sustained effort.

Infrastructure in some Arab communities has lagged behind Jewish communities. Roads, public facilities, and municipal services have sometimes been neglected or underfunded. Israeli governments have launched major initiatives to address these gaps—billions of shekels directed specifically at Arab education, infrastructure, and economic development.

HAMAN'S LIES

But progress takes time, and more remains to be done. The gaps are being addressed, but they have not been eliminated.[3]

Social tensions exist. Some Israeli Jews hold prejudiced attitudes toward Arabs; some Israeli Arabs hold prejudiced attitudes toward Jews. This is the reality of a diverse society with a history of conflict—prejudice exists in both directions, as it exists in every diverse society on earth. Neither prejudice represents official policy, and both are challenged by those committed to equality and coexistence.

These challenges are real, and they deserve serious attention. But they are challenges of integration and development—the same challenges faced by minority communities in democracies worldwide, from African Americans in the United States to North Africans in France to Turks in Germany. They are not evidence of systematic discrimination as state policy. The gap between "more needs to be done" and "Israel systematically discriminates" is the gap between honest assessment and propaganda designed to delegitimize.

The Regional Comparison

As noted in Chapter 7, the regional comparison is devastating to this accusation. Israeli Arabs have more rights, more opportunity, and more legal protection than minorities in any neighboring country—indeed, more than most citizens of those countries.

What Israeli Arabs Say

Perhaps the most telling evidence comes from Israeli Arabs themselves. Surveys consistently show that while Israeli Arabs have criticisms of Israeli policy—as do Israeli Jews—majorities prefer to remain citizens of

Israel rather than become citizens of a future Palestinian state. They would rather stay in Israel than join the country critics say would liberate them.

This preference is deeply revealing. If Israel systematically discriminated against its Arab citizens, why would they prefer Israeli citizenship? They prefer it because they know the reality of their lives—the rights they enjoy, the opportunities available, the protection of law, the freedom to speak and organize and worship. They know what they have in Israel and what they would likely have elsewhere.[4]

The Accusation Refutes Itself

The human rights organizations claiming suppression continue publishing from Israeli offices. The critics operate freely, funded often by foreign governments, protected by Israeli law, heard in Israeli courts.

The very existence of constant, vocal, well-funded criticism of Israel from within Israel proves the accusation false. Israel has the freest press in the Middle East. It has the most robust civil society in the region. Organizations like B'Tselem, Breaking the Silence, and Adalah operate openly, criticizing Israeli policies in the harshest terms, and are protected by the same legal system they criticize. The accusation is not a description of reality—it is a weapon wielded by those who enjoy the very freedoms they claim are suppressed.

This accusation endures because it offers certainty without understanding and judgment without responsibility. It replaces careful analysis with moral shorthand and rewards outrage over accuracy. But when measured against history, law, and lived reality, it cannot stand. What emerges instead is a clearer picture—one that challenges easy conclusions and demands intellectual honesty. Truth does not fear scrutiny. Lies do.

23

Lie #18

"Israel's Security Measures Are Really Designed to Oppress Palestinians"

This accusation reframes every Israeli security measure as oppression in disguise. Checkpoints are not security measures to prevent terrorism—they are deliberately designed to deprive and humiliate. The security barrier is not protection against suicide bombers—it is a land grab stealing Palestinian territory. Military operations are not counterterrorism—they are collective punishment of an innocent population. Administrative detention is not prevention of imminent attacks—it is arbitrary imprisonment designed to crush resistance. According to this narrative, security is merely a pretext, a convenient excuse for what Israel really wants: to dominate, control, and oppress Palestinians indefinitely for its own sake.

This accusation requires believing that Israel implements costly, complicated, politically damaging, diplomatically destructive security measures not because they serve security purposes but because Israel enjoys making Palestinian life difficult. It requires ignoring the terrorism that prompted these measures, the documented lives they have saved, and the adjustments Israel makes when security conditions improve. It requires a cynicism about Israeli motives that ignores all evidence and assumes malicious intent in every case.

The reality is that Israel's security measures exist because of genuine, documented, ongoing threats that have killed thousands of Israelis. When those threats diminish, measures ease. When threats increase, measures tighten. The correlation between security conditions and security measures is clear to anyone willing to examine evidence rather than assume conclusions.

The Terrorism That Prompted the Measures

Every significant Israeli security measure in the West Bank was implemented in response to specific terrorist attacks or documented patterns of attack. Understanding this history is essential to evaluating the accusation honestly. These measures did not emerge from ideology or desire to oppress—they emerged from bloodshed, from funerals, from hospital wards full of maimed survivors.

The security barrier was not built to take land or humiliate Palestinians—it was built to stop the mass murder of Israeli civilians. And it worked. After the barrier was completed in key areas, suicide bombings dropped by over 90 percent (see Lie #8). The barrier saved lives—hundreds of lives, probably thousands of lives; Israeli and Palestinian alike since violence harmed everyone.

Checkpoints exist because terrorists have used vehicles to transport explosives and weapons into Israel. Car bombs packed with nails and bolts designed to maximize casualties. Weapons smuggled to cells planning attacks. Suicide bombers transported to their targets by handlers.

"Israel's Security Measures Are Really Designed to Oppress Palestinians"

Every checkpoint searches for the next car bomb, the next weapons cache, the next suicide bomber with an explosive vest. Every checkpoint delay represents, potentially, an attack prevented and lives saved.

Administrative detention—holding suspects without public trial for limited periods—exists because some terrorist plots must be stopped before they are executed, and some evidence cannot be presented in open court without compromising intelligence sources who would then be murdered by the organizations they have infiltrated. Every democracy facing terrorism struggles with this tension between security and civil liberties. The United States used administrative detention at Guantanamo and elsewhere; the United Kingdom used it extensively in Northern Ireland. Israel is not unique in using such measures—it is unique only in the scrutiny and condemnation it receives for using them.[1]

The Costs Israel Bears

If security measures were really about oppression rather than security, why would Israel bear the enormous costs they impose? The costs make sense only if the measures serve genuine purposes—and the costs are substantial.

The security barrier cost billions of dollars to construct—over $2 billion in direct construction costs alone—and requires ongoing maintenance and staffing that costs hundreds of millions more annually. If Israel simply wanted to oppress Palestinians, there would be far cheaper ways to do so. The barrier exists because it serves a specific security function—preventing infiltration by terrorists—that Israel considered worth billions of dollars to achieve. No country spends billions for purposeless harassment.

Israeli soldiers face danger in these operations. They are shot at, attacked with explosives and firebombs, confronted with violence that sometimes proves fatal. If the purpose were merely oppression rather than security, why would Israel put its own citizens in harm's way? The danger Israeli soldiers face only makes sense if the operations serve genuine security purposes worth that risk to Israeli lives.

The Evidence of Calibration

If security measures were really about oppression, they would not vary with security conditions. An oppressor oppresses constantly, regardless of circumstances; security measures respond to threats. Israeli measures clearly respond to threats—they calibrate to security conditions in ways that make sense only if security is the actual purpose.

When violence decreases, checkpoints are reduced or removed. During periods of relative calm, many checkpoints are opened or closed entirely. Palestinians experience faster movement, easier access, and less friction in daily life. This happens because the security calculus has changed—when threats genuinely diminish, restrictions can genuinely ease. This would not happen if the purpose were oppression rather than security—an oppressor would not ease oppression simply because violence decreased.[2]

After terrorist attacks or during periods of heightened threat intelligence, checkpoints are reinforced, additional measures are implemented, and movement becomes more difficult. This is security calibration—adjusting measures to threat levels—not arbitrary oppression that would remain constant regardless of what Palestinians actually do.

The barrier's route has been adjusted multiple times in response to Israeli Supreme Court rulings that required reducing impact on Palestinian communities. Sections have been moved at great expense, routes changed through difficult terrain, and access points added. An oppressive state does not adjust its instruments of oppression in response to court rulings that favor the oppressed—a state committed to rule of law does. Israel's compliance with its own Supreme Court, often at significant cost and operational difficulty, demonstrates that law rather than oppression governs its actions.[3]

Work permits for Palestinians to enter Israel for employment fluctuate based on security assessments. During calm periods, permits are expanded dramatically and tens of thousands of Palestinians work in Israel, earning wages several times higher than available locally. During violent periods, permits are restricted.

What Oppression Would Actually Look Like

If Israel wanted to oppress Palestinians rather than protect its citizens, what would that actually look like? History and the contemporary world offer many examples of genuine oppression to serve as comparison.

- **Oppressive regimes do not adjust restrictions based on threat levels**—they maintain maximum pressure at all times because control, not security, is the goal. Israel demonstrably eases restrictions when security conditions permit, sometimes dramatically and quickly.
- **Oppressive regimes do not allow their highest courts to rule against security measures** and then comply with those rulings even when compliance is costly and difficult. Israel's Supreme Court has repeatedly ordered changes to security policies, and the government has complied—moving the barrier at the expense of billions of dollars, releasing detainees, changing procedures.
- **Oppressive regimes do not provide humanitarian aid to populations they are oppressing.** Israel coordinates the transfer of enormous quantities of goods into Gaza and the West Bank—food,

medicine, fuel, construction materials, consumer goods—even during active conflicts. Humanitarian corridors remain open during military operations. Trucks cross into Gaza even when rockets are flying in the other direction.[4]

- **Oppressive regimes do not treat enemy wounded in their hospitals.** Israeli hospitals have treated thousands of Palestinians, including from Gaza, including those wounded in conflicts. Doctors treat patients regardless of nationality or the circumstances of their injuries. Children from Gaza receive heart surgery in Israeli hospitals; cancer patients receive treatment; complex cases beyond Gaza's medical capacity are handled with sophisticated care. This is not oppression.

The gap between Israel's actual behavior and what oppression looks like is enormous. The accusation confuses security measures—which impose costs but serve legitimate purposes—with oppression, which serves no purpose but control. The confusion is either genuinely ignorant or deliberately dishonest.

The Alternative to Security Measures

Critics who accuse Israel of using security as a pretext for oppression rarely explain what alternative they propose. If checkpoints cause hardship, what should replace them? If the barrier is objectionable, how should Israel prevent suicide bombings? If administrative detention is wrong, how should Israel prevent attacks by people actively planning them?

The implied alternative is that Israel should simply accept attacks—should allow unrestricted movement and accept that some of those moving freely will murder Israeli civilians. It should remove barriers and accept that suicide bombers will again reach Israeli cities and detonate themselves in crowds. It should release all detainees and accept that some will carry out the attacks they were planning. It should absorb unlimited casualties as the price of not inconveniencing those who might murder its citizens.

No country would accept this. No government that allowed its citizens to be murdered when measures existed to prevent those murders would survive politically or morally. The primary duty of any government is to protect its citizens from violence. The accusation that security measures are really oppression offers no alternative that any responsible government could possibly adopt.

The Palestinian Authority's Role

The accusation ignores the Palestinian Authority's role in perpetuating the situation that makes security measures necessary. Under the Oslo Accords, the Palestinian Authority was supposed to provide security in areas under its control and prevent terrorism against Israel. It has failed to do so consistently—and often actively undermines security.

When the Palestinian Authority fails to prevent terrorism—or actively encourages it—Israeli security measures become more necessary, not less, yet the accusation perversely blames Israel for measures made necessary by Palestinian failure and Palestinian choice.

24

Lie #19

"Israel Suppresses Journalists and Civil Society"

This accusation portrays Israel as fundamentally hostile to press freedom and civil society—a country that suppresses journalists who cover inconvenient truths, silences critics who expose its crimes, and eliminates dissent wherever it appears. According to this narrative, Israel restricts media access to conflict zones, targets journalists covering Israeli actions, persecutes human rights organizations that document abuses, and generally behaves like authoritarian regimes that fear transparency. Israel, the accusation implies, has something terrible to hide and will silence those who try to expose it.

The reality is almost exactly opposite. Israel has the only genuinely free press environment in the region by every measure used to assess press freedom. It hosts dozens of human rights organizations—including organizations fiercely and relentlessly critical of Israeli policy—that operate openly, receive funding, publish constant condemnations, and testify before international bodies. Israeli journalists are among the most aggressive in the world in investigating their own government and military. The accusation of suppression is refuted by the very critics who make it, who operate freely in Israel while claiming to be suppressed.

Israel's Press Freedom

By every measure used to assess press freedom, Israel ranks as a free country—and by far the freest in its region, not even close to its neighbors. Freedom House, Reporters Without Borders, the Committee to Protect Journalists, and other organizations that monitor press freedom globally consistently rate Israel as having a free press, even as they rate Israel's neighbors as not free or only partly free. The gap between Israel and every neighboring country is vast and unbridgeable.[1]

Israeli media operate without government censorship of political content. Israeli newspapers publish criticism of the government daily—harsh criticism, personal attacks on leaders, exposure of scandals, demands for accountability. Israeli television broadcasts debates that would be unthinkable in neighboring countries—debates where government officials are challenged, contradicted, and ridiculed. Israeli journalists have brought down ministers, exposed corruption, forced policy changes, and challenged military decisions that the government wanted kept quiet.

Haaretz, one of Israel's major newspapers, publishes content that is among the most critical of Israeli policy anywhere in the world—more critical than much international coverage. Its columnists accuse Israel of racism, militarism, occupation, and worse. Its reporters document incidents that the government would prefer not publicized. It operates completely freely in Israel, employs Israeli journalists, is available at every newsstand, and has never been shut down, censored, or interfered with by any government. If Israel suppressed critical journalism, Haaretz would not exist—yet it thrives, it provokes, and it publishes daily.

"Israel Suppresses Journalists and Civil Society"

Foreign journalists operate extensively in Israel and the Palestinian territories without meaningful restriction. Major international outlets—*The New York Times*, BBC, CNN, Reuters, *The Guardian*, *Al Jazeera*, and dozens of others—maintain bureaus, employ correspondents, and report freely. They cover conflicts, interview critics, photograph controversial incidents, and publish reports that Israeli officials often find deeply unflattering.

We would add one point for clarification: Israel's international press freedom rankings have been lowered over the last two years due to restrictions tied primarily to national security concerns rather than broad suppression of dissent or opposition journalism. Israel operates under a unique and persistent security environment, including active military conflict, terrorism threats, and compulsory military service.

As a result, certain press restrictions—most notably military censorship laws inherited from the British Mandate period—remain in force. These regulations allow the military censor to restrict publication of specific information deemed to pose an immediate risk to national security, such as troop movements, intelligence operations, or classified capabilities. Most free nations have the ability to limit press access during wartime conditions.

Critics argue these measures can chill reporting, while defenders note that Israeli media regularly challenge the government, publish leaks, and litigate censorship decisions in court. Unlike authoritarian systems, such restrictions are narrowly scoped, legally reviewable, and coexist with a pluralistic and adversarial media culture.

The Regional Comparison

The accusation that Israel suppresses journalists becomes absurd when compared to what happens to journalists elsewhere in the region.

In Iran, journalists are imprisoned routinely for criticizing the government. Reporters have been executed for their work. International journalists are arrested, held hostage, and used as bargaining chips in negotiations. The entire media landscape is controlled by the state, and any deviation from the official line brings severe consequences. Wards in Evin Prison are filled with journalists whose crime was telling the truth.[2]

In Saudi Arabia, a journalist—Jamal Khashoggi—was murdered and dismembered inside a Saudi consulate for his critical writing. Other Saudi journalists have been imprisoned, tortured, and disappeared. The media operates under strict government control with no tolerance for dissent of any kind. Criticizing the royal family can result in imprisonment or death.

In Egypt, journalists are arrested, beaten, imprisoned, and disappeared. Al Jazeera journalists were imprisoned for years on fabricated charges. Independent media has been largely eliminated through a combination of legal pressure, arrest, and intimidation. Coverage of sensitive topics can result in lengthy prison sentences.

In the Palestinian territories—supposedly the beneficiaries of concern about press freedom—journalists who criticize Hamas or the Palestinian Authority face arrest, torture, and worse. Palestinian authorities have murdered Palestinian journalists. The Committee to Protect Journalists and Reporters Without Borders have documented systematic suppression of press freedom under both Hamas and the Palestinian Authority.[3]

Civil Society Organizations

Israel hosts a vibrant civil society that includes dozens of organizations dedicated to monitoring and criticizing Israeli policy—often in the harshest terms imaginable. These organizations operate freely, publish regular reports that receive international attention, testify before international bodies against Israel, and advocate for policy changes. Their very existence and flourishing refutes the accusation of suppression more powerfully than any argument could.

B'Tselem, the Israeli Information Center for Human Rights in the Occupied Territories, publishes constant criticism of Israeli policy. It documents incidents it considers violations, provides information to international organizations and media, and advocates internationally for changes to Israeli practices. It operates legally and openly from offices in Israel, employs Israeli staff, and has never been shut down or meaningfully restricted.[4]

Breaking the Silence collects and publishes testimonies from Israeli soldiers about their service in the Palestinian territories, often testimonies that portray Israeli actions in an extremely negative light. It organizes tours, publishes reports, cooperates with international media seeking critical stories, and testifies before foreign governments. It is controversial in Israel—many Israelis criticize it harshly—but it operates freely under Israeli law, protected by the same legal system it criticizes.

Adalah, the Legal Center for Arab Minority Rights in Israel, litigates cases challenging Israeli policies it considers discriminatory. It has won cases in Israeli courts, including the Supreme Court, forcing policy changes. It advocates for Arab citizens before international bodies and publishes reports critical of Israeli law and practice.

Numerous other organizations operate throughout the country, monitoring, criticizing, and challenging Israeli policies continuously. Many receive funding from European governments and international foundations specifically to criticize Israel. They are not suppressed—they are part of Israeli public discourse, heard and argued with rather than silenced.

The Transparency Law

Critics point to Israeli legislation requiring certain NGOs to disclose foreign government funding as evidence of suppression. This characterization dramatically misrepresents both the law and its actual effects.

The law, passed in 2016, requires organizations that receive more than half their funding from foreign governments to disclose this fact in their publications and when appearing before the Knesset. It does not prohibit the funding. It does not restrict the organizations' activities in any way. It requires transparency about funding sources—nothing more.

Similar transparency requirements exist in many democracies and are considered normal good governance. The United States' Foreign Agent Registration Act requires disclosure of activities on behalf of foreign governments and is far more restrictive than Israel's law. Other democracies have comparable requirements. The principle that the public should know who funds political advocacy is widely accepted and is not suppression.

The organizations affected by this law continue to operate freely. B'Tselem still publishes. Breaking the Silence still testifies. Adalah still litigates and wins cases. The disclosure requirement has not suppressed their activities in any meaningful way—it has required them to be transparent about funding that critics believe creates conflicts of interest. People of differing opinions can debate whether the law is good policy, but calling it suppression dramatically overstates its effects.[5]

Journalists in Conflict Zones

A specific version of the accusation focuses on journalists killed or injured while covering conflicts between Israel and Hamas or other armed groups. Critics claim Israel deliberately targets journalists, using tragic deaths as evidence of intentional suppression.

The reality is more complicated than the accusation allows. Conflict zones are inherently dangerous for everyone, including journalists who choose to cover them. In urban warfare—particularly against an enemy that deliberately operates from within civilian areas, uses civilian infrastructure, and does not wear distinguishing uniforms—tragic accidents occur despite precautions. Journalists who embed with armed groups, who approach active combat areas, who seek to cover ongoing operations take serious personal risks.

In some documented cases, individuals described as journalists were also affiliated with terrorist organizations—Hamas uses journalist credentials as cover for operatives engaged in military activities. This does not mean every journalist death is justified, but it complicates assessments of who is a protected journalist and who is a legitimate military target operating under false pretenses.[6]

Israel investigates journalist deaths and has faced criticism where investigations found problems. This accountability, imperfect though it may be, is itself evidence that Israel does not have a policy of targeting journalists. A state that deliberately targeted journalists would not investigate such deaths or acknowledge wrongdoing when found.

The Irony of the Accusation

There is deep irony in the accusation that Israel suppresses journalists and civil society. The accusation is typically made by journalists operating freely in Israel and by civil society organizations that publish from Israeli offices without any interference whatsoever.

The reports documenting alleged Israeli suppression are published openly in Israel. The human rights organizations claiming to be suppressed continue operating, funding staff, and publishing criticisms. If the accusation were true, making it would be impossible—yet it is made constantly, loudly, and freely.

Palestinian Press Freedom

Those accusing Israel of suppressing journalists rarely focus on Palestinian press freedom—which is far more restricted than Israeli press freedom by any measure.

Hamas does not tolerate critical journalism in Gaza. Journalists who report unfavorably on Hamas face arrest, beating, and worse. Foreign journalists operating in Gaza do so with Hamas minders watching and under implicit threat—coverage that Hamas considers unfavorable can have severe consequences. The result is coverage that reflects Hamas narratives because independent coverage is too dangerous.

The Palestinian Authority has arrested and detained journalists who criticize it. Palestinian journalists have reported being threatened, intimidated, and physically assaulted for critical coverage.[7]

The contrast is instructive: Journalists can criticize Israel from Israel freely, protected by Israeli law. They cannot criticize Palestinian authorities from Palestinian-controlled areas safely. Yet the accusation of press suppression is directed at Israel, not at the Palestinian authorities that actually suppress journalists covering them.

25

Lie #20

"Israel Fabricates or Exaggerates Security Threats to Justify Its Policies"

This accusation suggests that Israel manufactures threats to justify its existence, its policies, and its military actions. Palestinian terrorism is exaggerated or even fabricated. Iran's nuclear program is not really a threat—*Israeli hysteria inflates a manageable situation into an existential crisis*. Hamas's ideology is misrepresented to make a legitimate resistance movement look like a terrorist organization. Hezbollah's arsenal is overstated to justify Israeli aggression. According to this narrative, Israel uses invented or deliberately inflated threats to maintain a permanent state of emergency, justify excessive military spending, manipulate international opinion, and deflect attention from its real agenda of expansion and oppression.

This accusation requires denying documented reality—reality recorded in bodies, in hospital records, in rocket impact sites, in the testimony of survivors, in the statements of Israel's enemies themselves. The threats Israel faces are not fabricated—they are verified, documented, and undeniable to anyone willing to look at evidence. Thousands of rockets have fallen on Israeli territory, tracked by radar, and captured on video. Suicide bombers have murdered over a thousand Israeli civilians in attacks claimed proudly by the organizations that sent them. Iranian leaders have explicitly and repeatedly called for Israel's destruction in statements broadcast worldwide. Hamas's founding charter calls for the elimination of the Jewish state in language anyone can read. These are not Israeli inventions—they are facts that anyone can verify independently.

The accusation reveals more about those who make it than about Israel. Denying threats that have killed thousands is not healthy skepticism—it is denial of reality in service of ideology, a refusal to see what is plainly visible.

The Documented Reality of Terrorism

Palestinian terrorism against Israel is not alleged or claimed—it is documented in excruciating detail that anyone can verify. Every attack is recorded in police files. Every victim is named and mourned. Every method is cataloged by security services. The terrorist organizations themselves claim credit for attacks, issue statements explaining their motivations, and celebrate their "martyrs" publicly. This is not Israeli propaganda; it is historical record created largely by the perpetrators themselves.

The Second Intifada's toll—over 140 suicide bombings, more than a thousand Israeli deaths (see Lie #8 for full documentation)—is not alleged but meticulously recorded by police, media, and the terrorist organizations themselves.

Hamas, Palestinian Islamic Jihad, and other organizations have fired over twenty thousand rockets and mortars at Israeli territory since 2001.

"Israel Fabricates or Exaggerates Security Threats to Justify Its Policies"

These rockets are physical objects that can be counted, photographed, traced to their launch sites, and analyzed for their components. Many have been recovered and displayed to international observers. The launches are detected by radar systems operated by multiple countries, recorded by satellites, tracked in real time, and often filmed by journalists and civilians who share video instantly worldwide. This is not exaggeration—it is documented, verified, observable fact.[1]

On October 7, 2023, Hamas launched the largest terrorist attack in Israel's history—an attack documented in extraordinary detail because the perpetrators filmed themselves committing atrocities and shared the footage proudly. Over 1,200 people were murdered in a single day. This is not Israeli fabrication; it is Hamas documentation of Hamas atrocities.

The Iranian Threat

Critics claim Israel exaggerates the threat from Iran to justify military preparations, to manipulate American foreign policy, and to distract from its treatment of Palestinians. The documented evidence tells a completely different story.

Iranian leaders have explicitly and repeatedly called for Israel's destruction—not in private conversations that Israel has allegedly intercepted, but in public speeches broadcast worldwide. Supreme Leader Khamenei has called Israel a "cancerous tumor" that must be eliminated. Former President Ahmadinejad said Israel should be "wiped off the map"—and while the precise translation has been debated, the intent was unmistakably clear. These statements are public, recorded, translated by multiple independent sources, and available for anyone to review. Israel did not fabricate them; Iranian leaders said them publicly.[2]

The International Atomic Energy Agency documents Iran's nuclear program—an independent international organization, not an Israeli intelligence service. The International Atomic Energy Agency (IAEA) has repeatedly found Iran in violation of its nuclear agreements, has documented undeclared nuclear activities, has expressed concern about possible military dimensions to Iran's program, and has struggled to gain access to sites where suspicious activities have been detected.[3]

Iran funds, arms, and trains Hamas and Hezbollah—terrorist organizations dedicated to Israel's destruction. This support is not disputed; it is acknowledged by Iran, by Hamas, and by Hezbollah as a matter of pride. Iranian weapons are found in Gaza after conflicts—rockets, missiles, and military equipment traced to Iranian manufacture. Iranian advisers work with these organizations openly. Iranian officials meet with terrorist leaders publicly. This is not Israeli accusation but Iranian policy, proclaimed rather than hidden.

In April 2024, Iran conducted a direct military attack on Israel, launching over 300 drones and missiles at Israeli territory. These attacks were witnessed by the entire world, tracked by radar systems of multiple countries, confirmed by Iran itself, and defended against with international cooperation. Israel did not need to fabricate an Iranian threat when Iran demonstrated it openly, unmistakably, and on camera.

Hamas and Hezbollah

The accusation often suggests that Israel misrepresents Hamas and Hezbollah—that these organizations are legitimate resistance movements rather than terrorist groups, and that Israel exaggerates their threat to justify its actions against them.

Hamas's founding charter—its own document, written by Hamas, published by Hamas, available for anyone to read—explicitly calls for the destruction of Israel and contains antisemitic passages citing *The Protocols of the Elders of Zion*. The charter calls for jihad against Jews, not just

"Israel Fabricates or Exaggerates Security Threats to Justify Its Policies"

against Israel or Zionism specifically. Hamas has never fully renounced this document despite occasional tactical statements for Western audiences. Its ideology is not Israeli characterization—it is Hamas's own stated position in its own foundational document.[4]

Hezbollah's leader, Hassan Nasrallah, made clear statements about his organization's goals before his death—statements recorded on video, broadcast throughout the Arab world, and translated independently. He called for Israel's destruction and expressed antisemitic views that would be recognized as such in any context. Hezbollah's arsenal—estimated at over 150,000 rockets and missiles pointed at Israel, far more than most national armies possess—is documented by multiple intelligence services worldwide and proudly acknowledged by Hezbollah itself as evidence of its power.

The United States, the European Union, Canada, Australia, and numerous other governments independently designate Hamas and Hezbollah as terrorist organizations based on their own assessments, their own intelligence, their own analysis of these groups' actions and statements. This is not solely an Israeli position; it is the consensus of many democratic governments.[5]

The Threats Israel Did Not See Coming

If Israel fabricated threats, one would expect Israeli intelligence to consistently overstate dangers and predict attacks that never materialize—to cry wolf repeatedly about threats that prove imaginary. The historical record shows precisely the opposite: Israel has repeatedly been surprised by attacks it did not anticipate and failed to adequately prepare for.

On October 7, 2023, Israeli intelligence catastrophically failed to anticipate Hamas's massive, coordinated attack despite warning signs that, in retrospect, should have been recognized. The intelligence community did not predict the scale, timing, or methodology of what became the deadliest day in Israeli history. If Israel fabricated threats to justify its policies, surely its intelligence services would have exaggerated warnings about Gaza; instead, they dramatically underestimated a real threat that killed over 1,200 people.

These failures demonstrate that Israeli threat assessment is imperfect and sometimes dangerously wrong—but wrong in the direction of underestimating threats rather than fabricating them. A country that fabricated threats would not be caught by surprise; Israel has been surprised, with devastating consequences.

"False Flag" Conspiracies

No discussion of fabricated or exaggerated threats is complete without mentioning one of the most grotesque claims circulating after October 7—the allegation that Israel itself orchestrated, allowed, or staged the massacre as a "false flag." This theory collapses under even the most superficial examination.

Hamas filmed its own atrocities in real time—body-camera footage, livestreamed executions, hours of video proudly posted by the perpetrators themselves. Thousands of Israeli civilians were murdered in broad daylight, in multiple locations, by attackers whose identities, movements, and communications are documented on video, cell-site data, forensic evidence, eyewitness testimony, intercepted calls, and Hamas's own public statements.

Israel's military and intelligence establishment suffered one of the most humiliating failures in its history that day; no nation engineers its own worst disaster, its own deadliest day, and its own global disgrace. "False flag" claims require the listener to ignore the perpetrators, ignore the evidence, and ignore the basic logic of human behavior.[6]

"Israel Fabricates or Exaggerates Security Threats to Justify Its Policies"

Why the Accusation Persists

If the threats Israel faces are so obviously real and documented, why does the accusation of fabrication persist? Several factors explain its endurance despite its falsehood.

First, acknowledging the threats would require acknowledging Israel's right to respond to them. If Hamas is a genuine terrorist threat, Israel's operations against Hamas become more defensible. If Iran genuinely seeks Israel's destruction, Israeli concerns about Iran's nuclear program become more reasonable. Denying threats allows critics to deny the legitimacy of Israeli responses to those threats—to treat Israeli self-defense as aggression.

Second, some critics apply different evidentiary standards to Israel than to any other country. When Israel describes a threat, skepticism is automatic and evidence is dismissed; when Israel's enemies describe their intentions, they are not taken at their word or their statements are explained away. This double standard—believing critics of Israel while disbelieving Israel—produces systematically biased conclusions.

Third, distance and safety make threats seem abstract to those who do not face them. People who have never lived under rocket fire, never experienced suicide bombing campaigns, never sent children to school wondering if the bus would explode can easily dismiss threats as exaggerated. What feels urgent and terrifying to Israelis who have buried children murdered by terrorists seems distant and theoretical to those who live in safety.

The Evidence Standard

Those who accuse Israel of fabricating threats should ask themselves honestly: What evidence would convince them the threats are real?

HAMAN'S LIES

If 1,200 murdered on a single day does not demonstrate a threat, what number would? If twenty thousand rockets falling on civilian areas does not demonstrate a threat, what weapon would? If explicit statements by national leaders calling for Israel's destruction do not demonstrate a threat, what language would? If a nuclear weapons program pursued by a regime pledging Israel's elimination does not demonstrate a threat, what capability would?

If no evidence could establish that the threats are real, then the accusation of fabrication is unfalsifiable—it cannot be disproven because no evidence would be accepted regardless of how overwhelming. This is not rational analysis subject to evidence; it is ideological commitment impervious to facts.

26

Lie #21

"Israel Controls Water Resources Unfairly"

This accusation paints Israel as a water thief, stealing this precious resource from Palestinians to irrigate Jewish settlements while Palestinian children go thirsty. According to this narrative, Israel controls aquifers, restricts Palestinian access to water, and uses resource control as a weapon of oppression. Palestinians suffer shortages while Israelis enjoy swimming pools and lush gardens.

The reality is far more complicated—and far more favorable to Israel—than the accusation suggests. Israel has actually increased Palestinian water access dramatically, shares water beyond its legal obligations, has developed revolutionary water technology that benefits the entire region, and works cooperatively on water issues even amid political conflict. The water shortages that do exist in Palestinian areas result primarily from Palestinian Authority mismanagement, not Israeli restriction.

The Legal Framework

Water allocation between Israel and the Palestinian Authority is governed by the Oslo II Accord of 1995 (for broader Oslo context, see Chapter 20)—an agreement negotiated and signed by both parties. This agreement established specific allocations from shared aquifers and created a Joint Water Committee to manage water resources cooperatively. Israel has consistently met and exceeded its obligations under this agreement, providing more water to Palestinians than the agreement requires.

Under Oslo II, Israel agreed to provide specific quantities of water—and has consistently exceeded those allocations, as documented by Israeli, Palestinian, and international records.[1]

The agreement also established that final water arrangements would be negotiated as part of permanent status talks. Those talks have never concluded because Palestinian leadership has repeatedly rejected comprehensive peace offers, leaving interim water arrangements in place.

Israel's Water Innovation

Israel has transformed itself from a water-scarce country into a country with a net reliable water surplus through technological innovation that has revolutionized water management worldwide. This transformation benefits not only Israel but also Palestinians and the entire region.

Drip irrigation—invented in Israel—has transformed agriculture worldwide by delivering water directly to plant roots with minimal waste. This technology, developed at Kibbutz Hatzerim and commercialized globally, has enabled farming in arid regions throughout the world. It reduces water consumption dramatically while increasing crop yields. Israeli companies have shared this technology internationally, including with Palestinian farmers who benefit from higher yields with less water.[2]

Desalination technology developed in Israel has made the country independent of rainfall for its drinking water supply. Israel now produces more fresh water from desalination than it consumes from natural sources—a remarkable achievement for a country in one of the world's most water-stressed regions. Israeli desalination plants produce water at costs that were unimaginable a generation ago, making the technology viable for countries worldwide.[3]

Water recycling in Israel leads the world—over 85 percent of wastewater is treated and reused, primarily for agriculture. This is more than four times the rate of any other country. The technology and expertise Israel has developed in water recycling is shared internationally and could transform water management in Palestinian areas if Palestinian authorities chose to implement it.[4]

Israel sells water to Jordan under a peace agreement and provides water to Palestinian areas beyond its Oslo obligations. A country using water as a weapon of oppression would not develop technology that creates abundance; it would hoard scarcity. Israel's massive investment in water technology proves its interest is in solving water challenges, not exploiting them.

Water Provided to Palestinians

The amount of water Israel provides to Palestinian areas has increased dramatically since the Oslo Accords—the opposite of what the accusation implies. This increase is documented and verifiable through official records.

In 1967, when Israel took control of the West Bank, Palestinian water consumption was approximately sixty million cubic meters annually. Today, Palestinians receive over two hundred million cubic meters annually—more than a threefold increase. This increase has occurred even as final-status negotiations have stalled, with Israel expanding water provision unilaterally to address Palestinian needs.

Mekorot, Israel's national water company, supplies water directly to Palestinian communities throughout the West Bank. This water is sold at the same price Mekorot charges Israeli communities—there is no discriminatory pricing. Palestinian municipalities receive reliable water supply from Israeli infrastructure even when political relations are tense or hostile.

Israel has connected Palestinian communities to its water grid that were never connected before, extending infrastructure into areas that lacked reliable water supply. This expansion of service is ongoing and continues regardless of the political situation. A country using water as a weapon would not extend water infrastructure to the population it supposedly wants to deprive.[5]

Palestinian Authority Mismanagement

Where water shortages exist in Palestinian areas—and they do exist—the primary cause is Palestinian Authority mismanagement, not Israeli restriction. This is documented by international organizations and evident from the data on water loss and infrastructure investment.

The Palestinian water system loses approximately 33 percent of its water to leaks and theft—one of the highest loss rates in the world. Aging pipes, poorly maintained infrastructure, and illegal connections drain water that never reaches consumers. By comparison, Israel's water loss rate is approximately 10 percent. The difference represents hundreds of millions of cubic meters of water lost annually to mismanagement rather than Israeli restriction.[6]

The Palestinian Authority has failed to build wastewater treatment facilities that would allow water recycling like Israel practices. International donors have offered hundreds of millions of dollars for such facilities; the Palestinian Authority has failed to implement the projects. Sewage flows untreated into the environment, wasting water that could be recycled and contaminating aquifers that provide drinking water.

The Joint Water Committee established under Oslo requires both Israeli and Palestinian approval for new water projects. For years, the Palestinian Authority refused to convene the committee, blocking projects that would have increased Palestinian water supply. When the Palestinian Authority boycotts institutions it agreed to participate in, and water projects consequently stall, blaming Israel for the resulting shortages is misleading.

The Gaza Situation

Gaza faces a genuine water crisis—but its causes lie with Hamas governance and geographic reality, not Israeli malice. Gaza's coastal aquifer—its primary natural water source—has been devastated by over-pumping and contamination. Palestinians in Gaza have extracted water far beyond sustainable rates for decades, causing saltwater intrusion that has made most of the aquifer undrinkable.

Sewage contamination—from untreated wastewater that Hamas has failed to manage—has further polluted Gaza's groundwater. Treatment facilities exist but are poorly maintained. Raw sewage flows into the aquifer. This contamination is entirely under Hamas control; Israel has no role in Gaza's internal sewage management.

Despite hostility from Hamas—despite rockets fired at Israeli cities—Israel continues to supply water to Gaza and has increased that supply over time. Israel also provides electricity that powers Gaza's water pumps and treatment facilities. A country using water as a weapon would cut supply to a hostile territory; Israel maintains and increases it.

International donors have funded desalination projects for Gaza that could solve its water crisis. These projects have been delayed by Hamas priorities, by conflict, by Hamas's diversion of construction materials to military purposes rather than civilian infrastructure. Gaza could have abundant water; Hamas has chosen otherwise.[7]

Cooperation Despite Conflict

Perhaps the strongest refutation of the accusation is the ongoing cooperation on water issues that continues even during periods of intense conflict. Water professionals from Israel and the Palestinian Authority work together on technical issues, share data, coordinate infrastructure, and solve problems cooperatively. This cooperation persists because both sides recognize that water challenges require cooperation regardless of political disagreements.

Israeli and Palestinian water engineers meet regularly to coordinate supply, address emergencies, and plan infrastructure. These meetings continue even when political negotiations have collapsed, even during military operations, even when relations are at their most hostile. Water is treated as a shared challenge requiring shared solutions—the opposite of water as a weapon.

When pipes break or pumps fail in Palestinian areas, Israeli technicians often assist with repairs. This practical cooperation continues quietly while accusations of water theft circulate loudly. The professionals who actually manage water know the accusations are false; they work together daily.

The Regional Comparison

Palestinians have better access to water than populations in many neighboring countries—a fact that demolishes the accusation of deliberate deprivation. The comparison is instructive.

Jordan—at peace with Israel and facing no accusations of water theft—has lower per capita water availability than Palestinian areas. Jordanians receive less water than Palestinians, yet Jordan is not accused of oppressing its own people. The disparity reveals that the accusation against Israel is political rather than based on actual water availability.

Syria's water infrastructure has been devastated by civil war, leaving millions without reliable access. **Iraq's** water systems have deteriorated dramatically. **Yemen** faces catastrophic water shortages that receive minimal international attention.[8]

The Accusation's Purpose

The water accusation serves propaganda purposes regardless of its falsehood. It transforms Israel into a villain depriving innocents of life's most basic necessity. It creates emotional response that bypasses rational analysis. It fits into a broader narrative of Israeli oppression that delegitimizes Israel's existence.

The accusation also deflects responsibility from Palestinian leadership. If Israel is blamed for water shortages, Palestinian Authority mismanagement escapes scrutiny. If Israel is the oppressor, Palestinian leaders are absolved of their failures to invest in infrastructure, maintain systems, or implement projects that donors have funded. The accusation serves Palestinian leaders who prefer blaming Israel to addressing their own failures.

27

Lie #22

"Israel Assassinates Political Leaders and Scientists Abroad"

This accusation frames Israel as a rogue state that murders people around the world—assassinating political leaders, killing scientists, operating death squads that strike wherever Israel's enemies are found. According to this narrative, Israel ignores international law, violates the sovereignty of other nations, and kills people without trial or due process. The Mossad becomes a sinister force reaching anywhere on earth to eliminate those Israel has decided must die. Israel, the accusation implies, is a lawless state that murders at will.

The accusation conflates fundamentally different categories: targeted operations against terrorists actively planning mass murder, actions against individuals developing weapons intended for Israel's destruction, and the assassination of legitimate political figures. It treats all Israeli actions abroad as equivalent and equally illegitimate, ignoring the crucial distinctions that international law and basic morality recognize between targeting terrorist masterminds and murdering innocents.

The reality is that Israel conducts targeted operations against specific individuals who pose genuine, documented, imminent threats—terrorists who have killed or are actively planning to kill, and scientists working on weapons programs explicitly designed to destroy Israel. These operations are not assassination for political purposes; they are acts of self-defense against those who have declared war on the Jewish people and are actively working toward Jewish annihilation.

The Distinction That Matters

International law and moral philosophy recognize a fundamental distinction between assassination—the murder of political figures for political purposes—and targeted killing of combatants in armed conflict.

Assassination typically refers to killing political leaders to change political outcomes—murdering a president to install a different government, killing a prime minister to alter policy. Such killings are generally prohibited because they target people for their political roles rather than their participation in armed conflict. Political opposition does not make someone a legitimate military target.

Targeted killing of combatants is fundamentally different. International humanitarian law permits the targeting of combatants in armed conflict—individuals who are actively participating in hostilities, planning attacks, or commanding forces at war. A military commander can be targeted regardless of where he is located. A terrorist planner can be targeted because he is engaged in warfare, not because of his political views.

Israel does not target people for their political opposition to Israel. It targets terrorist leaders who have planned and ordered attacks that have killed Israeli civilians—attacks these leaders proudly claim and promise to repeat. It targets individuals working to develop weapons of mass destruction specifically intended to annihilate the Jewish state. These are not political assassinations; they are military operations against combatants in an ongoing conflict.[1]

Terrorists Targeted

The terrorist leaders Israel has targeted were not politicians peacefully advocating for their cause. They were commanders of organizations at war with Israel, personally responsible for ordering attacks that killed hundreds or thousands of civilians. Understanding who these individuals were reveals the absurdity of calling their deaths "assassinations" in the political sense.

Ahmed Yassin, founder and spiritual leader of Hamas, was killed in 2004. He was not a politician—he was the head of a terrorist organization that had sent dozens of suicide bombers into Israeli cities, killing hundreds of civilians in buses, restaurants, and shopping centers. He personally authorized attacks and blessed suicide bombers before their missions—making him a military commander in an organization at war, not a political figure assassinated for his beliefs.[2]

Yahya Sinwar, Hamas leader in Gaza and architect of the October 7, 2023, massacre that killed over 1,200 Israelis, was one of the most wanted terrorists in the world. He planned and ordered the largest terrorist attack in Israeli history—an attack documented in horrifying detail by the perpetrators themselves. Targeting Sinwar was not assassination; it was pursuit of a mass murderer who promised to repeat his crimes.

Hassan Nasrallah, Hezbollah's leader for over three decades, commanded an organization with over 150,000 rockets aimed at Israeli cities. He explicitly called for Israel's destruction and the killing of Jews worldwide. Under his command, Hezbollah conducted terrorist attacks across multiple continents, killing hundreds. He was a military commander of an organization at war, armed with an arsenal larger than most national armies possess.

These individuals were not killed for opposing Israel politically. They were killed because they commanded military forces actively engaged in killing Israelis and planning to kill more. Calling their deaths assassinations applies a term that implies illegitimacy to actions that international law permits against military commanders in armed conflict.

The Iranian Nuclear Program

The accusation often focuses on Iranian nuclear scientists—individuals killed in incidents attributed to Israel, though Israel has not officially confirmed responsibility. These scientists were working on a program explicitly intended to develop weapons capable of annihilating Israel, led by a regime that has repeatedly called for Israel's destruction.

Iran's nuclear program is not peaceful energy development—it is a weapons program designed to produce nuclear bombs. The IAEA has documented undeclared nuclear activities, hidden facilities, and research with no civilian application. Iranian leaders have explicitly stated their desire to destroy Israel; the nuclear program is the means to make that destruction possible.

The scientists working on this program were not innocent civilians. They were military personnel—often holding military ranks—working on weapons specifically intended to kill millions of Jews. They knew what they were building and for whom. They were participants in a program of potential genocide, not neutral academics pursuing knowledge.[3]

If a nation announces its intention to destroy another nation and actively develops weapons to accomplish that destruction, does the targeted nation have the right to act in self-defense? Must Israel wait until nuclear weapons are complete and launched before it may respond? The logic of the accusation requires Israel to accept annihilation rather than act to prevent it.

"Israel Assassinates Political Leaders and Scientists Abroad"

What Other Nations Do

Israel is hardly unique in conducting targeted operations against terrorists and military threats abroad. The United States, the United Kingdom, Russia, and numerous other nations conduct similar operations—yet only Israel faces condemnation framed as accusation of illegitimate assassination.

The United States killed Osama bin Laden in Pakistan in 2011—a targeted operation in another country's territory against a terrorist leader. It killed Qasem Soleimani, commander of Iran's Quds Force, in Iraq in 2020. It has conducted hundreds of drone strikes against terrorist targets in multiple countries. American operations receive debate, but they are not generally characterized as illegitimate assassination the way Israeli operations are.[4]

The United Kingdom killed ISIS terrorists through drone strikes. France has conducted operations against terrorists in Africa. Russia conducts operations against those it considers threats. Every major power reserves the right to act against imminent threats beyond its borders—yet Israel alone is characterized as a rogue state for doing so.

The double standard is revealing. When America kills bin Laden, it is celebrated as justice. When Israel kills terrorists, it is condemned as assassination. The selective outrage reveals that something other than principled objection to targeted killing drives the accusation against Israel.

The Alternative

Critics who condemn Israeli targeted operations rarely explain what alternative they propose. When terrorist leaders sit safely in other countries planning attacks on Israeli civilians, what should Israel do?

Arrest is often impossible—the terrorists operate in hostile territories or failed states where no functioning legal system exists to arrest and try them. Hamas leaders operated from Gaza under Hamas control, or from Qatar, which refuses to extradite them. Hezbollah leaders operated from Lebanon, where Hezbollah is more powerful than the state. Iranian scientists work under the protection of the Iranian regime. No legal process exists to bring these individuals to justice.

Waiting for attacks means accepting that Israelis will die. Terrorist leaders who have ordered previous attacks and promise future attacks will fulfill their promises if given the opportunity. Every month of inaction is a month for planning, recruiting, training, and eventually executing attacks that kill civilians.

The alternative the critics imply is that Israel should simply accept terrorism—should allow those planning its citizens' murder to plan in safety, should permit weapons programs designed to annihilate it to proceed unimpeded, should absorb whatever attacks come and respond only after the bodies are counted. No nation accepts this, and no nation should.

Precision and Restraint

Israeli targeted operations are characterized by precision and restraint that distinguish them from both terrorism and indiscriminate military action. Israel invests enormous resources in intelligence to identify specific individuals, track their movements, and strike when civilian casualties can be minimized.

Operations are called off when civilians are unexpectedly present. Strikes are timed to minimize collateral damage. Weapons are chosen for their precision rather than their destructive power. This care costs time, money, and sometimes allows targets to escape—but Israel maintains these standards because it values civilian life even when operating against those who deliberately target civilians.

Compare this to Israel's enemies. Hamas deliberately targets civilians—the more the better. Iranian-backed militias launch rockets at cities without any pretense of targeting military objectives. Hezbollah fills its rockets with ball bearings designed to maximize civilian casualties.

Historical Justice

Some Israeli operations have targeted individuals responsible for historical atrocities against Jews—most famously the capture of Adolf Eichmann, architect of the Holocaust's logistics, who was living safely in Argentina. Eichmann was brought to Israel for trial, convicted, and executed—the *only* execution in Israeli history. Was this an illegitimate assassination or the pursuit of justice against a mass murderer who had escaped punishment?

After the Munich Olympics massacre in 1972, when Palestinian terrorists murdered eleven Israeli athletes, Israel pursued and killed those responsible over subsequent years. These were not political leaders assassinated for their views—they were terrorists who had personally participated in murdering bound and helpless athletes, broadcast their crimes to the world, and escaped to safety in countries that refused to extradite them. Pursuing them was justice, not assassination.[5]

When legal systems fail—when murderers escape to safety, when host countries refuse to act, when justice is unavailable through normal channels—does justice become impossible? The accusation implies that once terrorists reach a safe haven, their crimes must go unpunished and their future crimes must be permitted. This is not a moral position; it is an abdication of responsibility.

28

Lie #23

"Israel Uses Collective Punishment"

This accusation charges Israel with punishing populations for the actions of individuals—demolishing the family homes of terrorists, restricting movement for whole communities after attacks, maintaining a blockade on Gaza that affects all residents rather than only Hamas fighters. According to this narrative, Israel deliberately inflicts suffering on innocents to deter terrorism.

The accusation conflates fundamentally different concepts: punitive measures intended to harm innocents for the acts of others, and security measures that unavoidably affect broader populations while targeting genuine threats.

The reality is that Israel's measures target genuine security threats and are calibrated to minimize impact on uninvolved populations while achieving necessary security objectives. Where broader effects occur, they often result from the nature of the threat and the tactics of Israel's enemies—particularly the deliberate embedding of military operations within civilian populations.

What Collective Punishment Means

International humanitarian law prohibits collective punishment—the infliction of penalties on people for offenses they did not personally commit. The prohibition emerged from historical atrocities where occupying powers punished entire populations—massacring entire villages or starving civilians—not for individual acts, but for group identity.

The prohibition does not mean that security measures are unlawful whenever they affect people beyond their immediate targets. A curfew imposed during active military operations affects everyone in the area, not just combatants—but it is not collective punishment if its purpose is operational security rather than punishment of a population. A checkpoint that slows everyone's movement to screen for terrorists affects innocent travelers—but screening is not punishment.

The distinction matters: *Collective punishment requires punitive intent toward a group for acts of some members.* Security measures that incidentally affect broader populations while addressing genuine threats are not collective punishment even when they impose hardship. Critics of Israel collapse this distinction deliberately, characterizing any measure with broad effects as collective punishment regardless of purpose or justification.[1]

House Demolitions

The accusation frequently cites Israel's practice of demolishing the homes of terrorists who have killed Israelis. Critics call this collective punishment because family members lose their homes for acts they did not personally commit. The practice is controversial and deserves serious examination rather than reflexive condemnation.

The purpose of demolitions is deterrence, not punishment. Studies have shown that the practice reduces terrorism by changing the calculus for potential attackers who might be willing to sacrifice their own lives but hesitate to impose costs on their families. When attackers know their families will retain benefits—or even receive payments—the incentive structure favors attacks. When attackers know their families will lose their home, some are deterred.

The homes demolished are often those from which attacks were planned, where weapons were stored, or where the family was complicit in the attack. The demolition policy addresses this incentive structure by imposing costs that offset the benefits.[2]

Israel's Supreme Court has reviewed the demolition policy multiple times and permitted it with restrictions—demolitions must be linked to specific terrorist acts, must be proportionate, and can be appealed. The judicial oversight, the limitations, and the ongoing debate within Israel all demonstrate that this is not arbitrary collective punishment but a carefully considered security measure subject to legal constraints.

Compare Israel's approach to genuine collective punishment historically: Nazi reprisals that killed hundreds of civilians for single acts of resistance, Soviet deportations of entire ethnic groups, or Assad's destruction of entire cities. Israel demolishes specific homes of specific terrorists. The scale and nature are entirely different from actual collective punishment.

The Gaza Blockade

The accusation that Israel's restrictions on Gaza constitute collective punishment mischaracterizes both the nature of the restrictions and their purpose.

HAMAN'S LIES

Hamas—a terrorist organization committed to Israel's destruction—seized control of Gaza in 2007 through violent coup, killing Palestinian Authority officials and establishing a hostile armed statelet on Israel's border. Since then, Hamas has launched thousands of rockets at Israeli civilians, built attack tunnels into Israeli territory, and conducted the October 7, 2023, massacre that killed over 1,200 Israelis. Gaza under Hamas is not a civilian population arbitrarily restricted—it is a territory controlled by an organization at war with Israel.[3]

Israel's restrictions focus on preventing weapons and materials usable for military purposes from reaching Hamas. Civilian goods flow into Gaza regularly—food, medicine, consumer products, and even construction materials when monitoring systems can ensure they are not diverted to tunnel construction. The restrictions target military capability, not civilian welfare.

Egypt maintains its own restrictions on Gaza's southern border—restrictions that receive virtually no international criticism. If restrictions on Gaza constitute collective punishment, Egypt is equally guilty. The selective focus on Israel reveals that the accusation is political rather than principled.

Israel's restrictions target military capability while permitting civilian supplies. The accusation of collective punishment ignores both the legal framework and the reality of ongoing armed conflict initiated and maintained by Hamas.

Movement Restrictions

Checkpoints, roadblocks, and movement restrictions in the West Bank are frequently cited as collective punishment—measures that affect all Palestinians, not just those involved in terrorism. This characterization ignores both the reason for these measures and their calibration to security conditions.

Movement restrictions exist because terrorists have used vehicles to transport explosives, weapons, and suicide bombers. Every checkpoint searches for the next attack. The restrictions are not punishment for past acts but prevention of future ones—security measures, not penalties. Restrictions are calibrated to threat levels.[4]

Tens of thousands of Palestinians enter Israel daily for work when security conditions permit—they pass through checkpoints designed to screen for threats while allowing legitimate movement. A policy of collective punishment would not permit this movement at all; security screening allows it while managing risk.

Who Creates These Conditions?

The accusation of collective punishment ignores a crucial question: *Who creates the conditions that make security measures necessary?* When terrorist organizations deliberately embed themselves within civilian populations, use civilian infrastructure for military purposes, and launch attacks from residential areas, who bears responsibility for measures that affect those populations?

Hamas deliberately operates from within Gaza's civilian population, stores weapons in homes and mosques, launches rockets from schoolyards and hospital grounds, and builds tunnels beneath residential neighborhoods. This strategy is designed precisely to ensure that any Israeli response affects civilians—either Israel refrains from responding and Hamas operates freely, or Israel responds and civilians are affected, generating the accusations Hamas seeks.

International humanitarian law assigns responsibility for civilian harm to parties that deliberately use human shields and civilian cover for military operations. When Hamas fires rockets from a neighborhood and Israel responds, Hamas bears legal and moral responsibility for exposing that neighborhood to return fire. The same logic applies to broader measures—when terrorist tactics make broad security measures necessary, those who employ those tactics bear responsibility for the consequences. Blaming Israel while ignoring Palestinian policies that create the need for Israeli responses inverts cause and effect.

The Comparative Standard

The accusation of collective punishment is applied to Israel with a selectivity that reveals its political rather than principled motivation.

Russia has destroyed entire Ukrainian cities, deliberately targeting civilian infrastructure including power plants, water systems, and hospitals. These are war crimes and collective punishment on a scale Israel has never approached—yet Russia faces less sustained condemnation in international forums than Israel faces for demolishing a terrorist's house.

Syria's Assad regime killed hundreds of thousands of its own citizens, used chemical weapons against civilian areas, and deliberately starved besieged populations. This was collective punishment in its purest form—punishment of populations for living in opposition-controlled areas. International response was largely ineffective, and Syria faced less criticism than Israel.

The disparity is clear: Israel's calibrated security measures generate more condemnation than vastly greater atrocities committed by other nations. This selectivity proves the accusation against Israel is not principled concern about collective punishment but political weaponization of legal concepts against the Jewish state.

What Would Satisfy Critics?

Critics who accuse Israel of collective punishment rarely specify what alternative they propose. If house demolitions are prohibited, what deterrent should replace them? If checkpoints are collective punishment, how should Israel screen for terrorists? If the Gaza blockade is illegitimate, how should Israel prevent weapons from reaching Hamas?

The implied answer is that Israel should simply accept terrorism—should permit free movement regardless of security implications, should allow weapons to flow freely to those pledged to Israel's destruction, should impose no consequences that might deter future attacks.

Calibrated Response to Terrorism

The collective punishment accusation misunderstands both international law and Israeli practice.

Collective punishment means imposing penalties on populations for acts they did not commit—reprisals against civilians for the actions of others. But security measures designed to prevent terrorism are not punishment. They are protection.

Israeli security measures are not static penalties imposed regardless of circumstances. They respond to threat levels. This calibration to actual conditions is the opposite of collective punishment—it is security policy adjusted to reality.

The measures are also subject to judicial review. Israel's Supreme Court has struck down policies it deemed excessive and required modifications to others. This accountability—imperfect but real—distinguishes Israeli practice from actual collective punishment that operates without constraint.

If Palestinian civilians face hardship from security measures, the primary responsibility lies with those who create the conditions requiring such measures—with Hamas, with terrorist organizations, with leadership that incentivizes attacks. The accusation inverts responsibility —blaming Israel for responding to terror while excusing those who deliberately create it.

Engaging the Harder Questions

We have explained the legal distinction between collective punishment and security measures. We have argued that checkpoints, the Gaza blockade, and house demolitions serve security purposes.

But sophisticated critics will argue that the distinction between "security" and "punishment" is semantic—that the effect on civilian populations is the same.

"House Demolitions Punish Families for Acts They Didn't Commit"

The critique:
A terrorist's mother didn't strap on the bomb. His siblings didn't plan the attack. Why should they lose their home? Western legal systems don't demolish murderers' families' houses.

The honest response:
The practice is controversial. Many Israelis oppose it. Israel's Supreme Court has upheld the practice with restrictions. Demolitions must be linked to specific terrorist acts. They can be appealed. This is not arbitrary destruction but a judicially supervised measure.

The honest concession:
Deterrence arguments are cold comfort to a family made homeless. Even if the practice reduces terrorism, it imposes suffering on people who may be genuinely innocent. Collective responsibility sits uneasily with most free societies.

The honest answer:
The practice exists because less severe measures failed. It is not collective punishment in the sense of random reprisal—it is targeted, legally reviewed, and proportionate to specific acts. But it remains morally uncomfortable, and we should be honest about that discomfort.

"The Gaza Blockade Punishes Two Million People"

The critique:
Two million people are affected by restrictions they have no power to change. Civilians can't disarm Hamas. Why should they bear the cost?

The honest response:
The blockade restricts military goods, not civilian supplies. Egypt maintains similar restrictions on its border. If the blockade is collective punishment, Egypt is equally responsible.

The honest concession:
The distinction between "military" and "civilian" goods is not always clear. Dual-use items are restricted. Two million people did not vote for October 7. They are trapped between a government that uses them as shields and restrictions they cannot change. Their suffering is real and not their fault.

The honest answer:

The blockade exists because unrestricted access would enable Hamas to rearm. The alternative—Hamas with unlimited weapons—would produce far greater suffering through renewed war. The situation is tragic but not arbitrary.

29

Lie #24

"Israel Detains Minors and Uses Harsh Interrogation Methods"

This accusation paints Israel as a nation that arrests Palestinian children arbitrarily, interrogates them harshly without parental presence, holds them in abusive conditions, and uses the military court system to deny them rights that should protect the young. According to this narrative, Israel deliberately targets children as a form of intimidation, traumatizing an entire generation to crush the spirit of resistance. The image of Palestinian minors handcuffed and blindfolded is presented as a symbol of Israeli cruelty toward the most vulnerable.

The accusation relies on emotional power—children should be protected, and any system that detains children can be portrayed as monstrous. It ignores crucial context: why these minors are detained, what acts they have committed, who bears responsibility for involving children in violence, and how Israel's treatment compares to detention of juveniles elsewhere, including in Western democracies facing far less severe security threats.

The reality is that Palestinian minors detained by Israel are charged with violent security offenses under military law—most commonly stabbing attempts, firebombings, or rock-throwing attacks that have caused fatal crashes and serious injuries—or are apprehended while attempting such acts. Israel does not arrest children because they are Palestinian; it arrests individuals who have committed violent crimes that endanger lives. The tragedy is not Israeli detention but the systematic recruitment and incitement of children to violence by Palestinian leadership and society.

Why Minors Are Detained

Palestinian minors are detained because they commit attacks—not because Israel targets children as a policy of intimidation. Understanding why these minors are in custody requires understanding what they have done.

Stabbing attacks have been conducted by Palestinian minors as young as thirteen. In numerous documented incidents, teenagers have approached Israeli soldiers, civilians, or security guards and stabbed them with knives. Some victims have died; many have been seriously wounded. These are not accidents or misunderstandings—they are premeditated attacks, often recorded on security cameras showing minors approaching victims and attacking without provocation.[1]

Firebombing—throwing Molotov cocktails at vehicles and homes—is frequently committed by minors. These attacks can and do kill; firebombs have burned families alive in their cars, killed infants in their cribs, and caused horrific injuries. When a sixteen-year-old throws a firebomb at a passing car, potentially burning a family to death, detention is not persecution—it is response to attempted murder.

Rock-throwing may sound minor, but children have hurled rocks that killed drivers when stones crashed through windshields at highway

"Israel Detains Minors and Uses Harsh Interrogation Methods"

speeds. Rock-throwing at soldiers has caused serious head injuries. These are not children throwing pebbles; they are attacks with potentially lethal weapons.[2]

When Israeli security forces detain a minor, it is almost always because that minor has committed or attempted to commit a violent act. The detention is a response to what the individual has done, not collective punishment of Palestinian youth. Israel does not randomly arrest children—it arrests attackers who happen to be young.

Who Sends Children to Attack?

The suffering of Palestinian minors caught in cycles of violence is real. But its cause is not Israeli cruelty—it is Palestinian incitement. Palestinian society systematically pushes children to violence, glorifies those who attack Israelis, and creates conditions where children become attackers. Focusing on Israeli detention while ignoring Palestinian incitement inverts cause and effect.

Palestinian Authority educational materials glorify violence against Jews. Textbooks describe terrorists as heroes and martyrs. Schools are named after suicide bombers. Children grow up in an environment where attacking Israelis is presented as the highest form of honor. This is not Israeli propaganda—these textbooks have been documented by international researchers, funded by international donors who have demanded reforms that the Palestinian Authority has refused to implement.[3]

Palestinian media aimed at children encourages violence. Television programs show children singing about attacking Jews, learning to praise martyrdom, playing games where killing Israelis is the goal. Social media content celebrating attacks and attackers saturates the Palestinian online environment. Children are immersed in messaging that normalizes and glorifies violence from their earliest years.

Hamas specifically recruits children, runs summer camps that train minors in military tactics, and celebrates child "martyrs" who die attacking Israelis. The organization deliberately uses children because their deaths generate international sympathy and propaganda value. Hamas benefits from children's deaths in ways that create perverse incentives to encourage children to attack.

When a thirteen-year-old attempts a stabbing attack, the question should not only be "why did Israel detain this child" but "who taught this child that stabbing strangers was noble?" The answer is Palestinian leadership, Palestinian education, Palestinian media, and Palestinian society. Israeli detention is response to violence; Palestinian incitement is its cause.

The Legal Framework

Palestinian minors in the West Bank are subject to Israeli military law because the West Bank is under military administration following the 1967 war. This legal framework applies to all residents of the West Bank regardless of age, just as military law applies in all military occupations worldwide. It is not a system designed to persecute children—it is the legal framework that governs the territory.

Israel has established a separate military juvenile court to handle cases involving minors—a recognition that children require different treatment than adults. The court has specialized judges, modified procedures, and considers the age of defendants in sentencing. This is not common in military justice systems; Israel created it specifically to address concerns about juvenile treatment.[4]

The age of criminal responsibility in the military system is twelve, lower than in Israeli civilian law where it is fourteen. Critics note this disparity, but it reflects the reality that Palestinian minors as young as twelve have committed serious attacks. The alternative—releasing attackers without consequence because of their age—would create incentives for terrorist organizations to use ever-younger attackers knowing they face no accountability.

Israel has implemented reforms over the years in response to criticism and its own internal reviews. Notification requirements, time limits on interrogation, provisions for parental involvement, and protections against abusive treatment have been strengthened. The system is imperfect—all justice systems are—but it has evolved toward greater protection for minors while maintaining the ability to respond to genuine security threats.[5]

Interrogation Concerns

Critics raise legitimate concerns about interrogation practices—questioning without parental presence, pressure techniques, and conditions of detention. These concerns deserve serious attention, and Israel has addressed many of them through reforms.

Israeli law now requires that parents be notified of a minor's arrest and be permitted to be present during questioning under most circumstances. While exceptions exist for security reasons—as they do in many countries' laws—the baseline requirement is parental involvement. Implementation has improved over time as monitoring and advocacy have highlighted problems.

Abusive treatment, when documented, is subject to investigation and prosecution. Israeli human rights organizations monitor detention conditions and bring cases to Israeli courts. These organizations operate freely in Israel, access detention facilities, and achieve results—improvements in conditions, prosecution of abusers, and policy changes. The system's openness to criticism and reform distinguishes it from systems where abuse occurs without any accountability.

The conditions of detention are subject to review by Israeli courts, by the International Committee of the Red Cross, and by other monitoring bodies. Facilities are not perfect, but they are subject to oversight that produces accountability. Comparisons to torture regimes elsewhere in the region—Syrian prisons, Egyptian detention facilities, Hamas's treatment of prisoners—reveal the gulf between Israel's flawed but accountable system and genuine abuse that operates without constraint.

The Comparative Perspective

The accusation implies that Israel's treatment of juvenile offenders is uniquely harsh. The comparative reality tells a different story. Many countries, including Western democracies, detain minors for serious offenses in conditions and under legal frameworks comparable to or less favorable than Israel's.

The United States has detained juveniles associated with terrorist organizations, including cases at Guantanamo Bay and in the juvenile justice system under conditions that have been widely criticized. American juveniles can be tried as adults for serious crimes, can receive lengthy sentences, and have faced conditions documented as abusive by human rights organizations. The American juvenile justice system detains hundreds of thousands of minors annually, many in conditions that have been condemned.

The United Kingdom has detained asylum-seeking minors in controversial circumstances. France has faced criticism for juvenile detention conditions. Germany, the Netherlands, and other European countries all operate juvenile justice systems that face critiques. Israel's system is not uniquely harsh by democratic standards—and it operates against far more severe security threats than most democracies face.

"Israel Detains Minors and Uses Harsh Interrogation Methods"

Regional comparison is even more revealing. Egyptian security services detain minors without meaningful legal process. Syrian prisons have held children under conditions amounting to torture. Hamas in Gaza detains children accused of collaboration without any legal rights. Palestinian Authority security services have detained and abused minors for political activity. Israel's system, with its flaws, operates under legal constraints unknown elsewhere in the region.[6]

The Real Tragedy

The real tragedy is not Israeli detention—it is the systematic sacrifice of Palestinian children by their own leadership. Children who should be in school, playing sports, dreaming of futures are instead taught to hate, trained to kill, and sent to attack knowing they will likely die or be captured. The loss of these children to violence is a tragedy—but the blame lies with those who create child attackers, not with those who must respond to their attacks.

Palestinian leadership has chosen to sacrifice generations of children to a conflict it refuses to resolve. It could educate for peace but educates for war. It could discourage violence but incentivizes it. It could protect children but sends them to attack. Nearly every Palestinian child in Israeli detention represents a child failed by Palestinian leadership—failed before Israel ever encountered them.

International organizations that focus exclusively on Israeli treatment while ignoring Palestinian incitement enable this tragedy. They create a framework where Palestinian leaders face no accountability for creating child attackers while Israel faces condemnation for responding to them. This inverted accountability encourages more incitement, more attacks, more children in detention. Those who truly care about

Palestinian children should demand an end to incitement, not an end to Israeli security responses.

Engaging the Harder Questions

We have discussed the security context—that children have been used in attacks, that interrogation prevents terrorism. But sophisticated critics will argue that treatment of Palestinian detainees violates international standards regardless of security justifications.

"Administrative Detention Without Trial Violates Basic Rights"

The critique:
Israel holds Palestinians in administrative detention—imprisonment without charge or trial, based on secret evidence. This violates fundamental due process.

The honest response:
Administrative detention is not unique to Israel. The United States used it at Guantanamo. The United Kingdom used it during the height of hostilities in Northern Ireland. Israeli administrative detention is subject to judicial review, time-limited, and must be renewed. Detainees have legal representation.

The security justification is real. Intelligence sometimes cannot be revealed without compromising sources who would be killed. Administrative detention allows incapacitation when prosecution would cost lives.

The honest concession:
The practice is uncomfortable for anyone who values due process. No one celebrates the necessity of holding someone without revealing the

full case against them. But the alternative—releasing individuals who would kill civilians or revealing intelligence sources who would then be murdered—is worse. Israel operates in an environment where these are not hypotheticals but realities. The international community holds Israel to standards it does not apply to its own counterterrorism operations, but the tension remains real, and we should not pretend otherwise.

"Interrogation Practices Are Coercive"

The critique:
Human rights organizations have documented problematic practices—sleep deprivation, stress positions. International law prohibits torture.

The honest response:
Israel's Supreme Court banned torture in 1999 and has enforced that ban. Interrogators who cross lines can be prosecuted. The question of what constitutes prohibited treatment is genuinely contested—sleep deprivation is used by many countries and is not universally classified as torture.

The honest concession:
Detainees have reported treatment that, if accurate, would violate Israeli law. We should not defend abuses. Security needs explain why interrogation is necessary—they do not excuse bad actors.

The honest answer:
Israel operates one of the most judicially supervised security systems in the world. The system is imperfect, and violations occur. When they do, they should be prosecuted. The existence of a legal framework with genuine enforcement distinguishes Israeli practice from actual torture regimes.

30

Lie #25

"Israel Manipulates Demographics to Maintain Jewish Majority"

This accusation claims that Israel is engaged in a dark project of demographic engineering—pulling levers behind the scenes to shape who can live where, who can become a citizen, who can marry whom, and even who can have children. According to the charge, Israel's residency laws, family reunification rules, immigration standards, and security policies are all expressions of a single agenda: maintaining a Jewish majority by suppressing Palestinian existence.

In this telling, every part of Israel's legal system becomes a weapon. Immigration policy becomes ethnic control. Security vetting becomes racial exclusion. Healthcare access becomes a tool of population management. Housing policy becomes an instrument of domination. And the story concludes that Israel's Jewish identity is not the result of history, peoplehood, or the right of a nation to define itself—but the product of a deliberate demographic war against Palestinians.

This accusation takes normal, universal functions of national sovereignty and recasts them as evidence of malevolence. Every nation on earth controls its borders. Every nation sets standards for citizenship. Every nation decides who may enter in times of conflict and who may not. These are the basic responsibilities of a state. But when Israel exercises the same rights, the normal becomes sinister. What other nations call immigration policy, Israel is accused of turning into demographic warfare.

The reality is very different. Like every other nation-state, Israel's citizenship and immigration laws reflect its national character, its history, and its security needs. The Law of Return—often singled out as proof of discrimination—is simply Israel's version of a policy that dozens of countries maintain. Many nations give automatic or preferred immigration rights to members of a dispersed people, ethnic group, or historical nation. Israel is not unique in this; it is normal.

Restrictions on family reunification from territories governed by hostile entities are not tools of demographic control. They are responses to real and ongoing security concerns—concerns that have been tragically validated many times over. These are not abstract fears; they reflect the lived reality of a nation targeted by terror organizations that openly call for its destruction.

And when we look at the demographic evidence itself, the accusation collapses. A country attempting to suppress a population does not preside over that population's dramatic growth. Yet that is exactly what has happened. Palestinian populations under Israeli governance have risen sharply, consistently, and measurably. That is the opposite of demographic manipulation aimed at erasure. It is historical fact, not political narrative.

The claim that Israel is conducting demographic warfare is not supported by the policies themselves, by international comparison, or by the population data. It is a lie that turns normal national functions into evidence of evil and then uses that distortion to delegitimize the very existence of the Jewish state.

The Law of Return

Critics point to Israel's Law of Return—which grants Jews worldwide the right to immigrate to Israel and receive citizenship—as evidence of demographic manipulation. This characterization ignores both the law's purpose and its commonality among nations.

The Law of Return was enacted in 1950, two years after Israel's founding and five years after the Holocaust. Its purpose was to ensure that Jews fleeing persecution would always have a refuge—that the tragedy of Jews being turned away during the Holocaust, when ship after ship of refugees was denied entry to country after country, would never recur. The law is a response to genocide, not an instrument of demographic engineering.

Many nations have similar provisions. Germany grants citizenship to ethnic Germans from Eastern Europe. Ireland grants citizenship to those of Irish descent. Greece, Italy, Poland, Hungary, Armenia, and dozens of other countries have laws allowing members of their diaspora populations to return and claim citizenship. Japan has provisions for ethnic Japanese. China facilitates immigration by ethnic Chinese. These laws recognize historical connections between peoples and ancestral homelands—exactly as Israel's Law of Return does.

The selectivity of the accusation is revealing. Germany's law for ethnic Germans is not characterized as demographic manipulation aimed at suppressing non-German populations. Ireland's provisions are not condemned as ethnic engineering. Only Israel's comparable law—applying to Jews, history's most persecuted people—is portrayed as sinister. The double standard is itself a form of discrimination against the Jewish state.

Jerusalem Residency

Critics often turn to Jerusalem as supposed proof that Israel is quietly manipulating demographics. They argue that because Palestinians in the city hold permanent residency rather than automatic citizenship, Israel can use residency rules to shrink the Palestinian population—demographic engineering disguised as bureaucracy.

But this accusation ignores the actual history of Jerusalem and the choices made by the city's Palestinian residents. When Israel unified Jerusalem in 1967, Palestinians living there were offered full Israeli citizenship. That offer was real, available, and documented. Most declined—not because it was denied to them, but because accepting citizenship would have required swearing loyalty to a state they opposed politically. They chose permanent residency instead, and Israel respected that choice by granting a status that provided nearly all the practical benefits of citizenship without the political obligations that many at the time rejected.[1]

Permanent residency—whether in Jerusalem or anywhere else in the world—comes with standard conditions. If someone relocates abroad for long periods, residency can lapse. That is not unique to Palestinians in Jerusalem. Israeli Jews who move overseas can lose certain residency benefits as well and must reestablish their status if they return. The rules apply based on where a person actually lives, not on their ethnicity. Palestinians who maintain residence in Jerusalem keep their status. Those who move away may lose it, just as residents in countless other countries forfeit residency when they relocate.

And the demographic facts dismantle the accusation entirely. Since 1967, the Palestinian population of Jerusalem has grown from roughly 66,000 to more than 370,000. That is a more than fivefold increase. A city engaged in demographic suppression does not preside over the explosive growth of the very population it is accused of trying to reduce. The numbers themselves reveal the truth: The accusation is simply false.

The Demographic Reality

If Israel were suppressing Palestinian population growth, you would expect to see shrinking communities, stalled birth rates, and declining populations. But the exact opposite has happened. Under Israeli governance, Palestinian populations have expanded at some of the highest growth rates in the world.

Inside Israel, the Arab population has grown from 156,000 in 1948 to more than two million today. That is a twelvefold increase. Arabs now make up roughly 21 percent of the country's population, and that proportion has remained stable as both Jewish and Arab communities have grown. Nothing about this resembles demographic suppression. It is the picture of a population growing, building, and expanding in every measurable way.[2]

In the West Bank, the Palestinian population has risen from around six hundred thousand in 1967 to more than three million today. In Gaza, the population has surged from roughly 350,000 to over two million. These growth rates are not only high compared to Israel—they rank among the fastest population increases worldwide. A country supposedly bent on suppressing these populations has somehow produced a demographic boom.

If we look at the broader picture—the total number of Palestinians in Israel, the West Bank, Gaza, and the global diaspora—the story is even clearer. Their population has grown from approximately 1.4 million in 1948 to more than 14 million today. A tenfold increase. A population experiencing demographic suppression does not multiply by ten in the space of a few generations. The numbers speak for themselves: The accusation is not just false; it is mathematically impossible.

What Real Demographic Manipulation Looks Like

The charge of demographic manipulation is leveled at Israel while some of the clearest, most brutal examples of real demographic engineering take place elsewhere—often with barely a whisper of international outrage. When you compare the claim against Israel with what actual demographic manipulation looks like, the accusation collapses instantly.

Look at what China has done to the Uyghurs. This is demographic engineering in its most literal form: forced sterilizations, children separated from their families, and state-directed birth restrictions aimed specifically at shrinking the Uyghur population. The impact has been immediate and devastating. Birth rates in Uyghur regions have plummeted. Communities are shrinking. Families are being broken apart. This is what true demographic suppression produces—declining populations, not the explosive growth we see among Palestinians.[3]

The former Yugoslavia offers another stark example. In Serbia, Croatia, and Bosnia, ethnic cleansing violently removed entire populations in order to create homogeneous territories. Villages emptied. Families fled or were killed. Communities that had existed for generations were wiped out in a matter of months. This was demographic manipulation enforced through terror—state power used to erase populations from the map.

And look at what happened to Jewish communities in the Arab world after 1948. Roughly 850,000 Jews were expelled from countries where they had lived for thousands of years. Their homes taken. Their property seized. Their communities dismantled. Today, outside of Israel, *fewer than four* thousand Jews remain across the entire Arab world. That is demographic engineering through ethnic cleansing, and it resulted in a population reduced to almost nothing.

The contrast is unavoidable. Real demographic manipulation produces disappearing communities. Populations that shrink. People who flee or are forced out. Under Israeli governance, Palestinian populations haven't declined—they have multiplied many times over. The accusation against Israel describes the opposite of what actually occurs.

The Nation-State Law

Critics point to Israel's 2018 Nation-State Law—which declares Israel the nation-state of the Jewish people—as evidence of demographic intent. This characterization misunderstands both the law and its context.

The Nation-State Law declares something that has been true from the first day of Israel's existence: Israel is the nation-state of the Jewish people. That identity has shaped the country since its founding. It is woven into the Declaration of Independence, into every stage of state-building, and into the lived experience of the people who established the nation after centuries of exile. The 2018 law didn't create a new reality; it simply put into constitutional language what had always been the foundation of the state.[4]

Many nations have similar constitutional provisions defining their national character. The constitutions of numerous European countries reference specific ethnic, religious, or cultural identities. Islamic countries define themselves as Muslim states. The law did not change minority rights in Israel—Arab citizens retain full legal equality, voting rights, and civil liberties. It defined Israel's identity without restricting anyone's rights.

The debate surrounding the law was largely symbolic. Critics argued it sent the wrong message about belonging. Supporters argued it clarified what was already a historical fact. But what it did not do is alter immigration policy, citizenship law, residency rules, or anything that would constitute demographic engineering. It did not shift the demographic landscape in any direction. It put into constitutional form what Israel has always been: the national homeland of the Jewish people.

PART THREE

Stepping Into Your Esther Moment

31

America's Best Investment

For years, people have framed US support for Israel as if America were simply writing checks out of goodwill. But those who have actually seen the partnership up close know better. A US military colonel who served as an attaché to the IDF once put it plainly: "We get far more than we give." He wasn't exaggerating. He was describing a strategic truth that lawmakers, critics, and many taxpayers have never been shown.[1]

The more you examine the evidence, the more you understand how right the colonel was. Supporting Israel is not a burden on American taxpayers—it is one of the most strategically profitable partnerships the United States maintains anywhere in the world.

The Military Technology Partnership

The US–Israel military relationship is not a one-way street where America simply provides weapons to Israel. It is a genuine partnership where both nations contribute, innovate, and benefit. Israeli battlefield experience, technological creativity, and rapid innovation cycles have produced military technologies that American forces use every day—technologies that save American lives and make American weapons systems more effective.

Consider what happened after the 1973 Yom Kippur War. The US Department of Defense undertook an extensive evaluation of the conflict, commissioning thirty-seven separate studies to analyze the strategies and technologies that enabled Israel to prevail against overwhelming odds. American military personnel walked the battlefields alongside Israeli commanders, learning lessons that would reshape American military doctrine for decades. The insights from Israel's experience significantly influenced the development of America's AirLand Battle doctrine and the "Big Five" weapon systems—Apache helicopters, Bradley Fighting Vehicles, Patriot missile systems, Abrams tanks, and Black Hawk helicopters. These weapons have defined American military capability for a generation, and their development was shaped by Israeli experience and expertise.[2]

The partnership continues producing innovations that protect American soldiers today. Israeli companies developed technologies to detect, map, and destroy tunnels used by Hamas and Hezbollah—and those same technologies were shared with America. The United States has used Israeli tunnel-detection systems to find and neutralize drug-smuggling tunnels under our southern border, tunnels that could also be used by terrorists to infiltrate the United States. American troops deployed to the Middle East used these same Israeli technologies to defeat ISIS and other terrorists who used tunnels to approach, surveil, and attack American positions.[3]

The Israeli Emergency Bandage—a simple yet highly effective hemorrhage control dressing developed by an Israeli military medic—has saved countless American lives. First introduced in the 1990s, it features a built-in pressure applicator that allows soldiers to treat severe wounds with one hand. The US military adopted it in the early 2000s as American casualties from improvised explosive devices (IEDs) and small arms fire increased in Iraq and Afghanistan. It is now standard issue in the individual first aid kits of American soldiers, special operations forces, and first responders. How many American families have their loved ones home today because of an Israeli invention? That number is beyond calculation, but it is not small.[4]

The Iron Dome missile defense system exemplifies how joint US–Israel development benefits both nations. The United States has invested over $1.3 billion in missile defense since 2011, and the system has intercepted thousands of rockets in real combat conditions—providing invaluable data that no amount of testing could replicate. American engineers have learned from every engagement, applying those lessons to improve our own missile defense capabilities. The US military has incorporated Iron Dome–derived technologies and combat data into its own missile defense systems, improving protection for American forces. This is not foreign aid disappearing overseas; it is investment in a weapons system that protects Americans while being perfected in the most demanding battlefield laboratory in the world.[5]

Israel's newest breakthrough, the Iron Beam laser defense system, represents the next generation of this mutually beneficial partnership. Delivered to the IAF in December 2025, Iron Beam is the world's first operational high-energy laser air defense system. The technology fundamentally changes the economics of defense: While each Iron Dome Tamir interceptor missile costs $40,000–$50,000, an Iron Beam interception costs mere dollars in electricity. In December 2022, Lockheed Martin and Rafael signed a teaming agreement to jointly develop, test, and manufacture a variant of the system for the American market—meaning that once again, Israeli combat innovation will directly strengthen American capabilities. As with Iron Dome before it, the Iron Beam will be battle-tested against real threats, generating data that enhances systems destined for American forces.[6]

The financial architecture of the US–Israel Iron Beam partnership illustrates how shared investment yields asymmetric returns for America. Israel and Rafael invested over three decades of research and development—funded primarily by Israel's Ministry of Defense—before the United States contributed $1.2 billion in 2024 for procurement and deployment. In exchange, Lockheed Martin and Rafael signed a teaming agreement to jointly develop a variant for the American market, and Israeli officials confirm the technology is already being shared with the US Army's directed energy program. The US Army's acquisition chief, Doug Bush, called the Israeli approach "intriguing" and noted it offers a complementary technological path to America's own laser development efforts—meaning the US essentially bought into a proven system rather than bearing the full cost and risk of independent development. While precise figures on Israel's total R&D expenditure remain undisclosed, the strategic calculus is clear: America invested in a technology that Israel spent decades perfecting and is now battle-testing in real combat, and in return gains access to a system where each interception costs a few dollars rather than the $40,000–$50,000 per missile required by current air defense systems. Over thousands of interceptions—the scale Israel routinely faces—the savings are transformational.[7]

When Israeli fighter jets struck Iranian air defense systems in 2024, they demonstrated something of enormous value to the United States: the superiority of American aircraft and weapons over Russian air defense systems. In widely reported operations, Israeli pilots flying American-made F-15I, F-16I, and F-35I aircraft—enhanced with Israeli technology—successfully defeated Russian-made S-300 air defense systems. Any country that relies on Russian air defenses now knows they can be defeated by American technology. This demonstration degrades

Russian military export sales, deprives Vladimir Putin of revenue for his war in Ukraine, and increases orders for American weapons systems. It employs more Americans, bolsters our economy, and helps revitalize our defense industrial base. The intelligence and tactical lessons from Israeli operations flow back to American engineers, military planners, and pilots, improving our own systems and procedures.[8]

Intelligence That Protects America

Intelligence cooperation between the United States and Israel is one of the most valuable—and least visible—aspects of the partnership. Former CIA Director George Tenet publicly stated that Israeli intelligence sharing is equivalent to having five additional CIA stations in the Middle East. Think about that: A single ally provides intelligence value equivalent to five major American intelligence operations. The cost savings alone would justify the investment, but the benefits go far beyond dollars.[9]

Israel's geographic position and regional expertise make it uniquely valuable for intelligence gathering on threats that matter to America. Israeli intelligence on Iran's nuclear program, on terrorist networks, on weapons proliferation, on the intentions and capabilities of hostile actors throughout the region—this information flows to American decision-makers and helps protect American interests and American lives. Israel is, as the saying goes, America's eyes and ears in one of the world's most dangerous regions.

Israeli radar systems and intelligence installations provide early warning of missile launches and military movements throughout the Middle East, information immediately shared with American forces. This real-time intelligence helps protect American bases, American ships, and American personnel deployed across the region. The presence of a strong, capable ally with world-class intelligence services reduces the burden on

American intelligence resources and provides independent verification of threats that American policymakers need to understand.

Medical Innovation That Saves American Lives

Israel has become a global leader in medical innovation, and American patients are among the primary beneficiaries. Israeli scientists have developed innovative cancer therapies, breakthrough medical devices, and pharmaceutical treatments that save American lives and improve American healthcare every day. The US–Israel partnership in healthcare has expanded dramatically in recent years, with cooperation spanning regenerative medicine, disease prevention, cancer research, digital health, and artificial intelligence applications in medicine.

Israel's national health system has created one of the largest databases of medical information anywhere in the world—decades of electronic health records covering virtually the entire population. This data has become invaluable for medical research, enabling researchers to track treatment outcomes, identify patterns, and accelerate the development of new therapies. American pharmaceutical companies and research institutions partner with Israeli counterparts precisely because Israel's comprehensive health data allows for research that would take far longer or be impossible elsewhere. This partnership accelerates medical breakthroughs that benefit American patients.

Israel is home to approximately one thousand medical device companies and leads the world in medical patents per capita. Major American companies like Abbott, Medtronic, and General Electric maintain research and development operations in Israel precisely because Israeli innovation in medical technology is world-class. American patients receiving treatment with cutting-edge medical devices are often benefiting from Israeli innovation without ever knowing it. The partnership makes

American healthcare better and American medical companies more competitive globally.[10]

Cybersecurity Protection for Critical Infrastructure

Israel has become a global leader in cybersecurity technology, and Israeli companies protect critical American infrastructure from state-sponsored cyberattacks every day. Israeli cybersecurity firms secure major US banks, power grids, telecommunications networks, and government systems against increasingly sophisticated threats from nations like China, Russia, and Iran. With more than 10 percent of global cybersecurity investment going to Israeli companies, Israel has become a key partner for protecting America's digital infrastructure.

The economic value of preventing major cyberattacks on American infrastructure is immeasurable. A successful attack on the US power grid could cause trillions of dollars in economic damage and threaten national security. Israeli cybersecurity expertise and real-time threat intelligence help protect against such scenarios. When it comes to digital security in the twenty-first century, Israel is not a charity case—it is a strategic asset that helps keep America's economy and infrastructure safe from adversaries who would do us harm.[11]

Economic Benefits and American Jobs

The US–Israel economic relationship supports over 255,000 American jobs. That is not a projection or an estimate—it is documented reality. Israeli stakeholders have contracts with over one thousand American companies in forty-eight states, the District of Columbia, and Puerto Rico. The military assistance America provides to Israel is largely spent on products manufactured in America, directly supporting American workers and American communities. By 2028, Israel is required to spend all of its military aid—roughly $3.8 billion annually—on products manufactured in America.

The economic partnership extends far beyond military aid. The US–Israel Free Trade Agreement, signed in 1985, was America's first free trade agreement with any country. Since then, bilateral trade has grown to over fifty billion dollars annually. Israel is America's twenty-fourth largest trading partner—a remarkable position for a country of only nine million people. Israeli firms represent the second-largest source of foreign listings on NASDAQ after China, and more than Indian, Japanese, and South Korean firms combined. This is a dynamic, innovative economy that creates opportunities for American businesses and American workers.

Joint research programs between the United States and Israel consistently produce remarkable returns on investment. The Binational Agricultural Research and Development Fund (BARD) has generated a $16.50 return for every dollar invested, translating to $2.7 billion to the US economy. Similar programs in science and industrial development have created tens of thousands of American jobs and produced technologies that benefit American farmers, American industries, and American consumers. This is not foreign aid—it is investment in a partnership that pays substantial returns.[12]

Innovation and Technology Leadership

Israel ranks first in the world in research and development investment as a percentage of gross domestic product and in the number of engineers and scientists per capita. It ranks fifth in patents per capita and seventh in overall innovation. It ranks first in artificial intelligence startups per capita and third in total AI startups, behind only the United States and China. More than three hundred US technology companies have established research and development centers in Israel to tap into this extraordinary innovation ecosystem.

Bill Gates observed in 2006 that "the innovation going on in Israel is critical to the future of the technology business." That observation has only become increasingly true in the years since. Critical components of leading American high-tech products are invented and designed in Israel, making American companies like Intel, Cisco, Motorola, Applied Materials, and Hewlett-Packard more competitive and more profitable globally. The "Startup Nation" generates ideas, technologies, and companies that American businesses partner with, invest in, acquire, and bring to global markets. American technology leadership is strengthened, not weakened, by the partnership with Israel.

Water technology provides a perfect example. Israel has solved its own water scarcity challenges through breakthrough technologies in desalination, recycling, conservation, and irrigation. Now Israeli companies are helping America—especially the drought-plagued Southwest—address our own water challenges. An Israeli company designed the largest water desalination plant in the United States. It creates American jobs, supplies water to over four hundred thousand Americans, and contributes $50 million dollars annually to the US economy. Israeli drip irrigation technology, invented and commercialized by Israeli companies, is used on American farms to produce more food with less water.[13]

Strategic Value Without American Troops

Unlike many American allies around the world, Israel does not ask American troops to fight its wars. No American soldiers die defending Israel because Israel defends itself. American support is primarily financial and diplomatic, not military deployment. The Israeli Defense Forces fight with their own soldiers, their own blood, their own sacrifice. American families do not receive flags from Israeli conflicts.

A strong Israel contributes to regional stability and serves as a counterweight to Iranian expansion—objectives that serve American interests without requiring American military intervention. A weakened Israel would invite adventurism from hostile actors in ways that could ultimately require American military response. The cost of maintaining large US military bases and forces in the Middle East would far exceed the aid provided to Israel if Israel were not capable of defending itself and deterring regional aggression.

The Numbers That Tell the Story

What does America actually receive for its $3.8 billion annual investment in Israel? According to General Alexander Haig—former NATO Supreme Commander and US Secretary of State—if Israel were not in the Middle East, the United States would have to invest $15 billion to $20 billion annually to manufacture and deploy aircraft carriers and ground divisions to the Mediterranean and Indian Ocean to protect American interests, secure our Arab allies, and counter threats from hostile powers. That means America's $3.8 billion investment saves $11 billion to $16 billion every year—a return of four to five dollars for every dollar invested. Admiral Elmo Zumwalt, former Chief of Naval Operations, made the same comparison: Israel functions as America's largest aircraft carrier, deployed in one of the world's most critical regions, requiring no American soldiers on board and proving unsinkable.

The intelligence value alone is staggering. General George Keegan, former Chief of US Air Force Intelligence, assessed that the intelligence Israel shares with the United States is equivalent to five CIA agencies.

With the CIA's annual budget at approximately $15 billion, that suggests intelligence value worth $75 billion—from a partnership that costs $3.8 billion. Senator Daniel Inouye, who chaired both the Appropriations Committee and the Intelligence Committee, stated that the scope of Israeli intelligence shared with America exceeded the intelligence provided by all NATO countries combined. Add to this the hundreds of Israeli-driven upgrades to American weapons systems—the F-16 alone received over six hundred improvements from Israeli innovation, saving American manufacturers billions of dollars. By any honest accounting, America does not give aid to Israel; America makes an investment that yields returns no other partnership in the world can match.[14]

The Bottom Line

Those who characterize the US–Israel relationship as a burden on American taxpayers either lack understanding of the comprehensive benefits or choose to ignore the evidence. The intelligence cooperation, technological innovation, economic returns, and strategic positioning provided by Israel deliver benefits worth many times the annual investment. American soldiers are safer because of Israeli technology. American infrastructure is more secure because of Israeli cybersecurity. American patients are healthier because of Israeli medicine. American workers have jobs because of Israeli partnerships. American military capabilities are stronger because of Israeli innovation and battlefield experience.

The United States provides approximately $3.8 billion annually in military assistance to Israel. But the return on that investment—in saved lives, prevented attacks, technological advancement, economic activity, and strategic benefit—is exponentially greater. This is not charity. This is partnership. This is investment. And by any rational measure, it is one of the best investments America makes anywhere in the world.

HAMAN'S LIES

Support for Israel has historically been one of the few genuinely bipartisan commitments in American foreign policy—and for good reason. Members of Congress who sit on intelligence and armed services committees, who receive classified briefings, who understand what Israel actually provides to American security, vote overwhelmingly to maintain this partnership. They do so not because of lobbying or campaign contributions, but because the evidence is overwhelming. The $1.2 billion for Iron Beam passed with bipartisan support even amid the most polarized Congress in modern memory.

The members who oppose this relationship are not the serious ones. They are not the ones reading intelligence assessments or visiting military installations or understanding the threat matrix in the Middle East. They are ideologues—often the same voices who have never met an American defense interest they wouldn't sacrifice for applause on social media. The real question isn't why so many in Congress support Israel. The real question is why a small, loud faction pretends the evidence doesn't exist.

Informed members of Congress—Republican and Democrat—understand that weakening this alliance doesn't save money; it costs American lives, American security, and American technological advantage. Those who claim otherwise are either uninformed or unserious. The grown-ups in the room know better.

When you hear critics claim that America gives too much to Israel, remember this: We get far more than we give. The partnership makes America stronger, safer, and more prosperous. It is good for America. It is good for Israel. And it represents the kind of alliance—built on shared values, shared interests, and mutual benefit—that serves both nations and advances the cause of freedom in a dangerous world.

32

A Moment That Demands More Than Understanding

You have walked through twenty-five lies—old spirits wearing new language, ancient accusations dressed in modern vocabulary. As you have seen, not one of them is new. They trace the same spiritual pattern that has sought to destroy the Jewish people from Haman to Herod to Hitler to Hamas. They move through history like a shadow, reappearing in every generation with fresh intensity. You now understand that these lies are not simple misunderstandings or political disagreements; they are part of a demonic, coordinated assault against God's Covenant People, woven into the fabric that has fueled antisemitism for thousands of years. And once your eyes are opened to that pattern, you cannot unsee it.

But understanding alone is not enough. Esther understood the danger, but her understanding did not save her people—her courage did. Mordecai perceived the threat clearly, but he did more than perceive. He challenged, he confronted, he called for action. Knowledge without obedience is unfinished faithfulness, and insight without response accomplishes nothing. Because every generation eventually faces a moment when clarity must become courage.

We have reached that point.

You Were Born into This Moment

The world is being conditioned—spiritually, culturally, politically—to turn against Israel. The pressure is rising. The lies are intensifying. Truth is being drowned out by accusation, and deception is spreading faster than most people realize. You have been given the gift of understanding in a time when understanding is rare. That is not accidental. That is an assignment. And with understanding comes responsibility.

You are not reading this by coincidence. You are alive in this moment for a reason. You have been placed where you are, with the influence you have, for such a time as this.

If the people of God ever needed clarity, courage, and conviction, it is now. Not because Israel is perfect—not because any nation is—but because God has chosen them, because God has spoken concerning them, and because the spirit of antisemitism has always opposed God's purposes in the world. To stand with Israel is not merely to take a political position; it is to align yourself with the heart of God in perhaps the most defining spiritual battle of our time.

Become a Person of Unshakable Truth

First, commit yourself to becoming a person of truth. Lies thrive in places where truth has not been taught. Most who repeat the accusations against Israel do so because they've only heard fragments, not the story itself. They inherit opinions from headlines, absorb

A Moment That Demands More Than Understanding

misinformation from social media, and accept narratives built on fragments divorced from context.

You cannot confront lies with vague impressions. You need substance. You need depth. You need to know the story of Israel—not just the modern story, but the ancient one. The Covenant with Abraham. The promises recorded by the prophets. The continuous connection of the Jewish people to the land for more than three thousand years—and a persistent Jewish presence there across the centuries. The miraculous return after centuries of dispersion. The wars of survival. The peace offers extended and rejected. The resilience of a people who refused to disappear.

When you know the truth, you cannot be shaken. When you understand the story, you cannot be manipulated. When you recognize the spiritual pattern behind these accusations, you cannot mistake them for isolated criticisms. Educating yourself is not an academic exercise; it is spiritual preparation. It forms conviction, and conviction is what gives your voice strength.

Your Voice Carries More Weight Than You Realize

And your voice is needed.

Most people will never read a chapter like this one. Most will never study Israel's history, examine accusations critically, or recognize the biblical significance of what is unfolding. That means the people in your life—your friends, your coworkers, your family members, your church community—will form their views based largely on conversations. They will draw conclusions from what they hear around them. In many cases, you may be the one person God uses to interrupt a lie before it takes root.

When someone repeats an accusation casually, your gentle, informed correction may be the only truth they hear. You do not need to lecture or argue. Truth isn't fragile. It doesn't need theatrics. It simply needs a voice willing to speak it. When someone says Israel is committing genocide, you can calmly point out that the Palestinian population has multiplied—a fact incompatible with genocide. When someone says Israel is an apartheid state, you can describe Arab citizens voting, serving in the Knesset, sitting on the Supreme Court, leading hospitals and universities. Simple truth stated with calm conviction is often more powerful than passionate argument.

And questions are sometimes even more powerful than statements.

- Why is Israel singled out when far worse abuses occur elsewhere every day?
- Why do accusations against Israel so closely mirror antisemitic tropes from centuries past?
- Why are Palestinian leaders never held accountable for rejecting peace?

A well-placed question can disarm an entire narrative. But your influence doesn't stop in personal conversations.

Strengthen the Church's Biblical Foundation

Your influence extends into your church. Churches today are often hesitant to speak about Israel—not because the Bible is unclear, but because culture is loud. Many pastors feel overwhelmed, intimidated, or fearful of controversy. Others have been influenced, knowingly or unknowingly, by replacement theology—the belief that the Church has replaced Israel in God's plans. That doctrine disconnects Christians from their own roots, opens the door to apathy toward Jewish suffering, and prepares hearts to shrug when Israel is under demonic attack.[1]

But the Bible tells a different story. The promises to Abraham have not been revoked. Paul says the gifts and calling of God are irrevocable. Jesus Himself teaches that how we treat *His brothers*—the Jewish people—will be remembered by Him.

Encourage your church, lovingly and respectfully, to teach on Israel—not politically, but biblically. Suggest small groups or classes that explore Israel's role in Scripture, prophecy, and history. Invite speakers who can bring clarity and context. Encourage prayer for Israel—not because prayer is symbolic, but because prayer aligns hearts with God's purposes. When churches pray for the peace of Jerusalem, they participate in a command of Scripture and join a spiritual battle older than any of us.

Let Your Support Take Visible, Practical Form

Supporting Israel also takes practical forms. There are organizations working every day to counter antisemitism, provide relief to victims of terrorism, and strengthen ties between Christians and Jews. Your support—financial, relational, or simply intentional—makes a real difference. Visiting Israel strengthens not only Israel's economy but your own understanding. Walking in the land, talking with Israelis, seeing what the news never shows, gives you a clarity that no book or video can match. You come home with a voice that carries weight because you have seen it for yourself.

Supporting Israel can be as simple as what you buy, where you invest, and what you share. The BDS movement seeks to isolate Israel economically; your everyday choices can break that isolation. These choices are not small—they are seeds. And seeds become legacies.

Stand for Truth in the Public Square

There is also a public dimension to this calling. Lies spread through media, education, politics, and social platforms. Truth must be present in those spaces too. Writing a letter to the editor when a newspaper distorts reality is not insignificant. Contacting an elected official when they stand against Israel is not futile. Politicians respond to people who speak. Policies change when enough voices demand it. Engaging on social media, when done wisely, can shift minds you will never meet.

If you work in education—or influence those who do—you have a role in ensuring curricula present Israel accurately. Generations are shaped by what they are taught when young. This is spiritual formation as much as academic instruction.

Choose Relationship Over Distance

But as important as all these actions are, they rest upon something deeper: relationship.

The most powerful stand you take may not occur in debate or public advocacy, but in friendship. Attend synagogue events open to your community. Stand with Jewish neighbors in times of fear. Check in when antisemitism surges. Make your solidarity visible. Let your Jewish friends know they are not alone. The rise in antisemitism is not abstract—it affects real people. And the presence of even one Christian friend who stands with them can provide immeasurable encouragement. In a world becoming colder, presence is a form of protection.

Courage Will Cost You—But Silence Costs More

Yet none of this is without cost. You will pay a price for standing for Israel today. You may face criticism, pressure, or distance from people you care about. You may be called names. You may be misunderstood. You will certainly face spiritual opposition. *Truth is costly—but the cost of silence is far greater.* If this moment asks for courage, then courage is what faithfulness requires.

Esther faced death. You will face discomfort. Mordecai faced Haman. You will face hostility. But the principle remains unchanged: Standing with God's truth always invites opposition. You must decide now that truth matters more than approval.

Why This Battle Matters to God

And why does all this matter?

Because this is not just about geopolitics. **This is about spiritual warfare.** About Covenant. About Bible prophecy. About the heart of God and the hatred of the enemy. Israel is the center of God's redemptive plan, the stage on which history will conclude, and the nation through whom God gave His Word and His Messiah to the world. Satan's hatred for Israel is not political—it is theological. And when you stand for Israel, you are standing with God against the oldest hostility on earth.

You have been given understanding at a moment when many are confused. You have seen what others refuse to see. And Jesus Himself said that the way we treat His "brothers" will not be forgotten. That is why this matters. That is why your voice matters. That is why your courage matters.

Your Answer Will Be Written in What You Do Next

The genius of Jewish survival across millennia has been faithful presence—engaging the world without losing identity, blessing their neighbors while holding fast to God's Covenant, enduring hatred without surrendering hope. That same calling rests on you now. To be faithfully present in your moment. To speak truth when lies prevail. To bless the people God has blessed. To stand where God stands.

Mordecai's question still echoes through Scripture and through history. It was not rhetorical when he asked it. It is not rhetorical now. And your answer will not be written in words, but in what you choose to do next.

CONCLUSION

The People Who Cannot Be Erased

Across the pages of this book, we have traced a pattern older than any modern nation-state, older than any ideology, older even than the empires that once ruled the known world. It began with the Amalekites. Then it found a home in the royal court of ancient Persia, where an Agagite named Haman stood before a king and spoke words that would echo for millennia. He argued that the Jewish people were different, disloyal, dangerous, and disposable—and that life would be better if they were destroyed altogether (Esther 3:8–9). Those charges did not remain trapped in the scroll of Esther. They reappeared in Rome, in medieval Europe, in the Ottoman courts, in Nazi Germany, in Soviet propaganda halls, and today in the resolutions of international bodies, on the campuses of elite universities, and across the platforms of social media. The slogans change; the substance does not.

This book showed how the same demonic spirit of slander resurged with stunning speed after October 7, 2023—how accusations once recognized as antisemitic tropes were repackaged as moral truth, shouted in the streets, posted by influencers, and echoed even by some who claim to love the Bible.[1] What followed in the intervening chapters was a careful dismantling of twenty-five modern lies about Israel. Each lie, no matter how contemporary it sounded, belonged to the same old pattern. Whether it was the claim that Israel is an apartheid state, or that it commits genocide, or that it manipulates world powers, or that it does not belong in its homeland, every one of these accusations drew from the ancient well Haman dug.[2] This book exposed them not merely with facts, but with the biblical and historical clarity that reveals their spiritual origin.

But if this book has shown you anything, it is that the Jewish people have faced far worse than headlines and hashtags.[3] They have encountered empires determined to erase them, rulers intent on extinguishing them, policies designed to scatter them, and ideologies that sought to bury their identity forever. Yet they remain—resilient, recognizable, rooted. Why? Because the God who scattered them also preserved them. The God who disciplined them also restored them. The God who promised Abraham that his seed would never disappear watched over them in Babylon, in Persia, in the camps of Europe, and in their rebirth in 1948.[4]

The Miracle of Survival

Consider the empires that tried to destroy the Jewish people: Egypt, Assyria, Babylon, Persia, Greece, Rome, the medieval kingdoms of Europe, the Russian Empire, the Nazi regime. Every one of these powers once dominated the world. Every one boasted armies, wealth, influence, and pride. And every one now sits in the dustbin of history. Yet the people they oppressed remain—still reading the same Scriptures, still celebrating the same festivals, still praying in the same language, still gathering in communities across the world, still connected to the Covenant God made with Abraham.

Historians marvel at it. Skeptics cannot erase it. Empires have tried—and failed. The survival of the Jewish people is nothing less than a living testimony to God's faithfulness—a sign written across history that the promises of the Bible are not empty words but realities that outlast every power that rises against them.

The genius of their survival was not military might or political power or economic leverage. It was faith rooted in God, enacted through consistent practice, embedded in families, reinforced by community, and strengthened by hope. Wherever they went—Babylon, Persia, Europe, the Americas—they carried a portable faith that could flourish anywhere. They made their homes sanctuaries of identity, their tables altars of memory, their children the carriers of Covenant across generations. Empires worked through force; God worked through faithfulness. Empires crumbled; the Covenant endured.[5]

Remember the Danish rescue during World War 2 that we described earlier? About the fishing boats and the 7,200 Jews ferried out of Denmark to safety in Sweden? One story from that rescue captures this truth with heartbreaking clarity. A Jewish man in Berlin, preparing to send his son on a train to Denmark—knowing he would likely never see him again, knowing the darkness closing in around his family—offered his final words. Not instructions for survival. Not warnings about danger. Not bitterness at a world gone mad. Simply this: "Don't forget there's a God." His son, recounting the story decades later, marveled at the impossibility of it: "How can you say that when you know things are that bad?" And yet that is precisely how the Jewish people endured. In the worst moments—on trains to uncertain futures, in the holds of fishing boats fleeing occupation, in cattle cars bound for death camps—they carried not just their lives but their faith. The father who spoke those words did not survive. But his words did. His son did. His grandchildren did. The Covenant continued. Empires built on hate crumbled into history; a people built on faith remained.

The Prophetic Moment

We are living in the days the prophets foresaw. Israel reborn in a day (Isaiah 66:8), Jerusalem restored after nineteen centuries (Luke 21:24), millions regathered from the nations (Jeremiah 16:14–15)—these are not random events or geopolitical accidents.[6] They are milestones on God's prophetic timeline, fulfillments of promises spoken through Isaiah, Jeremiah, Ezekiel, and Zechariah. The very existence of modern Israel is a statement that the God of the Bible is still acting in history, still keeping Covenant, still moving events toward the conclusion He has ordained.

The prophets also foretold that the nations would turn against Israel in the last days—that Jerusalem would become "a cup of drunkenness to all the surrounding peoples" and "a very heavy stone for all peoples" (Zechariah 12:2–3).[7] We are watching this unfold in real time. The lies documented in this book are not merely political arguments; they are spiritual strategies meant to oppose the purposes of God. They prepare nations to stand against Jerusalem just as the Bible said they would (Joel 3:1–2). But this does not mean fear for the believer. It means clarity. It means discernment. It means recognizing that we are watching prophecy rather than chaos unfold.

The spirit of Haman is alive in modern propaganda. The pattern of accusation, isolation, and destruction that he pioneered continues in new forms with new vocabulary but the same ancient hatred. Esther reveals that this hatred is not merely political—it is demonically inspired.[8] Haman was not merely a villain; he represented an ongoing spiritual war over Israel's existence. The book of Esther is prophetic because it shows a pattern that continues until the end of the age.[9] And it shows that God always raises up those who will stand against that pattern—those who will speak when speech is costly, who will act when action is risky, who will refuse to let lies stand unchallenged. As Isaiah declared, "No weapon formed against you shall prosper, and every tongue which rises against you in judgment you shall condemn" (Isaiah 54:17).

The King's Standard

It is here that Jesus' own words speak with piercing relevance. In Matthew 25, He describes a future judgment of the nations and separates the sheep from the goats based on one standard: how they treated "the least of these My brethren" (Matthew 25:40). That phrase has been debated, but in context—given that Jesus was speaking to Jewish disciples about the trials coming upon Israel in the last days—"His brethren" has been interpreted in different ways, but at minimum it cannot be severed from His Jewish identity, His Jewish disciples, and the coming trials tied to Jerusalem and Israel. This does not deny a broader application of compassion—it simply restores the original context Jesus' disciples would have understood. He was not giving a generic teaching about kindness; He was revealing that in the climactic season of human history, when Israel is surrounded, pressured, slandered, and attacked, He will remember who stood with them and who turned away.

The King Himself said that whatever is done to them in their moment of need is counted as done to Him.

> **This is not peripheral to prophecy; it is central.**
> **This is not optional for believers; it is commanded.**
> **This is not a vague concept; it is a measure of faithfulness.**

The nations will be judged—and every person will answer for their choices within those nations—by how they responded when Israel was slandered, isolated, and attacked. That time is upon us. The testing has begun. The lies are circulating. The hostility is rising. And every person who has read this book, who has understood what is happening, who has seen the pattern—that person now faces a choice. Not a political choice, but a biblical one. Not a partisan decision, but a prophetic one.

Why the Scapegoat Always Returns

We want to show you something that helps explain why this hatred never dies—why it keeps resurfacing century after century, no matter how enlightened a civilization claims to be.

Scripture gives Satan a title: "the accuser of our brethren" (Revelation 12:10). That's not just a description. That's his job. That's what he does. Day and night, the Bible says, he accuses. Jesus called him "the father of lies" (John 8:44). And his lies always follow the same pattern: isolate, accuse, destroy. He did it in Eden. He did it in Persia. He's doing it right now through phone screens all over the world.

There's a philosopher named René Girard who spent his whole career studying something he called the "scapegoat mechanism."[10] His research showed that when a society gets overwhelmed—by chaos, by guilt, by problems it can't solve—it looks for someone to blame. Not just criticize. *Blame.* The community finds one group, loads all its anxieties onto that group, and then turns on them. And here's the strange part: It works. For a little while. The society feels unified. It feels righteous. It feels like it's doing something. All at the cost of the innocent.

Girard saw this as a human problem—something broken deep in our nature. And he was right about that. But he could only see part of the picture.

Scripture shows us what's really going on. There is a spiritual force that *exploits* this broken tendency in human nature. The accuser didn't invent scapegoating—but he weaponizes it. He takes humanity's instinct to shift blame and he aims it, century after century, at the same target: *God's Covenant People.*

The People Who Cannot Be Erased

This is why Haman's template never goes away. This is why the same accusations keep reappearing in new vocabulary. Pharaoh, Haman, Antiochus, the Inquisitors, Hitler, the Soviet propagandists, today's campus activists—different people, different centuries, same demonic spirit. The accuser whispers the same lies through different mouths. He stirs the same hatred through different movements. And he always directs the accusation toward the Jews.

Why? *Because he knows what's at stake.*

If he can destroy Israel, he thinks he can prove God is a liar. If he can break the Covenant, he thinks he can break the One who made it.

He can't. But he will never stop trying.

This explains something that baffles a lot of people: *Why does Hamas so often disappear from the moral conversation?*

Think about it a minute. Hamas massacres families. Hamas takes hostages. Hamas fires rockets from schoolyards. Hamas slaughters Palestinians. And within hours—sometimes within minutes—the whole world is back to talking about what *Israel* did wrong. Hezbollah rains missiles on civilian towns, and UN voices demand Israeli "restraint." Iran funds terrorism on four continents, and somehow Israel is still "the obstacle to peace."

The scapegoat must carry all the blame. Everyone who attacks the scapegoat carries none of it.

There's a term researchers use that fits this pattern: *motive attribution asymmetry*. In studies of conflict perception—including Israeli–Palestinian contexts—people often explain their own side's aggression as defensive or love-driven, while explaining the other side's aggression as hatred-driven.[11] We fight because we love our families; they fight because they hate us. This bias makes conflict seem intractable because it strips all humanity from the other side's motives. Under this framework, Israel is the only actor in the Middle East with the power to choose—so Israel is the only one who can be blamed. Everyone else is just "reacting." The terrorist becomes a victim of circumstances. The aggressor becomes a product of oppression.

But this is more than psychology. This is the fingerprint of the accuser.

He assigns all guilt to one people. He absolves their attackers. He creates a moral universe where Israel is the only nation capable of sin. And the actual victims? The children pulled from their beds on October 7th? The hostages held or murdered in tunnels? They disappear. They don't fit the narrative. The accuser has no use for them.

And then there's projection.

Projection is when you take your own sin and see it in someone else instead.[12] It's one of the oldest tricks in the accuser's playbook. He did it in Eden—"Did God really say?"—twisting God's words to make the Creator look like the deceiver. He's *still* doing it.

Groups and leaders who openly call for genocide accuse Israel of genocide Those who target civilians accuse Israel of targeting civilians. Those whose founding documents call for killing Jews accuse Israel of Nazi-like crimes. Those who use hospitals as military bases accuse Israel of bombing hospitals.

The projection is so consistent, so predictable, that you can almost use it as a map. Whatever Israel's enemies accuse Israel of doing—look first at what *they* are doing. The accusation isn't analysis. It often becomes a confession. It's an unwitting admission of their own intent, projected onto the victim.

We wrote earlier in this book: "The projection is remarkable: Those who actually call for genocide accuse their intended victims of the crime they themselves proclaim. It is Haman accusing Mordecai of planning what Haman himself intends."

That's exactly what we're watching. Isaiah warned that a day would come when people would call evil good and good evil (Isaiah 5:20). We're living in that day. The father of lies has inverted every category—and the people who listen to him can no longer tell the difference between the arsonist and the firefighter.

But here's what history teaches us, and it's sobering: Scapegoating never solves the problems it promises to solve. It just blinds societies to their real dangers.

Europe's worst collapses came when nations redirected their fear and frustration onto Jews—while actual threats gathered strength in the shadows. The obsession consumed energy, attention, and moral clarity that should have been spent on real problems. And when the scapegoat was gone—expelled, murdered, fled—the problems didn't go away. They got worse.

The nations that turned on Jews didn't flourish. They declined. The civilizations that scapegoated Israel didn't find peace. They found judgment.

A society that cannot correctly identify its threats will not survive them.

This is one of the great paradoxes of antisemitism: It destroys the antisemite as surely as it targets the Jew. The accuser doesn't care about the nations he deceives. He'll use them and throw them away. His hatred isn't really for the nations—it's for God. The nations are just tools, manipulated through the scapegoat mechanism into opposing the very purposes that would have brought them blessing.

God told Abraham something that still echoes through history: "I will bless those who bless you, and I will curse him who curses you" (Genesis 12:3). That's not just a promise of protection for Israel. It's a warning to the nations. Align yourself with the accuser's agenda and you position yourself against God. No nation has ever prospered in that position for long.

HAMAN'S LIES

The ancient serpent knows his time is short. That's why the intensity is increasing. The global hostility toward Israel in our generation isn't random political friction. It's the acceleration of a spiritual war that Scripture told us would intensify as we approach the end.

But Haman lost. And the spirit behind him will lose again.

His strategy has never ultimately succeeded. Not in Egypt. Not in Persia. Not in Rome. Not in the death camps of Europe. The people he targeted still exist. The Covenant he tried to break still stands. The God he sought to discredit still reigns.

And in the end, the accuser himself will be thrown down. Revelation 12 tells us his time is coming. His accusations will be silenced forever.

Until that day, the battle continues. And every generation must choose which side of that battle they will stand on.

Esther's Answer

Earlier in this book, we told you about "Esther's answer"—the response of truth to each of Haman's lies. But Esther's answer was not only words. It was action. It was risk. It was courage when courage could have cost her everything.

Esther could have remained silent. She was safe in the palace, hidden in her position, protected by her concealed identity. Haman's decree threatened her people, but she might have escaped notice. She could have calculated the odds, weighed the risks, and concluded that speaking up was too dangerous. Many would have understood. Many would have made the same choice.

But Mordecai's words cut through her calculations:

"Do not think in your heart that you will escape in the king's palace any more than all the other Jews. For if you remain completely silent at this time, relief and deliverance will arise for the Jews from another place, but you and your father's house will perish. Yet who knows whether you have come to the kingdom for *such* a time as this?" (Esther 4:13–14).

These words contain a profound truth: God's purposes will be accomplished with or without any particular individual's participation. Deliverance will come from somewhere. But those who remain silent when called to speak, who shrink back when called to stand, who choose safety over faithfulness—they lose their place in the story. They survive, perhaps, but they perish in a deeper sense. They miss the purpose for which they were positioned.

Esther's response has echoed through centuries: "I will go to the king, which *is* against the law; and if I perish, I perish" (Esther 4:16). This is the voice of faith that has counted the cost and decided that faithfulness is worth the price. It is the voice that would rather perish doing right than survive doing nothing. It is the voice that trusts God's purposes more than personal safety. It is the voice this moment requires.

If I perish, I perish.

The Legacy You Will Leave

Esther's legacy is not merely that she survived or that her people survived—though both are true. Her legacy is that she acted when action was required. She is remembered across millennia not for her beauty, not for her position, not for her comfort in the palace, but for her courage at the moment of decision. Every year at Purim, her choice is celebrated. Her name means "star," and she shines still because she rose when rising was costly.

HAMAN'S LIES

What legacy will you leave? When this moment passes into history—and it will pass—how will you be remembered by those who knew you? More importantly, how will you be remembered by the King who sees all, who weighs all, who promised to remember what was done to the least of His brothers?

History always remembers the difference between those who stood and those who stayed silent. We remember Corrie ten Boom hiding Jews in her home (see Chapter 4 for her full story). We remember Dietrich Bonhoeffer speaking against Nazi ideology when the German church was silent. We remember Raoul Wallenberg saving thousands in Budapest. We remember Denmark's rescue of their Jewish neighbors (see Chapter 4). We remember because they chose faithfulness when faithfulness was costly. We remember because they understood that some moments demand response regardless of risk.

This is such a moment. The lies are rising. The pressure is building. The pattern is repeating. And you have been given understanding—understanding of what is happening, understanding of what Scripture says, understanding of what faithfulness requires. With understanding comes responsibility. With knowledge comes accountability. With position comes purpose.

The Survival That Cannot Be Explained

The people of Israel cannot be erased—not by Haman, not by Hitler, not by the Soviet Union, not by the clerics of Tehran, not by the slogans of activists, not by the resolutions of the UN, and not by the ferocity of digital mobs. Their survival is the proof of God's Covenant faithfulness. Their rebirth is the fulfillment of ancient promises. Their endurance is the sign that the God of Scripture is still acting in history. Their existence is a reminder that we are living in the days the prophets foresaw. And their future is secured not by the approval of nations, but by the word of the Lord: "The land shall not be sold permanently, for the land *is* Mine" (Leviticus 25:23).

But while they cannot be erased, you must choose whether you will stand with them or shrink back into silence. You must decide whether you will respond to this moment like Esther—courageous, clear, faithful—or like those who blend into the crowd and call it wisdom. You must choose whether your voice will strengthen the truth or strengthen the hostility gathering around God's Covenant People.

The Covenant will stand. God will keep His promises. The people of Israel will endure. These things are certain because God has spoken them. What is not certain is whether you will be part of the story of faithfulness or part of the backdrop of silence. That choice—your choice—remains open until you close it by action or inaction, by speech or silence, by courage or retreat.

For Such a Time as This

Mordecai's question was not written only for a queen in Persia. It was written for anyone God raises up when lies become fashionable and courage becomes costly. It was written for you, reading these words in this moment, with this understanding, at this point in history.

Who knows whether you have come to your position—your family, your church, your workplace, your community, your platform, your influence—for this very moment?

The question is not rhetorical. It demands an answer—not in words but in action. What you do with what you have learned, how you respond to what you now understand, whether you speak or stay silent, whether you act or merely agree—these will be your answer.

HAMAN'S LIES

This is your moment of decision. This is your generation's Esther hour. This is the season in which truth is costly, courage is rare, and silence is endorsement. And who knows—indeed, who can doubt—whether God has placed you in this moment, with this understanding, with this clarity, for such a time as this.

The people of Israel will endure.

The Covenant will stand.

God will keep His promises.

And when the King returns, He will remember how the nations—and how individuals—treated "these My brethren."

The only question left is the one this book places in your hands: **Will you give in to Haman's lies—or fight for Esther's truth?**

APPENDIX A

The 25 Lies at a Glance

#	THE LIE	BRIEF REBUTTAL
1	Jews Have No Right to the Land	3,000+ years of presence; God's covenant; 1922 Mandate recognized Jewish homeland.
2	Israel Is Apartheid	Arab citizens vote, serve in Parliament, Supreme Court, military. No segregation laws.
3	Founded Through Displacement	Arabs rejected partition and attacked; most fled at leaders' urging; 160,000 stayed.
4	Illegally Occupies West Bank	No prior Palestinian state existed; territory captured in defensive war.
5	Annexed Territory Illegally	Jerusalem unified after Jordan attacked; Golan secured after Syrian aggression.
6	Settler-Colonial Project	Jews are indigenous; returning from exile; no "mother country" sent them.
7	Commits Genocide	Palestinian population grown 5x since 1948. Genocide = elimination, not growth.
8	Targets Civilians	IDF uses roof-knocking, phone warnings, leaflet drops. Unprecedented precautions.
9	Disproportionate Force	International law requires proportionality to military objective, not equal casualties.
10	Punitive Gaza Blockade	Blockade began after Hamas coup; Egypt also blockades; humanitarian goods flow daily.

HAMAN'S LIES

#	THE LIE	BRIEF REBUTTAL
11	Violates Human Rights	Independent judiciary, free press, vibrant NGOs. Compare to neighbors.
12	Commits War Crimes	Strict rules of engagement; military lawyers review operations. Hamas uses human shields.
13	Restricts Holy Sites	Israel guarantees access to all faiths. Under Jordan, Jews barred from Western Wall.
14	Settlements Block Peace	Israel offered to remove settlements in peace deals; Palestinians rejected.
15	Doesn't Pursue Peace	Made peace with Egypt, Jordan, UAE, Bahrain, Morocco. Offered statehood multiple times.
16	Controls US Policy	Classic antisemitic trope. US supports Israel as strategic ally and only regional democracy.
17	Discriminates Against Arabs	Arab citizens vote, hold office, serve as judges. Arabic is official language.
18	Security = Oppression	Security barrier reduced suicide bombings 90%. Measures ease when violence decreases.
19	Suppresses Journalists	Freest press in Middle East. Critics operate openly. Compare to PA/Hamas.
20	Fabricates Threats	Oct 7 proved threats real. 20,000+ rockets from Gaza. Hamas charter calls for destruction.
21	Controls Water Unfairly	Israel supplies water per Oslo agreements. Shortages due to PA mismanagement.
22	Assassinates Leaders	Targeted killings of terrorists. Same policy US used against Bin Laden.
23	Collective Punishment	Home demolitions target terrorist families (documented deterrent). Security measures respond to threats.
24	Detains Minors Harshly	Separate juvenile court since 2009. Reforms ongoing. Minors detained for attacks.
25	Manipulates Demographics	Arab population has grown dramatically. Real manipulation: China's Uyghur policies.

APPENDIX B

Key Primary Sources

1. Haman's Accusation (Esther 3:8–9)

"There is a certain people scattered and dispersed among the people in all the provinces of your kingdom; their laws *are* different from all *other* people's, and they do not keep the king's laws. Therefore it *is* not fitting for the king to let them remain. If it pleases the king, let *a decree* be written that they be destroyed."

2. Hitler-Mufti Meeting (November 28, 1941)

From Documents on German Foreign Policy, 1918–1945:

The Mufti told Hitler that "the Arabs were Germany's natural friends because they had the same enemies... namely the English, the Jews, and the Communists." Hitler responded that Germany's goal was "solely the destruction of the Jewish element residing in the Arab sphere."

3. Hamas Charter (August 18, 1988)

Preamble: "Israel will exist and will continue to exist until Islam will obliterate it."

Article 7: "The Day of Judgment will not come about until Muslims fight the Jews and kill them."

Article 13: "There is no solution for the Palestinian question except through Jihad."

4. UN Resolution 3379 (1975)

"Determines that Zionism is a form of racism and racial discrimination."—Soviet-backed; revoked 1991.

5. Genesis 12:3

> "I will bless those who bless you,
> And I will curse him who curses you;
> And in you all the families of the earth shall be blessed."

APPENDIX C

Glossary of Key Terms

Antisemitism
Hostility to, prejudice against, or discrimination against Jews. Coined in 1879 by Wilhelm Marr.

Anti-Zionism
Opposition to Israel's existence as a Jewish state. Singles out Jews alone as unworthy of self-determination.

Apartheid
Institutionalized racial segregation (South Africa 1948–1994). Israel's Arab citizens have full legal equality.

BDS
Boycott, Divestment, and Sanctions movement (2005). Founders acknowledge goal is Israel's elimination.

"From the River to the Sea"
Slogan calling for Palestinian control from Jordan River to Mediterranean—Israel's elimination.

Genocide
Acts to destroy a national/ethnic/religious group (UN 1948). Palestinian population has grown 5x—opposite of genocide.

Intifada
Arabic: "uprising." First (1987–93) and Second (2000–05) were periods of Palestinian violence. Second included 130+ suicide bombings.

Nakba
Arabic: "catastrophe." 1948 displacement—omits that Arab armies invaded and 850,000 Jews were expelled from Arab countries.

Replacement Theology
View that Church replaced Israel in God's plan. Contributed to centuries of Christian antisemitism.

Settler-Colonialism
Colonizers replacing indigenous population. Inverts reality: Jews are indigenous, returned from exile.

Zionism
Movement for Jewish self-determination in ancestral homeland. Named for Zion (Jerusalem).

APPENDIX D

Select Bible Passages About Israel

The Land Covenant

Genesis 15:18

"To your descendants I have given this land, from the river of Egypt to the great river, the River Euphrates."

Genesis 17:7–8

"I will establish My covenant ... for an everlasting covenant,... Also I give to you and your descendants ... all the land of Canaan, as an everlasting possession."

Leviticus 25:23

"The land shall not be sold permanently, for the land is Mine."

The Regathering Prophecies

Isaiah 66:8

"Shall a nation be born at once? For as soon as Zion was in labor, she gave birth." (Fulfilled 14 May 1948)

Jeremiah 16:15

The Lord *"brought up the children of Israel from the land of the north and from all the lands."* (Soviet Jews 1989–2002)

Ezekiel 37:21

"I will take the children of Israel from among the nations … and bring them into their own land."

Amos 9:15

"I will plant them in their land, and no longer shall they be pulled up from the land I have given them."

The Blessing and the Curse

Genesis 12:3

"I will bless those who bless you, and I will curse him who curses you."

Joel 3:2

"I will enter into judgment with them there on account of My people, My heritage Israel, whom they have scattered among the nations; they have also divided up My land."

APPENDIX E

Answering Haman's Lies

A Quick Response Guide

How to use this guide: These are concise, factual responses to common accusations against Israel. Stay calm, stick to facts, and don't let emotion derail the conversation. For deeper understanding, see the corresponding chapters in *Haman's Lies*.

THE FOUNDATIONAL LIE

THE ACCUSATION	THE TRUTH
"Jews have no right to the land" / "Anti-Zionism isn't antisemitism" *(Book: Lie #1)*	Zionism simply means Jews have the right to self-determination in their ancestral homeland—the same right recognized for every other people. To oppose this for Jews alone is to single out one people as unworthy of what all others have. Jews are indigenous to Israel. Archaeological, historical, genetic, and biblical evidence confirms 3,000+ years of continuous connection. The word "Jew" comes from "Judean"—a person from Judea. When "anti-Zionism" leads to attacks on synagogues, Jewish students hiding their identity, and global spikes in anti-Jewish violence, the distinction between anti-Zionism and antisemitism collapses.

THE BIG ACCUSATIONS

THE ACCUSATION	THE TRUTH
"Israel is committing genocide" (Book: Lie #7)	Genocide means systematic extermination with intent to destroy a people. The Palestinian population has grown from 1.4 million in 1948 to over 14 million today—a tenfold increase. No genocide in history produces population growth. Compare to actual genocides: The Holocaust killed 6 million Jews. Rwanda: 800,000 Tutsis in 100 days. China's policies have reduced Uyghur birth rates by 84%. Hamas's charter actually calls for genocide against Jews (Article 7). Israel warns civilians before strikes; Hamas deliberately maximizes civilian deaths.
"Israel is an apartheid state" (Book: Lie #2)	Arab citizens of Israel vote, serve in parliament (the Knesset), sit on the Supreme Court, serve as military officers, and share all public spaces with Jews. An Arab party (Ra'am) was part of the governing coalition in 2021—helping choose Israel's prime minister. South African apartheid had pass laws, banned interracial marriage, and enforced total segregation. Israel has none of these. South Africans who lived under actual apartheid—including anti-apartheid activists—have rejected this comparison. The accusation was invented by Soviet propaganda in the 1970s as part of the "Zionism is racism" campaign.

THE ACCUSATION	THE TRUTH
"Israel is a settler-colonial state" (Book: Lie #6)	Colonialism requires a "mother country" sending settlers to exploit a distant territory. There was no Jewish empire. Jews came from 100+ countries—fleeing persecution—to rebuild their ancestral homeland. Jews are indigenous to Israel. Their language, religion, and culture originated there. Over half of Israeli Jews are Mizrahi—descended from 850,000 refugees expelled from Iraq, Yemen, Morocco, Egypt, and other Arab countries. They are Middle Eastern, not European colonizers. Arab presence began with the Islamic conquest in the seventh century—over 1,600 years after Jewish presence was established.
"From the river to the sea, Palestine will be free" (Book: Introduction)	The Jordan River to the Mediterranean Sea includes ALL of Israel. This chant calls for Israel's elimination—not coexistence. Ask: *"What happens to the 7 million Jews living between the river and the sea in your vision? Where do they go?"* This is a call for ethnic cleansing at best, genocide at worst.
"Israel is ethnically cleansing Palestinians" (Book: Lie #7)	Ethnic cleansing means forced removal of a population. The Palestinian population in the West Bank has grown from 600,000 in 1967 to over 3 million; in Gaza from 350,000 to over 2 million. Meanwhile, 850,000 Jews were expelled from Arab countries after 1948—communities that had existed for 2,500 years were destroyed. That was actual ethnic cleansing, yet it has been erased from history.

MILITARY & SECURITY ACCUSATIONS

THE ACCUSATION	THE TRUTH
"Israel targets civilians and children" *(Book: Lie #8)*	Israel drops leaflets, makes phone calls, sends texts, and uses "roof knocks" (warning strikes) to alert civilians before attacks—unprecedented precautions in military history.
	Hamas deliberately embeds fighters in hospitals, schools, and mosques. They fire rockets from schoolyards and store weapons in residential buildings. Under international law, responsibility for civilian deaths caused by human shields falls on the party using them.
	Israel's civilian-to-combatant casualty ratio is actually lower than in comparable urban warfare (Mosul, Raqqa).
"Israel uses disproportionate force" *(Book: Lie #9)*	"Proportionality" in international law does NOT mean equal casualties. It means the expected military advantage must be weighed against expected civilian harm for each specific strike.
	By the logic of "equal casualties," a country that builds bomb shelters and warning systems should be penalized for protecting its people, while a terrorist group that uses human shields should be rewarded.

HAMAN'S LIES

THE ACCUSATION	THE TRUTH
"Gaza is an open-air prison" *(Book: Lie #10)*	Gaza shares a border with Egypt—why is only Israel blamed? Egypt also enforces restrictions. The blockade exists because Hamas has fired over 20,000 rockets at Israeli civilians and uses imports to build attack tunnels. Before Hamas violently seized control in 2007, there was no blockade. Israel withdrew completely from Gaza in 2005—removing every soldier and settler. Even with restrictions, humanitarian goods flow through Israeli crossings daily. The problem is Hamas diverts resources to weapons and tunnels.
"Israel commits war crimes" *(Book: Lie #12)*	Israel has strict rules of engagement with military lawyers reviewing operations. It investigates allegations and prosecutes violations. It maintains an independent judiciary and free press that scrutinize military conduct. Hamas openly commits war crimes: targeting civilians, using human shields, executing prisoners, and taking hostages. October 7 was documented war crimes broadcast proudly by the perpetrators.
"Israel fabricates security threats" *(Book: Lie #20)*	October 7, 2023 proved the threats are real. Over 1,200 people were murdered in a single day. Hamas's charter explicitly calls for Israel's destruction. Over 20,000 rockets have been fired at Israeli civilians from Gaza. Hezbollah has 150,000+ missiles pointed at Israel. Iran openly calls for Israel's elimination. These are not fabrications.

HISTORY & LAND CLAIMS

THE ACCUSATION	THE TRUTH
"Israel stole Palestinian land" (Book: Lie #3)	Jews purchased land legally during the Ottoman and British periods—often at inflated prices from absentee landlords. Israel was established by UN partition in 1947 and recognized under international law. Arab nations rejected partition and invaded. Israel defended itself. Most Arab refugees fled at the urging of Arab leaders who promised a quick victory—160,000 Arabs who stayed became Israeli citizens. Jordan occupied the West Bank from 1948–1967. No one called it "occupation" or demanded a Palestinian state then.
"Israel illegally occupies the West Bank" (Book: Lie #4)	There was never a Palestinian state to "occupy." The territory was captured from Jordan in a defensive war Jordan started in 1967. Under international law, territory acquired in self-defense has a different status. Israel has offered to withdraw in exchange for peace multiple times. Palestinians rejected offers in 2000, 2001, and 2008 that would have created a state on virtually all the territory.

HAMAN'S LIES

THE ACCUSATION	THE TRUTH
"Settlements are the obstacle to peace" *(Book: Lie #14)*	Israel offered to remove settlements for peace at Camp David (2000), Taba (2001), and in Olmert's offer (2008). Palestinians rejected all three. The conflict existed before any settlements. Hamas controls Gaza, which has had zero settlements since 2005—and still fires rockets at Israel. If settlements were the issue, why did Palestinians reject statehood when Israel offered to remove them?
"Israel doesn't want peace" *(Book: Lie #15)*	Israel has made peace with every Arab party willing to make peace: Egypt (1979), Jordan (1994), UAE, Bahrain, Morocco, Sudan (Abraham Accords, 2020). Israel offered Palestinians statehood at Camp David (2000), Taba (2001), and through Olmert (2008). Each time, Palestinians walked away. Hamas's charter explicitly rejects any permanent peace with Israel. Article 13 states: "There is no solution for the Palestinian question except through Jihad."

US–ISRAEL PARTNERSHIP

THE ACCUSATION	THE TRUTH
"Israel controls US foreign policy" / "AIPAC controls Congress" (Book: Lie #16)	This echoes the ancient antisemitic trope of Jews secretly controlling governments—the same conspiracy theory in *The Protocols of the Elders of Zion*.
	AIPAC is not even in the top 50 lobbying spenders. The US supports Israel because it's the only democracy in the Middle East, shares American values, and is a strategic ally in a volatile region.
	The US and Israel have had significant policy disagreements (Iran deal, UN votes). If Israel "controlled" US policy, these disagreements wouldn't exist.
"Why do we give $3.8 billion to Israel?" (Book: Lie #16)	It's an investment, not charity. General Alexander Haig estimated the US would need $15–20 billion annually in military deployments if Israel weren't there. America gets $4–5 back for every $1 invested.
	By 2028, 100% of military aid must be spent on American-made products—supporting 255,000+ American jobs in 48 states.
	Israeli intelligence sharing is worth "five CIAs" according to former CIA directors. Israeli innovations protect American troops and civilians. No American soldiers die defending Israel—Israel defends itself.

QUESTIONS TO ASK

Sometimes the best response is a good question. These can expose contradictions and prompt genuine reflection:

WHEN THEY SAY...	.ASK...
"Genocide"	"Can you name another genocide where the targeted population grew tenfold? What's your definition of genocide?"
"Apartheid"	"Did you know Arab citizens vote and serve in Israel's parliament and Supreme Court? Have you heard what South Africans who lived under apartheid say about this comparison?"
"Colonizers"	"Where did Jews originate? What about the majority of Israeli Jews who are refugees from Arab countries?"
"River to the sea"	"That's the Jordan River to the Mediterranean—all of Israel. What happens to the 7 million Jews there? Where do they go?"
"Resistance"	"Have you read Hamas's charter? Is deliberately targeting a music festival 'resistance'? Is rape 'resistance'?"
"Both sides"	"One side warns civilians before strikes; one side targets civilians deliberately. One side investigates misconduct; one side celebrates atrocities. Are those really equivalent?"

The Ultimate Question

Ask: "Do you believe Israel has the right to exist as a Jewish state?"
This clarifies whether you're dealing with a policy critic or someone who opposes Israel's existence. Policy critics deserve engagement; eliminationists are simply repeating Haman's lie.

REMEMBER

- **You don't have to win every argument.** Sometimes the goal is simply to plant a seed of doubt in a borrowed conviction. Many people have never heard these facts.
- **Focus on one issue at a time.** Don't let your conversation partner overwhelm you with rapid-fire accusations. When someone throws ten claims at once, pick the weakest one and address it thoroughly. Trying to refute everything at once plays into their hands.
- **Stay calm and factual.** Emotional responses make you look defensive. Facts delivered calmly are more persuasive.
- **Know when to walk away.** Some people are not interested in truth—they are committed to a narrative. You cannot reason someone out of a position they didn't reason themselves into.
- **Others are listening.** Even if you don't convince the speaker, bystanders may be persuadable.
- **Pray for wisdom and courage.** This is ultimately a spiritual battle. The lies are ancient; so is the God who defeats them.

"Who knows whether you have come to the kingdom for such a time as this?"

—Esther 4:14

References

Introduction

1. Statistics on global antisemitic attitudes—including the 46% worldwide rate (2.2 billion people), the doubling since 2014, and the generational divide (50% under 35 versus 37% over 50)—come from the Anti-Defamation League's Global 100 Index. See https://global100.adl.org/.

2. Agenda Item 7 of the UN Human Rights Council, titled "Human rights situation in Palestine and other occupied Arab territories," is the only permanent agenda item dedicated to a specific country or conflict. No similar permanent item exists for any other nation, including those with documented large-scale human rights abuses. See "UNHRC Resolutions Database," *UN Watch*.

3. The official German record of the November 28, 1941, meeting between Hitler and Haj Amin al-Husseini—including the Mufti's statement about "natural friends," Hitler's pledge of "active opposition to the Jewish national home," and his promise regarding "destruction of the Jewish element"—is preserved in *Documents on German Foreign Policy, 1918–1945*, ser. D, vol. 13, doc. 515. Full English translation at Times of Israel.

4. The Mufti's wartime radio broadcasts to the Arab world are documented by the United States Holocaust Memorial Museum. He made regular broadcasts in Arabic calling for jihad against the Jews and urging Arabs to rise up against the Allies. See United States Holocaust Memorial Museum, "Hajj Amin al-Husayni: Wartime Propagandist," *Holocaust Encyclopedia*, https://encyclopedia.ushmm.org/content/en/article/hajj-amin-al-husayni-wartime-propagandist.

5. The 13th Waffen–SS Mountain Division, known as "Handschar" (Arabic for curved scimitar), was formed in 1943 with the Mufti's assistance. See United States Holocaust Memorial Museum, "Hajj Amin al-Husayni."

6. SS Chief Gottlob Berger's report describing the Mufti's recruiting tour as having "an extraordinarily successful impact" is documented in Nazi correspondence. The Mufti addressed military imams, identifying their "common enemies: World Jewry, England, and Bolshevism." The Handschar

division recruited between 24,000 and 27,000 men. See United States Holocaust Memorial Museum, "Hajj Amin al-Husayni."

7   The estimate that al-Husseini recruited at least 30,000 Muslim troops for Nazi Germany across multiple units, and his appointment as an SS officer with an office in the SS Main Office, is documented in "The Mufti and the Holocaust," *Jewish Virtual Library*, https://www.jewishvirtuallibrary.org/the-mufti-and-the-holocaust.

8   The Soviet strategy of equating Zionism with racism as a counter to Western proposals to condemn antisemitism in the International Convention on the Elimination of All Forms of Racial Discrimination is documented in Joel Fishman, "The Origins of Modern Anti-Zionism," *Jerusalem Center for Public Affairs*, https://jcpa.org/article/the-origins-of-modern-anti-zionism/.

9   The Soviet creation of "Zionology" as an academic discipline after the Six-Day War of 1967, and its dissemination as mandatory reading for military personnel, students, teachers, and Communist Party members, is documented in Fishman, "Origins of Modern Anti-Zionism."

10 The 1974 7-point plan adopted by the Party Central Committee to strengthen anti-Zionist propaganda throughout Soviet society is documented in Fishman, "Origins of Modern Anti-Zionism."

11 United Nations General Assembly Resolution 3379, "Elimination of All Forms of Racial Discrimination," A/RES/3379 (November 10,1975). The resolution declared that "Zionism is a form of racism and racial discrimination." Among those voting in favor were all Soviet bloc nations and most Arab states. The vote was 72 to 35, with 32 abstentions.

12 Daniel Patrick Moynihan, "Address to the United Nations General Assembly on Resolution 3379 (Zionism Is Racism)," speech delivered November 10, 1975, American Rhetoric, https://www.americanrhetoric.com/speeches/danielpatrickmoynihanun3379.htm.

13 United Nations General Assembly Resolution 46/86, A/RES/46/86 (December 16, 1991). The resolution revoking Resolution 3379 was adopted by a vote of 111 to 25, with 13 abstentions. Israel had made the revocation of the "Zionism is racism" resolution a condition for its participation in the Madrid Peace Conference.

1

1   Yehuda Bauer, "Franklin H. Littell—In Memoriam," *Yad Vashem Studies* 37, no. 2 (2009), accessed December 2024, https://www.yadvashem.org/research

References

/yv-studies/back-issues/37-2/franklin-littell.html. See also Franklin H. Littell, *The Crucifixion of the Jews: The Failure of Christians to Understand the Jewish Experience* (New York: Harper & Row, 1975). I (John) am grateful to say Dr. Littell was one of my professors.

2 "October 7 attacks," *Wikipedia,* last modified December 4, 2025, https://en.wikipedia.org/wiki/October_7_attacks.

3 "Israel, The West Bank and Gaza," Country Reports on Terrorism 2023, US Department of State, March 5, 2025, https://www.state.gov/reports/country-reports-on-terrorism-2023/israel-the-west-bank-and-gaza/.

4 "Audit of Antisemitic Incidents 2024," Anti-Defamation League, April 9, 2025, https://www.adl.org/resources/report/audit-antisemitic-incidents-2024.

5 "Antisemitic Incident Data Breaks All Previous Annual Records in 2024 for the Fourth Year in a Row," Anti-Defamation League, April 22, 2025, https://www.adl.org/resources/press-release/antisemitic-incident-data-breaks-all-previous-annual-records-2024-fourth.

6 ADL, "Audit of Antisemitic Incidents 2024."

7 Ibid.

8 Ibid.

9 Ibid.

10 "Antisemitic incidents surged 340% worldwide in 2024, alarming report says," *Ynetnews,* January 19, 2025, https://www.ynetnews.com/article/hkaj4t9vjl.

11 "Global Antisemitism Incidents Rise 107.7% in 2024, Fueled by Far-Left Surge, CAM Annual Data Study Reveals," Combat Antisemitism Movement, April 29, 2025, https://combatantisemitism.org/studies-reports/global-antisemitism-incidents-rise-107-7-in-2024-fueled-by-far-left-surge-cam-annual-data-study-reveals/.

12 "Antisemitic Incidents 2024," Community Security Trust, 2025, https://cst.org.uk/research/cst-publications/antisemitic-incidents-2024.

13 "Jewish Agency Report: Between 2022 and 2024 Global Antisemitism Surged 340%," Holocaust Remembrance Association, February 5, 2025, https://holocaustremembranceassociation.org/jewish-agency-report-between-2022-and-2024-global-antisemitism-surged-340/.

14 "Antisemitic incidents surge across Europe and the world, ADL's J7 Task Force report shows," *Euronews,* May 8, 2025, https://www.euronews.com/2025/05/08/antisemitic-incidents-surge-across-europe-and-the-world-adl-report-shows.

15 Ibid.

16 "80 years after Nazi Germany's surrender, antisemitism is rising worldwide, report finds," *Times of Israel,* May 7, 2025, https://www.timesofisrael.com/80-years-after-nazi-germanys-surrender-antisemitism-is-rising-worldwide-report-finds/.

17 Ibid.

18 "J7 Annual Report on Antisemitism 2025," Anti-Defamation League, May 2025, https://www.adl.org/sites/default/files/pdfs/2025-05/j7-annual-report-on-antisemitism-2025.pdf.

19 Holocaust Remembrance Association, "Jewish Agency Report."

20 "Australian police arrest second suspect in Melbourne synagogue arson attack," *Times of Israel,* August 24, 2025, https://www.timesofisrael.com/australian-police-arrest-second-suspect-in-melbourne-synagogue-arson-attack/.

21 "2024 Melbourne synagogue attack," *Wikipedia,* last modified November 2025, https://en.wikipedia.org/wiki/2024_Melbourne_synagogue_attack.

22 "Jews in Europe still face high levels of antisemitism," European Union Agency for Fundamental Rights, July 11, 2024, https://fra.europa.eu/en/news/2024/jews-europe-still-face-high-levels-antisemitism.

23 Ibid.

24 Combat Antisemitism Movement, "Global Antisemitism Incidents Rise 107.7%."

25 Ibid.

26 Ibid.

27 ADL, "Audit of Antisemitic Incidents 2024."

28 "Majority of Jewish College Students Say They Feel Less Safe Due to Encampments; 61% Report Antisemitism During Campus Protests," Hillel International, May 13, 2024, https://www.hillel.org/majority-of-jewish-college-students-say-they-feel-less-safe-due-to-encampments-61-report-antisemitism-during-campus-protests/.

29 "On campus, Jewish and Muslim students fear for their safety," *GBH News,* March 21, 2024, https://www.wgbh.org/news/education-news/2024-03-21/on-campus-jewish-and-muslim-students-fear-their-safety.

30 "Columbia University," ADL Campus Antisemitism Report Card, April 1, 2025, https://www.adl.org/campus-antisemitism-report-card/columbia-university.

31 Mathilda Heller, "Harvard, Columbia Quietly Promote Individuals Involved in Antisemitic Incidents," *The Jerusalem Post,* December 4, 2025, https://www.jpost.com/diaspora/antisemitism/article-879241.

References

32. Hannah Arendt, *Eichmann in Jerusalem: A Report on the Banality of Evil* (New York: Viking Press, 1963). Arendt's concept explains how institutions normalize atrocities by treating moral crimes as routine administrative tasks.
33. "Columbia University faces full-blown crisis as rabbi calls for Jewish students to 'return home,'" *CNN*, April 22, 2024, https://www.cnn.com/2024/04/21/us/columbia-university-jewish-students-protests/index.html.
34. "Campus Antisemitism Surges Amid Encampments and Related Protests at Columbia and Other US Colleges," Anti-Defamation League, June 20, 2025, https://www.adl.org/resources/article/campus-antisemitism-surges-amid-encampments-and-related-protests-columbia-and.
35. Ibid.
36. ADL, "Columbia University."
37. "Anti-Israel Activism on US Campuses, 2023–2024," Anti-Defamation League, February 7, 2025, https://www.adl.org/resources/report/anti-israel-activism-us-campuses-2023-2024.
38. "Red triangle, symbol associated with Hamas, is painted on Pittsburgh synagogue building," *Jewish Telegraphic Agency*, July 29, 2024, https://www.jta.org/2024/07/29/united-states/red-triangle-symbol-associated-with-hamas-is-painted-on-pittsburgh-synagogue-building.
39. Ibid.
40. "Congregation Mikveh Israel vandalized, hit by arson days apart," *NBC Philadelphia*, October 29, 2024, https://www.nbcphiladelphia.com/news/local/mikveh-israel-arson-vandalism/4007090/.
41. "Melbourne synagogue sustains massive damage in predawn attack by masked arsonists," *Times of Israel*, December 6, 2024, https://www.timesofisrael.com/melbourne-synagogue-sustains-massive-damage-in-predawn-attack-by-masked-arsonists/.
42. ADL, "Columbia University."
43. "We Jews cannot hide from hate," American Jewish Committee, June 17, 2025, https://www.ajc.org/news/we-jews-cannot-hide-from-hate.
44. "Jews Shouldn't Have to Hide Symbols of Their Identity," *Time*, November 18, 2024, https://time.com/7176312/jewish-identity-symbols-antisemitism/.
45. Ibid.
46. "Jewish Students Shouldn't Have to Hide Their Identity," *US News & World Report*, September 16, 2025, https://www.usnews.com/opinion

/articles/2025-09-16/college-university-students-campus-global-jewish-anti-defamation-league.

47 "North American Jews caught between Zionism, antisemitism," *Israel Hayom*, September 7, 2024, https://www.israelhayom.com/2024/09/07/north-american-aliyah-tanks-despite-rise-in-antisemitism/.

48 European Union Agency for Fundamental Rights, "Jews in Europe still face high levels of antisemitism."

49 Ibid.

50 "Antisemitism has declined from post-October 7 peak, but remains alarmingly high – TAU," *Times of Israel*, April 23, 2025, https://www.timesofisrael.com/antisemitism-has-declined-from-post-october-7-peak-but-remains-alarmingly-high-tau/.

51 "Global antisemitism remains high in 2024, with sharp surges in Italy and Australia, report finds," *Ynetnews*, April 23, 2025, https://www.ynetnews.com/article/hj8vbblkee.

52 Kenneth Stein, "US Generational Divide Solidifies on Views Toward Israel, Hamas," *Center for Israel Education*, September 2, 2025, https://israeled.org/u-s-generational-divide-solidifies-on-views-toward-israel-hamas/. Data from Harvard Center for American Political Studies (CAPS)–Harris poll, August 2025.

53 Sacha Baron Cohen made this assessment in December 2023. See also Gabriel Weimann and Natalie Masri, "TikTok's Spiral of Antisemitism," *Journalism and Media* 2, no. (November 4, 2021): 697–708, https://www.mdpi.com/2673-5172/2/4/41.

2

1 On the ceremony's location and timing: The declaration was held at the Tel Aviv Museum (today known as Independence Hall) on Rothschild Boulevard at 4:00 p.m. on Friday, May 14, 1948, 8 hours before the official end of the British Mandate. David Ben-Gurion, Chairman of the Jewish Agency Executive and head of the People's Council, read the Declaration of Independence before approximately 400 invited guests. See Israel Ministry of Foreign Affairs, "The Declaration of the Establishment of the State of Israel," May 14, 1948, https://www.gov.il/en/pages/declaration-of-establishment-state-of-israel; Israel State Archives, "The Declaration of Independence," https://catalog.archives.gov.il/site/en/chapter/the-declaration-of-independence/.

2 The United States was the first country to recognize Israel, with President Harry Truman granting *de facto* recognition just 11 minutes after the declaration of

independence at 6:11 a.m. Washington time. Truman's two-sentence statement read: "This government has been informed that a Jewish state has been proclaimed in Palestine and recognition has been requested by the provisional government thereof. The United States recognizes the provisional government as the de facto authority of the new state of Israel." *De jure* recognition followed on January 31, 1949. See Harry S. Truman Library and Museum, "Recognition of Israel," https://www.trumanlibrary.gov/education/presidential-inquiries/recognition-israel; National Archives, "Press Release Announcing US Recognition of Israel (1948)," https://www.archives.gov/milestone-documents/press-release-announcing-us-recognition-of-israel; US Department of State, Office of the Historian, "Creation of Israel, 1948," https://history.state.gov/milestones/1945–1952/creation-israel.

3   Between 1989 and 2006, approximately 1.6 million Jews and their relatives emigrated from the former Soviet Union, with about 979,000 (61%) immigrating to Israel under the Law of Return. The largest wave occurred in the early 1990s following the lifting of emigration restrictions under Mikhail Gorbachev and the subsequent collapse of the Soviet Union: 185,227 arrived in 1990 and 148,000 in 1991. By 2003, more than 950,000 Jews from the former Soviet Union had made their home in Israel. See Mark Tolts, "A Half Century of Jewish Emigration from the Former Soviet Union," Harvard University Davis Center for Russian and Eurasian Studies; Israeli Central Bureau of Statistics, Immigration Data 1989–2006; Jewish Virtual Library, "Immigration to Israel: Introduction & Historical Overview," https://www.jewishvirtuallibrary.org/introduction-and-historical-overview.

4   On June 7, 1967, the third day of the Six-Day War, Israeli paratroopers of the 55th Reserve Brigade under Colonel Mordechai "Motta" Gur entered the Old City of Jerusalem through the Lion's Gate at approximately 9:45 a.m. Upon reaching the Temple Mount, Gur broadcast the now-famous words over the IDF radio network: *"Har HaBayit b'yadeinu!"* ("The Temple Mount is in our hands!"). This marked the first time since AD 70 that the Temple Mount was under Jewish sovereignty. See Jewish Virtual Library, "The Liberation of the Temple Mount and Western Wall (June 1967)," https://www.jewishvirtuallibrary.org/the-liberation-of-the-temple-mount-and-western-wall-june-1967; Six-Day War Project, "1967: Reunification of Jerusalem," https://www.sixdaywar.org/jerusalem/1967-reunification-of-jerusalem/.

5   Following the destruction of Jerusalem and the Second Temple by Roman forces under Titus in AD 70, the city passed through the following rulers: Romans (70–324), Byzantines (324–614), Persians (614–629), Byzantines again (629–638),

Arab Caliphates including the Rashidun, Umayyad, and Abbasid dynasties (638–1099), Crusaders (1099–1187, with brief periods of control in 1229–1244), Ayyubids (1187–1250), Mamluks (1250–1517), Ottoman Empire (1517–1917), British Mandate (1917–1948), and Jordan (1948–1967, controlling East Jerusalem and the Old City). See Karen Armstrong, *Jerusalem: One City, Three Faiths* (New York: Ballantine Books, 1996); Simon Sebag Montefiore, *Jerusalem: The Biography* (New York: Alfred A. Knopf, 2011); Jewish Virtual Library, "Timeline for the History of Jerusalem," https://www.jewishvirtuallibrary.org/timeline-for-the-history-of-jerusalem-4500-bce-present.

6   We are aware that some Bible scholars believe the phrase "all nations" in Zechariah 12:2–3 and 14:2 could reflect a common prophetic convention in which universal language describes the full scope and intensity of opposition rather than a literal enumeration of every nation on earth. It is true that throughout the Bible, such language frequently denotes comprehensive involvement within a defined historical or theological frame (cf. Genesis 41:57; 1 Kings 10:24). In Zechariah, "all nations" may only refer to those drawn into opposition against Jerusalem as the focal point of divine judgment and redemption, not to the totality of all global political entities. This interpretation is reinforced by Zechariah 14:16, which anticipates surviving nations later worshipping the Lord, indicating that the phrase signifies representative global opposition rather than universal destruction. In summary, could some nations still support Israel? It's certainly possible and we take scholars who see it that way seriously. See Mark J. Boda, *The Book of Zechariah*, New International Commentary on the Old Testament (Grand Rapids: Eerdmans, 2016), 640–645.

3

1   The title "Agagite" (Hebrew: אגגי) appears five times in Esther (3:1, 3:10, 8:3, 8:5, 9:24). The Targum Sheni to Esther 3:1 provides Haman's complete genealogy tracing him through 16 generations back to Agag, then to Amalek, and finally to "the concubine of Eliphaz, firstborn son of Esau." *Jewish Encyclopedia* (New York: Funk and Wagnalls, 1906), s.v. "Haman the Agagite."

2   On Amalek's guardian angel being identified with Satan/Samael, see *Zohar* III, 282a (Ra'aya Mehemna, parashat Ki Tetze). See also Avi Sagi, "The Punishment of Amalek in Jewish Tradition: Coping with the Moral Problem," *Harvard Theological Review* 87, no. 3 (1994): 323–346; and David Golinkin, "Are Jews Still Commanded to Blot Out the Memory of Amalek?" Schechter Institute of Jewish Studies, March 2012, https://schechter.edu/are-jews-still-commanded-to-blot-out-the-memory-of-amalek-2/.

References

3   See Marc Zvi Brettler, "Megillat Esther: Reversing the Legacy of King Saul," TheTorah.com, March 5, 2017, https://www.thetorah.com/article/megillat-esther-reversing-the-legacy-of-king-saul.

4   On Amalekite territory, see Numbers 13:29 ("the land of the South"), 1 Samuel 15:7 (from Havilah to Shur), and Judges 6:3–4, which records Amalekite raids reaching "as far as Gaza."

5   Maimonides, *Mishneh Torah*, Hilkhot Melakhim uMilchamoteihem 5:4; see also *Mishneh Torah*, Hilkhot Teshuvah 3:2. For discussion of Amalek as a symbolic and ethical category in rabbinic thought, see Jonathan Sacks, *Not in God's Name: Confronting Religious Violence* (New York: Schocken Books, 2015), 61–66.

6   Elliot Horowitz, *Reckless Rites: Purim and the Legacy of Jewish Violence* (Princeton: Princeton University Press, 2006), 107–148.

7   The United Nations Human Rights Council established Agenda Item 7 ("Human rights situation in Palestine and other occupied Arab territories") on June 18, 2007. It is the only country-specific permanent item on the Council's agenda; no other nation—including North Korea, Iran, Syria, China, or Russia—receives equivalent standing scrutiny. UN Secretary-General Ban Ki-moon criticized the decision the following day: "The Secretary-General is disappointed at the Council's decision to single out only one specific regional item given the range and scope of allegations of human rights violations throughout the world." See "UN Human Rights Council makes Israel permanent agenda item," *Haaretz*, June 20, 2007; "Agenda Item 7," UN Watch, accessed December 2025, https://unwatch.org/item7/.

8   The Covenant of the Islamic Resistance Movement (Hamas) was issued on August 18, 1988. Its preamble quotes Muslim Brotherhood founder Hassan al-Banna: "Israel will exist and will continue to exist until Islam will obliterate it, just as it obliterated others before it." Article 7 invokes a hadith from Sahih al-Bukhari stating that "The Day of Judgment will not come about until Muslims fight the Jews" and kill them. Article 13 explicitly rejects "initiatives, and so-called peaceful solutions and international conferences" as "in contradiction to the principles of the Islamic Resistance Movement." Hamas issued a revised document in 2017 without formally revoking the 1988 charter. See "Hamas Covenant 1988," The Avalon Project, Yale Law School, accessed December 2025, https://avalon.law.yale.edu/20th_century/hamas.asp.

HAMAN'S LIES

4

1. For a comprehensive treatment of typological interpretation in Scripture—the understanding that certain figures, events, and institutions in the Old Testament foreshadow greater realities fulfilled in Christ and the last days—see Patrick Fairbairn, *The Typology of Scripture: Viewed in Connection with the Whole Series of the Divine Dispensations* (Grand Rapids: Kregel, 1989).

2. Arnold G. Fruchtenbaum, *The Footsteps of the Messiah: A Study of the Sequence of Prophetic Events*, rev. ed. (Tustin, CA: Ariel Ministries, 2003). Fruchtenbaum's treatment of the righteous remnant of Israel during the Tribulation, and the prophetic significance of Old Testament figures as types, is developed throughout this work.

3. Asher Intrater, "Ruth Ecclesiology and Esther Eschatology," Tikkun Global, February 2017, https://www.tikkunglobal.org/post/the-ruth-esther-keys. Intrater discusses the pattern by which the spirit of Esther rises in every generation to counter the spirit of Haman.

4. Corrie ten Boom, with John Sherrill and Elizabeth Sherrill, *The Hiding Place* (Washington Depot, CT: Chosen Books, 1971). The ten Boom family hid Jews and Dutch resistance members in a secret room behind a false wall in their Haarlem home until their betrayal and arrest on February 28, 1944. Corrie ten Boom was recognized by Yad Vashem as Righteous Among the Nations in 1967.

5. "Raoul Wallenberg and the Rescue of Jews in Budapest," United States Holocaust Memorial Museum, Holocaust Encyclopedia, https://encyclopedia.ushmm.org/content/en/article/raoul-wallenberg-and-the-rescue-of-jews-in-budapest. Wallenberg, a Swedish diplomat, arrived in Budapest in July 1944 and issued thousands of protective passports, established "Swedish houses" as safe havens, and personally intervened to remove Jews from deportation trains. He disappeared after being detained by Soviet forces in January 1945.

6. "Rescue in Denmark," United States Holocaust Memorial Museum, Holocaust Encyclopedia, https://encyclopedia.ushmm.org/content/en/gallery/rescue-in-denmark. See also "The Rescue of Denmark's Jews," Yad Vashem, https://www.yadvashem.org/righteous/stories/the-rescue-of-denmark-jews.html.

7. The survivor account of the nine-year-old child's memory—"When you hear boots on the deck, you have to be absolutely silent"—comes from testimony preserved in the Museum of Jewish Heritage exhibition on the Danish rescue. See "Rescue in Denmark," United States Holocaust Memorial Museum, Holocaust Encyclopedia.

References

8   The cargo boat *Gerda III* is now on permanent display at the Museum of Jewish Heritage in New York City. The estimate that approximately 50 Danes were involved for every Jew rescued comes from Jack Kliger, president of the Museum of Jewish Heritage, as quoted in James Barron, "A Boat That Conjures Up Denmark's Finest Hour," *The New York Times*, October 11, 2023. The "Elsinore Sewing Club" was one of several resistance groups operating under innocuous cover names.

9   The statistics that 7,200 Jews and 700 non-Jewish relatives were rescued, representing a 99% survival rate, and that only 102 Danish Jews died in the Holocaust—the highest Jewish survival rate of any Nazi-occupied country in Europe—are documented by Yad Vashem. See "The Rescue of Denmark's Jews," Yad Vashem.

10 William W. Hallo, "The First Purim," *The Biblical Archaeologist* 46, no. 1 (1983): 19–26. Hallo's analysis of the archaeological evidence for the Akkadian word *pur* ('lot'), including the ninth-century-BC clay cube (YBC 7058) from the Yale Babylonian Collection belonging to Yaḫalu, a minister of Shalmaneser III, demonstrates the connection between ancient Mesopotamian divination practices and the lots cast in the book of Esther.

11 *Encyclopaedia Judaica*, 2nd ed., s.v. "Purim," discusses the development of customs intended to blot out Haman's name in connection with Deuteronomy 25:19.

12 Abraham ben Nathan of Lunel, *Sefer HaManhig*, Hilkhot Purim, describing the custom of writing Haman's name on stones or wood and striking them together to fulfill the command to blot out Amalek.

13 Israel Isserlein (Maharil), *Sefer Maharil*, Hilkhot Purim, notes the practice of writing Haman's name on the soles of shoes and stamping when his name is mentioned during the Megillah reading.

14 Moses Isserles (Rema), gloss to *Shulchan Aruch*, Orach Chaim 690, on the evolution of Purim noise-making customs and their symbolic intent.

15 Fruchtenbaum, *The Footsteps of the Messiah*. Fruchtenbaum's interpretation of Esther as a type of the Jewish remnant during the Tribulation, including the parallels between Esther's experience and the prophesied events of the last days, is developed throughout his eschatological framework.

16 "The Tribes of Israel in the End Times," *Israel My Glory*, Friends of Israel Gospel Ministry, https://israelmyglory.org/article/the-tribes-of-israel-in-the-end-times/. This article discusses the identification of the 144,000 sealed servants of Revelation 7 and 14 as a Jewish remnant during the Tribulation.

17 The "gallows" mentioned in Esther (Hebrew ʿēts, 'tree' or 'wood') likely refers not to a rope-and-platform structure but to a wooden stake or pole used for impalement or public suspension, a common Persian form of execution. The Hebrew verb tālāh ('to hang' or 'to suspend') does not specify the method of death and is used elsewhere for postmortem display (cf. Deuteronomy. 21:22–23). Many scholars note that the structure's extreme height (fifty cubits) supports this interpretation. See Carey A. Moore, *Esther*, Anchor Yale Bible 7B (New Haven: Yale University Press, 1971), 52–53; Adele Berlin, *Esther: The Traditional Hebrew Text with the New JPS Translation* (Philadelphia: Jewish Publication Society, 2001), 47–48.

18 The concept of the "spirit of Elijah" coming upon John the Baptist is found in Luke 1:17, where the angel Gabriel tells Zechariah that John will go before the Lord "in the spirit and power of Elijah." This establishes the biblical pattern by which a prophetic calling or mantle can be transferred across generations without requiring literal reincarnation (cf. John 1:21, where John denies being Elijah himself).

19 The observation that God's name is never mentioned directly in the book of Esther, yet His providential work is evident throughout, is noted in the Babylonian Talmud, *Chullin* 139b, which finds an allusion to Esther in Deuteronomy 31:18, where God says, "I will surely hide [*haster astir*] My face." The name "Esther" is connected to the Hebrew root *s-t-r*, meaning 'to hide' or 'to conceal.'

20 James Russell Lowell, "Once to Every Man and Nation," in *Poems of James Russell Lowell*, rev. ed. (Boston: Houghton, Mifflin and Company, 1890), 155–56.

21 Ibid.

5

1 Eric Metaxas, *Bonhoeffer: Pastor, Martyr, Prophet, Spy* (Nashville: Thomas Nelson, 2010); Corrie ten Boom, *The Hiding Place* (see Chapter 4, note 4). These works portray Christians whose convictions led them to risk—and in some cases sacrifice—their lives to protect Jews during the Holocaust."

2 Robert Conquest, *The Great Terror: A Reassessment* (New York: Oxford University Press, 1990). Conquest documents Stalin's purges and the widespread denial among Western intellectuals who praised the Soviet Union while atrocities were underway. His research underscores the chapter's point that distant supporters can become defenders of movements that would destroy them.

3 Jonathan Rauch, "The Constitution of Knowledge," *National Affairs*, no. 45 (Fall 2020). Rauch outlines how truth-seeking systems function—through criticism,

open debate, and institutional checks that keep error from spreading. His analysis sheds light on why movements built on deception must silence dissenters rather than answer them.

4   Jacques Ellul, *Propaganda: The Formation of Men's Attitudes* (New York: Alfred A. Knopf, 1965; reprint, New York: Vintage Books, 1973). Ellul explains how modern propaganda works primarily through emotional manipulation, especially appeals to compassion, which can bypass critical thinking. His insights support the chapter's discussion of "compassion as a weapon."

5   Hannah Arendt, *The Origins of Totalitarianism* (New York: Harcourt, Brace, 1951). Arendt analyzes how totalitarian systems invert moral categories, redefine reality, and isolate individuals from shared truth. Her work illuminates the chapter's explanation of societies calling evil good and good evil.

6   George Orwell, "Politics and the English Language," in *Shooting an Elephant and Other Essays* (London: Secker & Warburg, 1950). Orwell shows how political actors corrupt language in order to corrupt thought, masking moral outrage with euphemism. His essay strengthens the chapter's argument that linguistic manipulation precedes moral confusion.

7   Yascha Mounk, *The Identity Trap: A Story of Ideas and Power in Our Time* (New York: Penguin Press, 2023). Mounk documents how ideological frameworks have captured major Western institutions and reshaped their decision-making. His work supports the chapter's point that institutional consensus no longer guarantees truth.

8   Thomas Sowell, *Intellectuals and Society* (New York: Basic Books, 2009). Sowell argues that intellectuals often advocate ideas without bearing the consequences of those ideas, creating a harmful disconnect between theory and real-world impact. This directly informs the chapter's section on leaders who are insulated from the costs of their ideologies.

9   Hannah Arendt, *The Origins of Totalitarianism* (New York: Harcourt, Brace, 1951); Robert Conquest, *The Great Terror: A Reassessment* (New York: Oxford University Press, 1990). Read together, Arendt and Conquest provide historical models of deceptive systems in full operation—showing how ordinary people, bureaucracies, and entire cultures become instruments of destructive agendas they believe are righteous.

6

1   Captain Alfred Dreyfus, a Jewish officer in the French Army's General Staff, was arrested on October 15, 1894, and charged with passing military secrets

to Germany. The sole evidence against him was a handwritten document (the *bordereau*) retrieved from the German embassy. He was convicted by a military tribunal on December 22, 1894, and sentenced to life imprisonment on Devil's Island, French Guiana. The case was later revealed to be a cover-up protecting the actual spy, Major Ferdinand Walsin Esterhazy. Dreyfus was not fully exonerated until July 12, 1906. See "Alfred Dreyfus and the 'Dreyfus Affair,'" Holocaust Encyclopedia, United States Holocaust Memorial Museum, https://encyclopedia.ushmm.org/content/en/article/alfred-dreyfus-and-the-dreyfus-affair.

2   Theodor Herzl, *Der Judenstaat: Versuch einer modernen Lösung der Judenfrage* [The Jewish State: An Attempt at a Modern Solution of the Jewish Question] (Vienna: M. Breitenstein, 1896). The Dreyfus degradation ceremony took place on January 5, 1895, in the courtyard of the École Militaire in Paris. Herzl, then a correspondent for the Viennese *Neue Freie Presse*, reported on the event and witnessed crowds shouting "Death to the Jews" as Captain Dreyfus had his insignia stripped and his sword broken. The experience convinced Herzl that Jewish assimilation into European society would never provide security against antisemitism. See "Theodor (Binyamin Ze'ev) Herzl," Jewish Virtual Library, https://www.jewishvirtuallibrary.org/theodor-binyamin-ze-rsquo-ev-herzl.

3   The MS *St. Louis* departed Hamburg on May 13, 1939, carrying 937 passengers, almost all Jewish refugees fleeing Nazi Germany with Cuban landing permits. After Cuba revoked their permits upon arrival on May 27, the ship was denied entry by Cuba, the United States (which deployed Coast Guard vessels to prevent unauthorized landing), and Canada (June 7). Forced to return to Europe, passengers were accepted by the United Kingdom (288), France (224), Belgium (214), and the Netherlands (181). Of the 620 who disembarked in continental Europe, 254 later perished in the Holocaust. See "Voyage of the St. Louis," Holocaust Encyclopedia, United States Holocaust Memorial Museum, https://encyclopedia.ushmm.org/content/en/article/voyage-of-the-st-louis.

4   The United Nations Relief and Works Agency (UNRWA) defines Palestinian refugees as "persons whose normal place of residence was Palestine during the period 1 June 1946 to 15 May 1948, and who lost both home and means of livelihood as a result of the 1948 conflict," and uniquely extends this status to all patrilineal descendants regardless of citizenship acquired elsewhere. In 1965, UNRWA expanded eligibility to include third-generation descendants, and in 1982 extended it to all descendants of male refugees without limit. Under the 1951 UN Convention Relating to the Status of Refugees administered by UNHCR, a person ceases to be a refugee upon acquiring "a new nationality, and enjoy[ing] the protection of the country of his new nationality" (Article I[c][3]). UNRWA's

operational definition contains no such provision. The original 1948 refugee population of approximately 700,000 has grown to over 5.9 million registered refugees under UNRWA's criteria. See "Palestine Refugees," UNRWA, https://www.unrwa.org/palestine-refugees; James G. Lindsay, "Fixing UNRWA: Repairing the UN's Troubled System of Aid to Palestinian Refugees," Washington Institute for Near East Policy, Policy Focus #91, January 2009.

5   According to the Pew Research Center's comprehensive 2020 survey of Jewish Americans (4,718 respondents), 82% said that caring about Israel is an essential or important part of what being Jewish means to them, and 58% reported feeling "very" or "somewhat" emotionally attached to Israel. Among Jews by religion (as opposed to Jews of no religion), 67% reported emotional attachment to Israel. See "US Jews' Connections with and Attitudes toward Israel," Pew Research Center, May 11, 2021, https://www.pewresearch.org/religion/2021/05/11/u-s-jews-connections-with-and-attitudes-toward-israel/.

6   The blood libel—the false accusation that Jews murdered Christian children to use their blood in religious rituals—first emerged in medieval England. The earliest documented case occurred in Norwich in 1144, when the death of a 12-year-old boy named William was attributed to Jews by the monk Thomas of Monmouth in his hagiography *The Life and Miracles of St William of Norwich* (c. 1150). The accusation spread across England and continental Europe, provoking massacres, expulsions, and executions for centuries. Pope Innocent IV formally denounced the blood libel as false in the papal bull *Lacrimabilem Judaeorum* (1247). See E. M. Rose, *The Murder of William of Norwich: The Origins of Blood Libel in Medieval Europe* (New York: Oxford University Press, 2015); "Blood Libel," Holocaust Encyclopedia, United States Holocaust Memorial Museum, https://encyclopedia.ushmm.org/content/en/article/blood-libel.

7   The structural parallels between classical antisemitic tropes and contemporary anti-Zionist discourse have been extensively documented. On dual loyalty accusations, the American Jewish Committee (AJC) notes this canard "has existed for thousands of years" and "has been used to scapegoat, harass, and vilify Jews." The International Holocaust Remembrance Alliance (IHRA) working definition of antisemitism specifically identifies "accusing Jewish citizens of being more loyal to Israel... than to the interests of their own nations" as a contemporary example of antisemitism. On the "Israel Lobby" conspiracy theory, see John J. Mearsheimer and Stephen M. Walt, *The Israel Lobby and US Foreign Policy* (New York: Farrar, Straus, and Giroux, 2007). On classical tropes in anti-Zionist discourse, see David Hirsh, *Contemporary Left Antisemitism* (London: Routledge, 2017). See also "Dual

Loyalty," #TranslateHate, American Jewish Committee, https://www.ajc.org/translatehate/dual-loyalty.

8 The term "supersessionism" derives from the Latin *supersedere* (from *super*, 'upon,' and *sedere*, 'to sit'), conveying the notion of one thing sitting in the place of another. Scholars distinguish three forms: (1) *punitive supersessionism*, which holds that God rejected Israel as punishment for rejecting Jesus; (2) *economic supersessionism*, which views Israel's role as merely preparatory, rendered obsolete by Christ; and (3) *structural supersessionism*, which marginalizes Israel by constructing the biblical narrative without essential reference to God's covenant with Israel. These categories were systematized by R. Kendall Soulen in *The God of Israel and Christian Theology* (Minneapolis: Fortress Press, 1996), 1–21.

9 Michael J. Vlach, *Has the Church Replaced Israel? A Theological Evaluation* (Nashville: B&H Academic, 2010). Vlach traces supersessionism from Justin Martyr's *Dialogue with Trypho* (c. AD 160) through the medieval period, Reformation, and into modern theology, documenting how supersessionist teaching "has been the dominant view of the church concerning Israel for much of church history" (p. 23). Gerald R. McDermott, *Israel Matters: Why Christians Must Think Differently about the People and the Land* (Grand Rapids: Brazos Press, 2017). McDermott demonstrates that supersessionism created a theological environment in which Christian indifference to Jewish suffering became normalized.

10 The Greek word ἀμεταμέλητα (*ametameléta*) appears only twice in the New Testament (Romans 11:29 and 2 Corinthians 7:10). The term is a compound of the alpha privative (negation) and *metamelomai* ("'to regret'"), yielding "'not to be regretted,'" "'without change of purpose,'" or "'irrevocable.'" Douglas J. Moo writes that the term means God "will never take back" his gifts to Israel. See Douglas J. Moo, *The Letter to the Romans*, 2nd ed., New International Commentary on the New Testament (Grand Rapids: Eerdmans, 2018), 733–736; Thomas R. Schreiner, *Romans*, 2nd ed., Baker Exegetical Commentary on the New Testament (Grand Rapids: Baker Academic, 2018), 615–617.

11 David M. Friedman served as United States Ambassador to Israel from 2017 to 2021. His statement was made in response to a June 2025 interview between Senator Ted Cruz (R–TX) and commentator Tucker Carlson regarding US support for Israel. Friedman continued: "This is the same nation of Israel referred to in the Bible." See "Ted Cruz Defends Support For Israel With Bible Verse in Fiery Exchange With Tucker Carlson," Beliefnet, June 23, 2025, https://www.beliefnet.com/columnists/news/2025/06/ted-cruz-defends-support-for-israel-with-bible-verse-in-fiery-exchange-with-tucker-carlson.

12 Doron M. Behar et al., "The Genome-Wide Structure of the Jewish People," *Nature* 466, no. 7303 (July 8, 2010): 238–242, https://doi.org/10.1038/nature09103. The international research team used high-density bead arrays to genotype individuals from fourteen Jewish Diaspora communities and compared patterns of genome-wide diversity with sixty-nine Old World non-Jewish populations. The study found that "most Jewish samples form a remarkably tight subcluster" with genetic origins tracing to the Levant. A parallel study reached similar conclusions: Gil Atzmon et al., "Abraham's Children in the Genome Era," *American Journal of Human Genetics* 86, no. 6 (June 2010): 850–859.

13 Jeremiah 31:35–37 conditions God's rejection of Israel on cosmological impossibilities—the departure of the sun, moon, and stars—thereby affirming the unconditional permanence of Israel's national existence. This text appears in the immediate context of the New Covenant promise (Jeremiah 31:31–34).

14 Vlach, *Has the Church Replaced Israel?*, 185. Vlach presents 7 arguments for Israel's restoration: (1) the Bible explicitly teaches the restoration of Israel (Deuteronomy 30:1–10; Ezekiel 36–37; Amos 9:11–15); (2) the Bible promises the perpetuity of Israel (Jeremiah 31:35–37); (3) the New Testament reaffirms Israel's future restoration (Romans 11:26–27); (4) New Testament authors affirm Old Testament promises will be fulfilled with Israel; (5) the New Testament presents the Church as something new, not "the new Israel"; (6) the doctrine of election supports Israel's restoration; (7) the biblical covenants support Israel's future restoration. See pages 177–202.

15 McDermott, *Israel Matters*, 35–52. McDermott traces "Christian Zionism before Zionism" through Thomas Draxe (*The Worldes Resurrection*, 1608), Thomas Brightman (*A Revelation of the Apocalypse*, 1615), Sir Henry Finch (*The Worlds Great Restauration*, 1621), Increase Mather (*The Mystery of Israel's Salvation*, 1669), and Jonathan Edwards. These theologians—writing centuries before modern dispensationalism—interpreted Scripture as teaching a future restoration of the Jewish people to their land.

7

1 Pass laws were one of the central tools of South Africa's apartheid system. They were racially discriminatory internal passports designed to control where Black South Africans could go, live, or work.

2 For a comprehensive history of South African apartheid and its legal structure, see Leonard Thompson, *A History of South Africa*, 4th ed. (New Haven: Yale University Press, 2014).

HAMAN'S LIES

3   Israel's Central Bureau of Statistics reports that Arab citizens comprise approximately 21% of Israel's population as of 2024. See "Statistical Abstract of Israel," Israel Central Bureau of Statistics, https://www.cbs.gov.il/.

4   Arab political representation in the Knesset spans multiple parties. The Joint List coalition and Ra'am (United Arab List) are predominantly Arab parties, but Arab citizens also serve in mainstream parties. See "Members of the Knesset," The Knesset, https://www.knesset.gov.il/.

5   Justice Salim Joubran served on Israel's Supreme Court from 2004 to 2017. He was part of the three-judge panel that unanimously rejected the appeal of President Moshe Katsav, who was convicted of rape in 2011. See "Katsav to Serve 7 Years for Rape Conviction," *Jerusalem Post*, November 10, 2011.

6   Arab physicians constitute a significant portion of Israel's medical workforce, with some hospitals reporting that Arab doctors comprise 30–40% of medical staff. See reports from Israel's Ministry of Health and academic studies on healthcare demographics in Israel.

7   The exemption of Arab citizens from mandatory military service dates to Israel's founding and reflects the state's recognition of the complex position of Arab citizens. See Oren Barak and Gabriel Sheffer, "Israel's 'Security Network' and Its Impact," *International Journal of Middle East Studies* 38, no. 2 (2006): 235–61.

8   Druze citizens have served in the IDF since 1956 under a compulsory service agreement reached with Druze community leaders. Bedouin citizens serve in significant numbers as volunteers, particularly in tracking units. See "Minorities in the IDF," Israel Defense Forces.

9   Israel's Declaration of Independence (May 14, 1948) states: "THE STATE OF ISRAEL... will ensure complete equality of social and political rights to all its inhabitants irrespective of religion, race or sex; it will guarantee freedom of religion, conscience, language, education and culture." Full text available through Israel Ministry of Foreign Affairs.

10 The Israeli government has launched several multi-billion shekel programs to address disparities in Arab communities, including Government Resolution 922 (2015), allocating 15 billion shekels over five years for economic development in Arab municipalities. See Israel Ministry of Finance documentation.

11 For comprehensive documentation of the Oslo Accords, see Chapter 20, note 3.

12 The Second Intifada (2000–2005) resulted in over 1,000 Israeli civilian deaths from suicide bombings and other terror attacks. See Israel Ministry of Foreign Affairs casualty documentation and B'Tselem statistics.

13 Following construction of the security barrier (begun 2002), terrorist attacks originating from the West Bank decreased by over 90%. See Israeli Security Agency (Shin Bet) statistics and academic analyses in *Terrorism and Political Violence*.

14 Richard Goldstone, "Israel and the Apartheid Slander," *New York Times*, October 31, 2011. Goldstone wrote: "In Israel, there is no apartheid. Nothing there comes close to the definition of apartheid under the 1998 Rome Statute."

15 For documentation of Soviet anti-Zionist propaganda campaigns, see Izabella Tabarovsky, "Soviet Anti-Zionism and Contemporary Left Antisemitism," *Fathom Journal*, May 2019; and Joel Kotek, "Major Anti-Israeli Fictions," *Jewish Political Studies Review*. The USSR's campaign culminated in UN Resolution 3379 (1975), which was revoked by Resolution 46/86 in 1991.

16 Freedom House consistently rates Israel as "Free" in its annual Freedom in the World reports—the only country in the Middle East and North Africa region to receive this designation. See https://freedomhouse.org/.

8

1 Testimony of Awni Abd al-Hadi, Secretary of the Arab Higher Committee, before the Peel Commission (British Royal Commission of Inquiry), 1937. The Peel Commission investigated the causes of unrest in Mandatory Palestine. Similar testimony was given before UNSCOP (UN Special Committee on Palestine) in 1947.

2 Kenneth W. Stein, *The Land Question in Palestine, 1917–1939* (Chapel Hill: University of North Carolina Press, 1984). Stein's research documents the political objectives of Arab leadership during the Mandate period.

3 Statement of the Arab Higher Committee to the UN Ad Hoc Committee on the Palestinian Question, 1947. See UN documentation and Benny Morris, *1948: A History of the First Arab–Israeli War* (New Haven: Yale University Press, 2008).

4 On May 15, 1948, armies from Egypt, Jordan, Syria, Iraq, and Lebanon invaded the newly declared State of Israel. Arab League Secretary-General Azzam Pasha declared: "This will be a war of extermination and momentous massacre." The original source is an interview with Azzam Pasha published in *Akhbar al-Yom* (Cairo), October 11, 1947. See David Barnett and Efraim Karsh, "Azzam's Genocidal Threat," *Middle East Quarterly* 18, no. 4 (Fall 2011): 85–88; Morris, *1948*.

5 The causes of Palestinian flight in 1948 are debated by historians. Factors include fear of violence, Arab leadership instructions, psychological warfare, and

direct expulsion in some cases. See Benny Morris, *The Birth of the Palestinian Refugee Problem Revisited* (Cambridge: Cambridge University Press, 2004) for a comprehensive analysis.

6   Between 1948 and the early 1970s, approximately 850,000 Jews were expelled or fled from Arab countries. Their property was confiscated and their communities destroyed. See JIMENA (Jews Indigenous to the Middle East and North Africa), https://www.jimena.org/; and "Jewish Refugees from Arab Countries," Israel Ministry of Foreign Affairs.

7   Khaled al-Azm, *Mudhakkirat* (Memoirs), Volume 1, Beirut, 1973, 386–387.

8   Mahmoud Abbas interview with Palestinian TV (Falastin), March 2008. Also cited in *The Wall Street Journal*, June 5, 2011.

9   British Mandate census data from 1922 and 1931 show a 37% increase in the Muslim population—far exceeding natural growth rates. See *A Survey of Palestine*, prepared by the British Mandate government for UNSCOP (1946–1947), and Roberto Bachi, *The Population of Israel* (Jerusalem: Hebrew University, 1977).

10 Population growth figures from British Mandate census records. See Justin McCarthy, *The Population of Palestine: Population History and Statistics of the Late Ottoman Period and the Mandate* (New York: Columbia University Press, 1990).

11 On Ottoman resettlement policies and migration patterns, see Kemal Karpat, *Ottoman Population 1830–1914: Demographic and Social Characteristics* (Madison: University of Wisconsin Press, 1985); and Fred M. Gottheil, "The Smoking Gun: Arab Immigration into Palestine, 1922–1931," *Middle East Quarterly* 10, no. 1 (Winter 2003): 53–64.

12 UNRWA Consolidated Eligibility and Registration Instructions define Palestinian refugees as "persons whose normal place of residence was Palestine during the period 1 June 1946 to 15 May 1948, and who lost both home and means of livelihood as a result of the 1948 conflict." This status passes to descendants, unlike any other refugee population under UNHCR.

13 Jordan annexed the West Bank in 1950 (recognized only by the United Kingdom and Pakistan; rejected by the Arab League). Egypt administered Gaza as occupied territory without offering citizenship or statehood to its residents. See Yehuda Z. Blum, "The Missing Reversioner: Reflections on the Status of Judea and Samaria," *Israel Law Review* 3, no. 2 (April 1968): 279–301.

14 The San Remo Conference (April 1920) and League of Nations Mandate (July 1922) recognized the Jewish historical connection to Palestine and established the legal framework for the Jewish national home. See Howard Grief, *The Legal*

Foundation and Borders of Israel Under International Law (Jerusalem: Mazo Publishers, 2008).

15 Archaeological discoveries at Shiloh by the Associates for Biblical Research, directed by Dr. Scott Stripling, have uncovered evidence of Israelite cultic activity including altar horns and bone deposits consistent with biblical descriptions. Excavations beginning in 2017 have revealed a monumental building from the Iron Age I period (circa 1177–980 BC) that may correspond to the Tabernacle complex. See Associates for Biblical Research reports and Israel Antiquities Authority documentation.

16 Jewish presence in the Land of Israel dates to approximately 1200 BC, with continuous habitation documented through archaeological and historical records. The Arab conquest of the Levant occurred AD 634–638. See Anita Shapira, *Israel: A History* (Waltham, MA: Brandeis University Press, 2012).

17 For a comprehensive legal and historical analysis of Israel's founding, see Alan Dershowitz, *The Case for Israel* (Hoboken, NJ: Wiley, 2003); Eli E. Hertz, "This Land Is My Land" (Myths and Facts, 2008); and Eugene V. Rostow, "Palestinian Self-Determination: Possible Futures for the Unallocated Territories of the Palestine Mandate," *Yale Studies in World Public Order* 5, no. 2 (1979): 147–172.

9

1 No sovereign Palestinian state has existed in recorded history. The region was successively ruled by Israelite kingdoms, Babylonian, Persian, Greek, Roman, Byzantine, Arab Caliphate, Crusader, Mamluk, Ottoman (1517–1917), and British Mandate (1920–1948) authorities.

2 While only the United Kingdom and Pakistan recognized Jordan's annexation of the West Bank (April 24, 1950), the Arab League explicitly rejected it. See Yehuda Z. Blum, "The Missing Reversioner: Reflections on the Status of Judea and Samaria," *Israel Law Review* 3, no. 2 (April 1968): 279–301.

3 Under Jordanian rule (1948–1967), 58 synagogues were destroyed or desecrated, and the Mount of Olives cemetery—the oldest Jewish cemetery in continuous use—was vandalized with tombstones used for construction and latrines. Documentation available through Jerusalem Foundation archives and Israeli government records.

4 Egypt's closure of the Straits of Tiran on May 22–23, 1967 was considered a casus belli. Israel had declared in 1957 that such closure would constitute an act of war. President Lyndon Johnson later stated: "If a single act of folly was more

5 Nasser's statement of May 27, 1967: "Our basic objective will be the destruction of Israel. The Arab people want to fight." See Michael B. Oren, *Six Days of War: June 1967 and the Making of the Modern Middle East* (New York: Oxford University Press, 2002).

6 On the legal status of territories captured in defensive wars, see Julius Stone, *Israel and Palestine: Assault on the Law of Nations* (Baltimore: Johns Hopkins University Press, 1981); and Stephen M. Schwebel, "What Weight to Conquest?" *American Journal of International Law* 64, no. 2 (1970): 344–347.

7 The San Remo Conference (April 19–26, 1920) assigned the Mandate for Palestine to the United Kingdom with the stated purpose of establishing a Jewish national home. The resolution incorporated the Balfour Declaration and was ratified by the League of Nations on July 24, 1922.

8 The League of Nations Mandate for Palestine (1922), Article 6: "The Administration of Palestine... shall encourage, in cooperation with the Jewish agency... close settlement by Jews on the land, including State lands and waste lands not required for public purposes."

9 UN Security Council Resolution 242 (November 22, 1967) called for "withdrawal of Israeli armed forces from territories occupied"—not "the territories" or "all territories." Lord Caradon, the resolution's chief drafter, confirmed: "We deliberately did not say that the old line... was an ideal demarcation line.... We did not put the 'the' in, we did not say 'all the territories' deliberately."

10 Jordan formally renounced its claim to the West Bank on July 31, 1988. King Hussein's address severed all legal and administrative ties to the territory.

11 Oslo I (1993) and Oslo II (1995) divided the West Bank into Areas A, B, and C. See Chapter 20, note 3 for full documentation.

12 Israel's unilateral disengagement from Gaza (August 15–September 12, 2005) involved the evacuation of approximately 8,000 Israeli settlers from 21 settlements and the removal of all IDF forces. See "The Disengagement Plan," Israel Ministry of Foreign Affairs.

10

1 Jordan's annexation of the West Bank (April 24, 1950) was recognized only by the United Kingdom and Pakistan. The United States extended de facto recognition but excluded Jerusalem. The Arab League rejected the annexation, with Egypt, Syria, Saudi Arabia, and Lebanon demanding Jordan's expulsion. See Yehuda Z.

References

Blum, "The Missing Reversioner: Reflections on the Status of Judea and Samaria," *Israel Law Review* 3, no. 2 (April 1968): 279–301.

2 By the 1860s, Jews constituted the largest single religious group in Jerusalem, a majority they maintained into the twentieth century. See Yehoshua Ben-Arieh, *Jerusalem in the 19th Century: The Old City* (Jerusalem: Yad Izhak Ben-Zvi Institute; New York: St. Martin's Press, 1984). Ottoman census data and Montefiore census records analyzed in Ben-Arieh corroborate these findings.

3 Under Israeli administration since 1967, all faiths have access to their holy sites in Jerusalem. The Temple Mount/Haram al-Sharif remains under the administration of the Islamic Waqf, an arrangement formalized by Defense Minister Moshe Dayan in June 1967. See Nadav Shragai, "The 'Status Quo' on the Temple Mount," Jerusalem Center for Public Affairs, 2014.

4 Syrian forces used the Golan Heights to shell Israeli communities from 1948 to 1967. Israeli farmers worked fields under fire for nearly two decades, and Syrian snipers targeted civilians below. Documentation available in IDF records and contemporary news accounts.

5 On March 25, 2019, President Donald Trump signed Presidential Proclamation 9852 recognizing Israeli sovereignty over the Golan Heights, citing "aggressive acts by Iran and terrorist groups, including Hizballah, in southern Syria." The Biden administration reaffirmed this recognition. Full text at Trump White House Archives.

11

1 Israeli Jews trace their origins to over 100 countries across Europe, Asia, Africa, and the Americas. See Israel Central Bureau of Statistics, "Immigration to Israel," available at cbs.gov.il; Israel Ministry of Immigration and Absorption, "The Ingathering of the Exiles."

2 Jewish holidays are tied to the agricultural calendar of the Land of Israel: Passover (Pesach) marks the spring barley harvest; Shavuot marks the wheat harvest; Sukkot marks the fall fruit harvest. The Jewish calendar's intercalation ensures holidays remain in their proper agricultural seasons in Israel. See Encyclopedia Britannica, "Shavuot;" Chabad.org, "From Barley to Wheat."

3 Ephraim Stern, *Archaeology of the Land of the Bible, Volume II: The Assyrian, Babylonian, and Persian Periods (732–332 B.C.E.)* (New York: Doubleday, 2001). See also Yigael Yadin's excavations at Masada, Hazor, and Megiddo, which documented extensive Jewish presence from the Second Temple period and earlier.

4   The Hebron massacre of August 24, 1929, killed 67 Jews and destroyed the ancient Jewish community of Hebron. Survivors were evacuated to Jerusalem by British authorities. See Jerold S. Auerbach, *Hebron Jews: Memory and Conflict in the Land of Israel* (Lanham, MD: Rowman & Littlefield, 2009).

5   Approximately half of Israeli Jews are Mizrahi or Sephardi, descended from communities in Arab and Muslim countries. Over 850,000 Jews were expelled from Arab lands between 1948 and the early 1970s. See Lyn Julius, *Uprooted: How 3000 Years of Jewish Civilization in the Arab World Vanished Overnight* (London: Vallentine Mitchell, 2018).

6   Harry Ostrer, *Legacy: A Genetic History of the Jewish People* (Oxford: Oxford University Press, 2012). Genetic studies consistently show that Jewish populations share significant Middle Eastern ancestry despite centuries of diaspora.

7   The Arab conquest of the Levant occurred AD 634–638 under the Rashidun Caliphate. Jerusalem fell in AD 637 or 638. This was over 1,600 years after the establishment of the Israelite kingdoms and over 600 years after the destruction of the Second Temple in AD 70. See World History Encyclopedia, "Early Muslim Conquests (622–656 CE)."

8   Anti-Defamation League, "Slogan: 'From the River to the Sea Palestine Will be Free,'" January 2024.

9   Howard Grief, *The Legal Foundation and Borders of Israel Under International Law* (Jerusalem: Mazo Publishers, 2008); Eugene V. Rostow, "Palestinian Self-Determination: Possible Futures for the Unallocated Territories of the Palestine Mandate," *Yale Studies in World Public Order* 5 (1979): 147–172.

12

1   Raphael Lemkin, *Axis Rule in Occupied Europe: Laws of Occupation, Analysis of Government, Proposals for Redress* (Washington, DC: Carnegie Endowment for International Peace, 1944). Lemkin, a Polish-Jewish lawyer who lost 49 family members in the Holocaust, coined the term "genocide" from the Greek *genos* ('race,' 'people') and the Latin *-cide* ('killing').

2   Convention on the Prevention and Punishment of the Crime of Genocide, December 9, 1948, Article II. The Convention defines genocide as "any of the following acts committed with intent to destroy, in whole or in part, a national, ethnical, racial or religious group." See United Nations Office on Genocide Prevention and the Responsibility to Protect, "Definitions of Genocide and Related Crimes," available at un.org/en/genocide-prevention.

References

3   The term "ethnic cleansing" gained prominence during the Yugoslav Wars. The UN Commission of Experts established pursuant to Security Council Resolution 780 defined ethnic cleansing in its 1994 Final Report as "rendering an area ethnically homogenous by using force or intimidation to remove persons of given groups from the area." See UN Doc. S/1994/674 (May 27, 1994).

4   Israel Central Bureau of Statistics. In 1948, approximately 156,000 Arabs remained within Israel's borders. As of 2024, Israel's Arab population exceeds 2 million, comprising approximately 21% of Israel's citizenry—a more than twelvefold increase. See "Israeli Arab Statistics," Jewish Virtual Library; Israel Central Bureau of Statistics, "Population and Demography."

5   Palestinian Central Bureau of Statistics and World Bank demographic data. The West Bank Palestinian population grew from approximately 600,000 in 1967 to over 3 million today. Gaza's population increased from approximately 350,000 in 1967 to over 2 million before the October 7, 2023, war. See World Bank, "Palestinian Territories Population Data."

6   COGAT (Coordinator of Government Activities in the Territories) documentation of humanitarian coordination. Israel provides electricity, water, and facilitates humanitarian aid to Gaza. See COGAT, "Humanitarian Aid to Gaza," available at gov.il/cogat.

7   Israel reopened the Kerem Shalom crossing for humanitarian aid in mid-December 2023, citing "urgent security need" to increase humanitarian deliveries. Additional crossings were subsequently opened, including a new Northern Crossing in late 2024 specifically designed to increase aid flow to northern Gaza. The Erez crossing was opened in April 2024. See COGAT, "Humanitarian Activity Reports," cogat.mod.gov.il; IDF timeline of humanitarian aid efforts.

8   In a report published by the IDF in April 2024, Israel reported facilitating the entry of 19,776 trucks of humanitarian aid into Gaza through the Kerem Shalom and Nitsana border crossings, bringing in 369,990 tons of aid. This was supplemented by at least 50 airdrops of approximately 3,000 packages and six field hospitals. See IDF, "Humanitarian Aid Efforts," April 2024.

9   According to AJC, citing COGAT data, since May 2025, over 10,000 aid trucks have entered Gaza, with approximately 80% carrying food, alongside 5,000 tons of baby food and more than 2,500 tons of medical supplies. Airdrops by 12 countries have delivered more than 2,300 food packages. See AJC, "Humanitarian Aid in Gaza: What's Really Happening," September 2025.

10   COGAT stated in August 2025 that there were "dramatic and severe gaps" between its figures and UN reports—nearly 6,000 trucks uncounted. COGAT

explained that UN monitoring includes only trucks handled by UN agencies, excluding assistance delivered by other countries, international organizations, the private sector, airdrops, and US-operated distribution hubs. See *Ynet*, "UN misrepresents Gaza aid flow," August 19, 2025.

11 United Nations Office for Project Services data showed that from May 19 to August 5, 2025, of 4,659 trucks that entered Gaza, 4,107 (approximately 88%) were "intercepted"—meaning cargo was taken before reaching intended destinations. The UN clarified that the majority of interceptions were by hungry civilians, not armed gangs. See *Times of Israel*, "Almost 9 in 10 aid trucks looted before reaching Gaza destinations," August 5, 2025.

12 COGAT Major General Ghassan Alian posted video in November 2024 showing 600 trucks worth of humanitarian aid in Gaza that the UN had not distributed. ILTV reported from the Gaza side of Kerem Shalom in August 2025 that "thousands and thousands of tons of humanitarian aid [...] is sitting here in the boiling sun." See COGAT statements; ILTV reporting from Kerem Shalom, August 2025.

13 UNRWA reported that 98 of 109 trucks in a convoy were looted near Kerem Shalom in November 2024, calling it "one of the worst" incidents of its kind. UNRWA stated it was unable to identify perpetrators due to "total breakdown of civil order." Hamas subsequently announced it had killed 20 "gang members" involved in looting. See *Times of Israel*, "UN says nearly 100 Gaza aid trucks looted," November 19, 2024.

14 The Hamas Covenant (1988), also known as the Hamas Charter, explicitly calls for the destruction of Israel and contains virulently antisemitic passages. Article 7 cites a hadith calling for Muslims to kill Jews. Article 22 propagates conspiracy theories about Jewish control of world events. Article 32 states: "Their scheme has been laid out in '*The Protocols of the Elders of Zion*.'" The Preamble declares: "Israel will exist and will continue to exist until Islam invalidates it." Full text available at Yale Law School, Avalon Project.

15 Iranian leaders have repeatedly called for Israel's elimination. Former President Mahmoud Ahmadinejad called for Israel to be "wiped off the map." Supreme Leader Ayatollah Khamenei has called Israel a "cancerous tumor" that must be removed. See Anti-Defamation League, "Iranian Leaders' Statements Calling for Israel's Destruction."

16 Hezbollah leader Hassan Nasrallah stated in 2002: "If they [Jews] all gather in Israel, it will save us the trouble of going after them worldwide." See MEMRI

References

(Middle East Media Research Institute), Special Dispatch No. 426, October 23, 2002.

17 The Boycott, Divestment, and Sanctions movement was launched on July 9, 2005, by a coalition of 170 Palestinian organizations. Its three demands include ending Israel's "occupation and colonization of all Arab lands," full equality for Arab citizens of Israel, and the return of Palestinian refugees and their descendants—which, if implemented, would transform Israel into a Palestinian-majority state. BDS founder Omar Barghouti has stated that the goal is to end the existence of Israel as a Jewish state. See BDS Movement, "What is BDS?," bdsmovement.net; Encyclopedia Britannica, "Boycott, Divestment, Sanctions (BDS)."

13

1 Documentation of Israeli warning systems is extensive. During Operation Protective Edge (2014), the IDF employed multiple warning methods: phone calls to buildings about to be struck, text messages to cell phones, leaflets dropped over Gaza (over 5 million during the 2014 conflict), and "roof knock" warning munitions. See Israel Defense Forces, "How is the IDF Minimizing Harm to Civilians in Gaza?," idf.il; UN Office for the Coordination of Humanitarian Affairs (OCHA), "Gaza Crisis Atlas," August 2014; CNN, "Israeli military's 'knock on roof' warnings criticized by rights groups," July 15, 2014.

2 During Operation Protective Edge in 2014, the IDF made tens of thousands of phone calls warning Gaza residents of impending strikes. Israel also sent mass text messages and dropped millions of leaflets. See Israel Defense Forces, "Operation Protective Edge," official reports, 2014; Anti-Defamation League, "Operation Protective Edge: July–August 2014," adl.org; Michael N. Schmitt, "The IDF, Hamas, and the Duty to Warn," Lieber Institute, West Point, September 2024.

3 The IDF has documented numerous aborted missions due to civilian presence. Israeli pilots and drone operators have standing orders to abort strikes if civilians appear unexpectedly in target areas. Video evidence released by the IDF shows missiles being diverted and strikes called off when civilians were identified. See IDF Spokesperson, "IDF calls off airstrike after children spotted," July 2014; Jerusalem Center for Public Affairs, "Israel, Gaza and Humanitarian Law: Efforts to Limit Civilian Casualties," 2015.

4 During the 2014 conflict, the Israeli Air Force dropped over 5 million leaflets warning civilians of operations and advising them where to go for safety. These leaflets included maps showing safe areas, evacuation routes, and warnings about which neighborhoods would see military activity. See Israel Ministry of Foreign

HAMAN'S LIES

Affairs, "Operation Protective Edge: IDF Warnings to Civilian Population," 2014; CNN, July 15, 2014.

5   Hamas's practice of placing military infrastructure in civilian areas has been documented by the United Nations, international journalists, and captured Hamas materials. Hamas has operated from schools, mosques, hospitals, and residential buildings. Foreign correspondents in Gaza have reported seeing rockets launched from civilian neighborhoods and Hamas fighters operating in plainclothes among civilians. See UN Secretary-General's Board of Inquiry Summary, S/2015/286, April 2015; NATO, "Lawfare: Use of Human Shields in Gaza," strategic analysis.

6   The United Nations Relief and Works Agency (UNRWA) confirmed that weapons were found in its schools on three separate occasions during the 2014 conflict—on July 16, July 22, and July 29. UN Secretary-General Ban Ki-moon stated: "I am dismayed that Palestinian militant groups would put United Nations schools at risk by using them to hide their arms." A 2015 UN Board of Inquiry found that Palestinian armed groups "highly likely" stored weapons and fired rockets from UNRWA school premises. See UNRWA Press Releases, July 17, 22, and 29, 2014; UN Secretary-General Report S/2015/286, April 27, 2015.

7   Hamas official Fathi Hamad stated on Al-Aqsa TV on February 29, 2008: "For the Palestinian people, death has become an industry, at which women excel, and so do all the people living on this land. The elderly excel at this, and so do the mujahideen and the children. This is why they have formed human shields of the women, the children, the elderly, and the mujahideen, in order to challenge the Zionist bombing machine." See MEMRI (Middle East Media Research Institute), Clip No. 1710, "Hamas MP Fathi Hammad: We Used Women and Children as Human Shields," March 13, 2008.

8   Protocol I Additional to the Geneva Conventions (1977), Article 51(7), explicitly prohibits the use of human shields: "The presence or movements of the civilian population or individual civilians shall not be used to render certain points or areas immune from military operations, in particular in attempts to shield military objectives from attacks or to shield, favour or impede military operations." Article 51(8) further states that violation of this prohibition "shall not release the Parties to the conflict from their legal obligations with respect to the civilian population." See International Committee of the Red Cross, "Customary IHL Database," Rule 97; Rome Statute of the International Criminal Court, Article 8(2)(b)(xxiii).

9   Colonel Richard Kemp, CBE, former commander of British Forces in Afghanistan, testified before the United Nations Human Rights Council on October 16, 2009,

References

during the emergency session examining the Goldstone Report on Operation Cast Lead: "Based on my knowledge and experience, I can say this: During Operation Cast Lead, the Israeli Defense Forces did more to safeguard the rights of civilians in the combat zones than any other army in the history of warfare." Kemp repeated similar assessments after Operation Protective Edge in 2014 and subsequent Gaza conflicts. See UN Watch, "Colonel Kemp Addresses UN Human Rights Council," October 2009; *Mishpacha Magazine*, "British Defender," May 2021.

10 General Martin Dempsey, Chairman of the US Joint Chiefs of Staff (the highest-ranking US military officer), stated at the Carnegie Council for Ethics in International Affairs on November 6, 2014: "I actually do think that Israel went to extraordinary lengths to limit collateral damage and civilian casualties." Dempsey also confirmed that the Pentagon sent a team to Israel to learn lessons from IDF practices, including "the measures they took to prevent civilian casualties." See US Department of Defense, "Chairman Says Israel Acted Responsibly in Gaza Operation," November 7, 2014; Haaretz, "Dempsey: Israel Went to 'Extraordinary Length' to Avoid Civilian Casualties in Gaza," November 7, 2014; The Tower, November 2014.

11 Hamas has invested extensively in military infrastructure—including an estimated 500 kilometers of tunnels beneath Gaza—rather than civilian protection. Unlike Israel, which has invested in their missile defense system, bomb shelters in every building, and early warning sirens, Hamas has built no bomb shelters for Gazan civilians and has explicitly instructed civilians not to evacuate areas targeted by Israeli warnings. See Israeli Security Agency assessments; Hamas Ministry of Interior statements calling on civilians to reject IDF evacuation warnings, July 10, 2014; Israel Defense Forces, "Hamas Tunnels," documentation and captured materials.

14

1 Protocol Additional to the Geneva Conventions of 12 August 1949, and Relating to the Protection of Victims of International Armed Conflicts (Protocol I), June 8, 1977, Article 51(5)(b). The rule prohibits attacks "which may be expected to cause incidental loss of civilian life, injury to civilians, damage to civilian objects, or a combination thereof, which would be excessive in relation to the concrete and direct military advantage anticipated." This proportionality standard is also recognized as customary international law. See ICRC, *Customary International Humanitarian Law*, Rule 14.

HAMAN'S LIES

2   Michael N. Schmitt and John J. Merriam, "The Tyranny of Context: Israeli Targeting Practices in Legal Perspective," *University of Pennsylvania Journal of International Law* 37, no. 1 (2015): 53–139. The authors conducted extensive interviews with IDF personnel and found that "IDF lawyers figure heavily in this process. Once planners identify and propose targets based on anticipated or actual missions and operational goals, lawyers from the International Law Department (ILD) review each." The Military Advocate General's Corps operates independently from combat commanders and provides binding legal advice. See also IDF, "The IDF Military Justice System," available at idf.il.

3   Israeli defense officials estimate Hamas's tunnel network extends 350–450 miles beneath Gaza. Hamas leader Yahya Sinwar claimed in 2021 that Hamas possessed over 500 kilometers of tunnels. According to Israeli military estimates, each advanced tunnel costs approximately $3 million to construct and requires a year to dig one kilometer. The tunnels are reinforced with concrete, equipped with electricity, ventilation, and communication lines. See John Spencer, "Gaza's Underground: Hamas's Entire Politico-Military Strategy Rests on Its Tunnels," *Modern War Institute*, West Point, January 18, 2024; *New York Times*, January 16, 2024.

4   Protocol I Additional to the Geneva Conventions (1977), Article 51(7): "The presence or movements of the civilian population or individual civilians shall not be used to render certain points or areas immune from military operations, in particular in attempts to shield military objectives from attacks or to shield, favour or impede military operations." This prohibition reflects customary international law. See ICRC *Customary International Humanitarian Law*, Rule 97; Rome Statute Article 8(2)(b)(xxiii) (criminalizing human shields as a war crime).

5   Since Israel's withdrawal from Gaza in 2005, terrorists have fired more than 22,500 rockets and mortars at Israeli civilian areas. Data compiled from Israeli Security Agency (Shabak) reports shows a dramatic increase after the 2005 disengagement: fewer than 2,000 rockets were fired in the five years prior to disengagement, compared to approximately 10,000 in the five years following. Between October 7, 2023, and December 2023 alone, over 12,000 rockets were fired at Israel. See Israel Security Agency annual reports; ACLED, "Middle East Crisis: A Year of War in Numbers," October 2024.

6   Hamas has constructed no public bomb shelters for Gaza's civilian population, despite spending hundreds of millions of dollars on its tunnel network. The tunnels are reserved exclusively for military use and Hamas fighters. Hamas's Ministry of Interior instructed civilians to ignore Israeli evacuation warnings

during the 2014 conflict. See *CNN*, "The 'Gaza metro': The mysterious subterranean tunnel network used by Hamas," October 2023; IDF documentation of Hamas Interior Ministry statement, July 13, 2014.

7 Associated Press investigation, December 2017. The nine-month battle to liberate Mosul from ISIS (October 2016–July 2017) resulted in between 9,000 and 11,000 civilian deaths—nearly 10 times higher than officially acknowledged figures. The US-led coalition acknowledged responsibility for only 326 deaths. The AP cross-referenced morgue records, databases from Amnesty International, Iraq Body Count, and UN reports. See Susannah George et al., *Associated Press*, December 20, 2017; *PBS NewsHour*, December 21, 2017.

8 The High Level Military Group report specifically addressed the disparity between international criticism of Israel and other conflicts: "In reference to the disparity of our findings with the widely noted condemnations of the IDF's conduct ... by the United Nations Human Rights Council Commission of Inquiry, Amnesty International and other NGOs, and parts of the international media, we believe that, where ideological motivation can be discounted, the principal reason for this disparity is the absence of the appropriate military and legal expertise and judgement." High Level Military Group, *An Assessment of the 2014 Gaza Conflict* (2015), 12.

9 High Level Military Group (HLMG), *An Assessment of the 2014 Gaza Conflict* (October 2015), 11. The HLMG comprised former military chiefs and senior officers from Germany, Italy, United States, Spain, Australia, India, France, the United Kingdom, and Colombia. After extensive fact-finding visits to Israel, they concluded: "Israel's conduct in the 2014 Gaza Conflict met and in some respects exceeded the highest standards we set for our own nations' militaries ... The IDF not only met its obligations under the Law of Armed Conflict, but often exceeded these on the battlefield at significant tactical cost." Available at high-level-military-group.org.

15

1 Israel completed the disengagement from Gaza in September 2005. See Chapter 20 for full details. The disengagement was unilateral, designed by Prime Minister Ariel Sharon to improve Israel's security and international standing. See Israel Ministry of Foreign Affairs, "Israel's Disengagement Plan: Renewing the Peace Process," April 2005; *Encyclopaedia Britannica*, "Israel's disengagement from Gaza" (updated October 2023); NPR coverage of the withdrawal, September 2005.

2 American Jewish donors, with support from former World Bank President James Wolfensohn (who contributed $500,000 personally), purchased approximately

3,000 greenhouses from Israeli settlers for $14 million and transferred them to the Palestinian Authority. On September 13, 2005, the day after the last Israeli soldier left Gaza, Palestinian crowds entered the former settlements and looted dozens of greenhouses, stripping irrigation hoses, water pumps, plastic sheeting, and equipment. Palestinian police were inadequately staffed to prevent the looting, and in some cases joined the looters. See Associated Press, "Looters Strip Gaza Greenhouses," September 13–14, 2005; *NBC News*; *Al Jazeera*.

3   Human Rights Watch, *Internal Fight: Palestinian Abuses in Gaza and the West Bank*, July 2008. The report documents the June 2007 battle for Gaza in which Hamas forcefully seized control from Fatah forces. The fighting killed at least 161 people and wounded over 700. Both sides committed serious violations including summary executions, torture, and throwing captives from buildings. Human Rights Watch documented that "Hamas's internal takeover in Gaza in June 2007 was perhaps the bloodiest" episode of Palestinian internal conflict. See also Human Rights Watch, "Gaza: Armed Palestinian Groups Commit Grave Crimes," June 12, 2007.

4   Egypt closed the Rafah crossing after Hamas's 2007 takeover and has maintained strict restrictions since. By September 2021, Egypt had destroyed more than 3,000 smuggling tunnels over six years by flooding them or pumping in toxic gas. In 2014–2015, Egypt created a buffer zone up to five kilometers wide, demolishing at least 3,255 buildings and forcibly evicting thousands. In 2020, Egypt began constructing a concrete wall along the Gaza border. Egypt views Hamas as connected to the Muslim Brotherhood, which Egypt considers a terrorist organization. See Human Rights Watch reports; *Washington Institute for Near East Policy* analysis, October 2023; University of Sydney analysis, February 2024.

5   In 2016, Israeli security personnel prevented 1,226 attempts to smuggle illicit goods (drones, scuba gear, explosives, commando knives) through the Kerem Shalom crossing—a 66% increase over 2015. Israel maintains a list of prohibited dual-use materials that could be diverted for military purposes. The IDF confirmed on October 26, 2023, that Hamas used tunnels under the Egyptian border to smuggle weapons before the October 7 attack. Former Egyptian President Morsi tacitly allowed weapons smuggling through the tunnel system. See *Times of Israel*, January 15, 2017; Foundation for Defense of Democracies, "10 Things to Know About Hamas Tunnels," November 2023.

6   Hamas has developed a tunnel network estimated at 350–450 miles, with close to 5,700 separate shafts. Construction costs are estimated at up to $1 billion, using more than 6,000 tons of concrete and 1,800 tons of metal. Individual advanced tunnels cost approximately $3 million each. Tunnels feature telephone lines,

electricity, railways, ventilation, and air conditioning. The network includes luxury sections with painted walls, tile floors, and ceiling fans. See John Spencer, "Gaza's Underground: Hamas's Entire Politico-Military Strategy Rests on Its Tunnels," *Modern War Institute at West Point*, January 18, 2024; IDF Intelligence Directorate reports; Foundation for Defense of Democracies analysis.

7   Fourth Geneva Convention, Article 33: "No protected person may be punished for an offence he or she has not personally committed. Collective penalties and likewise all measures of intimidation or of terrorism are prohibited. Pillage is prohibited. Reprisals against protected persons and their property are prohibited." The prohibition applies specifically to penalties imposed on civilians for acts they did not personally commit. See ICRC Customary International Humanitarian Law Rule 103; *Cambridge Guide to Humanitarian Law*, "Collective Punishment."

8   Hamas's military budget increased from 15% of annual spending in 2014 to 55% in 2016, while civilian affairs budget decreased. The IDF estimates Hamas invested over $150 million specifically in tunnel building activities (earlier estimate) to potentially $1 billion for the complete underground network. Hamas leader Moussa Abu Marzouk stated that Hamas built no bomb shelters for Gaza's civilian population because it was the UN's responsibility to "protect" civilians. See IDF, "The Gaza Tunnel Industry;" *Modern War Institute at West Point*; *Fox News* investigation, January 2024.

9   *Report of the Secretary-General's Panel of Inquiry on the 31 May 2010 Flotilla Incident* (Palmer Report), September 2011. The panel, chaired by former New Zealand Prime Minister Geoffrey Palmer, found: "Israel faces a real threat to its security from militant groups in Gaza. The naval blockade was imposed as a legitimate security measure in order to prevent weapons from entering Gaza by sea and its implementation complied with the requirements of international law." The report also found that Israel used "excessive and unreasonable" force during the flotilla boarding and that the humanitarian situation in Gaza was "unsustainable." Available at UN Digital Library.

16

1   Israel is the only country with a permanent agenda item (Item 7) at the UN Human Rights Council. Every session features debate on "Human rights situation in Palestine and other occupied Arab territories." No other country—not Iran, Russia, Syria, or North Korea—has a dedicated agenda item. UN Secretary-General Ban Ki-moon criticized this selectivity on June 20, 2007, expressing "disappointment at the Council decision to single out Israel as the only specific regional item on its agenda." The UK, US, Australia, Denmark, and

other democracies have formally opposed Item 7 as representing "systematic institutional bias." UN Watch, "Item 7," https://unwatch.org/item7; World Jewish Congress, "Israel is the only country that the UNHRC has a standing agenda item against," https://www.worldjewishcongress.org/en/unhrc; UK Foreign Office, "Human Rights Council 40: UK Explanation of Vote," March 22, 2019.

2 Freedom House, *Freedom in the World 2025* (Washington, DC: Freedom House, 2025). Israel scored 73 out of 100 and remains the only "Free" country in the Middle East. Syria scored 1, Saudi Arabia 8. Over 93% of people in the region live in countries rated "Not Free." The report notes Israel is "a parliamentary democracy with a multiparty system and independent institutions that generally guarantee political rights and civil liberties." See also Freedom House, "New Report: Freedom in the Middle East Remains Out of Reach for Most," 2024; Washington Institute, "Political Rights and Civil Liberties in the Middle East: Trends in Freedom House Data Since 2010," 2023.

3 During the Second Intifada (September 2000 to 2005), approximately 138 suicide bombings killed over 1,000 Israelis and wounded thousands more. The International Institute for Counter-Terrorism documented that 78% (887) of the 1,137 Israelis killed were civilians. Between 1994 and 2005, suicide bombings killed 735 Israelis and wounded 4,554. The 2007 study from University of Haifa found 39.9% of attacks were by Hamas, 26.4% by Fatah, and 25.7% by Palestinian Islamic Jihad. Major attacks included the March 27, 2002, Park Hotel Passover massacre (30 killed, 140 injured) and the June 1, 2001, Dolphinarium disco bombing (21 killed). Israel Ministry of Foreign Affairs, https://embassies.gov.il/MFA/AboutIsrael/Maps/Pages/Situation-on-the-eve-of-the-Second-Intifada.aspx; Washington Institute, "The Implications of the Second Intifada on Israeli Views of Oslo;" Wikipedia, "Palestinian suicide attacks," "Second Intifada," "Civilian casualties in the Second Intifada."

4 Studies on the effectiveness of the security barrier in reducing terrorism, including Israeli Security Agency data. Research confirms the West Bank security barrier's effectiveness in reducing suicide bombings. Suicide attacks dropped from 73 between 2000–July 2003 to only 12 between August 2003–end of 2006. A 2017 study in the *Journal of Quantitative Criminology* found the barrier "was effective in preventing suicide bombings and other attacks and fatalities with little if any apparent displacement." The study noted that when only half the barrier was completed (early 2005), suicide bombings had already dropped to near zero. Approximately 75% of suicide bombers prior to construction had crossed in areas where the first phase was built. Washington Institute, "Israel's Security Fence: Effective in Reducing Suicide Attacks," 2004; Perry et al., "The Situational

References

Prevention of Terrorism: An Evaluation of the Israeli West Bank Barrier," *Journal of Quantitative Criminology* (2017); Jewish Virtual Library, "Background & Overview of Israel's Security Barriers."

5   Human Rights Watch (HRW) has extensively documented abuses by Hamas in Gaza. See Human Rights Watch, *Under Cover of War: Hamas Political Violence in Gaza*, April 20, 2009 (documenting 32 killings, arbitrary arrests, torture, and maimings during and after 2008–09 conflict); *Internal Fight: Palestinian Abuses in Gaza and the West Bank*, July 29, 2008 (documenting Hamas's "arbitrary arrests of political opponents, tortured detainees, clamped down on freedom of expression"); *Two Authorities, One Way, Zero Dissent: Arbitrary Arrest and Torture Under the Palestinian Authority and Hamas*, October 23, 2018. HRW documented arrests for Facebook posts, detention of journalists, and that "security forces routinely taunt, threaten, beat, and force detainees into painful stress positions."

6   LGBTQ persecution under Palestinian authorities is extensively documented. UN Watch reported to the UN Committee Against Torture in July 2022 that "LGBTQ persons living under the Palestinian Authority and Hamas control suffer severe persecution and ostracism." One gay Gaza Palestinian in exile recounted: "They arrested me, hanged me from the ceiling, beat me up and interrogated me for five days." In February 2016, Hamas tortured and murdered Mahmoud Ishtiwi, commander of Hamas's armed wing, reportedly for being gay. Many gay Palestinians have fled to Israel seeking refuge. UN Watch, "Rights Group Exposes Palestinian Torture Ahead of First UN Review," July 14, 2022; NGO Monitor, "Omissions and Oversimplifications: HRW's Report on PA and Hamas Torture," December 16, 2018.

7   Hamas has executed numerous Palestinians accused of "collaboration" with Israel. Amnesty International documented Hamas summarily executing at least 23 Palestinians during the 2014 Gaza war, with "severe beatings with truncheons, gun butts, hoses and wire." In one incident, six men were executed outside a mosque in front of hundreds of spectators, including children. Since seizing control in June 2007, Hamas authorities have executed at least 28 people following trials that "lacked appropriate due process protections." Human Rights Watch and Amnesty International reports; UN Watch submissions to UN Committee Against Torture; US State Department, *West Bank and Gaza Strip 2022 Human Rights Report*.

8   Human Rights Watch has documented Palestinian Authority detention practices and restrictions on freedom. See *Two Authorities, One Way, Zero Dissent* (2018), documenting arbitrary arrests, torture, and that PA security forces "detained

HAMAN'S LIES

65,415 Palestinians in the West Bank in 2018 and the first three months of 2019." Torture methods include "beatings, solitary confinement, feet whipping, threats and taunts, and forcing detainees into various painful positions for extended periods." Under Palestinian law, selling land to Jews is punishable by death. At least eight Palestinians have been executed for this offense. Human Rights Watch, "Palestine: No Letup in Arbitrary Arrests, Torture," May 29, 2019; "Palestine: Impunity for Arbitrary Arrests, Torture," June 30, 2022.

9   The Israeli Supreme Court has ordered rerouting of the security barrier to reduce impact on Palestinian communities. In the 2004 Beit Surik case, the Court ordered 30 km of barrier rerouted, ruling the route "injures the local inhabitants in a severe and acute way" and failed the "proportionality" test. In 2009, responding to Association for Civil Rights in Israel (ACRI) petitions, the Court ordered sections dismantled, returning 6,000 dunams to the Palestinian side. Palestinians can and do petition the Israeli Supreme Court. The Court has heard hundreds of cases from the territories and sometimes rules in petitioners' favor. HCJ 2056/04 Beit Sourik Village Council v. The Government of Israel; HCJ 7957/04 Mara'abe v. Prime Minister of Israel; Association for Civil Rights in Israel, "Following ACRI Petitions, Separation Barrier Ordered Rerouted," September 9, 2009.

10   Israel has a robust civil society and functioning press freedom. Israeli human rights organizations including B'Tselem, Breaking the Silence, and the Association for Civil Rights in Israel operate freely, publish criticism, testify before international bodies, and receive government funding. Freedom House's 2025 report gave Israel 3 out of 4 for Freedom of Expression, noting media is "generally free to criticize the government." In 2022, a Muslim judge (Khaled Kabub) was appointed to the Supreme Court—not the first Israeli Arab to serve. An Arab judge, George Karra, presided over the trial of former President Moshe Katsav and sent him to prison. Arab citizens vote, serve in parliament, and hold positions throughout Israeli society. Freedom House, *Freedom in the World 2025: Israel*; Wikipedia, "Arab citizens of Israel," "Mass media in Israel."

11   Iran's penal code explicitly criminalizes same-sex relations and prescribes the death penalty for sodomy. Human Rights Watch documented multiple executions for homosexual conduct, including two men publicly hanged in November 2005 in Gorgan. In January 2022, two gay men (Mehrdad Karimpour and Farid Mohammadi) were executed in Maragheh after six years on death row. LGBT rights activists Zahra Seddiqi Hamedani and Elham Choubdar were sentenced to death in 2021. UN human rights experts have repeatedly demanded stays of execution for LGBTQ activists. Iran is considered "one of the most repressive

References

places in the world for lesbian, gay, bisexual and transgender people." Human Rights Watch, "Iran: Two More Executions for Homosexual Conduct," November 21, 2005; UN OHCHR, "Iran: UN experts demand stay of execution for two women, including LGBT activist," September 28, 2022; *NBC News*, February 2, 2022.

12 Israeli efforts to reduce checkpoint friction include humanitarian expedited passage, medical emergency prioritization, and technology deployment. COGAT (Coordinator of Government Activities in the Territories) coordinates humanitarian access and has implemented measures to reduce waiting times at crossings. When security conditions permit, checkpoints are reduced or removed. The goal is minimum necessary security rather than maximum restriction. See COGAT official reports and statements.

13 Comparative human rights documentation for regional states: For Egypt, Freedom House rates it "Not Free" (18/100), documenting killings of protesters, imprisonment of journalists and activists. For Turkey, Reporters Without Borders notes it has "imprisoned more journalists than any other country." For Syria, Saudi Arabia, and other regional states, see Freedom House annual reports and Committee to Protect Journalists documentation. Freedom House, *Freedom in the World* annual reports; Committee to Protect Journalists annual prison census; Human Rights Watch and Amnesty International country reports.

14 Documentation of Syrian chemical weapons use available from Syrian Network for Human Rights and OPCW-IIT reports.

17

1 Geneva Conventions (1949) and Additional Protocols (1977), particularly Protocol I, Articles 48–58. Article 48 establish the basic rule of distinction requiring parties to "distinguish between the civilian population and combatants and between civilian objects and military objectives." Article 51 protects civilians from attack and prohibits indiscriminate attacks, while Article 51(5)(b) defines proportionality, prohibiting attacks "which may be expected to cause incidental loss of civilian life, injury to civilians, damage to civilian objects, or a combination thereof, which would be excessive in relation to the concrete and direct military advantage anticipated." Articles 57 and 58 establish precautionary obligations, requiring parties to take "constant care" to spare civilians and to "do everything feasible" to minimize incidental harm. The ICRC's *Customary International Humanitarian Law Study* (2005) confirms these principles as customary law binding all parties to armed conflict regardless of treaty ratification. See also

International Committee of the Red Cross, "The Practical Guide to Humanitarian Law," accessed 2025, guide-humanitarian-law.org.

2   Israel Defense Forces, "The IDF Military Justice System," idf.il, accessed 2025. The Military Advocate General's Corps (MAG Corps) provides legal advice to all military authorities and enforces both military and criminal law throughout the IDF. The MAG is appointed by the Minister of Defense and is "subject only to the law on professional matters," operating with full professional independence from the Chief of Staff. The MAG Corps includes an International Law Department providing "operational advice at various levels of command on international law in terms of what can and cannot be targeted, what weaponry is lawful to employ under international humanitarian law, and how operations must be conducted to comply with the principles of distinction, proportionality, and precautions in attack."

3   On IDF targeting procedures with legal oversight: *Times of Israel*, "Is the IDF's ongoing Gaza operation complying with the laws of war?" October 24, 2023. The report describes how the MAG Corps International Law Department provides "operational advice at various levels of command" and how "legal advisers are fully integrated into the planning and fire-control groups. Every target must receive their approval." Former MAG International Law Department head Pnina Sharvit Baruch (2003–2009) confirmed that "the IDF only attacks military targets" while acknowledging these "may include residential buildings that are used by Hamas and other terror groups." Professor Michael Schmitt of the University of Reading and West Point noted that IDF evacuation warnings, while imperfect, represent a genuine effort to protect civilians before combat operations.

4   Israel Defense Forces, "Addressing Alleged Misconduct in the Context of the War in Gaza," idf.il, February 24, 2024. The IDF reported that since the beginning of the current conflict following October 7, 2023, the MAG ordered the launching of 74 criminal investigations regarding incidents raising suspicion of criminal misconduct. These include 44 criminal investigations concerning deaths of detainees (consistent with IDF policy requiring immediate criminal investigation when detainees die), 8 criminal investigations concerning alleged detainee mistreatment, 3 criminal investigations concerning alleged destruction of civilian property without military necessity, and 13 additional criminal investigations. The General Staff's Fact-Finding and Assessment Mechanism conducts initial factual assessments using "advanced digital applications" including "collection of open-source material, preservation of operational records, and geo-location of ground forces."

References

5   On Hamas rocket attacks: The ICRC's Customary International Humanitarian Law Study, Rule 11, prohibits indiscriminate attacks, defined as attacks "not directed at a specific military objective" or employing "methods or means of combat which cannot be directed at a specific military objective." Hamas rockets fired at Israeli population centers meet this definition as they are unguided weapons directed at civilian areas rather than military targets. US State Department, *Country Reports on Terrorism 2023*: "That the crimes allegedly committed by Hamas were intentional goes without saying—its rockets were purposefully and indiscriminately aimed at civilian targets." Goldstone, in his 2011 reconsideration, emphasized: "That comparatively few Israelis have been killed by the unlawful rocket and mortar attacks from Gaza in no way minimizes the criminality. The UN Human Rights Council should condemn these heinous acts in the strongest terms."

6   Documentation of the October 7, 2023, attack from multiple authoritative sources: Israeli government officials confirmed approximately 1,200 people were killed in the Hamas-led attack, revised from earlier estimates of 1,400 after determining some unidentified remains belonged to attackers. Foreign Ministry spokesperson Lior Haiat stated, "Around 1,200 is the official number of victims of the October 7 massacre." US State Department, *Country Reports on Terrorism 2023*, states: "On October 7, Hamas terrorists and armed Palestinian militants from other terrorist organizations in Gaza invaded Israel by land, sea, and air and murdered an estimated 1,200 people. Terrorists killed men, women, children, babies, and elderly people; raped, sexually assaulted, and mutilated women and men; and took hostage 253 Israeli and foreign citizens." Human Rights Watch conducted interviews with 144 people including 94 survivors and verified over 280 photographs and videos. The attack occurred during Simchat Torah and targeted 21 communities including kibbutzim Be'eri, Kfar Aza, and Nir Oz, as well as the Nova music festival where approximately 360 people were killed.

7   For documentation of sexual violence during October 7 attacks: UN Special Representative of the Secretary-General on Sexual Violence in Conflict, Pramila Patten, conducted a fact-finding mission in early 2024 and found "clear and convincing information" of sexual violence during the Hamas attacks. The *New York Times* investigation "Screams Without Words" (December 2023) documented evidence from "at least 7 locations where sexual assaults and mutilations of Israeli women and girls were carried out," concluding these were "not isolated events but part of a broader pattern." Israeli police investigators confirmed building "several sexual assault cases" based on "video evidence, testimony from terrorists, and photographs of victims' bodies." Human Rights

Watch's 2024 report includes sexual violence among documented crimes. The Rome Statute, Article 7(1)(g) and 8(2)(b)(xxii), classifies rape and other forms of sexual violence as crimes against humanity and war crimes respectively.

8   Human Rights Watch, "'I Can't Erase All the Blood from My Mind': Palestinian Armed Groups' October 7 Assault on Israel," hrw.org, July 17, 2024. This comprehensive investigation documents war crimes including deliberate killing of civilians, hostage-taking, sexual violence, and mutilation. The report states: "Human Rights Watch documented Hamas-led and other Palestinian armed groups' indiscriminate rocket attacks against Israeli population centers; deliberate killing of civilians, including children; deliberate destruction of civilian property; hostage-taking; torture and other inhumane treatment of hostages; desecration of dead bodies; and sexual violence." The UN Independent International Commission of Inquiry confirmed similar findings in its report to the Human Rights Council (A/HRC/56/26), documenting that "children were also intentionally targeted for abduction" with 36 children taken hostage.

9   Geneva Convention Relative to the Protection of Civilian Persons in Time of War (Fourth Geneva Convention), Article 34: "The taking of hostages is prohibited." Article 147 classifies hostage-taking as a "grave breach" of the Convention, imposing obligations on states parties to "provide effective penal sanctions for persons committing, or ordering to be committed, any of the grave breaches" (Article 146). The Rome Statute of the International Criminal Court, Article 8(2)(a)(viii), classifies "[t]aking of hostages" as a war crime. The International Convention Against the Taking of Hostages (1979) further codifies this prohibition. The ICRC confirms in Rule 96 of its Customary International Humanitarian Law study that "the taking of hostages is prohibited" in both international and non-international armed conflicts. See also Michael N. Schmitt, "Hostage-Taking and the Law of Armed Conflict," Lieber Institute, West Point, 2023.

10 Human Rights Watch, "'I Can't Erase All the Blood from My Mind': Palestinian Armed Groups' October 7 Assault on Israel," hrw.org, July 17, 2024, documenting "torture and other inhumane treatment of hostages." The UN Independent International Commission of Inquiry confirmed similar findings in its report to the Human Rights Council (A/HRC/56/26), documenting that hostages included 36 children who were "intentionally targeted for abduction."

11 Protocol I Additional to the Geneva Conventions, Article 41, prohibits ordering "that there shall be no survivors." Article 35(2) prohibits weapons "of a nature to cause superfluous injury or unnecessary suffering." Common Article 3 of the Geneva Conventions requires humane treatment of "persons taking no active part

in the hostilities, including members of armed forces who have laid down their arms." Human Rights Watch's July 2024 report documents instances during the October 7 attack where "people who emerged from safe rooms with hands raised were shot," characterizing such acts as violations of these fundamental protections for those who surrender or are *hors de combat*.

12   Colonel John Spencer, Chair of Urban Warfare Studies at the Modern War Institute at West Point, has conducted extensive assessments of IDF operations. In September 2024, speaking at the United Nations, Spencer stated: "In my extensive career studying and advising on urban warfare for the US military, I've never known an army to take such measures to attend to the enemy's civilian population, especially while simultaneously combating the enemy in the very same buildings." Spencer has argued that "Israel has taken precautionary measures even the United States did not do during its recent wars in Iraq and Afghanistan." These assessments address IDF practices including advance warnings, evacuation orders, phone calls, and text messages to civilians in proximity to targets, and "roof knocking" techniques. See also JINSA (Jewish Institute for National Security of America).

13   Richard Goldstone, "Reconsidering the Goldstone Report on Israel and War Crimes," *Washington Post*, April 1, 2011. Justice Goldstone, who chaired the UN Fact-Finding Mission on the Gaza Conflict that produced the 2009 Goldstone Report, wrote: "We know a lot more today about what happened in the Gaza war of 2008–09 than we did when I chaired the fact-finding mission... If I had known then what I know now, the Goldstone Report would have been a different document." He specifically stated that subsequent Israeli investigations "indicate that civilians were not intentionally targeted as a matter of policy." Goldstone praised Israel's commitment to investigating allegations: "Israel has dedicated significant resources to investigate over 400 allegations of operational misconduct in Gaza," while noting that Hamas "conducted no investigations" and "hundreds more rockets and mortar rounds have been directed at civilian targets in southern Israel." He acknowledged that his inquiry was "in no way a judicial or even quasi-judicial proceeding" and that the UN Human Rights Council's "history of bias against Israel cannot be doubted."

18

1   General Armistice Agreement between Israel and Jordan, April 3, 1949, Article VIII, guaranteed access to holy sites and cultural institutions, including "free access to the Holy Places and cultural institutions and use of the cemetery on the Mount of Olives." Jordan violated this provision from the outset, barring all

HAMAN'S LIES

Jewish access to the Western Wall and Old City for 19 years. See United Nations, "Hashemite Jordan Kingdom–Israel: General Armistice Agreement," UN Treaty Series, April 3, 1949.

2   For 19 years under Jordanian control (1948–1967), no Jew was permitted to pray at the Western Wall or enter the Old City. The Jordanian authorities enforced a complete ban on Jewish access despite armistice commitments. See Martin Gilbert, *Jerusalem in the Twentieth Century* (New York: Wiley, 1996); Dore Gold, *The Fight for Jerusalem: Radical Islam, the West, and the Future of the Holy City* (Washington: Regnery, 2007).

3   Martin Gilbert, *Jerusalem in the Twentieth Century* (New York: Wiley, 1996), documenting the destruction of 58 synagogues, the desecration of the Mount of Olives cemetery, and the systematic erasure of Jewish presence from the Old City during Jordanian rule. See also Yehuda Hakohen, "The Destruction of the Jewish Quarter," Jerusalem Center for Public Affairs, 2017.

4   Documentation of Christian conditions under Jordanian rule. Christian access was restricted and Christian institutions faced discrimination under Jordanian rule. Christian property ownership was limited by law, and Christian schools were required to teach the Quran. The Christian population of Jerusalem declined during this period. See Justus Reid Weiner, "Christian Access to Holy Sites in Jerusalem Under Jordanian and Israeli Rule," Jerusalem Center for Public Affairs, 1999.

5   On June 7, 1967, Defence Minister Moshe Dayan announced at Al-Aqsa Mosque: "We have returned to the holiest of our sites, and will never again be separated from it. To our Arab neighbours we extend, especially at this hour, the hand of peace. To members of the other religions, Christians and Muslims, I hereby promise faithfully that their full freedom and all their religious rights will be preserved." See Moshe Dayan, *Story of My Life* (London: Weidenfeld & Nicolson, 1976); Israel Ministry of Foreign Affairs, "Preservation of Holy Places Law," June 27, 1967.

6   Israel allowed the Jordanian-appointed Islamic Waqf to continue administering the Temple Mount, including Al-Aqsa Mosque and the Dome of the Rock. This arrangement, known as the "status quo," restricts Jewish prayer on the Temple Mount while permitting Muslim worship. See Nadav Shragai, "The 'Status Quo' on the Temple Mount," Jerusalem Center for Public Affairs, 2014; Yitzhak Reiter, *Jerusalem and Its Role in Islamic Solidarity* (New York: Palgrave Macmillan, 2008).

References

7   The Church of the Holy Sepulchre is administered by six Christian denominations—Greek Orthodox, Roman Catholic, Armenian Apostolic, Coptic, Ethiopian Orthodox, and Syriac Orthodox—under the "Status Quo" arrangement dating to the Ottoman period (1852). Israel has scrupulously maintained these arrangements. See Raymond Cohen, *Saving the Holy Sepulchre: How Rival Christians Came Together to Rescue Their Holiest Shrine* (Oxford: Oxford University Press, 2008).

8   Israel Central Bureau of Statistics, "The Christian Population of Israel," December 24, 2023. The Christian population of Israel has grown from approximately 34,000 in 1949 to over 185,000 in 2023. Christians comprise approximately 1.9% of Israel's population and enjoy full religious freedom, political participation, and civil rights.

9   Pew Research Center, "The Changing Global Religious Landscape," April 5, 2017; "Christians in the Middle East," December 13, 2011. The Christian population of Iraq fell from approximately 1.5 million in 2003 to fewer than 200,000 by 2020. Christians in Syria declined from approximately 10% of the population before the civil war to less than 2%. Bethlehem's Christian population fell from approximately 86% in 1950 to less than 12% today. See also Todd M. Johnson and Gina A. Zurlo, eds., *World Christian Encyclopedia*, 3rd ed. (Edinburgh: Edinburgh University Press, 2020).

10 Israel Police and Waqf records document daily Muslim prayer at Al-Aqsa Mosque. During Ramadan, attendance regularly exceeds 300,000 worshippers for Friday prayers. On Laylat al-Qadr (Night of Power) in 2023, approximately 450,000 Muslims prayed at Al-Aqsa. See Israel Police spokesperson statements; Times of Israel, "Some 450,000 worshippers attend Laylat al-Qadr prayers at Al-Aqsa," April 18, 2023.

11 Israel Police documentation records multiple incidents of weapons, rocks, and fireworks stockpiled inside Al-Aqsa Mosque and used to attack worshippers at the Western Wall below. See Israel Police spokesperson statements, April 2022, and April 2023; Israel Ministry of Foreign Affairs, "Violence on the Temple Mount," 2022–2023.

12 Under the status quo arrangement, the Islamic Waqf administers the Temple Mount compound and mosques. Israeli police provide external security. Jews may visit during limited hours (typically Sunday–Thursday mornings) but are prohibited from visible prayer, prayer books, or religious articles. See Nadav Shragai, "The 'Status Quo' on the Temple Mount," Jerusalem Center for Public Affairs, 2014.

13 Israel Police and security services have documented repeated incidents of weapons, rocks, fireworks, and Molotov cocktails stockpiled inside Al-Aqsa Mosque. Rioters have used the mosque as a staging ground to attack Jewish worshippers at the Western Wall below. See Israel Police statements, April 2021, April 2022, April 2023; Israel Ministry of Foreign Affairs documentation.

14 The Temple Mount Sifting Project, established in 2004, examines debris illegally removed from the Temple Mount by the Waqf during construction of an underground mosque in Solomon's Stables (1999) and subsequent excavations. The project has recovered thousands of artifacts from the First and Second Temple periods, demonstrating the archaeological significance of material the Waqf discarded as rubble. See Gabriel Barkay and Zachi Dvira, "The Temple Mount Sifting Project," *Biblical Archaeology Review*, 2016; Temple Mount Sifting Project, templemount.wordpress.com.

15 Joseph's Tomb in Nablus has been attacked, burned, and vandalized repeatedly since being transferred to Palestinian Authority control in 2000. Documented attacks occurred in October 2000 (destroyed by Palestinian mob), April 2011, December 2013, October 2015, April 2022, and March 2024, among others. The ancient synagogue in Jericho (Shalom Al Yisrael) was also damaged. See Israel Ministry of Foreign Affairs documentation; *Times of Israel*, "Palestinians set fire to Joseph's Tomb in West Bank's Nablus," April 10, 2022.

19

1 Geneva Convention Relative to the Protection of Civilian Persons in Time of War (Fourth Geneva Convention), August 12, 1949, Article 49, paragraph 6: "The Occupying Power shall not deport or transfer parts of its own civilian population into the territory it occupies."

2 Eugene V. Rostow, former US Undersecretary of State and Dean of Yale Law School, argued that Article 49 was drafted to address Nazi-era forced deportations and does not apply to voluntary civilian movement. Rostow noted that the provision prohibits "deportation or transfer"—both involving compulsion—not voluntary settlement. See Eugene V. Rostow, "Palestinian Self-Determination: Possible Futures for the Unallocated Territories of the Palestine Mandate," Yale Studies in World Public Order 5, no. 2 (1979): 147–172; Eugene V. Rostow, "Resolved: Are the Settlements Legal? Israeli West Bank Policies," The New Republic, October 21, 1991.

3 Jordan seized the West Bank during the 1948 Arab–Israeli War and formally annexed it in 1950. The Arab League, the United Nations, and the broader international community refused to recognize Jordanian sovereignty over the

References

territory. See Yehuda Zvi Blum, "The Missing Reversioner: Reflections on the Status of Judea and Samaria," Israel Law Review 3, no. 2 (1968): 279–301.

4   League of Nations, "Mandate for Palestine," July 24, 1922, Article 6: "The Administration of Palestine… shall encourage, in cooperation with the Jewish agency referred to in Article 4, close settlement by Jews on the land, including State lands and waste lands not required for public purposes." The principle of *uti possidetis juris* (Latin: 'as you possess under law') holds that newly formed states inherit the administrative boundaries that existed at the time of their independence. Applied to the former Mandate territories, this principle suggests that the boundaries and settlement rights established under the Mandate remain legally relevant.

5   On August 24, 1929, Arab rioters massacred 67 Jews in Hebron, including women, children, and elderly, following incitement by the Grand Mufti of Jerusalem, Haj Amin al-Husseini, who spread false claims that Jews threatened Al-Aqsa Mosque. The surviving Jewish community was evacuated by British authorities. In 1948, Jordanian forces expelled all remaining Jews from the West Bank, including the ancient Jewish community of the Old City of Jerusalem. See Tom Segev, *One Palestine, Complete: Jews and Arabs Under the British Mandate* (New York: Metropolitan Books, 2000); Martin Gilbert, *In Ishmael's House: A History of Jews in Muslim Lands* (New Haven: Yale University Press, 2010).

6   Every major peace proposal since the 1990s—including the Clinton Parameters (2000), the Geneva Initiative (2003), and the Olmert offer (2008)—has assumed that major settlement blocs would remain part of Israel, with equivalent land swaps to compensate Palestinians. See David Makovsky, "Imagining the Border: Options for Resolving the Israeli–Palestinian Territorial Issue," Washington Institute for Near East Policy, January 2011.

7   Israel Central Bureau of Statistics, "Population of Localities: Judea and Samaria," 2024. Approximately 80% of Israeli settlers (over 500,000 people) live in major settlement blocs close to the pre-1967 lines, including Ma'ale Adumim, Modi'in Illit, Beitar Illit, Gush Etzion, and Ariel. An additional approximately 220,000 Israelis live in East Jerusalem neighborhoods built after 1967.

8   The Israeli Supreme Court has repeatedly ruled on settlement land disputes, ordering demolition of structures built on privately owned Palestinian land. In 2020, the Court ordered the demolition of buildings in the Netiv Ha'avot outpost. In 2017, the Knesset passed a law retroactively legalizing certain outposts, which the Supreme Court struck down as unconstitutional in 2020. See HCJ 2055/17, *Silwad Municipality v. Knesset* (2020); HCJ 1308/17, *Netiv Ha'avot* (2018).

HAMAN'S LIES

9   Dennis Ross, *The Missing Peace: The Inside Story of the Fight for Middle East Peace* (New York: Farrar, Straus, and Giroux, 2004), 650–711. Ross, the chief US negotiator at Camp David, documents that Prime Minister Ehud Barak offered approximately 94% of the West Bank, all of Gaza, a capital in East Jerusalem, and shared arrangements for the Temple Mount. Palestinian Chairman Yasser Arafat rejected the proposal without making a counter-offer. See also Bill Clinton, *My Life* (New York: Knopf, 2004), 936–944.

10 The Taba negotiations (January 21–27, 2001) represented the closest the parties came to a final agreement. Israeli negotiators offered approximately 97% of the West Bank with land swaps, a capital in East Jerusalem, and creative solutions for refugees and holy sites. The talks ended without agreement when Israeli elections were called. See Miguel Moratinos, "EU Non-Paper on Taba Negotiations," 2001 (the "Moratinos Document"); Gilead Sher, *The Israeli–Palestinian Peace Negotiations, 1999–2001* (London: Routledge, 2006).

11 Israel unilaterally withdrew from the Gaza Strip in August–September 2005, evacuating all 8,000 settlers from 21 settlements and withdrawing all military forces. In January 2006, Hamas won Palestinian legislative elections. In June 2007, Hamas violently seized control of Gaza, killing Fatah officials and security personnel. Between 2005 and 2023, Hamas and other groups fired over 25,000 rockets and mortars at Israeli civilian communities. See Israel Ministry of Foreign Affairs, "The Israeli Disengagement Plan," 2005; Israel Security Agency statistics on rocket fire.

12 In a 2015 interview, Palestinian Authority President Mahmoud Abbas acknowledged that Prime Minister Ehud Olmert presented him with a map offering the equivalent of 100% of the West Bank (with land swaps), a divided Jerusalem, and a creative solution for refugees. Abbas stated: "He showed me a map. He didn't give me the map... I told him I couldn't decide... I rejected it out of hand." See "Abbas Admits He Rejected 2008 Peace Offer," *Times of Israel*, November 19, 2015; Jackson Diehl, "Abbas's Rejection," *Washington Post*, May 29, 2009; Bernard Avishai, "A Plan for Peace That Still Could Be," *New York Times Magazine*, February 7, 2011.

20

1   Camp David Accords, September 17, 1978, signed by Egyptian President Anwar Sadat, Israeli Prime Minister Menachem Begin, and witnessed by US President Jimmy Carter. The Egypt–Israel Peace Treaty, signed March 26, 1979, ended 30 years of war between the two nations. Israel returned the entire Sinai Peninsula—approximately 23,000 square miles of territory, including oil fields and

strategic military installations—in exchange for peace and normalized relations. See William B. Quandt, *Camp David: Peacemaking and Politics* (Washington: Brookings Institution Press, 1986).

2   Treaty of Peace Between the State of Israel and the Hashemite Kingdom of Jordan, signed October 26, 1994, at the Arava/Araba Crossing. The treaty resolved border disputes, established water-sharing arrangements, and normalized diplomatic and economic relations. King Hussein and Prime Minister Yitzhak Rabin had maintained secret contacts for years before the public agreement. See Moshe Zak, "Israeli–Jordanian Negotiations," *Washington Quarterly* 18, no. 4 (1995): 155–176.

3   Declaration of Principles on Interim Self-Government Arrangements (Oslo I Accord), signed September 13, 1993, by Israeli Prime Minister Yitzhak Rabin and PLO Chairman Yasser Arafat, witnessed by US President Bill Clinton. The Israeli–Palestinian Interim Agreement on the West Bank and the Gaza Strip (Oslo II), signed September 28, 1995, established the Palestinian Authority and divided the West Bank into Areas A, B, and C with varying degrees of Palestinian and Israeli control. See David Makovsky, *Making Peace with the PLO: The Rabin Government's Road to the Oslo Accord* (Boulder: Westview Press, 1996).

4   Prime Minister Yitzhak Rabin was assassinated on November 4, 1995, by Yigal Amir, an Israeli extremist opposed to the Oslo peace process. Rabin was shot after addressing a peace rally in Tel Aviv attended by approximately 100,000 supporters. His death shocked the nation and the world. See Dan Ephron, *Killing a King: The Assassination of Yitzhak Rabin and the Remaking of Israel* (New York: W. W. Norton, 2015).

5   Ehud Olmert, *In First Person* [Hebrew] (Tel Aviv: Yedioth Ahronoth, 2018). Olmert has described the 2008 offer in numerous interviews and his memoir. He proposed land swaps that would give Palestinians territory equivalent to 100% of the West Bank, Palestinian sovereignty in Arab neighborhoods of East Jerusalem, international administration of the Old City's holy sites, and admission of several thousand Palestinian refugees to Israel on humanitarian grounds. See also Bernard Avishai, "A Plan for Peace That Still Could Be," *New York Times Magazine*, February 7, 2011; Condoleezza Rice, *No Higher Honor: A Memoir of My Years in Washington* (New York: Crown, 2011), 651–653.

6   In a 2015 interview with Israel's Channel 2, Palestinian Authority President Mahmoud Abbas acknowledged that Olmert showed him a map of the proposed borders: "He showed me a map. He didn't give me the map... I told him I couldn't decide... I rejected it out of hand." Abbas later claimed he asked to take the map but was refused, though Olmert and US officials present contradict this account.

HAMAN'S LIES

See "Abbas Admits He Rejected 2008 Peace Offer," *Times of Israel*, November 19, 2015; Jackson Diehl, "Abbas's Rejection," *Washington Post*, May 29, 2009.

7   Israel's unilateral disengagement from Gaza was implemented in August–September 2005 under Prime Minister Ariel Sharon. All 8,000 Israeli settlers were evacuated from 21 settlements, and all military installations were dismantled. Some settlers had to be removed by force. In January 2006, Hamas won Palestinian legislative elections, and in June 2007, Hamas violently seized control of Gaza from the Palestinian Authority, executing Fatah members and throwing rivals from rooftops. Between 2005 and 2023, over 25,000 rockets and mortars were fired from Gaza at Israeli communities. See Israel Ministry of Foreign Affairs, "The Disengagement Plan," 2005; Israel Security Agency statistics.

8   The Abraham Accords, signed September 15, 2020, normalized relations between Israel and the United Arab Emirates and Bahrain. Sudan announced normalization in October 2020, and Morocco in December 2020. The agreements established full diplomatic relations, direct flights, economic cooperation, and security coordination. The accords were brokered by the Trump administration and marked the first Arab–Israeli peace agreements since the 1994 Jordan treaty. See US Department of State, "The Abraham Accords," 2020; Michael Koplow and Shira Efron, "The Abraham Accords at One Year," Israel Policy Forum, September 2021.

21

1   Norman Cohn, *Warrant for Genocide: The Myth of the Jewish World Conspiracy and the Protocols of the Elders of Zion* (London: Eyre & Spottiswoode, 1967). Cohn traces the origins of *The Protocols of the Elders of Zion* to the Russian secret police (Okhrana) in the early 1900s, documenting how this fabricated text—which purported to reveal a Jewish conspiracy for world domination—was used to justify pogroms in Tsarist Russia and later became central to Nazi ideology. The *Protocols* remain in circulation today and continue to influence antisemitic movements worldwide.

2   Gallup has polled American sympathies in the Israeli–Palestinian conflict since 1988. Results consistently show Americans sympathizing more with Israel than with Palestinians, typically by margins of 3-to-1 or greater. In February 2024, 58% of Americans sympathized more with Israel versus 18% with Palestinians. Support for Israel spans both political parties, though Republicans show higher support than Democrats. See Gallup, "Americans Still Sympathize More with Israel Than Palestinians," March 2024; Lydia Saad, "Americans' Views Toward Israel Remain Firmly Positive," Gallup, March 14, 2022.

References

3   OpenSecrets.org, Center for Responsive Politics, "Lobbying Data Summary," 2023. The pharmaceutical and health products industry spent approximately $370 million on lobbying in 2023, the most of any sector. Oil and gas spent approximately $125 million; electronics manufacturing and equipment, $155 million; insurance, $150 million. Pro-Israel groups, including AIPAC, spent approximately $5 million on direct lobbying in the same period. Saudi Arabia's registered foreign agents spent over $27 million on lobbying and public relations in 2023, while the United Arab Emirates spent over $20 million. See also OpenSecrets.org, "Foreign Lobby Watch," 2023.

4   US–Israel intelligence cooperation is extensive and mutually beneficial. Israel provided critical intelligence on Soviet weapons systems during the Cold War, on Iraqi nuclear facilities before the 1981 Osirak strike, and on terrorist networks including Al-Qaeda and ISIS. The United States shares satellite imagery, signals intelligence, and threat assessments with Israel. Former CIA Director George Tenet described the relationship as "the most productive bilateral intelligence relationship the United States has." See Bob Woodward, *Veil: The Secret Wars of the CIA 1981–1987* (New York: Simon & Schuster, 1987); Ronen Bergman, *Rise and Kill First: The Secret History of Israel's Targeted Assassinations* (New York: Random House, 2018).

5   The Authorization for Use of Military Force Against Iraq Resolution of 2002 (Public Law 107–243) passed the House of Representatives on October 10, 2002, by a vote of 296–133 and the Senate on October 11, 2002, by a vote of 77–23. The resolution was debated publicly for months, with extensive media coverage and congressional hearings. Israeli officials were divided on the wisdom of the war; some, including military and intelligence figures, warned that removing Saddam Hussein would strengthen Iran's regional position—a prediction that proved accurate.

6   Relations between the Obama administration and Israeli Prime Minister Benjamin Netanyahu were frequently tense, particularly over the Iran nuclear negotiations and settlement policy. On December 23, 2016, the United States abstained on UN Security Council Resolution 2334, allowing it to pass 14–0. The resolution declared Israeli settlements in the West Bank and East Jerusalem to have "no legal validity" and demanded Israel "immediately and completely cease all settlement activities." This was the first time since 1979 that the United States had not vetoed a UN Security Council resolution critical of Israel. The abstention demonstrated American policy independence from Israeli preferences. See US Department of State archives; UN Security Council Resolution 2334 (2016).

HAMAN'S LIES

22

1. In June 2021, Ra'am (United Arab List), led by Mansour Abbas, became the first Arab party to join an Israeli governing coalition, supporting the government of Prime Minister Naftali Bennett. The coalition agreement included approximately 53 billion shekels ($16 billion) in funding for Arab communities over five years, addressing infrastructure, education, housing, and public safety. Abbas stated that he joined the government to address the needs of Arab citizens rather than remaining in perpetual opposition. See "Historic First: Arab Party Joins Israeli Government," *Times of Israel*, June 13, 2021.

2. Israel's Defense Service Law exempts Arab citizens (except Druze and Circassians) from mandatory military service. This exemption was established in 1948 to avoid placing Arab citizens in conflict with their ethnic and religious kin in neighboring states. The exemption is not a prohibition—Arab citizens may volunteer for military service, and many do. Bedouin Arabs have a long tradition of IDF service, particularly in tracking and reconnaissance units. The Druze community has been subject to mandatory conscription since 1956 by agreement with Druze leaders. Christian Arab volunteers have increased in recent years. See Israel Defense Service Law, 1986 (Consolidated Version); Rhoda Ann Kanaaneh, *Surrounded: Palestinian Soldiers in the Israeli Military* (Stanford: Stanford University Press, 2008).

3. Israel Central Bureau of Statistics, "The Arab Population of Israel," Statistical Abstract, 2023. Economic indicators show gaps between Jewish and Arab communities: median household income in Arab localities is approximately 60–70% of that in Jewish localities; labor force participation among Arab women, while increasing, remains lower than among Jewish women. However, these gaps have been narrowing. Government Resolution 922 (2015) allocated 15 billion shekels over five years for Arab community development, followed by Government Resolution 550 (2021) allocating an additional 30 billion shekels. See also Hanna Herzog and Taghreed Yahia-Younis, "Men's Bargaining with Patriarchy: The Case of Primaries within Hamulas in Palestinian–Arab Communities in Israel," *Gender & Society* 21, no. 4 (2007): 579–602.

4. Multiple surveys have found that Israeli Arabs, despite criticisms of government policy, prefer Israeli citizenship to alternatives. A 2021 survey by the Israel Democracy Institute found that 68% of Arab citizens reported feeling proud to be Israeli. A 2017 survey by Professor Sammy Smooha of the University of Haifa found that only 11.2% of Israeli Arabs would prefer to become citizens of a future Palestinian state. A 2015 survey by the Palestinian Center for Public Opinion

found that 78% of Arab citizens of Israel would prefer to remain Israeli citizens rather than become citizens of a Palestinian state. See Israel Democracy Institute, "Israeli Arab Society Survey," 2021; Sammy Smooha, "Index of Arab-Jewish Relations in Israel," University of Haifa, 2017.

23

1. Israel's administrative detention authority derives from the Administrative Detention Order (Judea and Samaria) of 1988, permitting detention without charge for renewable periods of up to six months when security officials possess evidence that an individual poses an imminent threat. Detainees may appeal to military courts and the Israeli Supreme Court. Similar measures have been used by other democracies facing terrorism: the United States held detainees at Guantanamo Bay under the Authorization for Use of Military Force (2001); the United Kingdom used internment without trial extensively in Northern Ireland under the Civil Authorities (Special Powers) Act (1922) and later the Detention of Terrorists Order (1972); France has employed administrative detention under successive states of emergency. See Amnesty International, "Administrative Detention," 2023; Human Rights Watch, "Israel: 50 Years of Administrative Detention," 2017.

2. The Coordinator of Government Activities in the Territories (COGAT), a unit of the Israeli Ministry of Defense, administers checkpoints in the West Bank and publishes data on their operation. COGAT reports document significant reductions in checkpoint numbers and waiting times during periods of reduced violence. Between 2008 and 2010, Israel removed over 100 checkpoints and roadblocks in the West Bank as security conditions improved. During periods of heightened threat, checkpoints are reinforced and additional temporary checkpoints established. Work permits for Palestinians to enter Israel for employment have fluctuated from near zero during the Second Intifada to over 150,000 by 2023 based on security assessments. See COGAT, "Humanitarian Activity Reports," cogat.mod.gov.il; World Bank, "Movement and Access in the West Bank," 2023.

3. The Israeli Supreme Court has ruled on the security barrier's route in multiple cases, ordering adjustments to reduce impact on Palestinian communities. In *Beit Sourik Village Council v. Government of Israel* (HCJ 2056/04, June 30, 2004), the Court ordered rerouting of approximately 30 kilometers of barrier, ruling that the original route violated proportionality requirements. Chief Justice Aharon Barak wrote that security needs must be balanced against humanitarian concerns and that "the military commander must consider the needs of the local

HAMAN'S LIES

inhabitants." In *Mara'abe v. Prime Minister of Israel* (HCJ 7957/04, September 15, 2005), the Court ordered further modifications. The government complied with these rulings at significant expense, demonstrating judicial oversight of security measures. See Barak–Erez, Daphne, "Israel: The Security Barrier— Between International Law, Constitutional Law, and Domestic Judicial Review," *International Journal of Constitutional Law* 4, no. 3 (2006): 540–552.

4   COGAT coordinates the transfer of humanitarian goods into Gaza and the West Bank. According to COGAT data, approximately 500–700 trucks of goods enter Gaza daily during non-conflict periods, carrying food, medicine, fuel, construction materials, and consumer goods. During military operations, Israel maintains humanitarian corridors and coordinates with international organizations including the United Nations and International Committee of the Red Cross. Israel also facilitates medical evacuations from Gaza to Israeli and West Bank hospitals, treatment of Gaza patients in Israeli hospitals, and entry of international humanitarian personnel. See COGAT, "Gaza Crossings: Activities Report," cogat.mod.gov.il; United Nations Office for the Coordination of Humanitarian Affairs (OCHA), "Gaza Crossings Operations Status," various reports.

24

1   Freedom House, *Freedom in the World 2024*, rates Israel's press freedom status as "Free." Reporters Without Borders, *World Press Freedom Index 2024*, ranks Israel 101st globally but notes it is the highest-ranked country in the Middle East and North Africa region. By comparison, regional rankings include: Lebanon (140), Jordan (143), Egypt (170), Saudi Arabia (166), Iran (176), and Syria (179). The Committee to Protect Journalists includes Israel among countries with a free press while documenting concerns about journalist safety in conflict zones. See Freedom House, "Israel: Freedom of the Press," freedomhouse.org; Reporters Without Borders, "Middle East and North Africa," rsf.org.

2   The Committee to Protect Journalists has documented systematic persecution of journalists in Iran. As of 2024, Iran holds at least 17 journalists in prison, making it one of the world's worst jailers of journalists. Journalists have been executed for their work, including Rouhollah Zam, hanged in December 2020 for running a news channel critical of the government. International journalists including *Washington Post* contributor Jason Rezaian have been imprisoned and used as bargaining chips. Reporters Without Borders describes Iran as "one of the world's most repressive countries for journalists." See Committee to Protect Journalists, "Iran," cpj.org; Reporters Without Borders, "Iran," rsf.org.

References

3   The Committee to Protect Journalists (CPJ) and Reporters Without Borders have documented systematic suppression of press freedom under both Hamas in Gaza and the Palestinian Authority in the West Bank. Hamas has detained, beaten, and threatened journalists for critical coverage; CPJ documented at least 15 journalists detained by Hamas in 2023 alone. The Palestinian Authority has arrested journalists for social media posts critical of leadership, detained reporters covering protests, and pressured outlets to avoid unfavorable coverage. In 2021, the PA detained journalist Nizar Banat, who died in custody after being beaten—prompting widespread condemnation from press freedom organizations. See Committee to Protect Journalists, "Palestinian Territories," cpj.org; Reporters Without Borders, "Palestine," rsf.org; Human Rights Watch, "Palestine: Authorities Should Investigate Activist's Death," June 24, 2021.

4   B'Tselem (Hebrew for "in the image of," from Genesis 1:27) was founded in 1989 by a group of Israeli academics, attorneys, journalists, and Knesset members. It operates legally from offices in Jerusalem, employs Israeli and Palestinian staff, and publishes regular reports documenting incidents it considers human rights violations in the occupied territories. B'Tselem has provided testimony to the UN Human Rights Council, cooperated with international media investigations, and advocated internationally for policy changes. Its executive director and staff operate openly in Israel without legal restriction. See B'Tselem, "About B'Tselem," btselem.org; B'Tselem annual reports.

5   The Law on Disclosure Requirements for Recipients of Support from a Foreign State Entity, passed by the Knesset on July 11, 2016, requires nonprofit organizations that receive more than 50% of their funding from foreign governments to disclose this fact in official publications and when communicating with elected officials. The law does not prohibit foreign funding, does not restrict organizational activities, and does not require registration as a foreign agent. It applies only to funding from foreign governments, not private foundations or individuals. Comparable disclosure requirements exist in other democracies: the United States' Foreign Agents Registration Act (1938) requires registration and disclosure of activities on behalf of foreign principals; Canada's proposed Foreign Influence Transparency Registry (2023) imposes similar requirements. See Knesset, Law on Disclosure Requirements for Recipients of Support from a Foreign State Entity, 2016; US Department of Justice, "Foreign Agents Registration Act," justice.gov.

6   In several documented cases, individuals killed while holding journalist credentials were also affiliated with Hamas or other armed groups. In May 2021, Israel struck a Gaza building housing Al Jazeera and Associated Press offices,

stating it was used by Hamas military intelligence—a claim disputed by the news organizations. In separate incidents, Israel has presented evidence that specific individuals described as journalists were also operatives for armed groups. The use of journalist credentials as cover for military activities complicates assessments of who qualifies as a protected journalist under international law. Protocol I Additional to the Geneva Conventions, Article 79, protects journalists "engaged in dangerous professional missions in areas of armed conflict" provided they "take no action adversely affecting their status as civilians." See Israel Ministry of Foreign Affairs statements; Protocol I Additional to the Geneva Conventions, Article 79.

7   Human Rights Watch has documented Hamas treatment of journalists and civil society in Gaza, finding systematic suppression of press freedom. Reports document arbitrary detention of journalists, forced closure of media outlets, confiscation of equipment, and physical assaults on reporters covering protests against Hamas rule. In 2019, Hamas security forces violently dispersed protests against economic conditions, beating and detaining journalists covering the events. Human Rights Watch stated that "Hamas authorities have shown zero tolerance for public criticism" and called on Hamas to "end the systematic practice of arresting and torturing critics." See Human Rights Watch, "Two Authorities, One Way, Zero Dissent: Arbitrary Arrest and Torture Under the Palestinian Authority and Hamas," October 23, 2018; Human Rights Watch, "Gaza: Authorities Crack Down on Journalists, Activists," April 29, 2019.

25

1   Israel Defense Forces and Israel Security Agency statistics document over 20,000 rockets and mortars fired from Gaza at Israeli territory since 2001. Major escalations include: Operation Cast Lead (2008–2009), approximately 750 rockets; Operation Pillar of Defense (2012), approximately 1,500 rockets; Operation Protective Edge (2014), approximately 4,500 rockets; May 2021 conflict, approximately 4,400 rockets; October 2023–present conflict, over 12,000 rockets in the first months alone. Rockets are tracked by radar, recovered as physical evidence, and their launch sites identified through multiple intelligence means. See Israel Security Agency, "Rocket Fire from Gaza," shabak.gov.il; IDF Spokesperson statements.

2   Iranian leaders have made numerous public statements calling for Israel's elimination. Supreme Leader Ayatollah Ali Khamenei has repeatedly referred to Israel as a "cancerous tumor" that must be removed, including in speeches on May 22, 2020, and October 7, 2023. In 2014, Khamenei tweeted a nine-point

References

plan for Israel's elimination. Former President Mahmoud Ahmadinejad stated in October 2005 that Israel should be "wiped off the map" (*bayad az safheh-ye ruzgar mahv shavad*)—a statement broadcast on Iranian state television and translated by multiple independent sources. Iranian officials have described Israel as a "one-bomb country" referring to its small geographic size. See Middle East Media Research Institute (MEMRI) translations; Anti-Defamation League, "Iranian Leaders in Their Own Words," adl.org.

3   The International Atomic Energy Agency has issued numerous reports documenting concerns about Iran's nuclear program. In November 2011, the IAEA published a detailed annex documenting "possible military dimensions" to Iran's nuclear activities, including work on nuclear weapons design, high-explosive detonators, and missile reentry vehicles. Subsequent reports documented Iran's violations of the Joint Comprehensive Plan of Action, including exceeding limits on enriched uranium stockpiles, enriching uranium to 60% purity (far beyond civilian needs), and operating advanced centrifuges in violation of the agreement. In 2023, IAEA Director General Rafael Grossi stated that Iran's uranium enrichment had reached levels with "no credible civilian justification." See IAEA, "Implementation of the NPT Safeguards Agreement and Relevant Provisions of Security Council Resolutions in the Islamic Republic of Iran," GOV/2011/65, November 2011, and subsequent quarterly reports.

4   See Introduction, Endnote 2, and Chapter 12 for full documentation of the Hamas Charter.

5   Hezbollah's arsenal is estimated at 130,000 to 150,000 rockets and missiles by Israeli, American, and United Nations assessments—more than most national armies possess. The UN Interim Force in Lebanon (UNIFIL) has documented Hezbollah's military buildup in violation of UN Security Council Resolution 1701 (2006). Hezbollah Secretary-General Hassan Nasrallah (killed in September 2024) made numerous public statements calling for Israel's destruction, including: "If they [Jews] all gather in Israel, it will save us the trouble of going after them worldwide" (2002, broadcast on Al-Manar television). The United States, European Union, the United Kingdom, Canada, Australia, Israel, and the Arab League designate Hezbollah (or its military wing) as a terrorist organization. See US Department of State, "Foreign Terrorist Organizations," state.gov; UN Security Council Resolution 1701 (2006); Center for Strategic and International Studies, "Hezbollah's Missiles and Rockets," 2018.

6   Claims that Israel orchestrated or permitted the October 7 attacks as a "false flag" have been widely promoted on social media platforms and by fringe commentators, despite the abundance of primary-source evidence created by

HAMAN'S LIES

Hamas itself. Investigations by major news organizations—including *The New York Times*, *BBC*, and *Associated Press*—all independently verified that Hamas fighters filmed their own actions with body cameras, phones, and livestreams, and that the footage used by Israel to document atrocities originated from the attackers, not Israeli sources. See Adam Goldman et al., "How Hamas Carried Out the Deadliest Attack on Israel in Decades," *New York Times*, December 12, 2023; "What We Know About the Hamas Attack on Israel," *BBC News*, October 16, 2023; and Joseph Krauss, "Hamas Attackers Filmed Their Assault, Creating a Record of Brutality," *Associated Press*, October 19, 2023. Experts on disinformation note that "false flag" narratives often emerge after mass-casualty events as a way for ideological communities to avoid confronting uncomfortable truths; see Joan Donovan, "Crisis Actor Conspiracies After Mass Violence," *Harvard Kennedy School Shorenstein Center*, 2021.

26

1   Israeli–Palestinian Interim Agreement on the West Bank and the Gaza Strip (Oslo II), signed September 28, 1995, Annex III, Article 40: "Water and Sewage." The agreement established Israeli recognition of Palestinian water rights in the West Bank, allocated specific quantities from the Mountain Aquifer (estimated 70–80 million cubic meters annually for immediate Palestinian needs plus additional future needs), and created the Joint Water Committee to coordinate water management. Israel committed to maintaining existing water supply to Palestinian communities and facilitating increased supply. See Israeli–Palestinian Interim Agreement, Annex III, Article 40; US Department of State archives.

2   Drip irrigation was developed in Israel in the 1960s by Simcha Blass, an engineer who observed that a tree near a leaking pipe grew larger than surrounding trees. Blass partnered with Kibbutz Hatzerim to commercialize the technology, founding Netafim in 1965. Netafim is now the world's largest drip irrigation company, operating in over 110 countries and credited with transforming agriculture in arid regions worldwide. Drip irrigation reduces water consumption by 30–70% compared to conventional irrigation while increasing yields by 20–90%. Israeli agricultural technology companies, including Netafim, operate in Palestinian areas and have trained Palestinian farmers in water-efficient techniques. See Netafim, "Our Story," netafim.com; Seth M. Siegel, *Let There Be Water: Israel's Solution for a Water-Starved World* (New York: Thomas Dunne Books, 2015).

3   Israel operates five major desalination plants along its Mediterranean coast, producing approximately 600 million cubic meters of drinking water

References

annually—over 80% of Israel's domestic water supply. The Sorek desalination plant, the world's largest seawater reverse osmosis facility when it opened in 2013, produces water at approximately $0.50 per cubic meter, among the lowest costs globally. By contrast, Iran faces severe water shortages affecting over 50 million people despite possessing extensive coastline. Iranian officials have acknowledged a water crisis, with Lake Urmia shrinking by 90% and groundwater depletion reaching critical levels. Iran's failure to develop desalination capacity comparable to Israel's has contributed to protests, agricultural collapse, and internal migration. See *Financial Times*, "Israel's Desalination Success Offers Hope for Parched Middle East," March 7, 2023; *Associated Press*, "Iran's Water Crisis: Protests Erupt as Lakes Dry Up," November 15, 2021; Radio Free Europe, "Iran's Water Shortages Fuel Protests Across the Country," July 22, 2021.

4 Israel Water Authority, "Water Sector in Israel: OECD Review," 2023. Israel recycles approximately 87% of its wastewater, far exceeding any other country. Spain, the second-highest, recycles approximately 20%. Treated wastewater provides over 50% of Israel's agricultural irrigation water. The Shafdan wastewater treatment plant near Tel Aviv, one of the world's largest and most advanced, treats sewage from the Tel Aviv metropolitan area and supplies recycled water to the Negev desert for agriculture. This technology is available for implementation in Palestinian areas, where wastewater recycling rates remain minimal. See Israel Water Authority, "Treated Wastewater Reuse," water.gov.il; OECD, "Water Resources Allocation: Israel," 2021.

5 Israeli Civil Administration (COGAT) and Palestinian Water Authority data document increasing water supply to Palestinian areas. In 1967, Palestinian water consumption in the West Bank was approximately 60 million cubic meters annually. By 2020, total water available to Palestinians in the West Bank exceeded 200 million cubic meters annually, including approximately 64 million cubic meters purchased from Mekorot (Israel's national water company), Palestinian extraction from wells and springs, and additional allocations. Mekorot supplies water to Palestinian municipalities at the same regulated price charged to Israeli communities. Israel has exceeded its Oslo II commitments, providing approximately 64 million cubic meters annually compared to the agreed 31 million cubic meters. See COGAT, "Water in Judea and Samaria," cogat.mod.gov.il; Palestinian Water Authority annual reports.

6 World Bank, "Assessment of Restrictions on Palestinian Water Sector Development," April 2009; World Bank, "West Bank and Gaza: Securing Water for Development in West Bank and Gaza," 2018. These studies document that the Palestinian water system loses approximately 30–35% of water to

"non-revenue water"—leaks, theft, unbilled consumption, and poor metering—among the highest rates in the world. The World Bank estimated that addressing infrastructure losses and improving efficiency could provide Palestinians with 50% more water without any additional allocation from Israel. The reports noted that the Palestinian Authority had not fully utilized available water allocations and that donor-funded infrastructure projects faced implementation delays. See also Ido Zelkovitz, "The Politics of Water in the Israeli–Palestinian Conflict," Middle East Policy 24, no. 3 (2017): 133–148.

7   The Gaza coastal aquifer, the sole natural freshwater source for Gaza's population of over 2 million, has been severely depleted and contaminated. According to the United Nations Environment Programme and Palestinian Water Authority assessments, over-extraction has caused annual withdrawal of approximately 200 million cubic meters against a sustainable yield of 55 million cubic meters, leading to seawater intrusion. Approximately 97% of Gaza's groundwater now exceeds World Health Organization standards for salinity, nitrates, or other contaminants. Untreated sewage—approximately 100,000 cubic meters daily—flows into the Mediterranean and seeps into the aquifer due to inadequate treatment infrastructure. These problems predate and have accelerated since the 2005 Israeli withdrawal. See UNEP, "Environmental Assessment of the Gaza Strip," 2009; World Bank, "Assessment of Water Supply in the Gaza Strip," 2016; RAND Corporation, "The Costs of the Israeli–Palestinian Conflict: Gaza Water Crisis," 2015.

8   Regional water availability data from the World Bank, UN Food and Agriculture Organization (FAO), and World Resources Institute demonstrate that Palestinians have higher per capita water availability than populations in several neighboring countries. Jordan's per capita renewable freshwater availability is approximately 80 cubic meters annually, among the lowest in the world, compared to over 100 cubic meters for Palestinians in the West Bank. Yemen faces catastrophic water shortages with aquifers expected to be depleted within decades; Syria's water infrastructure has been devastated by civil war; Iraq's water availability has declined by 40% since the 1980s due to upstream damming and climate change. These crises receive far less international attention than Palestinian water issues despite affecting far larger populations with far greater severity. See World Bank, "Renewable Internal Freshwater Resources per Capita," data.worldbank.org; FAO AQUASTAT database; World Resources Institute, "Water Stress Rankings," 2023.

References

27

1. International humanitarian law permits the targeting of combatants in armed conflict regardless of their location. Protocol I Additional to the Geneva Conventions, Article 51(3), states that civilians "shall enjoy the protection afforded by this Section, unless and for such time as they take a direct part in hostilities." The International Committee of the Red Cross, in its 2009 "Interpretive Guidance on the Notion of Direct Participation in Hostilities," concluded that members of organized armed groups with a "continuous combat function" may be targeted at any time during the conflict. Legal scholars distinguish between assassination—killing political figures for political purposes—and targeted killing of combatants, which is permitted under the laws of armed conflict. See Nils Melzer, *Targeted Killing in International Law* (Oxford: Oxford University Press, 2008); Gary Solis, *The Law of Armed Conflict: International Humanitarian Law in War* (Cambridge: Cambridge University Press, 2010), 538–550.

2. Sheikh Ahmed Yassin founded Hamas in 1987 and served as its spiritual leader until his death in an Israeli strike on March 22, 2004. Under Yassin's leadership, Hamas conducted over 50 suicide bombings that killed more than 500 Israeli civilians between 2000 and 2004 alone. Yassin publicly endorsed suicide bombings as a religious obligation and personally blessed suicide bombers before their missions. He declared that "armed resistance and the armed struggle are the right and authentic means of liberating our land" and rejected any peace agreement recognizing Israel's existence. Hamas's charter, issued under Yassin's leadership, explicitly calls for Israel's destruction and contains antisemitic content citing *The Protocols of the Elders of Zion*. See Matthew Levitt, *Hamas: Politics, Charity, and Terrorism in the Service of Jihad* (New Haven: Yale University Press, 2006); Israel Ministry of Foreign Affairs, "Victims of Palestinian Violence and Terrorism," mfa.gov.il.

3. The International Atomic Energy Agency has documented extensive evidence of undeclared nuclear activities in Iran. The November 2011 IAEA report (GOV/2011/65) included a detailed annex describing "possible military dimensions" to Iran's nuclear program, including work on nuclear weapons design, high-explosive detonation systems, and missile reentry vehicles. The IAEA documented that Iran had constructed hidden enrichment facilities (including the Fordow facility built inside a mountain), conducted uranium enrichment beyond civilian needs, and failed to explain evidence of weaponization research. Iranian nuclear scientists, including Mohsen Fakhrizadeh (killed in November 2020), held military ranks and worked within Iran's defense establishment. Fakhrizadeh was identified by the IAEA and Western intelligence agencies as the head of Iran's

nuclear weapons development program. See IAEA, "Implementation of the NPT Safeguards Agreement in the Islamic Republic of Iran," GOV/2011/65, November 2011; David Albright and Andrea Stricker, *Iran's Perilous Pursuit of Nuclear Weapons* (Washington: Institute for Science and International Security, 2021).

4   The United States has conducted extensive targeted killing operations abroad. Operation Neptune Spear killed Osama bin Laden in Abbottabad, Pakistan, on May 2, 2011, without Pakistani government consent. A US drone strike killed Qasem Soleimani, commander of Iran's Islamic Revolutionary Guard Corps Quds Force, at Baghdad International Airport on January 3, 2020. The US drone program has conducted thousands of strikes in Pakistan, Yemen, Somalia, Libya, and other countries, killing senior al-Qaeda, ISIS, and other terrorist leaders. The US Department of Justice and executive branch have issued legal memoranda justifying targeted killing of terrorists, including American citizens abroad, under the Authorization for Use of Military Force and inherent self-defense authority. See US Department of Justice, Office of Legal Counsel, "Lawfulness of a Lethal Operation Directed Against a US Citizen," July 16, 2010; Daniel Klaidman, *Kill or Capture: The War on Terror and the Soul of the Obama Presidency* (New York: Houghton Mifflin Harcourt, 2012).

5   Adolf Eichmann, SS Lieutenant Colonel and chief architect of the logistics of the Holocaust, escaped to Argentina after World War II using false documents obtained through "ratlines" that helped Nazi war criminals flee Europe. Israeli Mossad agents identified and captured Eichmann in Buenos Aires on May 11, 1960, and transported him to Israel for trial. The trial, held in Jerusalem from April 11 to August 15, 1961, presented extensive documentary evidence and testimony from over 100 Holocaust survivors. Eichmann was convicted of crimes against humanity, crimes against the Jewish people, and war crimes, and was hanged on June 1, 1962—the only execution ever carried out in Israel. The trial was broadcast internationally and is credited with bringing worldwide attention to the Holocaust. See Hannah Arendt, *Eichmann in Jerusalem: A Report on the Banality of Evil* (New York: Viking, 1963); Deborah E. Lipstadt, *The Eichmann Trial* (New York: Schocken, 2011); State of Israel, *The Trial of Adolf Eichmann: Record of Proceedings in the District Court of Jerusalem* (Jerusalem: Ministry of Justice, 1992).

28

1   Geneva Convention Relative to the Protection of Civilian Persons in Time of War (Fourth Geneva Convention), August 12, 1949, Article 33: "No protected person may be punished for an offence he or she has not personally committed.

References

Collective penalties and likewise all measures of intimidation or of terrorism are prohibited." The prohibition emerged from World War II atrocities including Nazi reprisals against civilian populations—such as the Lidice massacre (1942), where German forces killed all men, deported women and children, and razed the village in retaliation for the assassination of Reinhard Heydrich. Legal scholars distinguish between punitive collective punishment (prohibited) and security measures that incidentally affect broader populations while addressing genuine threats (permitted). See Jean-Marie Henckaerts and Louise Doswald-Beck, *Customary International Humanitarian Law*, vol. 1 (Cambridge: Cambridge University Press, 2005), Rule 103.

2   Studies on the deterrent effect of house demolitions have produced mixed but significant findings. Research by Efraim Benmelech, Claude Berrebi, and Esteban Klor, "Counter-Suicide-Terrorism: Evidence from House Demolitions," *Journal of Politics* 77, no. 1 (2015): 27–43, found that punitive house demolitions significantly reduced suicide attacks, with the effect increasing with the number of demolitions in a given area. The study concluded that demolitions "cause an immediate, significant decrease in the number of suicide attacks." A separate study by the Israel Defense Forces found that demolitions deterred approximately 10–15% of potential attackers who cited family consequences as a factor in abandoning planned attacks. The Israeli Supreme Court has reviewed the policy in multiple cases, including HCJ 2006/97, *Ghanimat v. GOC Central Command*, permitting demolitions with restrictions including proportionality requirements and opportunity for appeal.

3   Hamas violently seized control of Gaza in June 2007, overthrowing the Palestinian Authority in a brief civil war. Hamas forces killed over 100 Fatah members, threw rivals from rooftops, and executed opponents in the streets. Since the takeover, Hamas has launched over 20,000 rockets and mortars at Israeli civilian communities, constructed cross-border attack tunnels, and conducted the October 7, 2023, massacre that killed over 1,200 Israelis. Hamas's charter (1988) explicitly calls for Israel's destruction and contains antisemitic content. The organization is designated as a terrorist organization by the United States, European Union, the United Kingdom, Canada, Australia, and other nations. See International Crisis Group, "After Gaza," Middle East Report No. 68, August 2, 2007; US Department of State, "Foreign Terrorist Organizations," state.gov.

4   The COGAT publishes data on checkpoint operations and adjustments in the West Bank. Between 2008 and 2010, Israel removed over 100 checkpoints and roadblocks as security conditions improved following the decline in suicide bombings. Work permits for Palestinians to enter Israel have fluctuated based

on security assessments, expanding from near zero during the Second Intifada to over 150,000 by 2023 during periods of relative calm. During periods of heightened violence, checkpoints are reinforced and permits restricted. This calibration to threat levels demonstrates that restrictions serve security purposes rather than punitive intent. See COGAT, "Humanitarian Activities Reports," cogat.mod.gov.il; World Bank, "Economic Monitoring Report to the Ad Hoc Liaison Committee," various years.

29

1. Israeli security services have documented numerous stabbing attacks by Palestinian minors. During the "Knife Intifada" (October 2015–2016), attackers as young as 13 committed stabbings. On October 12, 2015, a 13-year-old and a 15-year-old stabbed a 13-year-old Israeli boy riding his bicycle in Pisgat Ze'ev, seriously wounding him. On November 10, 2015, two 12-year-old Palestinians stabbed a security guard at Jerusalem's light rail. On February 23, 2016, a 14-year-old girl attempted to stab a guard at the Anatot checkpoint. These incidents were captured on security cameras and documented by Israel Police and Shin Bet. See Israel Ministry of Foreign Affairs, "Wave of Terror 2015–2016," mfa.gov.il; Israel Security Agency, "Terrorism and Security Data," shabak.gov.il.

2. Rock-throwing attacks have caused multiple fatalities and serious injuries. On September 14, 2011, Asher Palmer and his infant son Yonatan were killed when rocks thrown at their car near Kiryat Arba caused Palmer to lose control and crash. On September 22, 2013, Sergeant Gal Kobi was killed by a rock thrown at his head in Hebron. On March 13, 2013, Adele Biton, age two, was critically injured when rocks struck her mother's car; she died in 2015 from complications. In 2022, Yehuda Dimentman was killed when rocks caused a car crash near Homesh. Israeli medical facilities treat hundreds of injuries annually from rock attacks, including severe head trauma and injuries from crashes caused by rocks striking windshields. See Israel Police statistics; Israel Ministry of Foreign Affairs documentation.

3. IMPACT-se (Institute for Monitoring Peace and Cultural Tolerance in School Education) has conducted comprehensive reviews of Palestinian Authority and UNRWA educational materials. Their 2021–2023 reports document systematic problems including: glorification of terrorists as role models (e.g., Dalal Mughrabi, who led the 1978 Coastal Road massacre killing 38 Israelis, including 13 children); mathematical word problems using violence against Israelis; maps that omit Israel entirely; and poems praising martyrdom. Palestinian Authority textbooks have been funded by the European Union and other donors who

have repeatedly demanded reforms. The EU commissioned reviews in 2019 and 2021 that confirmed problematic content; limited reforms followed but core issues remain. See IMPACT-se, "Palestinian Authority Textbooks 2022–2023: Selected Examples," impact-se.org; European Commission, "Review of Palestinian Authority Textbooks," Georg Eckert Institute, 2021.

4   Israel established a separate Military Juvenile Court in September 2009 to handle cases involving minors in the West Bank. The court features judges with specialized training in juvenile justice, modified procedures including limits on detention periods before hearings, and consideration of age in sentencing. Military Order 1651 (2009) and subsequent amendments established specific provisions for minors including: requirement for parental notification within 24 hours of arrest; shorter maximum interrogation periods for minors; prohibition on nighttime arrests of children under 16 except in exceptional circumstances; and right to legal representation. The age of criminal responsibility in the military system is 12, compared to 14 in Israeli civilian law. See Military Order 1651 (2009); Israel Defense Forces Military Advocate General documentation; UNICEF, "Children in Israeli Military Detention," February 2013.

5   Israel has implemented multiple reforms to juvenile detention and interrogation procedures in response to domestic and international criticism. Military Order 1676 (2010) and subsequent amendments strengthened parental notification requirements, mandated audio-visual recording of interrogations of minors in most cases, limited the duration of interrogation sessions, and required that minors be informed of their rights in a language they understand. In 2015, Israel raised the age at which Palestinians could be prosecuted in military court from 16 to 18, aligning with international definitions of childhood. The Military Advocate General has issued binding directives on treatment of minors, and violations are subject to investigation and prosecution. Israeli human rights organizations including B'Tselem and HaMoked regularly monitor detention conditions and bring cases to Israeli courts, achieving policy changes and individual remedies. See Israel Defense Forces, "Treatment of Minors in Military Courts," 2015; HaMoked, annual reports on detention of minors.

6   Comparative analysis of juvenile justice systems shows Israel's treatment of Palestinian minors, while subject to legitimate criticism, is not uniquely harsh by international standards. The United States detains approximately 48,000 juveniles daily, including life sentences for minors. The UK, Australia, France, and Germany have all faced human rights criticism of their juvenile systems. In the Middle East, Egypt, Syria, Hamas, and the Palestinian Authority detain minors with far fewer legal protections than Israel provides. See Annie E. Casey Foundation, "'Youth

Incarceration in the United States,'" 2021; Human Rights Watch, country reports on juvenile justice; UN Committee Against Torture, country reports.

30

1. Menachem Klein, *Jerusalem: The Contested City* (New York: New York University Press, 2001), 118–123; and Michael Dumper, *The Politics of Jerusalem Since 1967* (New York: Columbia University Press, 1997), 64–76. Both works document Israel's offer of citizenship to Palestinians in Jerusalem after 1967, the widespread choice of permanent residency instead, and the standard residency regulations—comparable to residency rules worldwide—that apply regardless of ethnicity.

2. See Sergio DellaPergola, "Demography in Israel/Palestine: Trends, Prospects, Policy Implications," *Population Studies* 66, no. 2 (2012): 153–176; and United Nations Department of Economic and Social Affairs, *World Population Prospects 2022*. Both sources document long-term Palestinian and Arab population growth patterns in Israel, the West Bank, and Gaza, including historical baselines and contemporary totals.

3. See Adrian Zenz, "Sterilizations, IUDs, and Mandatory Birth Control: The CCP's Campaign to Suppress Uyghur Birthrates in Xinjiang," *The Jamestown Foundation* (2020); Norman M. Naimark, *Fires of Hatred: Ethnic Cleansing in Twentieth-Century Europe* (Cambridge, MA: Harvard University Press, 2001), 133–178; and Martin Gilbert, *In Ishmael's House: A History of Jews in Muslim Lands* (New Haven: Yale University Press, 2010), 295–314. These works document coercive birth-suppression policies in China, demographic cleansing in the former Yugoslavia, and the expulsion of Jewish populations from Arab countries after 1948.

4. For context and analysis of the Nation-State Law and comparable constitutional identity provisions worldwide, see Ruth Gavison, "What Is the Nation-State Law Trying to Do?" *Israel Studies* 24, no. 2 (2019): 1–14; and Asher Maoz, "Constitutional Identity and the Nation-State Law," in *Israel and International Law*, ed. Stephen Goldstein (Jerusalem: Hebrew University Press, 2020), 55–72.

31

1. Bradley Bowman and Ryan Brobst, "How America Benefits from Its Security Partnership with Israel," Foundation for Defense of Democracies, October 30, 2024, fdd.org. This analysis documents the extensive returns America receives from its investment in the US–Israel partnership across military technology, intelligence cooperation, and strategic positioning.

References

2. Following the 1973 Yom Kippur War, the US Department of Defense commissioned extensive studies of the conflict. American military officials walked Israeli battlefields and interviewed Israeli commanders, gathering lessons that shaped American military doctrine for decades. The insights directly influenced the development of AirLand Battle doctrine—emphasizing maneuver warfare, combined arms operations, and deep strikes—and the "Big Five" weapons programs: the M1 Abrams tank, M2 Bradley Fighting Vehicle, AH-64 Apache helicopter, UH-60 Black Hawk helicopter, and MIM-104 Patriot missile system. See John L. Romjue, *From Active Defense to AirLand Battle: The Development of Army Doctrine, 1973–1982* (Fort Monroe, VA: US Army Training and Doctrine Command, 1984).

3. Israeli companies, including Elbit Systems, developed advanced tunnel detection technologies in response to Hamas tunnels from Gaza and Hezbollah tunnels from Lebanon. The United States has deployed these technologies along the southern border to detect drug-smuggling tunnels, and American forces used similar systems to counter ISIS tunnel networks in Iraq and Syria. See US Customs and Border Protection statements; Bowman and Brobst, "How America Benefits from Its Security Partnership with Israel," Foundation for Defense of Democracies, October 30, 2024.

4. The Israeli Emergency Bandage (also called the "Emergency Bandage" or "Israeli Bandage") was invented by Bernard Bar-Natan, an Israeli military medic, in the 1990s. Its patented pressure applicator allows a wounded soldier to apply effective hemorrhage control with one hand. The US military adopted it as standard issue in individual first aid kits beginning in the early 2000s, and it has been credited with saving numerous American lives in Iraq and Afghanistan. The bandage is now used by military forces, emergency medical services, and first responders worldwide. See First Care Products Ltd., company documentation; US Army Medical Department documentation.

5. The United States has invested over $1.3 billion in Iron Dome development since 2011 under the US–Israel Missile Defense Cooperation program. Israel's missile defense has intercepted thousands of rockets in combat, providing real-world performance data unavailable from testing alone. In 2021, the US Army purchased two batteries for American use, deploying them to protect American forces. The combat-proven system continues to inform American missile defense development. See Congressional Research Service, "US Foreign Aid to Israel," updated 2024; US Army acquisition announcements.

6. Israel's Defense Ministry delivered the first operational Iron Beam high-energy laser system to the Israeli Air Force on December 28, 2025. The 100-kilowatt

system successfully intercepted rockets, mortars, and drones in testing. Each laser interception costs approximately $2–$3 in electricity versus $40,000–$50,000 per Iron Dome Tamir interceptor. In December 2022, Lockheed Martin and Rafael Advanced Defense Systems signed a teaming agreement to jointly develop a variant for the US market. Rafael has invested over 30 years in laser research and development with Israel's Ministry of Defense. Seth J. Frantzman, "Israel's new laser system goes active," *Breaking Defense,* December 29, 2025, https://breakingdefense.com/2025/12/israels-new-laser-system-goes-active/; "Lockheed Martin and Rafael Advanced Defense Systems to Collaborate on High-Energy Laser System," Lockheed Martin, December 5, 2022, https://news.lockheedmartin.com/2022-12-05-Lockheed-Martin-and-Rafael-Advanced-Defense-Systems-to-Collaborate-on-High-Energy-Laser-System; "Defense Ministry hands IDF first combat-ready Iron Beam laser interception system," *Times of Israel,* December 28, 2025, https://www.timesofisrael.com/defense-ministry-hands-idf-first-combat-ready-iron-beam-laser-interception-system/

7   The US Congress appropriated $1.2 billion for Iron Beam procurement in April 2024 as part of a broader Israel security assistance package. Rafael and the Israeli Ministry of Defense invested in laser weapons research for over 30 years, including 14 years of solid-state laser development specific to Iron Beam. Israel's 2024 defense budget allocated approximately NIS 2 billion (roughly $550 million) for initial Iron Beam batteries. Exact total Israeli R&D expenditure has not been publicly disclosed. In December 2022, Lockheed Martin and Rafael signed a teaming agreement to jointly develop an Iron Beam variant for the US market. US Army Assistant Secretary Doug Bush stated that Iron Beam technology "could be something the Army could think about leveraging." Each Iron Beam interception costs approximately $2–$3 in electricity versus $40,000–$50,000 for Iron Dome Tamir interceptors. Brandi Vincent, "US to give Israel $1.2B for Iron Beam laser weapon," *DefenseScoop,* April 25, 2024, https://defensescoop.com/2024/04/25/iron-beam-procurement-us-giving-israel-funding/; "Lockheed Martin and Rafael Advanced Defense Systems to Collaborate on High-Energy Laser System," Lockheed Martin, December 5, 2022, https://news.lockheedmartin.com/2022-12-05-Lockheed-Martin-and-Rafael-Advanced-Defense-Systems-to-Collaborate-on-High-Energy-Laser-System; Brandi Vincent, "US Army may look to procure Israel's Iron Beam laser weapon for air defense," *DefenseScoop,* November 8, 2023, https://defensescoop.com/2023/11/08/us-army-may-look-to-procure-israels-iron-beam-laser-weapon-for-air-defense/.

8   In October 2024, Israeli Air Force strikes against Iranian air defense sites demonstrated the vulnerability of Russian-made S-300 systems to American

References

aircraft flown by Israeli pilots. Israeli F-35I, F-15I, and F-16I aircraft—incorporating Israeli avionics and electronic warfare enhancements—successfully penetrated and destroyed Iranian air defenses. The operational lessons and intelligence from these strikes flow back to American defense planners and manufacturers, improving American systems and demonstrating American weapons superiority to potential customers worldwide. See Bowman and Brobst, "How America Benefits from Its Security Partnership with Israel," Foundation for Defense of Democracies, October 30, 2024.

9   Former CIA Director George Tenet described Israeli intelligence cooperation as equivalent to "five CIAs" in terms of the value of information shared with the United States. General George Keegan, former Chief of US Air Force Intelligence, made similar assessments. Senator Daniel Inouye, who chaired both the Senate Appropriations Committee and the Senate Intelligence Committee, stated that Israeli intelligence shared with America exceeded that provided by all NATO countries combined. See Bowman and Brobst, "How America Benefits from Its Security Partnership with Israel," Foundation for Defense of Democracies, October 30, 2024.

10 Israel has approximately 1,000 active medical device companies and leads the world in medical device patents per capita. Major American healthcare companies including Abbott, Medtronic, Johnson & Johnson, and General Electric maintain research and development operations in Israel. Israeli medical innovations used in American healthcare include the PillCam (capsule endoscopy), ReWalk exoskeleton for paralysis patients, Mazor robotic surgical guidance systems, and numerous cancer therapies and diagnostic technologies. See Israel Innovation Authority, "Life Sciences Industry Report," 2023; Startup Nation Central, "Israeli Life Sciences Sector Overview," 2024.

11 Israel receives approximately 10% of global cybersecurity investment and is home to over 500 cybersecurity companies. Israeli cybersecurity firms protect major American financial institutions, utilities, telecommunications companies, and government agencies. Check Point Software Technologies, founded in Israel, is among the world's largest cybersecurity companies. CyberArk, Palo Alto Networks (which acquired Israeli companies), and numerous other firms with Israeli origins or operations protect American critical infrastructure from state-sponsored cyberattacks. See Startup Nation Central, "Israeli Cybersecurity Sector Report," 2024; Bowman and Brobst, "How America Benefits from Its Security Partnership with Israel," Foundation for Defense of Democracies, October 30, 2024.

12 The US–Israel economic relationship supports over 255,000 American jobs according to analysis by the US–Israel Business Council and other sources. Israeli stakeholders maintain contracts with over 1,000 American companies across 48 states. Under the 2016 US–Israel Memorandum of Understanding, Israel is required to spend 100% of US military assistance on American-manufactured products by 2028 (previously, Israel could spend a portion domestically). The US–Israel Free Trade Agreement (FTA), signed in 1985, was America's first FTA. Bilateral trade exceeds $50 billion annually. Israeli companies represent the second-largest source of foreign listings on NASDAQ after China. See US–Israel Business Council documentation; Congressional Research Service, "US–Israel Relations," 2024.

13 The Claude H. (Poseidon) Desalination Plant in Carlsbad, California, designed by IDE Technologies (Israel), is the largest seawater desalination plant in the Western Hemisphere. It produces approximately 50 million gallons of fresh water daily, serving over 400,000 San Diego County residents. The plant contributes approximately $50 million annually to the local economy and employs American workers. Israeli drip irrigation technology, pioneered by Netafim (founded 1965), is used extensively on American farms. See IDE Technologies company documentation; San Diego County Water Authority, "Carlsbad Desalination Project."

14 General Alexander Haig, former NATO Supreme Allied Commander and US Secretary of State, assessed that without Israel, the United States would need to invest $15–20 billion annually in additional military deployments to protect American interests in the Middle East. Admiral Elmo Zumwalt, former Chief of Naval Operations, compared Israel to America's largest aircraft carrier—unsinkable and requiring no American crew. These assessments, while made decades ago, remain relevant: The cost of replacing Israeli capabilities with American deployments would far exceed the $3.8 billion annual investment in US–Israel military cooperation. See Bowman and Brobst, "How America Benefits from Its Security Partnership with Israel," Foundation for Defense of Democracies, October 30, 2024.

32

1 See Michael J. Vlach, *Has the Church Replaced Israel? A Theological Evaluation* (Nashville: B&H Academic, 2010), 45–78; and Gerald R. McDermott, *Israel Matters: Why Christians Must Think Differently About the People and the Land* (Grand Rapids: Brazos Press, 2017), 23–52. Both authors document how replacement theology and supersessionism historically contributed to Christian

References

indifference toward Jewish suffering, distorted the Church's relationship to its Jewish roots, and shaped negative Christian attitudes toward Israel.

Conclusion

1 See Introduction, note 1.
2 The Covenant of the Islamic Resistance Movement (Hamas) was issued on August 18, 1988. Its preamble quotes Muslim Brotherhood founder Hassan al-Banna: "Israel will exist and will continue to exist until Islam will obliterate it." Article 7 invokes a hadith stating that "The Day of Judgment will not come about until Muslims fight the Jews" and kill them. See "Hamas Covenant 1988," The Avalon Project, Yale Law School, https://avalon.law.yale.edu/20th_century/hamas.asp.
3 Documentation of the October 7, 2023, attack: Israeli government officials confirmed approximately 1,200 people were killed. US State Department, Country Reports on Terrorism 2023, states: "On October 7, Hamas terrorists and armed Palestinian militants invaded Israel by land, sea, and air and murdered an estimated 1,200 people." Human Rights Watch, "I Cannot Erase All the Blood from My Mind: Palestinian Armed Groups' October 7 Assault on Israel," hrw.org, 17 July 2024, documents war crimes including deliberate killing of civilians, hostage-taking, and sexual violence.
4 See Chapter 2, note 1.
5 "Courage to Act," Greater St. Petersburg, episode 2, PBS, https://www.pbs.org/video/courage-to-act-kcjloj/.
6 See Chapter 2, note 3.
7 See Chapter 2, note 4.
8 See Introduction, note 2.
9 See Chapter 3, notes 1–3.
10 René Girard (1923–2015) was a French philosopher and literary critic whose work on mimetic theory and the scapegoat mechanism has influenced anthropology, theology, sociology, and cultural studies. His key works include *Violence and the Sacred* (Baltimore: Johns Hopkins University Press, 1977) and *The Scapegoat* (Baltimore: Johns Hopkins University Press, 1986). Girard argued that human communities resolve internal tensions by projecting collective violence onto a single victim—a scapegoat—whose elimination temporarily restores social unity. Girard recognized that the Judeo-Christian Scriptures uniquely expose and condemn this mechanism, taking the side of the victim rather than the persecuting mob. For an accessible introduction, see Wolfgang

Palaver, *René Girard's Mimetic Theory* (East Lansing: Michigan State University Press, 2013).

11 The concept of "motive attribution asymmetry" was identified in a study involving 661 American Democrats and Republicans, 995 Israelis, and 1,266 Palestinians. Researchers found that in political and ethnoreligious conflict, adversaries tend to attribute their own group's aggression to love for their people but attribute the opposing group's aggression to hatred. This bias makes conflict seem intractable by stripping legitimate motivations from the other side. See Jeremy Ginges et al., "Motive Attribution Asymmetry for Love vs. Hate Drives Intractable Conflict," *Proceedings of the National Academy of Sciences* 111, no. 44 (November 4, 2014): 15687–92, https://doi.org/10.1073/pnas.1414146111.

12 Projection as a psychological defense mechanism was first conceptualized by Sigmund Freud and further developed by his daughter Anna Freud in *The Ego and the Mechanisms of Defence* (London: Hogarth Press, 1936). Projection involves attributing one's own unacceptable thoughts, feelings, or impulses to another person—for example, someone who feels guilty about dishonesty may accuse others of being dishonest. As the American Psychological Association defines it, projection is "the process by which one attributes one's own individual positive or negative characteristics, affects, and impulses to another person or group... often a defense mechanism in which unpleasant or unacceptable impulses, stressors, ideas, affects, or responsibilities are attributed to others." See "Defense Mechanisms," in *StatPearls* (Treasure Island, FL: StatPearls Publishing, 2023), https://www.ncbi.nlm.nih.gov/books/NBK559106/.

www.ingramcontent.com/pod-product-compliance
Lightning Source LLC
Chambersburg PA
CBHW050059170426
43198CB00014B/2389